OXFORD GEOGRAPHICAL AND ENVIRONMENTAL STUDIES

General Editors: Gordon Clark, Andrew Goudie, and Ceri Peach

THE GLOBALIZED CITY

The Globalized City

Economic Restructuring and
Social Polarization in European Cities

Edited by

Frank Moulaert
Arantxa Rodríguez
and
Erik Swyngedouw

OXFORD
UNIVERSITY PRESS

OXFORD

UNIVERSITY PRESS

Great Clarendon Street, Oxford OX2 6DP

Oxford University Press is a department of the University of Oxford.
It furthers the University's objective of excellence in research, scholarship,
and education by publishing worldwide in

Oxford New York

Auckland Bangkok Buenos Aires Cape Town Chennai
Dar es Salaam Delhi Hong Kong Istanbul Karachi Kolkata
Kuala Lumpur Madrid Melbourne Mexico City Mumbai Nairobi
São Paulo Shanghai Taipei Tokyo Toronto

Oxford is a registered trade mark of Oxford University Press
in the UK and in certain other countries

Published in the United States
by Oxford University Press Inc., New York

© Oxford University Press 2003

British Library Cataloguing in Publication Data
Data available

Library of Congress Cataloging in Publication Data
Data available

ISBN 0-19-926040-0

1 3 5 7 9 10 8 6 4 2

Typeset by SNP Best-Set Typesetter Ltd., Hong Kong
Printed in Great Britain
on acid-free paper by
Biddles Ltd,
Guildford and King's Lynn

Dedicated to the memory of

DANIÈLE LEBORGNE

EDITORS' PREFACE

Geography and environmental studies are two closely related and burgeoning fields of academic enquiry. Both have grown rapidly over the past few decades. At once catholic in its approach and yet strongly committed to a comprehensive understanding of the world, geography has focused upon the interaction between global and local phenomena. Environmental studies, on the other hand, have shared with the discipline of geography an engagement with different disciplines, addressing wide-ranging and significant environmental issues in the scientific community and the policy community. From the analysis of climate change and physical environmental processes to the cultural dislocations of post-modernism in and across the landscape, these two fields of enquiry have been at the forefront of attempts to comprehend transformations taking place in the world, manifesting themselves at a variety of interrelated spatial scales.

The Oxford Geographical and Environmental Studies series aims to reflect this diversity and engagement. Our goal is to publish the best and original research in the two related fields and, in doing so, demonstrate the significance of geographical and environmental perspectives for understanding the contemporary world. As a consequence, our scope is deliberately international and ranges widely in terms of topics, approaches, and methodologies. Authors are welcome from all corners of the globe. We hope the series will assist in redefining the frontiers of knowledge and build bridges within the fields of geography and environmental studies. We hope also that it will cement links with issues and approaches that have originated outside the strict confines of these disciplines. In doing so, our publications contribute to the frontiers of research and knowledge while representing the fruits of particular and diverse scholarly traditions.

Gordon L. Clark
Andrew Goudie
Ceri Peach

CONTENTS

LIST OF CONTRIBUTORS

John Andersen is a Professor at Roskilde University, Department of Social Sciences, Denmark. He worked for the European Commission, DG V, in the third European Anti-Poverty Programme 1991–4. His main research interests are social exclusion, and social and labour market policy in contemporary European welfare states.

Brendan Bartley is a lecturer in Urban Geography and Planning at the National University of Ireland Maynooth. He is also an Associate of the National Institute of Regional and Spatial Analysis (NIRSA) which is based in the National University of Ireland, Maynooth. His current research focuses on urban development and social polarization with a particular emphasis on the experiences of 'invisible' excluded communities in the city and the logic and impacts of 'high visibility' promotional and flagship urban development projects.

Guy Baeten is a lecturer at the Department of Geography, University of Strathclyde in Glasgow. His main research interest is in urban regeneration and social exclusion. He has also worked on regional-economic governance and critical transport ecology.

Joachim Becker is an economist and political scientist. He is Associate Professor at the Institute of Economics at Wirtschaftsuniversitant Wien, Vienna, Austria. In 1999 and 2001, he taught at Universidad de Buenos Aires in Argentina. His most recent publications include *Economía política de Montevideo. Desarrolo urbano y políticas locales* (Montvideo, 2001, co-author) and *Akkumulation, Regulation, Territorium. Zur kritischen Rekonstruktion der franzoesischen Regulationsthoerie* (Marburg, 2002).

João Cabral is Assistant Professor in Urban and Regional Planning at the University of Aveiro, Portugal. He has worked on urban and regional development and research and participated in several planning projects for local authorities and regional departments of the central government in Portugal.

Pavlos-Marinos Delladetsima is an Assistant Professor of Geography at the University of the Aegean in Greece. He has worked as Human Capital Mobility Research Fellow of the European Community at the Institut Federatif de Reserche sur les Economies et les Societes Industrielles (IFRESI) in Lille, France. He has also worked at the National Technical University of Athens. He has co-ordinated and been involved in numerous research programmes in Europe and Greece concerning land use and real estate development, local development, decision support systems and regional service economies.

Hartmut Häußermann has been Professor of Urban and Regional Sociology at the Humboldt University in Berlin since 1993; before that he was at the

University of Bremen. His fields of research are urban development and urban policy, transformation of cities in Eastern Europe, political-economic changes in Berlin, and socio-spatial structures in cities.

Elena Martínez is a doctoral student at the University of the Basque Country. She has worked on a number of research projects on urban regeneration and is currently completing a dissertation on social and spatial fragmentation in Bilbao.

Frank Moulaert is Professor in European Planning and Development at the University of Newcastle-upon-Tyne. Together with P.-M. Delladetsima and others, he recently published *Globalization and Integrated Area Development in European Cities* with Oxford University Press.

Andreas Novy is Associate Professor at the Department of City and Regional Studies, Wirtschaftsuniversitant Wien, Vienna, Austria. His research focuses on comparative analysis of political and economic developments in Europe and Latin America. His most recent publications include *A Desordem da periferia—500 anos de poder e espaco no Brasil* (Petropolis, 2001 which was presented at the World Social Forum in Porto Alegre, and *Entwicklung gestalten—Gesellschaftsveränderung in der Einen Welt* (Frankfurt and Vienna 2002).

Berta Rato has worked for the last few years for a Lisbon consulting company specializing in regional and local development projects and the evaluation of public policies. Since November 2001, she has been working in the field of co-operation for development for EUROSTAT.

Vanessa Redak is an urban and regional economist. She is currently a lecturer in economics at the University of Applied Studies in Banking and Finance (Vienna, Austria). Her current research activities include an EU 5th Framework research project on 'Social Innovation and Governance in the European City'.

Arantxa Rodríguez is Associate Professor in Urban and Regional Economics and Planning at the University of the Basque Country. Her research focuses on spatial development planning and regeneration strategies in disadvantaged areas.

Katja Simons is presently completing her Ph.D. in social sciences at the Graduate School, Metropolitan Areas in Comparison, Ruhr-University, Bochum, Germany. She has been a researcher and lecturer in Urban and Regional Sociology at the Humboldt University in Berlin. Her main research areas are urban development, global and local governance, and international migration.

Erik Swyngedouw is University Reader in Economic Geography at Oxford University and Fellow of St Peter's College. He is also associate Fellow of the Environmental Change Institute. His research interests include the political economy of capitalist societies, political ecology, the dynamics of urban and regional change, and the politics of globalization. He is co-editor (with A. Merrifield) of *The Urbanization of Injustice* (Lawrence and Wishart, 1996). He is currently completing *Flows of Power: The Political-Ecology of Water Urbanization in Guayaquil, Ecuador* (to be published by Oxford University Press in 2003) and *Re-Scaling Space: Glocalisation and the Politics of Scale* (to be published by Temple University Press in 2003).

Kasey Treadwell Shine is a doctoral candidate and researcher at the Department of Geography, National University of Ireland, Maynooth. Her research interests include urban geography; medical anthropology, especially in relation to health, discrimination, and marginalization; and issues of social justice. Her doctoral research investigates the applications of Complexity Theory for understanding the intersections of governance and exclusion in disadvantaged urban neighbourhoods.

Serena Vicari Haddock is Associate Professor in Urban Sociology at the University of Pavia (Italy). Her primary research interests include urban redevelopment, and initiatives for regeneration in Italian cities, in a comparative perspective. Among her recent publications in English are: 'The Political Economy of Urban Regimes: A Comparative Perspective' (with P. Kantor and H. V. Savitch), *Urban Affairs Review* (1997), and 'Naples: Urban Regeneration and Exclusion in the Italian South', *European Urban and Regional Studies* (2001).

LIST OF PLATES

LIST OF FIGURES

LIST OF TABLES

LIST OF ABBREVIATIONS

AB	Ayuntamiento de Bilbao
ADM	Area Development Management Limited
BAAG	Berlin Adlershof Aufbaugesellschaft mbH (development corporation)
CDN	Centro Direzionale di Napoli (Naples Business District)
CHDA	Custom House Docks Area
CIG	Cassa Integrazione Guadagni (Fund for Income Support)
CSF	Community Support Framework
DDDA	Dublin Docklands Development Authority
DM	Deutschmark
DOTVMA	Departamento de Ordenación del Territorio, Vivienda y Medio Ambiente-Gobierno Vasco
DUVMA	Departamento de Urbanismo, Vivienda y Medio Ambiente-Gobierno Vasco
ECSC	European Community of Steel and Coal
EEC	European Economic Council
EFIM	Ente Finanziario Industria Meridionale (Southern Manufacturing Industry Holdings Corporation)
EGA	Entwicklungsgesellschaft Adlershof mbH (development company)
ENI	Ente Nazionale Idrocarburi (Energy and Chemicals Holding Corporation)
EP	European Parliament
ERDF	European Regional Development Fund
EU	European Union
FIO	Fondo investimenti occupazione (Investment Fund for Employment Promotion)
FPÖ	Freiheitliche Partei Österreichs
FRG	Federal Republic of Germany
GBM	Guggenheim Bilbao Museo
GCC	Greater Copenhagen Council
HARP	Historic Area Rejuvenation Project
IAD	Integrated Area Development
IAP	Integrated Area Plan
IFSC	Irish Financial Services Centre
INPDAP	Istituto Nazionale Previdenza Dipendenti Amministrazione Pubblica (Pension Fund for State Employees)
IRI	Istituto Ricostruzione Industriale (Institute for Industrial Reconstruction)
IZ	Intervention Zone
LMA	Lisbon Metropolitan Area
MA	Magistratsabteilung
NEP	New Economic Policy
NUP	New Urban Policy

ODC	Orestad Development Corporation
OEK	Greek Social Housing Organization
OV	Olympic Village (Athens)
PERI	Plan Especial de Reforma Interior (Master Plan)
PPP	Public–Private Partnership
PROTAML	Regional plan for the Lisbon Metropolitan Area
R. & D.	Research and Development
SME	Small and Medium-Sized Enterprises
UDC	Urban Development Corporation
UDP	Urban Development Project
URSPIC	Urban Redevelopment and Social Polarization in the City (Acronym of EU Framework IV Research Project)
VIC	Vienna International Centre
WED	Wiener Entwicklungsgesellschaft für den Donauraum
WISTA MG	Wirtschafts- und Wissenschaftsstandort Management Gesellschaft (managing company of the Science and Business Park in Berlin-Adlershof)
WISTA	Wirtschafts- und Wissenschaftsstandort (Science and Business Park of Berlin-Adlershof)

Introduction

Erik Swyngedouw, Frank Moulaert, and Arantxa Rodríguez

This book and the nine city stories in it are written out of a love for the city, a love of large metropolitan places. Cities are brooding places of imagination, creativity, innovation, and the ever new and different. But cities also hide in their underbelly perverse and pervasive processes of physical decay and suffocation, social exclusion and marginalization, and are rife with all manner of social and political conflict, and often outright despair in the midst of the greatest affluence, abundance, and pleasure. Although these dynamics that define the urban experience have been part of urban life since the birth of the city, they have taken on a heightened intensity over the past two decades or so. There is no need to recount here the tumultuous reordering of urban social, cultural, and economic life that has rampaged through the city. Many urban communities were left in the doldrums of persistent decline and permanent upheaval and are still faced with the existential disorientation that comes with lasting unemployment. Other communities have risen to the challenge that restructuring sparks off, and have plunged into the cracks and fissures that have opened up a whole arena of new possibilities of action and intervention, as governments, economies, and civil society desperately seek out new niches for revitalizing the urban fabric.

These urban transformations, extensively documented in myriad academic research, governmental documents, the media, and even in literature, have invariably been situated in the context of transforming political, sociocultural, and economic systems. While economic processes were rapidly, but very unevenly, globalizing, and cities and city 'builders' were trying to carve out their place within the emerging new socio-spatial divisions of labour, of production, and of consumption, political transformations and policy reorientations—pursued by local, regional, and national governments from all ideological stripes and colours—were initiated in an attempt to align local dynamics with the imagined, assumed, or real requirements of a deregulated and increasingly neo-liberal international economic system. Heralded by some as the harbinger of a new era of potential prosperity, and vilified by others as perpetuating the social wastelands produced by enduring restructuring and accentuating polarization and marginalization, the urban arena became undoubtedly a key space where political-economic and social changes were enacted. A new urban policy, the urban expression of a new neo-liberal economic policy pursued at higher scale levels (see Chapter 2), squarely revolved around re-centring the city. Old forms and functions, traditional political and organizational configurations, had to give way for a new urbanity, a visionary urbanity that would stand the tests imposed by a global liberal world order. Re-positioning the city on the map of the competitive landscape meant re-imagining and re-creating urban space, not just in the eyes of the master planners and city fathers and mothers, but primarily for the outsider, the investor, developer, businesswoman or -man, the élite culture freak, or the money-packed tourist. And although the resistance to this re-positioning is very much alive, it is only in recent years that these mobilizations gained real momentum.

While many middle-sized cities kept prospering, the metropolitan world was ruined by the devastating restructuring of the 1970s and 1980s. Rebuilding the city—as in the aftermath of a war—became the leitmotif of urban governance. Large-scale and emblematic urban projects (UDPs) were the medicine for urban decline prescribed by the advocates of the new urban policy. The Guggenheim Museum in Bilbao, the new financial district in Dublin, the science-university–technology complex Adlershof in Berlin, the 1998 World Expo in Lisbon, Athens's bid to stage the Olympic Games, Vienna's new urban projects, among many other urban development experiences dotted over the map of urban Europe, testify to the unshakeable belief among city élites of the healing effect on the city's vitality of the production of new urban mega-projects and events.

It has been commonplace in much of the public debate as well as in academic analysis to present the emergence of a more competitive urban politics and the making of entrepreneurial cities as the outcome, the result, the crystallization of political and economic processes that operate outside and above the scale of the urban. It is, so the revived neo-liberal argument goes, global changes that 'force' urban governance and economies to move in a preordained direction if competitive survival in the global market-place is to be achieved. Occasionally, the local configuration is seen as the pivotal scale through which urban change ought to be understood. The new urban forms and functions are seen as the independent variables, whose emergence has to be theorized, explained, and situated in the context of the intertwining of local and national political and cultural processes, which, in turn, shape global processes. This book starts from a radically different premise.

While we agree that large-scale Urban Development Projects (UDPs) have, indeed, become one of the most visible and ubiquitous urban revitalization strategies pursued by cities in search of economic growth and competitiveness, we also insist that it is exactly this sort of new urban policy that actively produces, enacts, embodies, and shapes the new political and economic regimes that are operative at local, regional, national, and global scales. They are the material expression of a developmental logic that views mega-projects and place marketing as major leverages for generating future growth and for waging a competitive struggle to attract investment capital. Urban projects of this kind are, therefore, neither mere result or response, nor the consequence of political and economic change enacted elsewhere. On the contrary, we argue that such UDPs are the very catalysts of urban and political change; UDPs incorporate processes that are felt locally, but regionally, nationally, and internationally as well. UDPs are concrete interventions that embody, express, and shape transformations in the political and economic configurations but also in the physical networks and their nodes, and are often organized at other and higher geographical scales. They illustrate the real-life processes through which post-modern forms, post-Fordist economic dynamics, and neo-liberal systems of governance are crafted. UDPs are productive of and embody processes that operate in and over a variety of scales, from the local to the global. In sum, large-scale urban development projects are the mechanisms *par excellence* through which globalization becomes urbanized. In other words, 'urbanizing globalization' takes places through concrete interventions in urban space through which the socio-spatial and scalar relations of the political and economic processes become refashioned. Of course, 'urbanizing globalization' also includes new strategies of informal development, spontaneous reactions to mainstream urban 're-'development, visible in small-scale housing development, the mushrooming of small business in a variety of activities, new urban movements, and community initiatives and the like. However important these developments may be, we do not cover them in this book. This collection focuses on large-scale emblematic development projects. From our vantage point, the urban project becomes the lens that permits light to be cast on (i) how the global/national/local interplay is etched into particular urban schemes; (ii) how these projects, in turn, express the way global, national, and local forces intersect in the construction of new socio-economic environments; (iii) how social polarization and exclusion/integration are shaped in, and work through, these forms of socio-spatial restructuring; (iv) what the catalytic impact of the regulatory framework on social polarization and exclusion/integration is.

These Urban Development Projects constitute probably the main urban expression of global-local ('glocal') restructuring processes. Each is inevitably deeply embedded in local, regional, national, and supranational social, economic, and institutional frameworks. They are both associated with, and producers of, 'globalization'. In short, such projects seize and reflect urban restructuring processes in a synthetic way and, therefore, pave the way for the analysis of wider, more general processes of social inclusion/exclusion as they become magnified at the scale of the urban. This is the task we set in this book. Our principal aim is to show how the production of urban space is actually also the production of a new polity, a new economy, and a new form of living urban life.

This book excavates the dynamics that have accompanied the implementation of large-scale UDPs in nine European cities within the European Union (EU). The analysis is based on research undertaken as part of a Targeted Socio-economic Research Action (the Framework IV Research Program of the

EU), Urban Restructuring and Social Polarization in the City (URSPIC). A total of thirteen case studies were analysed in a comparative perspective. The research project intended to contribute to the analysis of the relationship between urban restructuring and social exclusion/integration in the context of the emergence of the new regimes of urban governance that parallel the European-wide—albeit geographically uneven and, on occasion, politically contested—consolidation of a neo-liberal and market-driven ideology and politics. The selected UDPs embody and express processes that reflect global pressures and incorporate changing systems of local, regional, and/or national regulation and governance. These projects, while being decidedly local, capture global trends, express new forms of national and local policies, and incorporate them in a particular localized setting. The selected UDPs are listed in Table 0.1, according to the city's ranking in the urban hierarchy and

Table 0.1. The thirteen case-study projects of the URSPIC Project

Type of City	Stage of the Project in 1997		
	Design	Construction	Commercialization
World cities		ROTTERDAM (*) (Randstad Holland) Kop Van Zuid	
		LONDON (*) The South Bank	
Euro-city	BERLIN Adlershof		BRUSSELS Espace Leopold/eu District
Big town	COPENHAGEN Orestaden	LISBON Expo 1998	
	DUBLIN Docklands— International Financial Services Centre	VIENNA Donau City	
	ATHENS Olympic Village		
Secondary town		BILBAO Abandoibarra	NAPLES Centro Direzionale
		BIRMINGHAM (*) Central Business District (CBD)	LILLE (*) Euralille

Source: http://www.ifresi.univ-lille1.fr (select Programmes de Recherche and then select URSPIC). The cities with an (*) were part of the case-study analysis, but have not been included in this book, although some of the findings from these studies have been incorporated in the introductory and concluding chapters.

their stage of development at the start of the research project in 1997. The large-scale urban interventions were deliberately chosen as reflections of a particular hegemonic and dominant expression of urban policy, as pursued during the 1990s. The book attempts, therefore, to provide a panoramic view of urban change in some of Europe's greatest cities.

The first three chapters will unravel the dynamics of urban transformation as they are expressed by the 'production' of these new project-based urban landscapes and situate the subsequent case studies within a common theoretical and methodological perspective. Chapter 1 will discuss the contemporary urban condition, with a particular eye towards elucidating the broader theoretical perspective that underpinned this collective research project. The chapter seeks to show the ways in which UDPs are 'grains of sand' that embody and express social, political, economic, and cultural processes operating at a variety of articulated geographical scales. Furthermore, it suggests that the analysis of the UDPs captures the new scale geometry that characterizes contemporary capitalism. Finally, we argue that the excavation of the UDPs permits us to cast substantive and empirical light on the actors, social relations, and contradictory political-economic process through which contemporary 'glocal' urbanization processes are fashioned. Chapter 2 elucidates the interrelated changes in urban and economic policy that emerged in the 1980s and shaped the particular neo-liberal political configurations through which these UDPs were envisioned, planned, and implemented. Despite the significant and important variations between cities, there are also striking similarities with respect to the political-economic transformations that invariably led to the, often contested, development of a New Urban Policy (NEP). Chapter 3 discusses the methodological perspective that was used and its relationship to the substantive processes we wished to excavate.

The subsequent nine chapters explore the particular trajectories of a single project in a single city. While retaining case-specific aspects, all chapters address a common range of issues. They describe and detail the nature of the urban project in each of the cities. For each case, the processes through which the UDP was planned and, depending on the case, implemented, is then used to shed light on changing economic, political, and institutional configurations and their consequences, with a particular sensitivity to their effects in terms of polarization and exclusion. This strategy permits comparability between cases while maintaining sensitivity to the particularities of each local, regional, or national framework. Moreover, this mode of presentation has helped to tease out general processes while insisting on the need to examine particular cases in detail in order really to grasp the dynamics of the changes that take place.

The first case, presented in Chapter 4, examines the tortuous process associated with the planning and implementation of the Olympic Village in Athens as part of the preparations in the run-up to the Olympic Games in 2004. Chapter 5 moves to northern Europe and considers how the planning and implementation of a new urban complex outside Copenhagen (Oresund) constitutes an emblematic example that illustrates contradictory and profound transformations in the Danish political-economic framework. The tumultuous and over-ambitious reordering of Berlin's cityscape is the subject of Chapter 6. Taking the planning and implementation of 'Adlershof, new science and technology city' as its particular 'lens', the authors examine the profound transformation of urban governance in Berlin after the *Wende* and how this became edged into Berlin's socio-spatial organization. In Chapter 7, the 'unplanned' development and expansion of the European Union's own spatialization in Brussels (the EU district) is presented as a vehicle to scrutinize both the changing global/local nexus that characterizes the contemporary urban condition in Brussels and the social and political exclusions that accompany this process. The remaking of Dublin's docklands into a high-level service and financial centre is discussed in Chapter 8. Here, the UDP's history is used as a vehicle to explore and analyse transforming systems of planning and governance in Dublin in their interrelation with national and European policies and the changing place of the 'Celtic Tiger' in global economic dynamics. Chapter 9, in turn, moves to 'Red' Vienna, where recent attempts to move into an entrepreneurial direction, while maintaining an inclusive welfare system, have met with significant problems and have been confronted with contradictions that may lead to a more polarized city, particularly articulated around the immigrant/Austrian nexus. Chapter 10 explores how the Guggenheim's strategy of urbanizing its own globalization strategy has joined with the reordering of Bilbao's socio-economic, institutional, and political framework, and highlights the polarizing and exclusive processes at work. The ambivalent attempts of Lisbon to reposition itself on the map of entrepreneurial and internationally competitive cities are excavated through the lens of EXPO-98, the international exhibition held in 1998. The contested dynamics of this emblematic project are presented in Chapter 11. In particular, the difficult balancing act between aspirations to maintain social cohesion on the one hand while improving urban competitiveness on the other will be the focus of this contribution. In Chapter 12, the remarkable urban transformation and partial renaissance of Naples are discussed via the analysis of the planning and construction of a new visionary and large-scale Central Business District.

While being sensitive to the formative importance of local and national configurations, the case studies suggest a series of similarities that point at more general processes of urban socio-economic restructuring and the reorganization of the system of governance. The localization of the global and the globalization of the local become crafted in a place-specific manner; yet exhale perplexing, and often disturbing, common threads. Their contradictory appearance will be summarized in the concluding chapter.

A project of this size and scope depends on the work and collaboration of many people. It requires 'speaking in tongues', as the team members spoke a variety of languages; it requires long discussions, friendly disagreement and a lot of good will from all sides. What makes projects like these worth while are, in the end, the friendships that are forged, the time spent together to try to hammer out a framework in which each could somehow find her- or himself. When international comparative research of this kind is criticized as being not sufficiently detailed, theoretically coherent, or methodologically sound, let us not forget that, at the end of the day, these multinational endeavours are precisely about negotiating difference, developing a sensitivity to 'otherness', while still pursuing a common objective in ways the participants find rewarding, insightful, stimulating, and, above all, pleasurable.

Many of the insights reported in this book come from the large number of participants in this project. We would like to acknowledge our debt in writing the first three chapters and the conclusion of this volume to all those who worked with us on this project. Their fieldwork, data collection, interviews, and surveys provided the foundation, material, and many of the insights for this project, and their thoughts and writings were used extensively in the preparation of this book. We are very much indebted to them: Serena Vicari Haddock (Pavia) and Lucia Cavola (Naples), Pavlos Delladetsimas (Athens), João Cabral (Lisbon), Elodie Salin and Thomas Werquin (Lille), Elena Martínez (Bilbao), Guy Baeten (Glasgow), Louis Albrechts (Leuven), Hartmut Häußermann and Katja Simons (Berlin), Andreas Novy, Vanessa Redak, and Joachim Becker (Vienna), John Andersen, Soeren H. Jensen, and Gestur Hovgaard (Copenhagen), Brendan Bartley, Caroline Creamer, and Kasey Treadwell Shine (Dublin), Alan Middleton and Patrick Loftman (Birmingham), and Gerard Oude Engberink and Frank Miedema (Rotterdam). We are also very grateful to Ailsa Allen of the School of Geography and the Environment of Oxford University for her meticulous and skilful redrafting of the figures and to Martin Barfoot for helping with the photographic work. This book is the final product of the URSPIC project. Kourosh Saljoghi created the URSPIC website, Cecile Soudan contributed to writing the proposal and leading the negotiations, Fariza Marecaille, Josèphe Lannoye, and Martine Ratajczak, all from IFRESI-CNRS in Lille, provided administrative and accounting support for the entire project. Finally we want to thank our EU Scientific Officer, Giulia Amaducci, who participated in many of our network meetings. This project was funded by the EU Framework IV TSER programme.

E.S.

F.M.

A.R.

1

'The World in a Grain of Sand': Large-Scale Urban Development Projects and the Dynamics of 'Glocal' Transformations

Erik Swyngedouw, Frank Moulaert, and Arantxa Rodriguez

> . . . by what route is it possible to attain a heightened graphicness . . . That is, to build up the large constructions out of the smallest, precisely fashioned structural elements. Indeed, to detect the crystal of the total event in the analysis of the small, individual moment.
>
> (Walter Benjamin, cited in Smith 1989)

1.1. Urbanizing Globalization

This book is structured around the view that large-scale Urban Development Projects (UDPs) are the embodiment of processes that operate in and over a variety of scales, from the local to the global. These urban interventions are as it were 'grains of sand', albeit of a particularly rough-edged variety, that hold the world's complex socio-spatial and political-economic configuration in their crystalline structure. They are part of a process of profound restructuring that over the past few decades has transformed the urban landscape in unexpected, perplexing, and often disturbing ways. This chapter seeks to address how urban revitalization projects refashion the city in the image of a new post-modern and post-Fordist urbanity, an urbanity articulated through a spectac-ularized commodification of urban space; one that redraws the boundaries between public and private, inside and outside, included and excluded (Sorkin 1993). UDPs combine the intersection of economic, social, cultural, and political processes and their articulation; processes that operate at a variety of nested, articulated and interacting spatial scales: the local, the regional, the national, the European Union, and the global. The interweaving of these scales and the mesmerizing complexity of cultural, social, economic, and political relations make it difficult, if not impossible, to capture them in all their dimensions. Hence, our objective is to read these multi-layered processes as they operate in and over space through their particular materialization in places as new urban forms. Whether we consider the territorialization of the European Union's bureaucratic and institutional apparatus in Brussels, the construction of Naples's New International Business District, or the sedimentation of the Guggenheim Museum's cultural-economic globalization in Bilbao, the resulting, often spectacular, built environments are exactly the outcome of processes operating at intertwined geographical scales.

Urban restructuring in general, and UDPs in particular, constitute the pivot of contemporary global-local (glocal) restructuring processes. Through such interventions, cities and city-builders attempt to relocate their position on the cartographic map of competitive globalization. This is one of the ways in which globalization becomes urbanized. Large-scale urban development projects, as expressions of new urban dynamics, often carried by local business élites, can provide key insights into both the mechanisms of global-local integration and the consequences in terms of new choreographies of social power, mechanisms of social polarization, and the dynamics of inclusion and exclusion.

Everyday life and the places that structure our everyday urban experiences operate through the internalization of continuously shifting articulations of complex, interwoven sets of particular, but socially produced, geographical (socio-economic, cultural, and institutional-political) scales through which action, meaning, sense, and explanation are constructed. In recent years, the problem of scale has become increasingly important, both academically and politically, as the contemporary maelstrom of social and cultural change and economic transformation is accompanied by transgressions of scale boundaries, the production of new scales, and the restructuring of others (Brenner 1997; 1999; Swyngedouw 1997a; 2002a). The hyper-modern pulverization of time and space, the transformations of everyday life, and the still accelerating globalization of commodification and commodified relations junk geographical scales we have taken too long for granted as fixed, stable, and frozen moments, as static containers that organize and regulate life. In recent years, however, the boundaries of the body, the city, and the nation are rapidly redefined in ways often enabling and emancipatory but also often in plainly and deeply disempowering ways. We seek to show through analysing the trajectory of project planning, implementation, and final operation how UDPs reflect and embody exactly the shifting scalar geographies that characterize the contemporary spatial rearrangements. The intention of this chapter, therefore, is (i) to contribute to a more sound foundation for theorizing scale and to bring out the political importance of the process of re-scaling of life and the contested production of a new '*Gestalt* of scale' (Smith 1993) in terms of strategies of empowerment and disempowerment, of repression and emancipation, and (ii) to explore how the production of new scaled articulations operates through, and becomes embodied in, urban interventions. Indeed, the reconfigurations of scale and the transformation of spatial processes become worked out and are mediated through the built environment. In many ways, therefore, urban environments, as constructed places, are the condensed expression and incarnation of the transformation of socio-spatial processes. Urban interventions become, as it were, the crystal or the lens through which we can begin to excavate the myriad processes of socio-spatial change that have reshaped, or are still in the process of refashioning, the co-ordinates of everyday life.

1.2. Situating Place, Space, and Scale

All social life is necessarily 'placed' or 'situated' and engaging place is fundamental to maintaining the process of life itself. This equally holds true for the process of capital circulation and accumulation. For accumulation to proceed, capital needs to territorialize, to become embedded in, and productive of, particular places and territorial configurations (Harvey 1981; Brenner 1998a). Yet, socio-spatial (power) relations always operate over a certain space and take a particular scalar geography. Place and space are, therefore, not two binary categories, but are materially and practically constituted through each other (Merrifield 2002). As Andy Merrifield (1993: 521) argues:

Social space must be posited as a material process. This process represents the rootless, fluid reality of material flows of commodities, money, capital and information which can be transferred and shifted across the globe . . . Capital is an inexorably circulatory process diffusive in space, which also fixates itself as a thing in space and so begets a built environment. The fixity nature (the thing quality) of the geographical landscape is necessary to permit the flow and diffuse nature of capital; and vice versa. Capital fixity must, of necessity, take place somewhere and hence place can be taken as the specific form emergent from an apparent stopping of, or as one specific moment in the dynamics of capitalist social space.

Urban 'things', then, are neither the outcome of processes operating over an abstract (globalizing) space nor the local determinants that shape a wider spatial order. 'Things' in place are moments, photographic stills, instances of socio-spatial processes in which the thing is defined and constituted through the process (Harvey, 1996). Therefore, grasping the processual character of urban change requires unravelling the process of production of particular places and 'things'. The 'Thing', i.e. building, spectacle, site, museum, house, body, workplace, state, etc., can only begin to make sense if viewed as an integral part of the process. Similarly, a spatialized intervention can become the entry, the window, or the crystal through which the flow and process of socio-spatial change can be unravelled and understood.

Engaging place(s) is inevitably a contradictory process as it necessarily implies some sort of 'creative destruction' or 'destructive creation' of an already historically constituted place. This importance of place does not offer the 'local' as the pre-eminent site for the construction of socio-spatial theory. 'Creative destruction' is always an already social *process*: it is a metabolic transformation that *takes place* in association with others and extends over a certain geographical space. Lefebvre (1989), Harvey (1981; 1985; 1996), and Massey (1992), among others, explore in a variety of ways this socio-spatiality of everyday life and its expression in 'the production of space(s)'. The process character of socio-spatial relations means that life is in a state of perpetual change, transformation, and reconfiguration (see Harvey 1996) in which 'everything that is solid melts into air' (Marx and Engels 1848).

These social relations are always constituted through temporal and spatial relations of power. That is what Massey (1992) refers to as 'the geometry of power', i.e. the multiple relations of domination/subordination and participation/exclusion through which social space is organized. These social relations are 'grounded' in the sense that they regulate (but in highly contested or contestable ways) control over and access to transformed place, but also that they are reproduced within a material/social/discursive space. Spatial scales, then, become the embodiment of, and the arenas through and in which, social relations of empowerment and disempowerment operate (Swyngedouw 1997a). It is here that the issue of geographical scale emerges centrally. The socio-spatial relations operate over a certain spatial reach that varies according to their type and concrete forms (Moulaert and Wilson 1983). In fact, scale emerges out of the socio-spatial character of the perpetual transformation of places. The scaling of the everyday, as Smith (1993) insists, is expressed in bodily, community, urban, regional, national, supranational, and global configurations, whose content and relations are fluid, contested, and perpetually transgressed. These scalar institutional, cultural, economic, and political configurations (and arenas) are woven together and become represented in the processes through which new places become constructed. The theoretical and political priority, therefore, never resides in a particular geographical scale, but rather in the process through which particular scales become (re)constituted (see Swyngedouw 1992b; 1997a; 1998).

1.3. A 'Glocal' City/Space? Large-Scale Urban Development Projects and the 'Glocalization' of the City

Urban restructuring in general, and Urban Development Projects in particular, have become emblems of contemporary global–local ('glocal') restructuring processes. These projects are each inevitably deeply embedded in local, regional, national, and supranational economic and institutional frameworks. They simultaneously exhale the shifting articulations between these scales as the parameters of political-economic dynamics and socio-political struggles work themselves out in new ways (Olds, 2001). These projects are wrought from and, in turn, shape local *and* global processes. Urban dynamics are, therefore, both a consequence of, and a key element in, the formation of a new global economy. In short, large-scale urban projects, as expressions of these new urban dynamics, can provide key insights into the mechanisms of global–local integration. In addition, by means of analysis, such grand urban intervention and the consequences of such new urban policy, in terms of social polarization and inclusion/exclusion mechanisms, can be assessed.First, large urban projects articulate with different processes of exclusion and polarization, i.e. job creation and destruction, the dynamics of housing markets, financial mechanisms, citizen participation or absence thereof. Second, such projects demand and exemplify different policy/strategy structures and measures enacted at a variety of interacting scale-levels, and illustrate varying views on how to deal with the general processes of polarization and exclusion. Third, they are, nevertheless, often part of internationally comparable urban strategies (networking, 'place' marketing, spectacularization, information technology, commodification of public space, shifting public/private relations, etc.) and express a common preoccupation with reasserting the competitive position of place in a globalizing world economy. Charting these changes in the light of the acceleration of high modernity is what we shall turn to next.

1.3.1. Re-ordering the urban

The past two decades have unleashed a profound restructuring process in virtually all aspects of daily life as well as in the broader spatial, social, and political ordering of our cities. City life has more than ever become the norm for most of the planet's inhabitants. In Europe, more than 70 per cent of the population lives in cities. On a world scale, we are rapidly approaching a situation in which more than half of the world's population lives in urban settings, many of them in mega-cities of over 1 million inhabitants (United Nations Centre for Human Settlement (HABITAT) (1996)). However, the 'Century of the City', as Mumford labelled the twentieth century, was not at its close a vision of a humane urban world such as the visionary planners at the beginning of the century imagined it to become. Not only cities in the global south but also many metropolitan cities in the north have become Malthusian battlegrounds in which a small élite enjoys a luxury beyond imagination, while many other social groups are engaged in a daily struggle for survival. If we consider the shifting urban realities of contemporary city life in the advanced capitalist economies, a series of rather disturbing tendencies have emerged. In an environment in which socio-spatial ordering by and for the market has become the dogma of the day, urban regions have become, more than ever before, landscapes of power (Zukin 1991) where islands of extreme wealth and social power are interspersed with places of deprivation, exclusion, and decline (Hamnett 1996). The accelerating and spatially deeply uneven processes of 'creative destruction' leave some urban communities uprooted and displaced while propelling others on to new commanding heights of privilege, money, and control. The process of 'globalization' that is trumpeted by a new global élite as announcing a 'new' world order of stability, prosperity, and growth, but vilified by others as the harbinger of irreversible decline is indeed a double-edged affair. For the privileged—those who are able to benefit from new technologies and new modes of communications—movement, access, and mobility have been augmented. Meanwhile, there are those at the receiving end of the process—such as the impoverished, the aged, the unemployed, and the immigrant labouring bodies—who have increasingly been imprisoned by it. Within Western cities, new forms of soft and hard technologies—including modes of managing social relations and spatial configurations—have enabled all manner of geopolitical zoning. The most powerful, for example, are now able, however permeable this may turn out to be, to insulate themselves in hermetically sealed enclaves, where gated communities and sophisticated modes of surveillance are the order of the day, both in the public spaces controlled by panoptical CCTV cameras, in the closely surveilled spaces of leisure and mass consumption malls, and in their suburban housing estates. Concurrently, the rich and powerful can decant and steer the poor into clearly demarcated zones in the city, where implicit and explicit forms of social control keep them in place (for a review, see Merrifield and Swyngedouw 1996). The efficacy of such a 'militarization of urban space' as Mike Davis appropriately calls it (Davis 1991), correlates directly with intensifying social polarization and processes of social exclusion and fragmentation. The contradictions of modernization reassert themselves with a vengeance in the reordering of our urban spaces (Swyngedouw 1997*b*). As the subsequent chapters will show, such general trends are cross-cut by all manner of variations and significant differences. In particular, local institutional settings, regional configurations, national political-economic regimes (and in particular, the degree and quality of welfare provision and income redistribution mechanisms), inter-state arrangements (such as the EU), and the constellation of multilevel systems of governance, produce outcomes that render each place unique and result in social and economic conditions of everyday life that make life in Dublin rather significantly different from the urban condition of, say, Naples or Copenhagen.

1.3.2. Globalizing the city?

In recent years, 'globalization' has emerged as the rhetorical vehicle and analytical device to describe recent important shifts in the economic and political organization of the world economy; and was quickly complemented by extensions of the concept into the cultural domain. The world economy has allegedly moved from a nation-state system to fundamentally and irrevocably new forms of institutional organization that have surpassed the traditional state-based and state-dominated world system. The propagation of this globalization ideology has become like an act of faith. Virtually all governments, in conjunction with economic élites, at every conceivable scale of governance, have taken measures to align their social and economic policy to the 'requirements' of this new competitive world (dis)order and the forces of a neo-liberal world economy. In the light of the real or imagined threat of owners of presumed (hyper)mobile capital that they might relocate their activities, regional and national states feel increasingly under pressure to assure the restoration of a fertile entrepreneurial culture. Budgetary and fiscal constraint has to be exercised, social expenditures kept in check, labour markets made more flexible, and social regulation minimized, while the terrain has to be cleared to permit the territorialization of those particular forms of capital that are deemed to be central to take on competitors on a global scale. This, then, is heralded as the golden path that will lead regional and national economies to the desired heaven of global competitiveness and sustained growth (Moulaert *et al.* 2000).

In production, local or regional subsidiaries, production and firm networks, deeply inserted in local/regional institutional, political, and cultural environments, co-operating locally, but competing globally, have become central to a reinvigorated—but often highly vulnerable and volatile—local, regional, or urban economy (Swyngedouw 2000*a*). A variety of terms have been associated with territorial economies such as learning regions, intelligent regions, *milieux innovateurs*, or reflexive economies. These territorial production systems are articulated with national, supranational, and global processes. In fact, intensifying competition on an expanding scale is paralleled exactly by the emergence of locally/regionally sensitive production milieus (Amin 1994). Yet, these localized or regionalized production complexes are organizationally, and in terms of trade and other networks, highly internationalized and globalized (Dicken *et al.* 2001). In fact, the 'forces of globalization' and the 'demand of global competitiveness' prove powerful leitmotifs for the economic élites to shape local conditions in their desired image: high productivity, low direct and indirect wages, and an absentee state. Companies have become simultaneously intensely local *and* intensely global (Drache and Gertler 1991; Group of Lisbon 1994; Ohmae 1995; Storper 1997; Cox 1997). All this is, of course, closely associated with hard and soft technologies that enable quick movement from place to place, and the 'annihilation of space by time' (Harvey 1981). Hard-nosed policies to impose free trade and the unhindered mobility of capital and commodities (but, of course, the free mobility of the labour force does not figure in the geopolitical reality of the neo-liberal utopian plans) coincide with the emergence of semi-global (really only North America, Western Europe, and parts of South-East Asia (and Japan)) material infrastructures and geographies to facilitate these integrated, networked flows. Needless to say, social power choreographies are consequently profoundly rearranged. Indeed, different groups and individuals bear different relationships to global flows of money, capital, technology, jobs, and information that become condensed in urban arenas, which have transformed into ever-greater containers of all sorts

of capital. The 'bulls and bears' of the urban financial enclaves and their associated business service districts—the smart buildings and office towers, neatly
packaged in decorative post-modern architectural jackets—have re- or displaced traditional urban economic activities and have begun to act as pivotal
relay centres in organizing and capitalizing on the flows of increasingly state-
less global capital. 'Traditional' activities have, of course, by no means disappeared from the urban, but have been relegated to suburban or marginalized
ex-urban spaces.

The breakdown of the post-war financial order on a global scale unleashed
a ballooning speculative flow of capital from one place to another that whizzed
through the digital lines of cybernetic information systems. These 'Spaces of
Flows' (Castells 1989) amount to a daily total turnover of over 2 trillion US$
that is moved from city to city (Swyngedouw 1996a). The practices of deterritorialization and re-territorialization by transnational corporate service,
leisure, real estate, and cultural capital have intensified the economic restructuring of urban regions. Many have seen a rampant de-industrialization, sometimes followed by a hesitant transformation into a business and financial
service economy. Big cities have become the central nervous system of these
flows, where financial managers and services reign over a service-based economy, whose support structure is maintained by a growing army of often part-
time and insecure jobs. As in the eighteenth and nineteenth centuries, when
many cities were equally functioning as major service-based hubs—although
the mix with manufacturing was much more explicit then than now—the service sector is not the glittering panacea to cure all socio-economic ills, as some
pundits of a high-tech service-based urban development model tend to make
us believe. While élite business services cater for the financial and other needs
of the newly organized firms, and for the new urban gentry, a large part of the
jobs have been created in the dead-end, low wage segments of personal services,
catering, and retailing, together with a booming 'sweated' industry in the construction, garment, and food industries of the world's major cities (Moulaert
and Tödtling 1995; Castells and Mollenkopf 1991; Sassen 1991). Needless to
say a new breed of city builders, the real estate developers in association with
banking interests, have moved in to replace or join the state and their Master
Planners in shaping the urban fabric. The development of the Leopold
Quarter in Brussels for European Union-related activities, the Guggenheim in
Bilbao, and London's Docklands are, of course, examples of this new form
of urban entrepreneurialism, but Berlin, Copenhagen, Vienna, Naples, and
Athens have also been thrown into this development frenzy, as the case
studies later in this book attest. While financial and service capitals flock to,
or flow through, the reconquered city—the 'revanchist' city as Neil Smith
(1997) appropriately labels it—industrial production either moves to the
exopolises surrounding the metropolitan areas or expands in the Third World
(Soja 1996).

1.4. Revitalization Strategies in the 'Glocal' City-as-Spectacle

The process of commodification of city spaces has taken unprecedented forms (Debord 1967). City imaging, city marketing, and the packaging of city life as chunks of commodified units for sale to a burgeoning tourist and business services industry, have taken root in most of our cities (Kearns and Philo 1993). Birmingham, Lisbon, Antwerp, Athens, and Dublin hustled to become the next 'Cultural Capital of Europe' or organizers of the Olympic Games. The spectacle of urban life has been transformed into the spectacle of the commodity (Swyngedouw 2002*b*). Time–space patterns have accelerated at an unprecedented rate: instantaneous production and consumption have reduced the turnover time of production, consumption, and even ideas to a minimum. Baudrillard's feeble post-modernism revels in the pleasures that some gain from a condition in which the sign and the image have seemingly become all there is to see and experience (Lash and Urry 1994). The transformation of cities into seductive theatres of accumulation collides with the permanent free time that characterizes daily life in the job-free zones of many urban and suburban neighbourhoods.

In face of the market tyranny that has become the triumphalist gospel of dominant political, economic, and cultural groups, it is not surprising to find that those most disempowered in cities often have had to resort to desperate forms of protest. The satellite cities of Paris and Lyons, for example, so captivatingly displayed in the French *film noir La Haîne*, testify to the crumbling social cohesion that feeds a rampant racism and to the boiling rancour that can easily blow the lid off the rumbling urban discontent. The frequent street upheavals in cities like Paris, Brussels, Lyons, or London, and the recent social inferno in England's racialized northern towns and cities, all illustrate the fragility of public acquiescence when marginalized citizens confront a deepening economic and socio-cultural crisis. Violence would seem the only effective conduit to communicate the voice of the dispossessed and politically disenfranchised. The élite's response usually amounts to a combination of mobilized counter-violence, political indifference, and verbal indignation.

Urban regions of the size and dynamics of today are globally connected in ways that reach every nook and cranny of the earth. The ecological footprint of the contemporary city extends from the local milieu to global problems. The bursting life of the city can only be sustained at the cost of unsustainable environmental degradation in other parts of the world. While companies in our cities and regions desperately try to instil an image and practice of environmental sensitivity, they continue to ransack the ecologies of less protected spaces in the post-colonial worlds (Harvey 1996). The mass migration of economic, political, and ecological refugees from Africa and elsewhere to the imagined honey-pots of Western Europe and the USA has resulted in a proliferation of urban asylums and refugee prisons, and contributed to greater urban socio-spatial inequality.

However myopic this evocation of contemporary urban restructuring may be, it casts a light on the condition of the urban that is somewhat different from the lustrous image most cities try to present. Surely, cities are still very much the pivotal sites where creative action and emancipatory practices emerge and reside. Cities are containers of the world; they are where the world, the global, becomes territorialized and rooted. The most remote of things appear just around the corner, the exotic has become our neighbour. The enabling and exhilarating experiences associated with this close encounter with the 'Other', the different, opens up the possibility of endless new configurations that are explored in new forms of music, art, design, and lifestyles. The process of global integration has reached its azimuth in the contemporary urban environment. But, at the same time, this very global–local condition is wrought with all manner of tension and conflict, as well as with benevolent chaos, potentially creative encounters, and enabling social practices. Each and every one of the above processes that summarize the contemporary urban condition hammer home how social, political, cultural, ecological, and economic action are inscribed in space and revolve around the meaning and (re)appropriation of space and place (Lefebvre 1989).

The urban-regional multiplex has become, more than ever before, a kaleidoscope of apparently disjointed spaces and places, a collage and patchwork of images, signs, functions, and activities that are nevertheless connected in myriad ways. The whirlwind of change that engulfed the urban has been defined by many as constituting a radical break with modernity, announcing the dawn of a new post-modern era. A small library of books has attempted to identify the contours of these assumed new times: ephemerality, fragmentation, disorder, uniqueness, collage, deconstruction, particularity, image, speed, time/space compression, open-endedness, non-totalitarian, aestheticized, vernacular—these are just some of the verbal gimmickry that has been identified with post-modernity (Soja 1989; Jameson 1991; Dear 2000). Contra the advocates of the 'post-modern turn', the last two decades have seen, if anything, the reassertion with a vengeance of the process of modernization, whose contradictory dynamics have been wrestling free from the cocoon in which the particular form of modernism that defined the managed capitalism and the planned urbanity of the post-war era had tried to contain it (Harvey 1989a). The flux and vagaries of modernization have taken over again and have left behind planners and policy-makers with their now redundant paper traces of a surpassed future. The contemporary period, however new the conditions may be, expresses the relentless restructuring of the spatiality of modern life that already impressed Baudelaire in nineteenth-century Paris and exhales the dictum that, under capitalism, 'everything that is solid melts into air' (Berman 1982).

These turbulent transformations are interspersed by, and articulated through, not only new forms of economic organization, but, perhaps more importantly, by a shift in institutional and political arrangements, alongside changing parameters of cultural and ideological scripting of the place of the urban. In particular, we shall argue that the re-scaling of the institutional and political domain, and its imprint on the urban fabric, is a major constitutive factor in producing growing social, economic, and cultural differentiations and heterogeneities. While this permits some to express new lifestyles and to explore emancipatory ways of living, others remain captive in a maze of exclusion, growing polarization, and reduced citizenship rights (Fainstein *et al.* 1992). The analysis of the reordering of the political and institutional framework that accompanies this change and that, ultimately, defines the choreographies through which global process become urbanized and territorialized in concrete urban projects is what we shall turn to next.

1.5. Re-Scaling the State, Governing the Urban

This section explores the intricate relationship between recent changes in the role and the position of the national state, and the formation of new and differently 'scaled' institutional forms on the one hand, and urban restructuring processes on the other (see Brenner 1999). We shall discuss the ways in which the drive to produce competitive spaces coincides with a more prominent position for both local and supranational state forms or sites of governance. This 're-scaling' of the state and the rise of 'glocal' forms of governance (Swyngedouw 1992*a*; 1997*a*; 2000*b*) takes place through the formation of new élite coalitions on the one hand, and the systematic exclusion or further disempowerment of politically and/or economically already weaker social groups on the other. Such exclusive homogenization of regional spaces erodes diversity and difference in highly oppressive ways. The glocal 'Entrepreneurial' (Harvey 1989*b*) or 'Schumpeterian Workfare' state (Jessop 1993; 1994*a*; Peck and Jones 1994; Peck 1995) becomes an 'Authoritarian' state (Swyngedouw 2000*b*).

Throughout Europe—and the case studies in this book will further attest to this—'glocalizing' tendencies of the state apparatus have been identified (Jessop 1993; 1994*b*; Morgan and Roberts 1993; Keating and Loughlin 1997; Brenner 1998*b*; Swyngedouw 1996*b*; Leitner 1997; MacLeod and Goodwin 1999; Baeten and Swyngedouw 2001; Boyle 2000). The re-scaling of the state is part and parcel of a wider and more global restructuring of the political economic geography of accumulation in the direction of what is invariably labelled as post-Fordism, flexible accumulation, or post-industrialization. However, much of the burgeoning literature in this field tends to focus on industrial, technological, and/or organizational changes (for a review, see Amin and Thrift 1994; Amin 1994; Berndt 2000; Moulaert and Swyngedouw 1989; Sadler 2000; Zeller 2000). We seek to argue and document that the reorganization of the post-war development model and the hesitant, highly contested, and still undecided restructuring is accompanied by quite important and powerful institutional changes. Moreover, these institutional changes are emerging through the processes by which the sort of interventions and large-scale urban development projects that are discussed in this book are implemented.

Although the thesis of state re-scaling has been advanced by a number of authors (see above), the actual mechanisms through which this process takes place remain vague and under-theorized. We maintain that urban restructuring processes, among others, provide the leverage for the national state to initiate such re-scaling. Even in traditionally social democratic political regimes, the tension between rising fiscal and monetary problems at the level of the national state (combined with the urgent need to revive ailing urban and regional economies in the context of mounting global competition), the erosion of democratic control and decision-making procedures, and the resorting to 'exceptional' procedures and institutional arrangements are seen as ways to restore the socio-economic basis for competitive economic growth. Needless to say, these processes do not unfold in an uncontested manner. At each moment, a variety of groups within civil society mount attacks on this increasing 'glocal' authoritarianism, while the power of others becomes consolidated and is often reinforced. In short, the relationship between state and civil society becomes more tense and riven with all manner of conflict, as the gap between the state and some strata within civil society widens. These exclusionary practices, in turn, silence a growing number of people, result in a fragmented urban-regional social fabric, and undermine the possibility of constructing an 'hegemonic vision' (Zukin 1996). Finally, the élite control over the new scales of governance results in strategies, which turn the future of the urban region into an image of their own interests (Harvey 1989*b*; Peck 1995). The outcome, then, further erodes socio-spatial cohesion and produces a new space, which includes the few and excludes the many. As will be documented in the empirical chapters of this book, we maintain that it is exactly through the production of new urban places that the above processes become manifest and concrete.

In the growing literature on the disputed development of 'post-Fordist' forms of socio-economic organization, relatively little attention has been paid to the state, its role, and the effects of recent state restructuring. Yet, it is evident that whatever form of restructuring takes place, the state is inevitably deeply caught up in this restructuring process. The state form is, in fact, central to Regulation theory, which maintains that changes in the form of the economy are always paralleled by changes in the form of the state (Lipietz 1987; Boyer 1986). While French regulation theory is indebted to state theorists like Poulantzas (1978) and Aglietta (1979) (see also Lipietz 1988), their theorization of the 'post-Fordist' state remains limited. With Jessop (1993), we agree that the state has to be brought back to centre stage in attempts to theorize and understand the form(s) of post-Fordist development. In addition, and perhaps more importantly, it is through the state (at whatever scale) that the position and role of the citizen and her/his relationship with society is defined, institutionalized, and, on occasion, contested and challenged. Of course, it is also through the state or other forms of governance that the territorialization and regulation of accumulation takes place. The state is an arena for the crystallization of political alliances and conflict, but also the site that has hegemonic control over legitimate forms of violence and mediates social conflict in the face of the requirement to maintain accumulation and economic development at the highest possible rate (Brenner 1998a). The politics of post-Fordism, therefore, need to be defined in relationship to these new state forms. Particularly if we are concerned with formulating emancipatory policies and strategies, the state or other forms of governance remain key arenas for challenging processes of exclusion and disempowerment.

Socio-economic urban restructuring illustrates and embodies these changes. We maintain that the analysis of urban/regional restructuring is not only a means of excavating the restructuring of the state apparatus, but perhaps more importantly, that the form of urban restructuring becomes, among other strategies, the way through which this reorganization of the state is achieved. As Lefebvre (1976) has argued, the state (at whatever scale—local, national, international) is always spatially organized, as its interventions are profoundly spatial strategies to regulate social and physical relations. Spatialized interventions are, consequently, one of the strategies where state tactics to control and mediate social relations among individuals, classes, class fractions, and social groups in the context of the maelstrom of perpetual shifts in the global economy are played out. The scale of governance, then, becomes an integral part of these tactics and strategies to mediate and control tension and social conflict. The re-scaling of the state redefines and reworks the relationship between state and civil society or between state power and the citizen (Swyngedouw 1996b).

One of the remarkable institutional–political (as well as economic—see Cooke, Moulaert, Swyngedouw, Weinstein, and Wells 1992) tendencies, over the past decade or so, has been the simultaneous internationalization and decentralization/devolution of key policy/regulatory/economic issues (see Swyngedouw 1992a; 1997a). A host of new institutional or regulatory bodies have been set up. They possess considerable decision-making and developmental powers, but operate in a shady political arena with little accountability and only limited forms of democratic control. These institutional changes have been invariably defined as part of a wider shift from government to governance. Increasingly, state regulation articulates with forms of governance in regulatory arrangements 'beyond-the-state' (Swyngedouw et al. 2002). Whereas, in the past, urban development was directly or indirectly under the control of a particular governmental scale, i.e. either at the national state and/or the local (municipal) level, in recent years there has been a proliferation of new, often project-related, institutions, bodies, and actors that are involved in policymaking and strategic planning at a variety of geographical scales, most notably at the scale of the European Union and at the sub-national or local scale. Of course, the partial 'privatization' of governance itself results in much greater power and autonomy in terms of strategic and other decision-making for corporations, private actors, and, occasionally, NGOs of a variety of stripes and colours. Privatization *de facto* means taking away some control from the public sector and transferring this to the private sector. This not only changes decision-making procedures and strategic developments, but also affects less tangible elements such as access to information and data.

The result is a new scalar gestalt of governance, characterized by a multi-scaled articulation of institutions and actors with varying degrees of power and authority. Traditional channels of democratic accountability are hereby cut, curtailed, or redefined. A plethora of new institutions has been formed at a variety of geographical scales. This proliferation of 'governing bodies' has diminished the transparency of the decision-making process and renders it more difficult to disentangle and articulate the power geometries that shape decision-making outcomes (Swyngedouw *et al.* 2002). Consequently, the level of the national state, which used to be the pivotal scale for negotiating and implementing (urban and regional) development policy, as well as regulating a host of socio-economic and even cultural tensions and relations during the post-war period, is not only profoundly redefined, but its discretionary powers have been eroded. In short, the denationalization of policy-making has altered the influence and diminished the relative importance of the national institutional level. This can be exemplified by the Europeanization of important regional, social, and economic policy initiatives and programmes and the devolution of state power to decentralized local or regional institutions, often newly created (MacLeod 1999). This new international/local ('glocal') state configuration parallels important changes in the nature and organizational structure of these 'local' institutional frameworks. Ironically, while the creation of local institutions is often defended and legitimized on the basis of their assumed potentiality to enhance democratic control from locally rooted organizations, the evidence often suggests the opposite—that is, a tendency towards a loss of democratic control and towards a political–institutional basis functioning on the basis of a very small, usually élite, basis (Swyngedouw 1996*b*). In addition, the privatization of governance (the displacement of state power outwards) increases the control and power of (inter)national or regional business élites which take centre stage in promoting a 'boosterist' entrepreneurial development vision (Cox and Mair 1989; Cox 1998).

1.6. A Preliminary Conclusion

The re-scaling of the state, therefore, does not suggest a diminishing role for the state apparatus. In fact, as we shall document further in this book, these new global/local institutions, in close co-operation with private capital, launch such redevelopment largely on the basis of public funds and state capital (Peck 1995; Peck and Tickell 1995). However, power and control over this public capital is increasingly diverted to a small élite, which shapes the urban/regional fabric in their own image and fashions and defines the very content of the restructuring process. The 'hollowed out' state is characterized, therefore, by an undemocratic and doubly authoritarian touch, both at the supranational and local (urban/regional) level. In short, disturbing political transformations and a redefined citizenship parallel the production of 'post-Fordist' spaces.

These new institutional forms are riven with all manner of conflicts and tensions. First, this double rearticulation of the scaling of the state is highly contested, particularly by those who become marginalized in, or excluded from, these new institutions. Second, the new alliances that are forged and their need to affirm their legitimacy accentuates the need on the part of the boosters to try to create an hegemony of vision, particularly through the spectacularization of both development perspectives and political programmes, which takes away the focus from the substantive, on-the-ground transformations of the urban-regional socio-economic fabric. This is particularly urgent, as channelling capital into speculative real estate-based projects and infrastructure tends to provide a more secure accumulation base in the long run as other investments become subject to increasingly global competition (see Harvey 1978). As Brenner (1997) suggests (*pace* Lefebvre 1989), a central role of state power is to mediate the tension between 'the territorialization of surplus-value realisation in the secondary circuit of landed property and the deterritorialization through the increasing globalisation of the world-economy in the primary circuit of capital circulation'. The production, control, and surveillance of social and physical spaces are central to this mediating process. As the tensions intensify with accelerating globalization, more authoritarian or strong forms of governance become increasingly important to allow the new élites to mine land rents through channelling capital into the built environment, while simultaneously producing a relative crisis-free and cohesive civic order. The built environment, then, becomes synonymous with real estate speculation and the production of a new built environment rather than with the provision of jobs.

Of course, new social movements (sometimes in alliance with the politically and socio-economically excluded) challenge the new élite programmes and question the legitimacy of the institutional framework from which they are excluded (Mayer 1994; Moulaert *et al.* 2000). Such strategies of resistance can take a variety of forms, ranging from the rise of deeply anti-state forms of anti-politics which feed the electoral support for extreme right-wing political parties to active contestation of the development vision by all sorts of groups, from discontented—since excluded—local business people to the green movement and immigrant groups.

It is exactly this relationship between Urban Development Projects, globalization dynamics, and the reconfiguration of the state on the one hand

and socio-economic polarization and political-economic exclusion on the other, to which we shall turn in the next chapter.

References

AGLIETTA, M. (1979). *A Theory of Capitalist Regulation—The U.S. Experience.* London: New Left Books (original work published 1976).

AMIN, A. (1994) (ed.). *Post-Fordism.* Oxford: Blackwell.

——and THRIFT, N. (1994) (eds). *Globalization, Institutions, and Regional Development in Europe.* Oxford: Oxford University Press.

BAETEN, G., and SWYNGEDOUW, E. (2001). 'Scaling the City: The Political Economy of 'Glocal' Development—Brussels' Conundrum'. *European Planning Studies,* 9/7: 823–49.

BERMAN, M. (1982). *Everything that is Solid Melts into Air.* New York: Simon & Schuster.

BERNDT, C. (2000). 'The Rescaling of Labour Regulation in Germany: From National and Regional Corporatism to Intrafirm Welfare?'. *Environment and Planning A,* 32: 1569–92.

BOYER, R. (1989). *Regulation Theory, a Critical Perspective.* New York: Columbia University Press (original work published 1986).

BOYLE, M. (2000). 'Euro-Regionalism and Struggles over Scales of Governance: The Politics of Ireland's Regionalisation Approach to Structural Fund Allocations 2000–2006'. *Political Geography,* 19: 737–69.

BRENNER, N. (1997). 'State Territorial Restructuring and the Production of Spatial Scale'. *Political Geography,* 16/4: 273–306.

——(1998a). 'Between Fixity and Motion: Accumulation, Territorial Organization and the Historical Geography of Spatial Scales'. *Environment and Planning D: Society and Space,* 16: 459–81.

——(1998b). 'Global Cities, Glocal States: Global City Formation and State Territorial Restructuring in Contemporary Europe'. *Review of International Political Economy,* 5: 1–37.

——(1999). 'Globalisation as Reterritorialisation: The Re-Scaling of Urban Governance in the European Union'. *Urban Studies,* 36/3: 431–51.

CASTELLS, M. (1989). *The Informational City.* Oxford: Blackwell.

——and MOLLENKOPF, J. (1991). *Dual City.* New York: Russell Sage Foundation.

COOKE, P., MOULAERT, F., SWYNGEDOUW, E., WEINSTEIN, O., and WELLS, P. (1992). *Towards Global Localization: The Computing and Communications Industries in Britain and France.* London: University College Press.

COX, K. (1997) (ed.). *Spaces of Globalization: Reasserting the Power of the Local.* New York and London: Guilford Press and Longman.

——(1998). 'Spaces of Dependence, Spaces of Engagement and the Politics of Scale, or: Looking for Local Politics'. *Political Geography,* 17/1: 1–23.

——and MAIR, A. (1989). 'Urban Growth Machines and the Politics of Local Economic Development'. *International Journal of Urban and Regional Research,* 13: 137–46.

DAVIS, M. (1991). *City of Quartz: Excavating the Future of L.A.* London: Verso.

DEAR, M. (2000). *The Postmodern Urban Condition.* Oxford: Blackwell.

DEBORD, G. (1967). *La Société du Spectacle.* Paris: Buchet-Chastel.

DICKEN, P., KELLY, P. F., OLDS, K., and WAI-CHUNG YEUNG, H. (2001). 'Chains and Networks, Territories and Scales: Towards a Relational Framework for Analysing the Global Economy'. *Global Networks*, 1/2: 89–112.

DRACHE, D., and GERTLER M. (1991) (eds.). *The New Era of Global Competition.* Montreal: McGill-Queens University Press.

FAINSTEIN, S., GORDON, I., and HARLOE, M. (1992) (eds). *Divided Cities: New York and London in the Contemporary World.* Oxford: Blackwell.

Group of Lisbon (1994). *Limits to Competition.* Cambridge, Mass.: Harvard University Press.

HAMNETT, C. (1996). 'Social Polarisation, Economic Restructuring and Welfare State Regimes'. *Urban Studies*, 33: 1407–30.

HARVEY, D. (1981). *Limits to Capital.* Oxford: Blackwell.

——(1985). 'The Geo-Politics of Capitalism', in D. Gregory and J. Urry (eds.), *Social Relations and Spatial Structures.* Macmillan: London.

——(1989a). 'From Managerialism to Entrepreneuralism: The Transformation in urban Governance in Late Capitalism'. *Geographiska Annaler Series B*, 71: 3–18.

——(1989b). *The Condition of Postmodernity.* Oxford: Blackwell.

——(1996). *Justice, Nature and the Geography of Difference.* Oxford: Blackwell.

JAMESON F. (1991). *Postmodernism or, the Cultural Logic of Late Capitalism.* London: Verso.

JESSOP, B. (1993). 'Fordism and Post-Fordism: Critique and Reformulation', in A. Scott and M. Storper (eds.), *Pathways to Regionalism and Industrial Development.* London: Routledge, 43–65.

——(1994a). 'Post-Fordism and the State', in A. Amin (ed.), *Post-Fordism: A Reader.* Oxford: Blackwell, 251–79.

——(1994b). 'The Transition to Post-Fordism and the Schumpeterian Workfare State', in R. Burrows and B. Loader (eds.), *Towards a Post-Fordist Welfare State?* London: Routledge, 13–37.

KEAINS, G., and PHILO, C. (1993) (eds.). *Selling Cities; The City as Cultural Capital, Past and Present.* Oxford: Pergamon Press.

KEATING, M., and LOUGHLIN, J. (1997) (eds.). *The Political Economy of Regionalism.* London: Frank Cass.

LASH, S., and URRY, J. (1994). *Economies of Signs and Spaces.* Thousand Oaks, Calif: Sage.

LEFEBVRE, H. (1976). *De l'Etat, II.* Paris: Union Générale d'Editions.

——(1989). *The Production of Space.* Oxford: Blackwell.

LEITNER, H. (1997). 'Reconfiguring the Spatiality of Power: The Construction of a Supranational Migration Framework for the European Union'. *Political Geography*, 16/2: 123–43.

LIPIETZ, A. (1987). *Mirages and Miracles: The Crisis of Global Fordism*, trans. D. Macey. London: New Left Books.

——(1988). 'Reflections on a Tale: The Marxist Foundations of the Concepts of Regulation and Accumulation'. *Studies in Political Economy*, 26: 7–36.

MACLEOD, G. (1999). 'Place, Politics and "Scale Dependence": Exploring the Structuration of Euro-Regionalism'. *European Urban and Regional Studies*, 6/3: 231–53.

MacLeod, G. and Goodwin, M. (1999). 'Reconstructing an Urban and Regional Political Economy: On State, Politics, Scale, and Explanation', *Political Geography*, 18: 697–730.

Marx, K., and Engels, F. (1848; 1997). The Communist Manifesto. CD-Rom eb0002, London: Electric Book Company.

Massey, D. (1992). 'Politics of Space/Time'. *New Left Review*, 196: 65–84.

Mayer, M. (1994). 'Post-Fordist City Politics', in A. Amin (ed.), *Post-Fordism: A Reader.* Oxford: Blackwell, 316–37.

Merrifield, A. (1993). 'Place and Space: A Lefebvrian Reconciliation'. *Transactions, Institute of British Geographers*, ns 18: 516-31.

——(2002). 'The Dialectics of Space and Place: Theory and Politics in the Age of Globalization'. Department of Geography, Clark University, Worcester, Mass. (mimeographed).

——and Swyngedouw, E. (1996) (eds.). *The Urbanization of Injustice*. London and New York: Lawrence and Wishart and New York University Press.

Morgan, K., and Roberts E. (1993). 'The Democratic Deficit: A Guide to Quangoland'. *Papers in Planning Research*, No. 144, Department of City and Regional Planning, University of Wales, College of Cardiff.

Moulaert, F., and Wilson, P. (1983). *Regional Analysis and the New International Division of Labour.* Boston: Kluwer Nijhoff Publishing.

——and Swyngedouw, E. (1989). 'A Regulation Approach to the Geography of Flexible Production Systems'. *Environment and Planning D*, 7: 327–45.

——and Tödtling, F. (1995). 'The Geography of Advanced Producer Europe. Special issue of *Progress in Planning*, vol. 43, parts 2–3, pp. 97–274.

——*et al.* (2000). *Globalization and Integrated Area Development in European Cities.* Oxford: Oxford University Press.

Ohmae, K. (1995). *The End of the Nation State.* London: Harper Collins.

Olds, K. (2001). *Globalization and Urban Change.* Oxford: Oxford University Press.

Peck, J. (1995). 'Moving and Shaking: Business Elites, State Localism and Urban Privatism'. *Progress in Human Geography*, 19: 16–46.

——(1996). *Work Place.* New York: Guilford Press.

——and Jones, M. (1994). 'Training and Enterprise Councils: Schumpeterian Workfare State or What?'. *Environment and Planning A*, 27: 1361–96.

——and Tickell, A. (1995). 'Business Goes Local—Dissecting the Business Agenda in Manchester'. *International Journal of Urban and Regional Research*, 19: 55–78.

Poulantzas, N. (1978). *State, Power, Socialism.* London: New Left Books.

Sadler, D. (2000). 'Organizing European Labour: Governance, Production, Trade Unions and the Question of Scale'. *Transactions, Institute of British Geographers*, ns 25: 135–52.

Sassen, S. (1991). *The Global City.* Princeton: Princeton University Press.

Smith, G. (1989) (ed.). *Benjamin: Philosophy, Aesthetics, History*. Chicago: Chicago University Press.

Smith, N. (1984). *Uneven Development: Nature, Capital and the Production of Space.* Oxford: Blackwell.

——(1993). 'Homeless/Global: Scaling Places', in J. Bird, B. Curtis, T. Putnam, G. Robertson, and L. Tickner (eds.), *Mapping the Futures Local: Cultures Global Change.* London: Routledge, 87–120.

——(1997). *The Revanchist City*. London: Routledge.

Soja, E. (1989). *Postmodern Geographies.* Oxford: Blackwell.

——(1996). *Thirdspace—Journeys to Los Angeles and other Real-and-Imagined Places.* Oxford: Blackwell.

Sorkin, M. (1993) (ed.). *Variations on a Theme Park—The New American City and the End of Public Space.* New York: The Noonday Press.

Storper, M. (1997). *The Regional World.* New York: Guilford Press.

Swyngedouw, E. (1992a). 'The Mammon Quest: "Glocalization", Interspatial Competition and the Monetary Order: The Construction of New Scales', in M. Dunford and G. Kafkalas (eds.), *Cities and Regions in the New Europe: The Global-Local Interplay and Spatial Development Strategies.* London: Belhaven Press, 39–67.

——(1992b). 'Territorial Organization and the Space/Technology Nexus'. *Transactions Institute of British Geographers,* ns 17: 417–33.

——(1996a). 'Producing Futures: Global Finance as a Geographical Project', in P. Daniels and W. Lewer (eds.), *The Global Economy in Transition.* Oxford and London: Longman, 135–63.

——(1996b). 'Reconstructing Citizenship, the Re-Scaling of the State and the New Authoritarianism: Closing the Belgian Mines'. *Urban Studies,* 33: 1499–1521.

——(1997a). 'Neither Global Nor Local: "Glocalization" and the Politics of Scale', in K. Cox (ed.), *Spaces of Globalization: Reasserting the Power of the Local.* New York and London: Guilford Press and Longman, 137–66.

——(1997b). 'The Specter of the Phoenix—Reflections on the Contemporary Urban Condition', in K. Bosma and H. Hellinga (eds.), *Mastering the City I.* Rotterdam, The Hague, and New York: Netherlands Architecture Institute, EFL Publications, and Distributed Art Publishers, 104–21.

——(1998). 'Homing In and Spacing Out: Re-Configuring Scale', in H. Gebhardt, G. Heinritz, and R. Weissner (eds.), *Europa im Globalisierungsprozess von Wirtschaft und Gesellschaft.* Stuttgart: Franz Steiner Verlag, 81–100.

——(2000a). 'Elite Power, Global Forces and the Political Economy of "Glocal" Development', in G. Clark, M. Feldman, and M. Gertler (eds.), *The Oxford Handbook of Economic Geography.* Oxford: Oxford University Press.

——(2000b). 'Authoritarian Governance, Power and the Politics of Rescaling'. *Environment and Planning D: Society and Space,* 18: 63–76.

——(2002a). 'Scaled Geographies: Nature, Place, and the Politics of Scale', in R. McMaster and E. Sheppard (eds.), *Scale and Geographic Inquiry: Nature, Society and Method.* Oxford and Cambridge, Mass.: Blackwell (forthcoming).

——(2002b). 'The Strange Respectability of the Situationist City'. *International Journal of Urban and Regional Research* (forthcoming).

——Page, B., and Kaika, M. (2002). 'Achieving Participatory Governance: Sustainability and Innovation Policies in Multi-Level Context', in P. Getimis, H. Heinelt, G. Kafkalas, R. Smith, and E. Swyngedouw (eds.), *Participatory Governance in Multi-level Context: Theoretical Debate and the Empirical Arena.* Frankfurt: Leske and Budrich (forthcoming).

United Nations Centre for Human Settlement (HABITAT) (1996). *An Urbanizing World: Global Report on Human Settlements.* Oxford: Oxford University Press.

Zeller, C. (2000). 'Rescaling Power Relations between Trade Unions and Corporate Management in a Globalising Pharmaceutical Industry: The Case of the Acquisition of Boehringer Mannheim by Hoffman-La Roche'. *Environment and Planning A,* 32: 1545–67.

ZUKIN, S. (1991). *Landscapes of Power.* Berkeley and Los Angeles: California University Press.

——(1996). 'Cultural Strategies of Economic Development and the Hegemony of Vision', in A. Merrifield and E. Swyngedouw (eds.), *The Urbanization of Injustice.* London and New York: Lawrence and Wishart and New York University Press, 223–4.

2

Urban Restructuring, Social-Political Polarization, and New Urban Policies

Arantxa Rodríguez, Erik Swyngedouw, and Frank Moulaert

2.1. Introduction

The dynamics of economic restructuring and globalization have radically reshaped the fortunes of cities and urban regions during the last two decades. For cities throughout the world, changing fortunes mean coming to terms with the consequences of socio-economic dislocation brought about by the reorganization of production and demand globally, including increasing polarization and social exclusion. To meet the challenges posed by the new economic realities, the policy agenda of cities has been drastically redefined. The new urban agendas reflect a shifting policy focus away from regulatory and distributive considerations towards the promotion of economic growth and competitiveness, a trend that has placed revitalization at the centre of urban intervention (Hall 1988; Oatley 1998; Roberts and Sykes 2000).

This strategic turn in the urban agenda is part and parcel of a critical reappraisal of the form, functions, and scope of urban policy and of the rise of new modes of urban governance (Brindley et al. 1989; Healey et al. 1995). Biased by the same neo-liberal pressures that have driven the restructuring of state intervention in all policy arenas, the emerging governance system reflects the fragmentation of governing responsibilities and the increasing involvement of private sector interests in urban policy design and implementation. And, while a variety of competing styles of planning and governance still provide for a great deal of differentiation, urban regeneration is increasingly framed in a common language of competitiveness, flexibility, efficiency, state entrepreneurship, partnership, and collaborative advantage (Healey 1997; Jessop 1997; Oatley 1998).

Changes in the urban policy arena have paved the path for competitive redevelopment by means of a variety of revitalization strategies (Moulaert et al. 2000). In the 1990s, urban revitalization strategies, aimed at repositioning cities on the map of globally competitive metropoles, strongly relied on the planning and implementation of large-scale Urban Development Projects (UDPs) to lead economic regeneration. These emblematic projects are non present all over the urban and regional landscape and are the material expression of a developmental logic that views them as major leverages for generating future growth and attracting investment capital and consumers.

This chapter focuses on the relationship between global restructuring and processes of integration and exclusion in the city through an analysis of large-scale urban redevelopment projects in European cities. The first part of the chapter discusses the socio-economic and political context in which UDPs develop and operate. In trying to understand why these mega-projects have become the dominant instruments for promoting and reviving ailing urban and regional economies, we discuss critical changes in the urban policy arena over the last two decades, underlining the links between the New Economic Policies and the New Urban Policies. In section 2.2, urban revitalization policy is set against a background of changing urban governance that incorporates critical shifts in scale, domains of intervention, actors and agents, institutional structures and relations, and policy tools, highlighting the significance of various innovative components of the New Urban Policies. Section 2.3 locates UDPs in relation to the local community and to integration and exclusion mechanisms. The fourth and final section addresses the limits of urban entrepreneurialism and the new urban governance and points to the need for new directions.

2.2. Restructuring Cities: Globalization, Economic Restructuring, and Social Exclusion

Intensifying processes of social exclusion and polarization have been among the most prominent and visible characteristics of urban socio-economic restructuring (Fainstein *et al.* 1992; Mingione 1995). In most major European cities, the crisis of Fordism and the reorganization of global production, consumption, and distribution conditions have altered in radical ways the hierarchy of sectors and the structure of labour markets and led to the emergence of a new socio-economic fabric as well as new forms of social and territorial fragmentation (Benko and Lipietz 1992; 2000; Moulaert 1996; Marcuse and van Kempen 2000). Persistent high levels of unemployment, shortage and casualization of job opportunities, homelessness, deteriorating housing and living conditions, widening income gaps, social violence, etc., have become an integral part of the new urban context, regardless of prevailing dynamics of economic growth or decline (Madanipour *et al.* 1998). New forms of deprivation and social exclusion have increased and reinforced the spatial segregation of Europe's urban areas and have led to new socio-spatial divisions (Martens and Vervaeke 1997; Pacione 1997). These tendencies towards increasing fragmentation and segregation in cities have been analysed predominantly in terms of the combination of, and articulation between, global socio-economic transformation, on the one hand, and local, regional, and/or national structural adjustment policies on the other (Hamnett 1994; Preteceille 1997).

The transformation of employment is, doubtless, the key axis of urban socio-economic restructuring and the primary factor shaping increasing inequality and social fragmentation in cities (Lawless *et al.* 1998). The crisis of Fordism and the transition to globalized flexible accumulation are accompanied by the radical recomposition of labour markets. The reorganization of production has brought in massive job loss and made it increasingly difficult for large sections of the urban population to (re-)enter the formal labour market and adjust to the new economic realities (Castells 1997). But unemployment is only the tip of an iceberg of increasing casualization of labour markets that involves increasing segmentation, skill polarization, flexibility, and externalization.

The recomposition of labour markets contributes directly to social exclusion because of the effects of high unemployment, income loss, and wage restraints on lowering purchasing power, but also through the exclusion of the unemployed from work and consumption-related social networks. At the same time, the transformation of employment also contributes to social exclusion because the required skills levels, the socialization norms on the shop floor or in the office, become increasingly less attainable by a larger portion of the active population, those least able to secure institutional access to social protection or welfare-based income. On the other hand, the promotion of growth and job creation, generally viewed as the most important means to combat unemployment and social exclusion, can also increase the risks of exclusion for vulnerable groups through the widespread extension of flexible and casualized employment (Moulaert *et al.* 2000). Indeed, the simultaneity of economic growth and the extension of poverty, vulnerability, and exclusion constitute, today, the basis for widening social and territorial cleavages (European Commission 1997).

The reorganization of labour markets has not been the only factor contributing to social polarization and exclusion; the extension of social and spatial fragmentation has also been strongly mediated by the fundamental reorganization of the Keynesian welfare state. The end of sustained growth has severely undermined both the capacity and commitment of the Keynesian state to maintain welfare, social integration, and demand management policies. The extension of needs and demands that followed the crisis of employment came up head-on against the fiscal and financial constraints imposed by economic austerity and shifting priorities of state intervention towards macroeconomic stability and supply-side crisis management policies (Navarro 1998). The emphasis on structural and international competitiveness has favoured a subordinated and productivist realignment of social policy to the imperatives of competitive restructuring. The strategic reorientation of the social and economic functions of the Keynesian welfare state has been explained as a tendency towards the gradual substitution of the Keynesian welfare state for a Schumpeterian workfare state more tuned to the needs and requirements of globalized flexible accumulation (Jessop 1993). The combination of global socio-economic restructuring processes, shifting policy priorities, and a changing and more restrictive social policy have led to the emergence of a wide diversity of new categories of urban poor (Mingione 1995; Benassi *et al.* 1997). But the growth of poverty and social exclusion is also linked to cultural and political factors. In the cultural sphere, the emergence of new urban élites, direct or indirect beneficiaries of restructuring processes, stand in sharp contrast to increasing deprivation, and the disempowerment and marginalization of other segments of the urban population (Merrifield and Swyngedouw 1996; Swyngedouw 1997*b*). Social and spatial differentiation and exclusion are, however, often disguised under ready-made image reconstruction strategies that provide the basis for new models of collective identification that mirror the lifestyles and aims of urban élites, excluding less successful or less marketable social groups from the new projected urban identity (Goodwin 1993; Kearns and Philo 1993).

Likewise, social exclusion can be reinforced through dynamics of political representation. In the political sphere, exclusion from social spaces and networks of power, from mainstream political processes, and from decision-making structures and dynamics are key factors of exclusion. In this sense, the social and spatial isolation of deprived sectors and communities from power centres and their absence—or direct exclusion—from decision-making processes about their future, contribute in a fundamental way to intensifying processes of social division and exclusion. The concentration of deprivation in particular urban areas and neighbourhoods fosters the formation of 'excluded communities' that are, often, reproduced by the very initiatives that purportedly aim at eradicating them (Geddes 1997).

In sum, heightening processes of social polarization and exclusion have accompanied the dynamics of economic restructuring and globalization. Processes of exclusion always operate in and through social space and nowhere has this been more evident than in urban areas. The rising concentration of excluded populations in certain geographical areas is an integral component of urban socio-economic change while social divisions are compounded by spatial segregation. The latter, in turn, is often re-enforced by a reorganization of land rents and housing prices that reflects the recomposition of urban space sought by the new urban policy. In this context, responding to increasing poverty and social exclusion in cities is gradually becoming an important point on the new urban agenda.

2.3. Urban Restructuring Policy: Large-scale Urban Development Projects (UDPs)

The new global economic realities, and the way they reshuffle urban land markets, as well as the reorganization of welfare, constitute the basic pillars of urban socio-economic restructuring. But the dynamics of urban transformation are also critically framed by the responses and strategies followed by cities to cope with change. It is increasingly recognized that the national, regional, and local state, as they create new socio-economic and political conditions for development, play a crucial part in shaping the fortunes of cities and urban regions as well as the processes of social inclusion/exclusion (Painter 1995). Urban policy has evolved in a context where globalization and restructuring processes raise important questions both about the changing functions and roles of cities as well as about the management and implementation of urban change in a globalized economy. Thus, in the same way cities are being thoroughly transformed by widespread economic, social and political re-composition, so has the emergence of a new urban policy been part and parcel of these shifts (Healey *et al.* 1995).

2.3.1. *Towards a New Urban Policy: searching for growth and competitive restructuring*

Changes on the urban agenda reflect a shifting policy focus away from regulatory and distributive considerations towards economic growth and competitive redevelopment. The reorientation of urban policy rests increasingly on economic regeneration and the promotion of competitiveness for tackling problems of urban decline, social disadvantage, and social exclusion derived from global restructuring. The emphasis on regeneration and competitiveness locates urban revitalization strategies at the centre of urban intervention (Hall 1988; Oatley 1998; Roberts and Sykes 2000).

Despite important differences among the case-study projects, they all share a common realignment of urban policy with the goals and means of a New Economic Policy (NEP). New Economic Policy is the policy platform of conservative liberalism. Contrary to what its ideology sustains, conservative liberalism is not against state intervention; rather it seeks to reorient state intervention away from monopoly market regulation, towards supporting economic growth and competitiveness. Likewise, NEP involves downplaying Keynesian redistribution policies in favour of more targeted social policies and indirect service provision. NEP involves, therefore, the restructuring of state intervention in line with principles of privatization and commodification (see Fig. 2.1).

2.3.2. *Urban revitalization: the choice of large-scale Urban Development Projects*

Changes in the urban policy arena have paved the path for competitive redevelopment by means of a variety of revitalization strategies, ranging from large-scale megadevelopments to integrated action plans and community-based

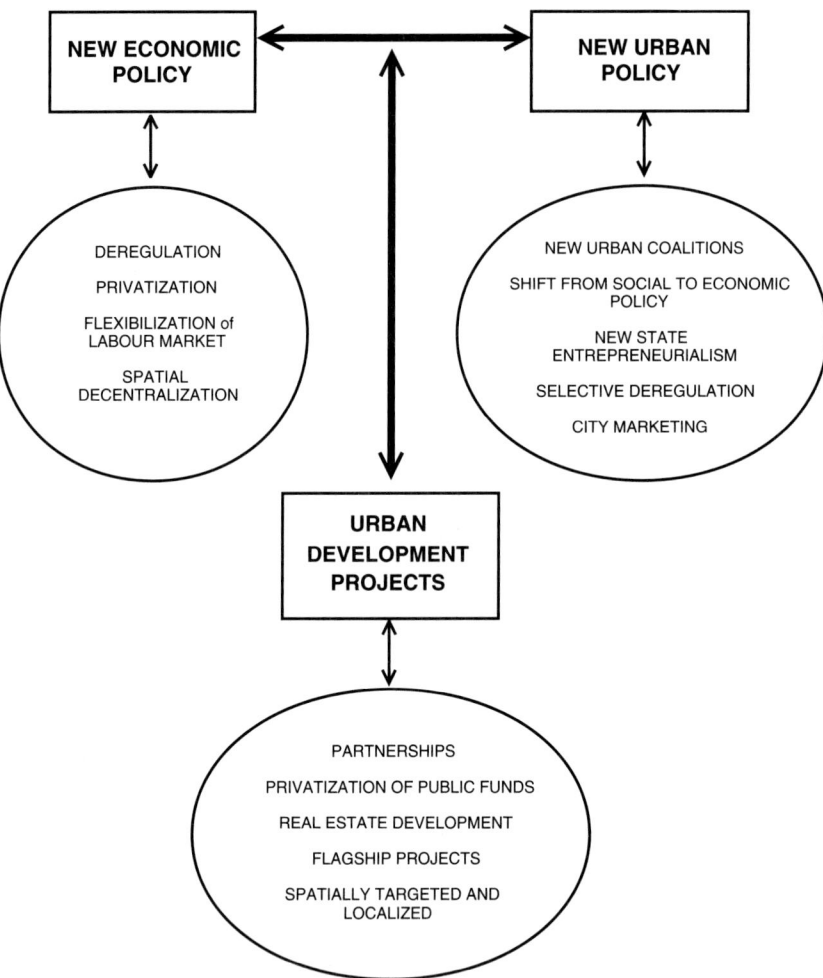

Fig. 2.1. Relationship between NEP, NUP, and UDPs

local restructuring efforts (Moulaert *et al.* 2000). These schemes are spread over the European urban and regional landscape, operating in a variety of regulatory, political, and socio-economic contexts, welfare regimes, and public policy frameworks and combine private and public initiatives and financial sources in a great diversity of institutional and organizational frameworks. However, they are comparable in the sense that they are inserted in, and grapple with, epochal European and global trends and attempt to reassert the position of the city in the new global economic competitive climate and its associated technological, cultural, and social transformations. Each of these set forth a series of exclusion/integration mechanisms that, in the end, shape or moderate the process of polarization and exclusion itself.

In Europe, during the 1990s, urban revitalization strategies, aimed at re-positioning cities on the map of globally competitive metropolises, have strongly relied on the planning and implementation of large-scale Urban Development Projects (UDPs) to lead a fundamental reconstruction of physical, socio-economic, political, and symbolic urban space. Of course, large-scale urban development projects are not particularly new. Ever since Haussmann's grand re-design of Paris, Robert Moses's plans for New York City, the post-war large housing schemes, or, more recently, Paris's *Grands Projets*, re-colonizing the city by means of major interventions has been part and parcel of urban development strategies. Yet, in recent years, such UDPs have emerged and been framed in a radically different political-economic and cultural context. Indeed, the new generation of UDPs sets itself apart from previous rounds of UDPs in the way they attempt to mediate between the spatial requirements of socio-economic restructuring and urban development. That is, the UDPs of the last decade take up the reconversion of derelict sites left behind by industrial closures or rationalization of obsolete infrastructure as an opportunity to create the physical conditions necessary to launch a new phase of development. Thus, the new generation of UDPs are the material expression of a developmental logic that views them as major leverages for generating future growth and for waging a competitive struggle to attract investment capital and consumers. Such projects seize and reflect urban restructuring processes in a uniquely synthetic way and, therefore, pave the way for the analysis of wider, more general processes of social inclusion/exclusion as they become magnified at the scale of the urban.

2.4. Managing Competitive Redevelopment: Towards a New Urban Governance

One of the salient features of the new urban context is the growing complexity of city government and urban politics that has favoured a gradual substitution of urban government for urban governance (Newman and Thornley 1996; Mayer 1994; Healey *et al.* 1995; Swyngedouw 1996). According to Stoker (1989; Stoker and Young 1993), the concept of urban governance incorporates the formal institutions of local government, changing government structures, and informal institutions as well as the direct involvement of private sector interests in the managing of cities. The expansion of the sphere of local political actions implies the fragmentation of local intervention decisions among a range of public, semi-public, and private actors. The emerging governance system places these actors, agencies, special planning bodies, private sector organizations, etc., alongside local government in designing and implementing urban strategies. The resulting institutional pattern is characterized by a proliferating number of institutions and organizations, usually organized as one or other form of public–private partnership. As is often the case for traditional forms of government that provide an arena to articulate state/civil society relationships, many among these new forms of governance tend to be based on a rather limited representation from civil society (Swyngedouw 1997*a*; 2000*a*; 2000*b*).

The emergence of new urban governance shows three parallel trends: (*a*) the greater role of local politics/institutions in staging proactive development strategies; (*b*) the increasing mobilization of local political, economic, and/or cultural power constellations in support of economic development and subordinating social policies to economic and labour market policies (a trend that has fostered a shift towards the 'entrepreneurial' city); and (*c*) the fragmentation of agencies among a range of private and semi-public actors co-ordinated through new forms of public–private collaboration (Mayer 1994).

This complex form of governance constitutes the institutional background against which the public sector's relations to the UDPs need to be situated. The local state defends the developmental logic of urban regeneration based on large-scale urban investment projects, following the rationale of global finance, real estate capital, and the real or imagined need for competitive restructuring. In other words, the local state proactively leads a New Economic Policy by promoting private investments through deregulation, providing fiscal relief and public city marketing actions (Cox 1997; Moulaert *et al.* 2000). At the same time, it has to wrestle in its social and political relations with the various parts of urban society: local SMEs, neighbourhood groups and their representatives, socio-economic interest groups (unions, professional organizations), political parties and activists, etc. (Judge *et al.* 1995). This unstable situation often drives local authorities to pursue rather exclusive or opportunist strategies for managing social relations. Among them, the growing importance of exceptionality procedures (circumventing standing rules and regulations), calls on the regional or national state for financial assistance, the establishment of non-governmental and non-accountable institutions, the formation of 'stakeholder' interest networks, the emergence of compensating—but unfortunately often low budget—social economy measures. In this way, local authorities become trapped in a triangular tension between the New Economic Policy, an ambiguous legitimization discourse in an attempt to forge a more harmonious coexistence of inherently conflicting development logics, and increasingly louder calls from populations in depressed neighbourhoods for new initiatives in the social economy and in fostering community social services.

The governance of project-led urban revitalization is highly revealing of these changes in urban policy-making and implementation. Like no other mechanism, UDPs reveal trends towards the formation of a new local mode of regulation of urban (re)development and management shaped by the pressures of competitive restructuring and changing social and economic priorities, as well as by major political and ideological shifts. Indeed, the emergence of the New Urban Policy rests significantly on the establishment of new forms of intervention at the local level, which, to a large extent, constitute a rupture with traditional institutional forms. Because, it is argued, the goals of urban regeneration cannot be achieved with traditional policy structures and processes, internalizing these goals requires a more proactive and entrepreneurial approach to city governance. This view has tied urban regeneration policy and practice to very fundamental changes in urban governance and the process of policy formulation and implementation.

2.4.1. Mediated entrepreneurialisms in urban regeneration

One of the key components of the new mode of socio-economic regulation in cities has been a gradual shift away from distributive policies, welfare considerations, and direct service provision towards more developmental approaches aimed at economic promotion and competitive restructuring. In most cities, urban revitalization is presented as an opportunity to change sector hierarchies and functions within the urban region, creating new jobs and strengthening the city's position in the division of labour among cities. The search for economic growth turns physical renewal into a mediated objective, a necessary precondition for economic regeneration.

Although this general trend adopts quite distinct forms in different cities, it generally involves critical changes in development priorities and the ascent of a more assertive and dynamic, albeit élitist, style of urban governance. Planners and local authorities are persuaded (and, on occasion, forced) to adopt a more proactive and entrepreneurial approach aimed at identifying market opportunities and assisting private investors to take advantage of them. The notion of entrepreneurialism highlights the increasing involvement of cities in the promotion of economic development and the parallel subordination of social policies to economic and labour market policies. Thus 'entrepreneurial' urban policy has assumed more direct forms of support for private capital including the use of leverage funding, direct subsidies, public–private partnerships, and the removal of regulatory constraints to make investments more attractive and secure private sector involvement in urban revitalization. But entrepreneurialism is also about the public sector running cities in a more business-like manner. This means that private sector management and accounting principles are increasingly applied in public sector administration.

Although most case studies documented in this book exhibit, to some extent, elements of entrepreneurialism, its particular form is crucially shaped by specific local contexts and regulatory traditions in each city. For example, while in Vienna entrepreneurialism means actively advertising the city as a strategic location with a business friendly environment, entrepreneurial rhetoric is mediated by a tradition of 'Fordist-type' social partnerships which

made, until recently, a single-minded discourse on efficiency and competitiveness by local politicians and planners unacceptable. A form of 'social
entrepreneurialism', combining business and social values, is rather in place
here. Similarly, in Copenhagen, the ambivalence between, on the one hand, a
participatory and welfare-oriented policy approach and, on the other, a neo-
corporate growth policy paradigm provides the conditions for a particular
form of social-democratic entrepreneurialism or 'new state-led entrepreneurialism'. And, in Dublin, while the principal direction of urban governance in
recent years has been towards making the Dublin Corporation more of a business and less of a bureaucracy, a modified entrepreneurial approach, with
a relatively strong interventionist bent, is more likely to develop. In Berlin,
limited entrepreneurial flexibility is guaranteed by strong state regulation. And
a limited entrepreneurial approach is also perceived in the cases of Lisbon and
Bilbao, although this does not necessarily imply a greater control of the public
institutions over the redevelopment process.

2.4.2. Institutional fragmentation and pluralistic governance

The case studies show that, over the last decade, the reorientation of urban
policy has been closely associated with fundamental shifts from traditional
government/governing structures to more diffused, fragmented, and flexible
modes of governance. Indeed, the combination of different spatial and administrative scales in urban policy-making and the increasing fragmentation of
competencies and responsibilities is one of the most relevant aspects identified
in the case studies. In most cities, the full dimension of urban regeneration
cannot be adequately apprehended without reference to the multiplicity of
agents and the fragmentation of agency responsibility within and beyond the
urban arena. In some cases, this trend seems to be linked to a shift from hierarchical relationships (in terms of the traditional territorial hierarchy of statutory planning procedures) to a more collaborative, but often socially highly
exclusive, scheme where partnerships between, and networks of, élites with various social, economic, or political backgrounds play a key role. However, at the
same time, fragmentation and diversity are also accompanied by tendencies
towards the exclusion of certain groups and collectives from participating in
the decision-making process; a democratic deficit emerges as a central element
of a strategic approach which is validated fundamentally on the grounds of its
'technical efficiency'. Ironically, as in the cases of Athens or Lisbon, the national state plays a pivotal role in setting up the élite development consortia that are
given 'free play' in implementing local programmes.

The emergence of a more fragmented and pluralistic mode of urban governance has contributed to redefining the roles played by local authorities.
Indeed, the new governance system involves the subordination of formal government institutions to more informal and quasi-private agencies with massive
redistribution of policy-making powers, competencies, and responsibilities. In

the name of greater flexibility and efficiency, these new institutions compete and often supplant local and regional authorities as protagonists and managers of urban renewal. In particular, the new governance has served to reinforce the tendency towards a more proactive approach, with local authorities acting simultaneously as enablers, partners, and clients. However, it has been often the case that local authorities are overrun and marginalized, even before such a process could be undertaken. In fact, the new governance structures express the provisional outcomes of an ongoing re-negotiation between the different levels of government, local, regional, or central administration, regarding competencies and powers in the management of urban revitalization. In addition, private capital equally operates at the interstices of public/private arrangements at the various scales of governance and, consequently, influence forms of state organization.

New inter-organizational bodies have been set up with an eye towards improving public sector performance, displacing traditional planning institutions, and subordinating formal government structures. The establishment of these new structures often involves the massive redistribution of policy-making powers, competencies, and responsibilities away from local governments to often highly exclusive partnership agencies, a process that has been described in terms of the 'privatization' of urban policy-making. In Dublin, for example, the establishment of the CHDDA as a planning authority in its own right took away significant powers from local authorities, excluding these from participating in one of the most important urban regeneration projects in Dublin. In Vienna, the shift from neo-corporatist and clientelist networks towards a more flexible and autonomous field of public planning has gone hand in hand with the proliferation of autonomous and semi-autonomous bodies assuming key functions in urban development. In Bilbao, Athens, Lisbon, Copenhagen, Berlin, Rotterdam, and Naples, the UDP is managed by a quasi-private organization with the legal status of a private company that acts as the main developer of the project area. Nevertheless, the state often plays a pivotal role and 'state executives' become part of the élite networks and management structures that run such new forms of governance, albeit in ways that are autocratic and outside the traditional procedures of democratic accountability.

Along with the increasing role of the central administration in shaping localized strategies for urban regeneration, several case studies also highlight the relevance of the metropolitan level in the planning process. The often missing metropolitan level is perceived as a relevant factor in explaining the fragmentation of the different powers and plans, the lack of co-ordination and of coherence in planning, the lack of an integrated administrative structure for planning, the overlapping and duplication of competencies, and even diminished accountability. In Lisbon, the missing linkages for planning and political decision-making at the metropolitan level are a main constraint for urban development that increasingly suffers from confrontations between local authorities, state departments, and public and private agencies. While in

Bilbao, the missing metropolitan level brings about significant disfunctionalities in urban policy in general and in revitalization initiatives in particular.

2.4.3. Market-led agenda, state guaranteed risks

The case studies reveal that, in contrast to discourses on market-led and entrepreneurial activity (risk-taking investments), UDPs are decidedly and almost without exception state led—even if managed by quasi-private structures—and often state financed. In a context of national deregulation, shrinking or stable social redistribution policies, and the outright exclusion of some groups at the national or European Union level (for example, immigrants) and an often narrowing fiscal basis for local urban intervention, UDPs are marshalled as panaceas to fight polarization, reinvigorate the local economy, and, most importantly, an explicit goal in many projects, to improve the tax basis of the city via a socio-spatial reorganization of the metropolitan space. In other words, urban redevelopment is considered to be a central strategy in rebalancing the problematic fiscal balance sheet of local government. Territorial policies, aimed at producing increasing rent income, altering the socio-economic tax basis, and producing profitable economic activities, are among the few options available, particularly in a context in which the structure of tax revenues is changing rapidly. As the financial services sector and profit-making via global speculative transactions drain major financial means, they simultaneously escape government control and generate only very limited fiscal returns.

Despite the rhetoric of market-led and privately covered investments, the state is still one of the leading actors in the process. Risks are taken by the state, on occasion shared with the private sector, but, given the speculative, real estate-based nature of the projects, deficits are likely to occur, especially when project-led strategies are carried out in less central areas. Well-known processes of socialization of the cost and risk, and privatization of the possible benefits, can be identified. While, in the past, such practices were legitimized by invoking the social return of the projects, they are now usually hidden behind a veil of creative accounting and the channelling of funds via quasi-governmental organizations and mixed private/public companies.

2.4.4. From community to élite partnerships: informal networks and co-ordinating structures

The fragmented character of many of the UDPs, often self-contained, isolated, and disconnected from the general dynamics of the city, contrasts sharply with the emphasis on co-ordinated action by different actors, the validation of partnerships, and the building of networks and support coalitions as a precondition for effective implementation. These networks or partnerships are presented as a superior form of urban management, more flexible and efficient, thus better adapted to the competitive and accelerating processes of global urban change. The growth of partnerships, in particular, is a fundamental component of a wider trend: the move towards increasing inter-organizational and collaborative networking of public policy and administration.

The case studies in the research reveal that the implementation of large-scale emblematic projects during the last decade has proceeded alongside a gradual move away from a centralist top-down relationship between the state and the local authorities towards more contractual modes of interaction between various institutional levels. And, parallel to this, has been the emergence of a new orientation of urban regeneration policy: contractual policy, fostered by the creation of specific instruments to promote public–private collaboration and investment. Berlin, Bilbao, Birmingham, Lisbon, and Vienna have, in different ways, followed this path. But while in Berlin, for example, most of these changes were state led and continued to involve state bureaucrats in key positions, in Vienna a trend towards a more flexible and less bureaucratic approach to planning emerged in the last decade as the planning department switched emphasis away from technical planning to a more network- and actor-based approach. The state-centred hierarchical planning approach was criticized as top-down and new planning procedures adopted more horizontal bargaining systems. Yet these new systems tended to cluster together élites while excluding ever-larger segments of the population at large.

The increasing role of informal networks of decision-making is also an important feature of the emerging urban governance model. Informal networks are, in fact, highly relevant in the tendering of large-scale projects. In Vienna, an informal network of decision-makers consisting of politicians, planners, private investors, representatives of banks and insurance firms, and construction and housing companies has emerged as key actors in the new local power field. In Brussels, there has been a shift from a centralist top-down relationship between the state and the local authorities, to contractual relations between various institutional levels. But, while there has been a growing role for public–private partnerships and local propulsive agencies, the maintenance of standard procedures for public spatial planning and project implementation has limited the autonomization of partnerships. At the same time, the establishment of local networks around national personalities can also be interpreted as the continuity of a vertical relationship in the decision-making process.

The trend towards a more flexible and network-oriented approach is often perceived as a validation of 'bottom-up', less hierarchical, and more participatory dynamics. Indeed, recourse to architectural competitions, expert procedures, and international workshops appears to open up the field of planning to greater participation. However, participation is often limited to selected professionals: architects, planners, economists, bankers, developers, engineers, etc., who have become increasingly influential while the non-professional sector and less powerful social groups are largely excluded. In the same way, several case studies also show that the shift from centralist, formalized, bureaucratized, hierarchical, top-down planning approaches to decentralized, more horizontal, informal, flexibilized, bottom-up, and network planning approaches has gone hand in hand with increasing inequality in access to decision-making. A strengthening of the role of experts is made at the expense of a diminishing role for the public in general and for traditional organized groups in particular, with a consequent loss of democratic accountability. Copenhagen, Vienna, Bilbao, and Lisbon illustrate this trend in a very clear way.

Thus, the mystique of an inclusive, non-hierarchical, and participatory network approach towards planning is undermined by the realities of a network based on the primacy of the expert, dominated by new technical and social élites and highly exclusionary in terms of access to decision-making processes. As is succinctly summarized in the Viennese case study, 'the advantage of these personalized networks is mutual trust and high adaptability; its disadvantage is a decrease of public accountability, a weakening of civil society, and an erosion of the existing parliamentary democracy'.

2.5. Conclusion

During the last decade and a half, urban regeneration policy has become an increasingly central component of urban policy. For the most part, urban regeneration schemes based on large-scale UDPs were aimed at combining physical upgrading with socio-economic development objectives. However, the new socio-economic realities pushed the focus of urban policy gradually away from managing city growth and the negative externalities of accelerated urbanization towards coping with the consequences of economic crisis and restructuring. The search for growth and competitive redevelopment became the leading objective of the new urban policies in an attempt to reassert the position of cities in the emerging global economy. But there is now a growing concern with increasing social and spatial polarization.

A fundamental component of many of the urban regeneration initiatives discussed in the case studies is the stress placed on developing and strengthening the competitiveness of cities. Enhancing the competitive advantage of cities is seen as largely dependent on improving and adapting the built environment to the demands and requirements of emerging sectors and firms. Therefore, physical reconversion and economic recovery tend to go hand in hand in these urban regeneration strategies and, very often, are perceived as quasi-simultaneous processes. At the same time, all UDPs respond to the imperatives of socio-economic change and are the material expression of a developmental logic that views mega-projects as major leverages for future growth and functional transformation. As such, they operate at the interstices between physical planning and development policies. But, although a radical transformation of the physical environment is, indeed, an integral part of urban regeneration, the overriding physical bias of these schemes renders economic recovery and growth almost an assumed automatic consequence. Moreover, it is increasingly recognized that UDP-led revitalization schemes rarely trickle down to deprived communities that—unless they are physically wiped out!—remain practically untouched by the revitalization dynamics induced by these projects. On the contrary, it is reasonable to assume that UDP-based strategies can actually contribute to exacerbating the exclusion mechanism for deprived communities because of the high opportunity costs of the massive allocation of resources to the UDPs. New Urban Policy has been accompanied by and has often facilitated the formation of a new form of urban governance that has rested principally on fostering new relations between the local state and the private sector and has, consequently, reshuffled social and political power relations in important ways. Accountability and participation often declined, while élite visions took over the actual restructuring of the city. In addition, these large-scale UDPs actively co-produced the processes that were later recognized as constituting globalization. UDPs are, in fact, the material and political-economic manifestations through which actual processes of economic globalization, cultural transnationalization, and increased inter-urban competition become constituted. As such, globalization is a process that is profoundly localized and is the result of concrete territorial restructuring dynamics. Pushing through this model of globalizing urbanization demands the cohesive formation of a growth-oriented élite configuration that will hold local governance under its hegemonic siege.

References

BENASSI, D., KAZEPOV, Y., and MINGIONE, E. (1997). 'Socio-economic Restructuring and Urban Poverty under Different Welfare Regimes', in F. Moulaert and A. Scott (eds.), *Cities, Enterprises and Society on the Eve of the 21st Century*. London and Washington: Pinter.

BENKO, G., and LIPIETZ, A. (1992) (eds.). *Les Régions qui gagnent. Districts et réseaux: les nouveaux paradigmens de la géographie economique*. Paris: Presses Universitaires de France.

—— and —— (2000). *La Richesse des régions: la nouvelle géographie socio-économique*. Paris: Presses Universitaires de France.

BRINDLEY, T., RYDIN, Y., and STOKER, G. (1989). *Remaking Planning: The Politics of Urban Change in the Thatcher Years*. London: Unwin Hyman.

CASTELLS, M. (1997). *La Era de la información. Economía, sociedad y cultura. El Poder de la identidad*, ii. Madrid.

Cox, K. (1997) (ed.). *Spaces of Globalization: Reasserting the Power of the Local*. New York and London: Guilford Press and Longman.

European Commission (1997). *Towards an Urban Agenda in the European Union*. Communication from the Commission. Brussels.

FAINSTEIN, S., GORDON, I., and HARLOE, M. (1992) (eds.). *Divided Cities: New York and London in the Contemporary World.* Oxford: Blackwell.

GEDDES, M. (1997). 'Poverty, Excluded Communities and Local Democracy', in N. Jewson and S. MacGregor (eds.), *Transforming Cities: Contested Governance and New Spatial Vision.* London: Routledge.

GOODWIN, M. (1993). 'The City as Commodity: The Contested Spaces of Urban Development', in G. Kearns and C. Philo (eds.), *Selling Places: The City as Cultural Capital, Past and Present.* Oxford: Pergamon Press.

HALL, P. (1988; 1996). *Cities of Tomorrow.* Oxford: Blackwell.

HAMNETT, C. (1994). 'Social Polarisation in Global Cities: Theory and Evidence'. *Urban Studies*, 31/3: 401–24.

HEALEY, P. (1997). *Collaborative Planning: Shaping Places in Fragmented Societies.* London: Macmillan.

——CAMERON, S., DAVOUDI, S., GRAHAM, S., and MADANIPOUR, A. (1995) (eds.). *Managing Cities: The New Urban Context.* London: Wiley.

JESSOP, B. (1993). 'Towards a Schumpeterian Workfare State? Preliminary Remarks on post-Fordist Political Economy'. *Studies in Political Economy*, 40: 7–39.

——(1997). 'The Entrepreneurial City: Re-imaging Localities, Redesigning Economic Governance, or Restructuring Capital?', in N. Jewson and S. MacGregor (eds.), *Transforming Cities: Contested Governance and New Spatial Vision.* London: Routledge.

JUDGE, D., WOLMAN, H., and STOKER, G. (1995) (eds.). *Theories of Urban Politics.* Sage: London.

KEARNS, G., and PHILO, C. (1993) (eds.). *Selling Places: The City as Cultural Capital, Past and Present.* Oxford: Pergamon Press.

LAWLESS, P., MARTIN, R., and HARDY, S. (1998) (eds.). *Unemployment and Social Exclusion: Landscapes of Labour Inequality.* London: Jessica Kingsley Publishers.

MADANIPOUR, A., CARS, G., and ALLEN, J. (1998) (eds.). *Social Exclusion in European Cities: Processes, Experiences and Responses.* London: Jessica Kingsley Publishers.

MARCUSE, P., and VAN KEMPEN, R. (2000) (eds.). *Globalizing Cities: A New Spatial Order?* Oxford: Blackwell.

MARTENS, A., and VERVAEKE, M. (1997) (eds.). *La Polarisation sociale des villes européennes.* Paris: Anthropos.

MASSEY, D. (1994). *Place, Space and Gender.* London: Polity.

MAYER, M. (1994). 'Post-Fordist City Politics', in A. Amin (ed.), *Post-Fordism: A Reader.* Oxford: Blackwell, 316–37.

MERRIFIELD, A., and SWYNGEDOUW, E. (1996) (eds.). *The Urbanization of Injustice.* London and New York: Lawrence and Wishart and New York University Press.

MINGIONE, E. (1995). 'Social and Employment Change in the Urban Arena', in P. Healey, S. Cameron, S. Davoudi, S. Graham, and A. Madanipour (eds.), *Managing Cities: The New Urban Context.* London: Wiley.

MOULAERT, F. (1996). 'Rediscovering Spatial Inequality in Europe: Building Blocks for an Appropriate "Regulationist" Analytical Framework'. *Society and Space*, 14: 155–79.

——et al. (2000). *Globalization and Integrated Area Development in European Cities.* Oxford: Oxford University Press.

NAVARRO, V. (1998). *Neoliberalismo y estado del bienestar.* Madrid: Ariel.

NEWMAN, P., and THORNLEY, A. (1996). *Urban Planning in Europe: International Competition, National Systems and Planning Projects.* London and New York: Routledge, 250–1.

OATLEY, N. (1998) (ed.). *Cities, Economic Competition and Urban Policy.* London: Paul Chapman.

PACIONE, M. (1997) (ed.). *Britain's Cities: Geographies of Division in Urban Britain.* London: Routledge.

PAINTER, J. (1995). 'Regulation Theory, Post-Fordism and Urban Politics', in D. Judge, H. Wolman, and G. Stoker (eds.), *Theories of Urban Politics.* London: Sage, 276–95.

PRETECEILLE, E. (1997). 'Socio-economic Restructuring of Cities and Public Policy', in F. Moulaert and A. Scott (eds.), *Cities, Enterprises and Societies on the Eve of the 21st Century.* London and Washington: Pinter.

ROBERTS, P., and SYKES, H. (2000) (eds.). *Urban Regeneration: A Handbook.* London: Sage.

STOKER, G. (1989). "Creating a Local Government for a Post-Fordist Society: The Thatcherite Project', in J. Steward and G. Stoker (eds.), *The Future of Local Government.* Basingstoke: Macmillan.

STOKER, G., and YOUNG, S. (1993). *Cities in the 1990's.* London: Longman.

SWYNGEDOUW, E. (1996). 'Reconstructing Citizenship, the Re-Scaling of the State and the New Authoritarianism: Closing the Belgian Mines'. *Urban Studies,* 33: 1499–521.

——(1997a). 'Neither Global Nor Local: "Glocalisation" and the Politics of Scale', in K. Cox (ed.), *Spaces of Globalization: Reasserting the Power of the Local.* New York and London: Guilford Press and Longman, 137–65.

——(1997b). 'The Specter of the Phoenix—Reflections on the Contemporary Urban Condition', in K. Bosma and H. Hellinga (eds.), *Mastering the City I.* Netherlands Architecture Institute, EFL Publications, and Distributed Art Publishers, Rotterdam, The Hague, and New York: 104–21.

——(2000a). 'Authoritarian Governance, Power and the Politics of Rescaling'. *Environment and Planning D: Society and Space,* 18: 63–76.

——(2000b). 'Elite Power, Gobal Forces, and the Political Economy of "Glocal" Development', in G. Clark, M. Feldman, and M. Gertler (eds.), *The Oxford Handbook of Economic Geography,* Oxford: Oxford University Press, 541–58.

3

Large-Scale Urban Development Projects, Urban Dynamics, and Social Polarization: A Methodological Reflection

Frank Moulaert, Arantxa Rodríguez, and Erik Swyngedouw

3.1. Introduction

'How can the relationship between large-scale Urban Development Projects (UDPs) and the multiple dimensions of urban socio-economic development be studied?' This is the main challenge of the URSPIC research presented in this book. In the previous two chapters, two main analytical perspectives have been discussed.

Chapter 1 addressed the dialectics between local and global dimensions of UDPs, and argued that UDPs are not just local answers to distant, abstract, and global forces driven by disembodied flows of international finance and corporate capital or by free trade-based global governance dominated by networks of financial and economic élites. They are also specifically localized projects that mobilize assets available at various interlocked spatial scales with a view towards increasing the accumulation and profitability of locally embedded capitals. In an allegedly globalized economy and polity, capital still needs to be territorialized in order to pursue its profitability objectives. Of course, the exploitation of differences between classes, social groups, and professional categories within a multi-scale geography as well as the mobilization of localized political, economic, and financial capabilities is central to capitalist strategies of territorialization.

The neo-liberal hegemony seeks to exploit these globally localized places by transforming them into competitive spaces. However, these transformations are necessarily accompanied by new, and often disciplining, regulatory regimes, and invariably hold local communities hostage to the credo of externally imposed competitive pressures. In this regard, it is not surprising that some observers see interesting parallels between the contemporary urban condition and the one that prevailed during the ultra-liberal periods of the second half of the nineteenth century when the premises of human existence were defined by the prerequisites of international competitive positions (Hirst and Thompson 1996).

In Chapter 2, it was argued that the globalization of the economy, in association with a politics of neo-liberalism, articulates with the dynamics of UDP development in a myriad of intricate manners. Of course, the local embedding of UDPs produces significantly different impacts on the local communities within metropolitan areas, depending on the specific territorial political-economic and physical embedding of the UDP. Large-scale housing projects, such as the Orestad in Copenhagen, contrast with the concentration of market-led international services found in the Quartier Léopold in Brussels, and lead to widely diverging urban development trajectories. The way these projects relate to the (pre-)existing local economy, the view and quality of urban development policy, and the governance dynamics in the cities also differ in important ways and lead, consequently, to very diverse outcomes. Yet, social polarization, political reorganization, and socio-economic transformation are common to all UDPs. It is exactly the particular articulation and mediations between the local and the transnational (often mediated via the policies of the national state and the EU) that shape and explain variations in the extent to which UDPs relate to processes of socio-economic polarization and exclusion. The territorialization of these projects is indeed a multifaceted and multidimensional affair. Whereas global forces are situated in the sphere of a market economy and the transnational politics of its regulation and law enforcement, local dynamism exhibits a mesmerizing complexity. The 'local' urban community is at the same time considered as economy, polity, social organization, space of regulation, and site for social or political movements and contestation. The key task is to unravel the processes and procedures of how social, political, and economic groups, communities, and organizations interact with the imposition of these sudden and often radical changes in the urban fabric. UDPs are frequently 'inorganic', in that they are mainly global strategies that have been planted in socio-spatial fabrics still carrying the sedimented imprint of earlier stages of urban development (nineteenth-century inner cities, semi-rural urban peripheries, derelict manufacturing sites, working-class neighbourhoods, etc.), and this creates interesting patterns of interaction with urban communities and neighbourhood organisms.

In Chapter 3, the task is to translate these dialectically grounded processes and mechanisms into guidelines for empirically informed research and analysis. In the case-study work, we focused on the following set of interrelated questions:

• How can the processes of social, economic, and political exclusion/integration in these cities be analysed?

- How can the conception, planning, implementation, and valorization of large-scale Urban Development Projects be studied, taking into account the structure of the cities and urban regions in which they are located?
- How can these processes be linked to the particular mechanisms of integration and exclusion generated by the UDP?
- How can large-scale urban development strategies be positioned with regard to trends in urban ideology and contemporary urban policy and strategic views?
- How can these 'local' research trajectories be made internationally comparable?

3.2. The Spatial Articulation of Social Exclusion

Any understanding of social exclusion processes is likely to be one-sided, unless reference is made to their spatial dimensions. The concentration of excluded populations in certain geographical areas is a fundamental part of socio-economic change. Processes of exclusion always operate in and through social space and nowhere has this been more evident than in urban areas. Worldwide economic restructuring has significantly altered the functions and hierarchy of cities and, consequently, their social structure (Sassen 1991; Fainstein 1994; Fainstein *et al.* 1992; Moulaert and Scott 1997; Scott 2001). For many cities, especially those in old industrial regions, this has meant systematic divestment from manufacturing activities, plant closures, environmental degradation, massive unemployment, and rising poverty and marginality (Andersen *et al.* 1995; Moulaert *et al.* 2000). These processes have had a significant impact on the displacement of urban populations and on the income and wealth distribution within and between cities (Moulaert, Swyngedouw, and Rodriguez 2001).

Since the end of the 1970s, and until very recently, research on socio-spatial exclusion mechanisms has been highly neglected. After some pathbreaking research by Harvey (1973), Castells (1973), Godard (1973), Preteceille (1974), and others, there has been silence from researchers and policy-makers alike. The relative success of the welfare state and the modernizing developmental views prompted a belief in a progressive, more or less socially balanced, future. The focus of research shifted to inter-regional differences and inequalities rather than intra-regional or intra-urban exclusion mechanisms. This shift took place in the context of a rapidly transforming society, which propelled new strata of economic, social, and cultural élites to the forefront. The result was significant social polarization, whereby affluence and success for one part of the population is counterposed with increasing deprivation, disempowerment, and marginalization of other social groups (Merrifield and Swyngedouw 1996; Madanipour, Cars, and Allen 1998; Mingione *et al.* 2002).

This trend prompted renewed interest in social exclusion mechanisms, but also positioned them in the context of urban and regional reorganization processes (Moulaert *et al.* 2000; Madapinour *et al.* 1998; Benassi, Kazepov, and Mingione 1997).

While economic restructuring is considered a major factor contributing to exclusion, it is increasingly recognized that the specific character of national, regional, and local state responses, changing regulatory regimes, and new modes of governance associated with the imperatives of structural change play a critical part in shaping the fortunes of cities and urban regions, as well as processes of social inclusion/exclusion. Economic restructuring generates exclusion in direct and indirect ways. Unemployment, income loss, wage cuts, etc., cause a direct lack of purchasing power, but also result in the exclusion of individuals from work and consumption-related social networks (Mommaas 1996). Indirectly, the required skill levels, the socialization norms on the shop floor or in the office, become increasingly less attainable by a larger portion of the active population. These citizens are often also less capable of negotiating institutional access to social protection or welfare incomes. The interaction between socio-economic restructuring processes (which affect, albeit to different degrees, most socio-professional categories), the shifts in focus of urban socio-economic policy, and more restricted access to the welfare system, have created a wide diversity of new categories of urban poor, whose socio-cultural identity is often hard to reconstruct (Mingione 1996; Madanipour *et al.* 1998).

The emergence of urban crisis during the 1980s and the early 1990s spurred a profound reappraisal of the form, functions, and scope of urban policy and led to shifting priorities, new modes of intervention, and the development of new planning goals, tools, and institutions (Thomas 2000; Keating, Krumholz, and Star 1996; Mayer 2000). In contrast to the 1970s, the 1980s witnessed a gradual move from (re)distribution towards a growing interest in economic promotion and competitive restructuring as the basis for urban and metropolitan revitalization. The imbalance between developmental and redistribution programmes increased as the lion's share of urban development funds was given to large infrastructure and property redevelopment projects, while support for growth initiatives meant enhancing the resources of the most dynamic and entrepreneurial sectors of the urban economy. Moreover, mega-projects and place marketing have been introduced as major leverage strategies for generating future growth and for waging a competitive struggle to attract investment capital (Voogd and Ashworth 1990; Kearns and Philo 1993; Haussermann and Kapphan 2000). Considerable attention is given to infrastructure and other major urban and regional projects which are seen to be essential for producing more jobs, and also for reinforcing the competitive position of the city and of the European Union as a whole (European Commission 1994). Whilst there is currently a significant body of knowledge available on the meaning and substance of poverty (Kazepov and Zajczyk 1997; Paugam 1996; Room 1994; Townsend 1993), its spatial variation, and the general processes contributing to its formation, there is also an important gap in our understanding of processes, mechanisms, and instruments through which polarization, exclusion, and integration are structured, organized, and institutionally geared. Previous research has focused almost exclusively on one side of the equation, i.e. poverty and exclusion. But poverty and exclusion must be understood in terms of polarization: poverty and exclusion are part of the process through which some negotiate and achieve superior positions of access (to jobs, education, housing, etc.), social status, and power, while others are weakened, marginalized, and disempowered (Moulaert 1995; 1996; Madanipour *et al.* 1998). This (neglected) relationship between the improved socio-economic situation of some groups and the worsening situation of others is one that needs to be explored further. Each of the UDPs presented in this book embodies to a certain extent the various dimensions of exclusion and integration signalled above. Yet, the analysis of these processes cannot be separated from the analysis of the development trajectories of the UDPs themselves. This is what we shall turn to next.

3.3. UDPs: Organic or Inorganic to the Existing City?

Building on previous research (Moulaert *et al.* 1994; Moulaert 1996; Swyngedouw 1996) that emphasized the highly localized processes and effects of polarization and exclusion, we intend to focus on how particular urban development projects influence and shape processes either of polarization and exclusion or, as the case may be, of socio-economic integration. Our emphasis is on the processes through which exclusion and polarization are generated. This entails the incorporation of social theory—particularly theories on class, ethnicity, and gender issues, global–local relations, state theory, welfare regimes and distribution theory, and the 'underclass' debate (Andersen and Elm Larsen 1995; Mommaas 1996)—in combination with a focus on the political economy of inter-place and inter-urban competition (Dunford and Kafkalas 1992; Kearns and Philo 1993). We have chosen to focus on large-scale urban redevelopment projects with a predominantly business-oriented urban renewal and city marketing logic, because these projects are particularly illustrative of the means through which current processes of social exclusion/inclusion operate in the urban areas in which the majority of the European Union's population lives. These mega-developments are increasingly portrayed as the most effective urban revitalization strategy, although this entails overlooking their exclusionary potential.[1] In addition, such development projects operate at the intersection of economic, social, cultural, and political processes and the point of articulation of different scale-levels (local, regional national, EU, and global). As most research indicates, the importance of the interweaving of these processes and their apparent complexity makes it difficult, if not impossible, to capture them in their rich totality at a global level (Swyngedouw and

Baeten 2001). Therefore, choosing to look at particular development projects from the perspective of the polarization/exclusion/integration processes enabled us to capture the relationships without sacrificing the complexity of their interactions. Comparing different local projects in several Member States not only contributes to the assessment of different institutional and policy environments, but also, and perhaps more importantly, enables the evaluation of the effects and the effectiveness of particular regulatory or policy conditions. As argued in Chapter 1, urban restructuring in general, and Urban Development Projects (UDPs) in particular, are the pivots of contemporary global–local ('glocal') restructuring processes. These projects are each inevitably deeply embedded in local/national social, economic, and institutional frameworks. Yet at the same time, they are eminently global in a double sense, both by responding to changing global (economic, cultural, technological) environments and by themselves contributing to these very global transformations. In other words, these UDPs are not merely responses to global change or emanations of local conditions; for the restructuring is wrought from and, in turn, shapes local *and* global processes. Urban dynamics are, therefore, both a consequence of, and a key element in, the formation of a new global economy. In short, UDPs as expressions of these urban dynamics can provide key insights into both the mechanisms of global–local integration and the consequences in terms of social polarization and inclusion/exclusion mechanisms that operate in the wider society.

3.3.1. *UDPs: multi-scalar complex development trajectories*

In order to study the real impact of mechanisms of global–local interaction, UDPs have been examined in various stages of development. In each of these stages, different articulations of local–global interactions can be found. For example, the formulation or conception stage truly takes place in an atmosphere of global competition between the world's leading architects and engineering consultancies. At the same time, it is a matter of fierce national and regional political struggle. Local politicians seek 'to bring their project home'. They do so by seeking to mobilize the 'cultural capital' of a small band of internationally renowned architects and designers, but also by mobilizing their political power position at local, regional, and national levels. The labour markets that are involved at this stage are highly élitist (very skilled professionals), often partly composed of a new nomadic international cultural and economic élite. The subsequent stage of construction and implementation will involve, among others, the employment of low-skilled construction workers hired by local, regional, or national firms who have various ethnic origins and legal status (illegal migrants, legal migrants, and nationals with varying levels of social protection). Needless to say, once completed, UDPs continue to interact with the urban labour markets, socio-spatial processes, and local policies in significant ways.

In sum, such comparative analysis of 'glocally' significant UDPs requires a methodology that allows us to reconstruct each of the case-study projects (UDPs) in terms of their economic, political, social, and cultural dimensions. It is important to excavate and reconstruct the interface of each of these dimensions in each UDP. In addition, there is need to identify 'who' (community groups, business and political élites, etc.) is involved in each stage of the project (design, planning, implementation) and, consequently, to indicate the processes of exclusion/integration at work in each stage. Moreover, we try to capture how local and higher scale processes are cemented into the structure, organization, and specific character of the UDPs. Table 3.1 shows a checklist of variables and processes that were analysed for each of the stages of the project. Of course, since not all UDPs were in the same stage of progress, this list had to be adjusted in light of the specificity of the cases.

A variety of sources and methods, such as published material, public and private documents, interviews, discourse analysis, statistics, actor network analysis, company reports, customer questionnaires, and the like were used to document these various dimensions of the UDP trajectories. Access to privileged insider knowledge holders simplified the research task, and using key witnesses as pivotal interlocutors helped us to understand the main features of the UDP and point at a first set of sources. However, much of the fieldwork can be compared to detective or grassroots intelligence work. The reconstruction of networks, financial links, political mechanisms, individual and collective responsibilities, etc., can be compared to the intelligence methodology used by the NGOs in John Le Carré's *The Constant Gardener* in their search to identify the role of transnational pharmaceutical companies in the production and distribution of an insufficiently tested drug against tuberculosis in Sub-Saharan Africa (Le Carré 2001).

3.3.2. The selection of UDPs

The selected projects incorporate global processes (such as global investment flows, dependence on immigrant labour, transnational information flows and value-added networks, supranational decision-making processes) and exemplify trend-breaking epochal changes (such as changes in cultural values and preferences, informalization of labour markets and relations, the nature of the competitive environment at a variety of scales, changes in labour and leisure time). At the same time, the projects are decidedly local, capturing these global trends and incorporating them in a particularly localized setting. For example, the Leopold Quarter development in Brussels combines national and international, private and public finance capital, uses formal and informal labour relations in its construction, including Portuguese and Polish subcontractors, necessitates policy arrangements and political compromises at the community, local, regional, national, and European level, and, last but not

Table 3.1. Organizational structure of empirical research format

---

1. Project formulation, design, and planning

Financial flows
    Direct investments flows (who, where, why, how much?)
    Indirect investments (who, where, etc.?)
    Public/private share
Employment structure
    Direct employment: number, structure, duration, qualifications
    Indirect employment relations (subcontracting, etc.)
Decision-making procedure
    Public/private rationales
    Rationales of decision-making
    Policy principles and global forces
    Ideologies, discourses, cultural visions, rhetoric
    Participatory Structure of Institutions of Governance: Who is financially, economically,
        ideologically, politically, and culturally involved and who is excluded?

---

2. Project construction and implementation

Financial flows
    Direct investments flows (who, etc.?)
    Indirect investment (who?)
    Cost/benefit analysis: who pays/who receives?
    Subcontractors for goods, services, and labour
Employment structure
    Direct employment: number, structure, length, qualifications
    Indirect employment relations (subcontracting, etc.)
    Local, national, or European dimensions of employment and welfare regimes
Effects of UDP construction on urban community
    Project site: displacement in terms of housing, cultural identity, jobs, and services
    Wider urban community impact (neighbouring areas; the wider city region)

---

3. Project operation

Financial structure
    Investment, operation, money flows
    Income, profits, distribution
Employment structure
    Number, FT/PT, M/F, ethnicity, gender relations, qualification structure, labour
        regulation system
    Subcontracting structure
    Direct impact on community
    Indirect community impact and strategic position in restructuring of the urban fabric,
        place in overall urban restructuring
Project participation
    Customers/end-users
    Profile of users/origin-destination structure of users (firms, employees, end users)
        accessibility and accessibility criteria

---

least, plays an important role in establishing and maintaining the competitive position of Brussels in the European and global inter-place competition and confirms the cultural role of Brussels as Europe's capital city. At the same time, the project has served to transform Brussels in highly polarizing ways (Papadopoulos 1996).

Care was taken to select initiatives that, at the time of the research, were in different stages of completion. Some of the chosen projects (for example, Adlershof in Berlin) were still in the planning and development formulation stage, others (such as Abandoibarra in Bilbao, or Expo 98 in Lisbon) were in various stages of implementation, while some had already been largely completed (the Leopold Quarter in Brussels), and one is still under construction (the Olympic Village Athens). This choice allowed us to identify how mechanisms of integration/exclusion are present in each phase of the process. Our aim is not to look solely at the *effects*, but, more importantly, to show how each stage in the UDP is an active and decisive element in the exclusion/integration process. Not only do the consequences of particular interventions need to be addressed (as is traditionally the case), but also the very intervention itself needs to be analysed in terms of the process of social polarization and exclusion it engenders. One urban project was chosen from each of the twelve participating countries (with the exception of the UK, in which both London and Birmingham were selected). Moreover, we worked with a sample of cities belonging to different tiers of the international urban hierarchy. This made the research even more interesting (see again Table 0.1 in the Introduction).[2]

3.3.3. UDPs and their urban fabric

In order to elucidate the central thesis of this project, i.e. the extent to which the exclusion/integration/polarization dynamics in a city are significantly co-determined by large-scale Urban Developments Projects (UDPs), the relative integration of UDPs in their urban fabric had to be analysed. For this purpose, we rely on a schematic representation of the interactions between various subsystems of the city and their spatial scales. These interactions summarize the dialectics of reproduction of localities and their subsystems (Moulaert 1996). Despite the apparent complexity of the methodological framework, earlier research undertaken for the European Commission has demonstrated both the feasibility and the power of this approach (Demazière 1996; Moulaert *et al.*, 1994; Moulaert 1996; Moulaert, Delvainquière, and Delladetsima 1997). The different types of subsystems presented in Table 3.2 must be considered from the point of view of their interaction with the UDP. Clearly, not each element in the reconstruction of the urban processes is of equal relevance for each case. In fact, identifying the relative importance of particular conditions and their interpenetration with the UDP is of central importance.

Table 3.2. The relationship between scales and urban processes

Spatial scale Subsystem	Local	Regional/national	Supranational
Production system Construction sector Labour process Technology Sector/market structure	Small/medium sized enterprises Branch plant Self-employed Family business Production/trade/technology networks	National/regional firms Technology Regional/national market Intermediate trade flows	Transnational corporation Intra-firm trade Alliances Subcontractor Networks
Labour market Skills Jobs Labour time	Local labour market mechanisms: formal and informal Self-employment	Integration in larger regional market: division of labour, migration and commuting	Integration in firm's international division of labour International migration
Real estate market	Residential segregation and urban social differentiation Spatial integration/separation of economic functions	Housing policy and regulatory framework Monetary policy	International real estate companies Financial flows International monetary system
Financial market	Local capital and business elites	National financial groups and financing mechanisms	Global capital market ERM and EMU Dynamics of money and financial markets
Reproduction of labour Housing and living environment	Housing stock, renovation processes, social quality of neighbourhood	Learning effects; development of regional lifestyle profiles	Internationalization and homogenization/ fragmentation of life and living styles
Political agencies and institutions	Local authorities and administrations	Regional/national authorities and administrations	Supranational authorities and administrations
Planning agencies and strategies	Local planning offices Investment and development corporations	Regional and national administration Specialized development services	Supranational bodies: European Commission (Structural Funds, DG XVI)
Issue-based social movements: political, ecological, . . .	Mobilization on local issues	Idem regional issues; regional mobilization on local issues	Idem international issues; international mobilization on issues of regions, localities, environment

3.4. UDPs and Social Integration and Exclusion Mechanisms

UDPs generate particular mechanisms of integration and exclusion. These are related to the dynamics of the subsystems. The interconnection between subsystems and the articulation between spatial scales are key issues in our methodology. Let us consider here the dynamics of some of the systems and how they affect exclusion/integration mechanisms.

- **Job creation and destruction for less skilled workers.** This is affected not only by the geographical origin of the workers and the way international migratory flows are regulated, but also by the interaction between the regulation of the labour market and work conditions by the European Union and by Member States. Practices of informal work processes are shared between countries and rapidly move from place to place, particularly in construction, retail, leisure, and other service activities. This may reinforce disequilibria in the local urban labour markets and create additional unemployment among less skilled residents, including national as well migrant workers. The recent movements of significant numbers of illegal migrants from the politically unstable Balkan area has catalysed disequilibrating mechanisms, and has resulted in severe job uncertainty for large groups of workers involved in the implementation of UDPs and the lower end of the service economy in which they are employed.
- **Job creation and destruction for skilled and highly skilled workers.** The observations about degrading work conditions and deregulation apply to these categories of workers as well, albeit to a lesser extent than for unskilled labour. Skilled and especially highly skilled professionals are in general more mobile: mobility from one construction site to another, or from one engineering team to another 'comes with the contract'. The consequences for the quality of work are hard to assess, but the labour market for engineers, planners, architects, managers, etc., itself becomes evidently more global. The consequences for the local urban labour market are not easily predictable, but it is obvious that the competitive environment for locally educated professionals in real estate, finance, architecture, construction engineering, etc., keeps stiffening. More mobile professionals tend to improve their income position, while those who limit their work radius to the local economy are often financially penalized.
- **Job creation and destruction at the sectoral level.** UDPs of the scale considered in this book have both a direct and indirect impact on the sectoral composition of the local labour market. These shifts are not neutral in terms of number of jobs created or destroyed, skill levels, wage levels, work conditions, etc. In fact, most of the UDPs we studied show a job creation effect with a high concentration of very skilled professionals in consulting, engineering, and architecture, and of particularly low-skilled jobs in the

personal, consumer, and producer services that accompany the establishment of UDPs.

- **Housing displacement.** Large-scale UDPs usually lead to the destruction of significant parts of the housing stock and of the socio-spatial environment of lower income classes in the neighbourhoods 'receiving' the UDP. With the exception of the few well-planned cities and *quartiers*, this means the loss of a house and familiar living environment for a large number of families, many of whom already have income problems. Access to alternative housing is difficult or impossible, and can seldom be obtained at the same cost. Moreover, UDPs usually provide new housing for higher income classes, so that existing patterns of social segregation are generally exacerbated.

- **Income generation and purchasing power.** Obviously, the processes described above directly interact with the real income distribution in neighbourhoods and cities. In fact, relocation of low-income families often happens in the direction of cheap, poorly designed suburban or new town locations, with low security levels, inadequate social services, lower quality schools, etc. This means a decline in well-being, or an increase in transportation and communication costs (to better schools, hospitals, public administration, etc.). For cities where poverty problems are already acute, this worsening income distribution at the expense of households already living at the margins of material well-being signals a severe policy problem.

- **Erosion of democratic decision-making.** In general, various public and private agents play a role in one or more stages of the implementation of a UDP. In the official discourse of city governments, Chambers of Commerce and similar institutions, UDPs are generally presented as positive examples of co-operation between the public and private sector, or between democracy and market. Still, social groups involved in the decision-making process seem to be selected from élites in the business, political, and planning worlds. Neighbourhood interest groups, grassroots movements, social agencies, social planners are, as a rule, only marginally involved in the conception and planning process. Democratic representation and accountability often include just the general 'economic interest' of the city, not the 'hosting' neighbourhoods; and the market interests tend to be more global than neighbourhood-bound.

- **Fragmentation of urban identities.** The exclusion from different social reproduction mechanisms (income, housing, urban environment, quality education and social services, political decision-making, etc.), combined with the upward mobility of groups of professional workers indirectly or directly involved in the UDP, is also reflected at the level of urban identities. If in the 'post-modern city' the fragmentation of urban self-images has become more complex and variegated, this demands a growing concern with issues of emancipation, affirmation of identity, and socio-cultural justice.

- **Money flows, investments flows, and the financial market.** UDPs embody investment assets that usually combine capital from a variety of places and institutions, from the local state and local investors, the European Union, and international financial institutions and developers. The interaction between investment flows and the reconstruction of the urban is a key element in the restructuring of socio-economic relations through global–local relationships. These restructuring processes often increase the power of supra-local financial interest groups and focus attention on projects with a high potential return, at the expense of neighbourhood development programmes or comparable initiatives.

3.5. The Importance of Comparative Urban Research

The 'places and cases' presented in this book are compared by using standardized lists of characteristics of subsystems at various spatial scales (see Table 3.2) and by describing the trajectories of UDPs in terms of common features (see Table 3.1). Obviously, not all variables and features are of equal weight or importance for each case-study UDP. In addition, the analysis of many of the characteristics of local subsystems and trajectories of UDPs are fine-tuned on the basis of qualitative information obtained from unpublished reports, privileged interlocutors, other published and unpublished research, interviews with politicians, activists, bureaucrats, planners, developers, users, and non-users, etc. The main objective, in addition to obtaining data and information on the development process, is to assess the relational positionality of all the relevant actors and to chart the power geometries between them. This often leads to contradictory or conflicting interpretations. There may be different reasons for this. In addition to personal interpretations related to the particular social, political, economic, or cultural roles taken by interlocutors (Moulaert 1979), there are also cultural identities and politico-institutional contexts that affect interpretation and presentation of information. For example, local residents may have a particular view of the role of social services and how they are used, and also have a better affinity with local cultural and other identities. This, in turn, affects their relative perception of exclusion/integration. In addition, different politico-institutional contexts act as catalysts for individual or collective, private or public strategies. Some local politico-administrative systems are very resistant to the introduction of exceptionality planning measures, while others flexibly and malleably adjust to changing regulatory and institutional contexts or service the agenda of private developers. Comparing the local fashioning of global dynamics, therefore, remains a precarious exercise. Still, as the following case studies show, such a comparison is worth undertaking, because it allows an analysis of the generality of some of the accumulation and exclusion/integration processes, while situating these processes within the thick embeddedness of local socio-economic and institutional dynamics. The 'generality of the local' then becomes a stimulus for further exchange of information among neighbourhoods and citizens, to formulate strategies of resistance to the New Urban Policy and ground movements that fight for alternative policies for urban redevelopment.

3.6. Conclusion

In this chapter we have attempted to collect and unite the various threads of 'glocal' case-study analysis pursued in the URSPIC project. To do this, we approached the localities and their 'glocal' dynamics through the lens of large-scale Urban Development Projects (UDPs). As argued in Chapter 1, UDPs are the grains of sand that reflect global–local dynamics. These dynamics are intrinsically localized, and researched through their particular historico-institutional trajectory. Yet, the research mobilized and used common categories that 'talk to' global dynamics. These shared categories enable a comparative analysis of the case studies by spelling out the common trends as they take shape through the local specificities of each UDP. These categories refer to various processes of the urban subsystems to which the UDPs relate: production systems, labour markets, real estate markets, financial markets, reproduction of labour, housing, political, institutions, and planning agencies. These systems are analysed with respect to their economic, social, political, and cultural processes on the one hand, and their articulation at various spatial scales (regional, national, European, global) on the other. UDPs are not only studied from the vantage point of their relationships to or their integration in urban processes, but are also considered as possessing development-trajectories in their own right, starting with project conception, design, and formulation, passing through planning and implementation, and continuing with the operation and valorization of activities housed in or generated by them. Each of these stages in the planning trajectory is researched from the vantage point of the various urban subsystems provided in Table 3.3 (see also Table 3.2).

The methodological challenge of URSPIC was not to develop an exhaustive social accounting system for the study of all dimensions of the UDPs in their various stages of development, but was rather to mobilize the multiple dimensions of the UDP with an eye towards answering the main research question of URSPIC: 'How and to what extent do UDPs increase or decrease the polarization and exclusion/integration of various social groups in the city?' Exclusion/integration is defined in relation to the various aforementioned subsystems of urban society. The use of common categories for the study of UDP trajectories in relation to their multidimensional inclusion/integration dynamics permits international comparison. The most powerful results appear when the relations between governance dynamics, real estate markets, and the various dimensions of inclusion/exclusion dynamics are related and confronted for a variety of UDPs. This comparative analysis is presented in

Table 3.3. The various logics explaining exclusion/integration in the city according to the URSPIC approach: overall methodological structure of the URSPIC Research Project

UDP Trajectory	Conception Design Decision-making	Planning Implementation	Operation Valorization
Urban Subsystem			
Production(s) Labour market(s) Real estate market(s) Financial market(s) Reproduction of labour (housing) Political system Planning agencies	*POLARIZATION: EXCLUSION—INTEGRATION* • *Economic* • *Social* • *Political* • *Cultural*		
Spatial Scales	**Regional** **National**	**European**	**'Global'**

the concluding chapter of this book. The following nine chapters analyse nine case studies along the methodological paths outlined above.

Notes

1. The risks of a two- or multi-speed metropolitanization and the polarizing potential of large-scale urban renewal operations have been highlighted in the 1990s. Social and spatial polarization where downtown prosperity contrasts with neighbourhood decline have been identified in many proclaimed urban revitalization 'successes' in places like Baltimore (Merrifield 1993), Pittsburgh and Cleveland (Holcomb 1993), London and New York (Fainstein *et al.* 1992).

2. Not all the case studies are reported on in this book. Presentations of other case-studies can be found in Moulaert *et al.* (2001; 2002), Rodríguez *et al.* (2001), and Vicari *et al.* (2001). Empirical details are available from the URSPIC website *(http://www.ifresi.univ-lille1.fr* select 'Programmes de Recherche' and then URSPIC).

References

ANDERSEN, J., ELM LARSEN, J. (1995). 'The Underclass Debate—a Spreading Disease?', in D. Mortensen and J. Olofsson (eds.), *Essays on Integration and Marginalisation*. Copenhagen: Samfundslitteratur.

BENASSI, D., KAZEPOV, Y., and MINGIONE, E. (1997). 'Socio-economic Restructuring and Urban Poverty under Different Welfare Regimes', in F. Moulaert and A. Scott (eds.), *Cities, Enterprises and Society on the Eve of the 21st Century*. London and Washington: Pinter, ch. 10.

CASTELLS, M. (1973). *La Question urbaine*. Paris: Maspéro.

DEMAZIÈRE, C. (1996). 'Développement economique et structuration de l'espace urbain. Le quartier ouvrier, la grande ville, l'Europe du Nord-Ouest. Etude de cas privilégiée: Anvers, ville portuaire'. Thèse de doctorat ès Sciences Economiques. Université de Lille I, Faculté des Sciences Economiques et Sociales.

DUNFORD, M., and KAFKALAS, G. (1992) (eds.). *Cities and Regions in the New Europe*. London: Belhaven Press.

European Commission (1994). White Paper on Growth, Competitivity and Employment, Luxembourg: Office for Official Publications of the European Communities.

FAINSTEIN, S. (1994). *The City Builders*. Oxford: Blackwell.

——GORDON, I., and HARLOE, M. (1992) (eds.). *Divided Cities: New York and London in the Contemporary World*. Oxford: Blackwell.

GODARD, F. (1973). *La Rénovation urbaine* à *Paris: structure urbaine et logique de classe*. Paris: Mouton.

HARVEY, D. (1973). *Social Justice and the City*. Baltimore: Johns Hopkins University Press.

HAUSSERMANN, H., and KAPPHAN, A. (2000). *Berlin: von der geteilten zur gespaltenen Stadt?* Opladen: Leske and Budrich.

HIRST, P., and THOMPSON, G. (1996). *Globalization in Question*. Cambridge: Polity Press.

HOLCOMB B. (1993). 'Revisioning Place: De- and Re-constructing the Image of the Industrial City', in G. Kearns and C. Philo (eds.), *Selling Places*. Oxford: Pergamon Press, 133–44.

KAZEPOV, Y., and ZAJCZYK, F. (1997). 'Urban Poverty and Social Exclusion: Concepts and Debates', in F. Moulaert and A. Scott (eds.), *Cities, Enterprises and Society on the Eve of the 21st Century*. London and Washington: Pinter, ch. 9.

KEARNS, G., and PHILO, C. (1993) (eds.). *Selling Places: The City as Cultural Capital, Past and Present*. Oxford: Pergamon Press.

KEATING, W. D., KRUMHOLZ, N., and STAR, P. (1996). *Revitalizing Urban Neighborhoods*. Lawrence, Kan.: University Press of Kansas.

LE CARRÉ, J. (2001). *The Constant Gardener*. London: Hodder and Stoughton.

LOGAN, J., TAYLOR-GOOBY, P., and REUTER, M. (1993). 'Poverty and Income Inequality', in S. Fainstein, I. Gordon, and M. Harloe (eds.), *Divided Cities: New York and London in the Contemporary World*. Oxford: Blackwell.

MADANIPOUR, A., CARS, G., and ALLEN, J. (1998) (eds.). *Social Exclusion in European Cities: Processes, Experiences and Responses*. London: Jessica Kingsley Publishers.

MAYER M. (2000). 'Post-Fordist City Politics', in R. LeGates and F. Stout (eds.), *The City Reader*. 2nd edn. London and New York: Routledge.

MERRIFIELD, A. (1993). 'The Struggle over Place—Redeveloping American Can in Southeast Baltimore'. *Transactions Institute of British Geographers*, NS 18: 102–21.

——and SWYNGEDOUW, E. (1996) (eds.). *The Urbanisation of Injustice*. London and New York: Lawrence and Wishart and New York University Press.

MINGIONE, E. (1996) (ed.). *Urban Poverty and the Underclass: A Reader*. Oxford: Blackwell.

——(1997). 'Socio-Economic Restructuring and the New Urban Poverty', in F. Moulaert and A. Scott (eds.), *Cities, Enterprises and Society on the Eve of the 21st Century*. London and Washington: Pinter.

——OBERTI, M., and PEREIRINHA, J. (2002). 'Cities and Local Systems', in C. Saraceno (ed.), *Social Assistance Dynamics in Europe: National and Local Poverty Regimes*. Bristol: Policy Press.

MOMMAAS, H. (1996). 'Modernity, Postmodernity and the Crisis of Social Moderniza-tion: A Case Study in Urban Fragmentation'. *International Journal of Urban and Regional Research*, 20: 196–216.

MOULAERT, F. (1979). 'On the Nature and Scope of Complex Conflicts'. *Papers Peace Science Society International*, 29: 48–66.

——(1995). 'Measuring Socio-Economic Disintegration at the Local Level in Europe', in G. Room, *Measurement and Analysis of Social Exclusion in Europe*. Bristol: Policy Press.

——(1996). 'Rediscovering Spatial Inequality in Europe: Building Blocks for an Appropriate Regulationist Framework'. *Society and Space*, 14: 155–79.

——DELLADETSIMA, P., and LEONTIDOU, L. (1994) (eds.). 'Local Economic Develop-ment: A Pro-Active Strategy Against Poverty in the European Community. Final Report'. Research Program European Commission, DG V—Poverty III.

——DELVAINQUIÈRE, J. C., and DELLADETSIMA, P. (1997). 'Le Rôle des mouvements sociaux dans le développement économique local. Contribution au colloque de AEP-UQAM, 18–19 octobre 1996, Montréal', in J. L. Klein (ed.), *Au delà du néolibéral-isme: quel rôle pour les mouvements sociaux?* Montreal: Presses Universitaires du Québec.

——and SCOTT, A. (1997) (eds.). *Cities, Enterprises and Society on the Eve of the 21st Century*. London and Washington: Pinter.

——*et al.* (2000). *Globalization and Integrated Area Development in European Cities*. Oxford: Oxford University Press.

——SWYNGEDOUW, E., and RODRÍGUEZ, A. (2001) (eds.). 'Social Polarization in the Metropolitan Areas: The Role of the New Urban Policy'. *European Urban and Regional Studies*, 8/2.

————and——(2002) (eds.). 'Urban Restructuring and Social Polarization in the City'. Special issue of *Geographische Zeitschrift*.

PAPADOPOULOS, A. G. (1996). *Urban Regimes and Strategies: Building Europe's Central Executive District in Brussels*. Chicago: University of Chicago Press.

PAUGAM S. (1996) (ed.). *L'Exclusion: l'état des Savoirs*. Paris: Editions La Découverte.

PRETECEILLE, E. (1974). *Jeux, modèles et simulations: critique des jeux urbains*. Paris and La Haye: Mouton.

RODRÍGUEZ, A., MOULAERT, F., and SWYNGEDOUW, E. (2001). 'Nuevas Politicas urbanas para la Revitalización de las Ciudades en Europa', *Ciudad y Territorio. Estudios Territoriales*, **33**, 129: 409–24.

ROOM, G. (1994). 'Poverty Studies in the European Union: Retrospect and Prospect'. Paper presented at the European Conference on Understanding Social Exclusion: Lessons from Transnational Research Institutes, London, 24–8. Nov.

SASSEN, S. (1991). *The Global City*. Princeton: Princeton University Press.

SCOTT, A. J. (2001). *Global City-Regions: Trends, Theory, Policy*. Oxford: Oxford University Press.

SWYNGEDOUW, E. (1989). 'The Heart of the Place: The Resurrection of Locality in an Age of Hyperspace'. *Geografiska Annaler*, 71 B (1): 31–42.

——(1996). 'Reconstructing Citizenship, the Re-Scaling of the State and the New Authoritarianism: Closing the Belgian Mines'. *Urban Studies*, 33/8: 1499–521.

SWYNGEDOUW, E., and BAETEN, G. (2001). 'Scaling the City: The Political Economy of "Glocal" Development—Brussels' Conundrum'. *European Planning Studies*, 9/7: 827–49.

THOMAS, H. (2000). *Race and Planning: The UK Experience.* London and New York: UCL Press.

TOWNSEND, P. (1993). *The International Analysis of Poverty.* New York and London: Harvester and Wheatsheaf.

VOOGD, H., and ASHWORTH, G. F. (1990). *Selling the City.* London: Belhaven.

4

The Olympic Village:
A Redevelopment Marathon
in Greater Athens

Pavlos-Marinos Delladetsima

4.1. Introduction

The city of Athens will host the 2004 Olympic Games, and the city is currently (2002) under considerable preparatory stress. The Olympic Games are considered to be a turning-point for Athens—as well as for Greek society and the economy as a whole. They constitute both a major challenge and an exceptional shift in economic investment priorities and in the city's social and organizational affairs. The rhetoric that has accompanied and served to legitimize the candidacy for the Games points to the potential political gains: 'increasing the competitive position of the country in the international and European setting' and 'promoting Athens as a metropolitan center of international caliber' (Law 2730/25 June 1999, Article 1); to anticipated positive macroeconomic effects (basically through the injection of foreign investment); and to sectoral employment gains: 'promoting Athens as a high-level service and innovative business activities center' (Committee for the Athens 2004 Candidacy 1997). As far as the Athens agglomeration is concerned, the Olympic Games are portrayed as a unique chance to overcome current functional, environmental, and traffic problems by implementing grand infrastructure schemes and public works.

It is, nevertheless, evident that the initial euphoria sparked by such rhetoric seems to have subsided somewhat and has been replaced by a widespread anxiety to meet the deadlines. Official announcements suggest that both the direct and (particularly) the indirect costs of the Games (basic urban infrastructure and organization costs) are increasing. The focus at the time of writing is to reduce spending to the minimum necessary for conducting the Games. The grand public works schemes are characterized by severe delays due to financing and legal technicalities. At a local level, many areas that will host Olympic works infrastructure are facing pressures on their landed assets. There has been considerable reaction to land use changes, the increase of real estate values (whether of a fictitious or real nature; see Peirounakis 1997; Stavrinou 1999; Jones Lang Lassale, 2001; Delladetsima 2001; Siomopoulos 2001), and with issues of environmental conservation. For example, the equestrian centre that will be constructed in the Marathon district has been a highly contested scheme, since the selected site is situated in an area that is both ecologically and archaeologically highly vulnerable. Most of the initial qualitative ambitions and expectations for the post-Olympic era of the agglomeration seem to have been abandoned for the time being. Even less attention has been paid to the potential benefits (or losses) to particular municipalities and neighbourhoods that are directly or indirectly located within the range of the Olympic Games redevelopment programme.

Taking this background into account, this chapter analyses one of the most important schemes that is taking place in Athens as part of the 2004 Olympic Games works general redevelopment programme: the Olympic Village. By Greek standards, this is an urban development programme *par excellence* and undeniably of the dimensions of a 'new town'. It is also a major initiative with particular characteristics. Firstly, as an 'event-led' intervention, the Olympic Village embodies a double planning objective, defined respectively by its Olympic and post-Olympic use. Secondly, this dual perspective poses compli- cated cost-benefit problems that, in turn, hamper both economic and social goals for the post-Olympic period.

This chapter on the Olympic Village (OV) also focuses on a very neglected aspect of the Olympiad's redevelopment programme, namely the impact (in physical, economic, and social terms) on localities within the Athens agglom- eration that host Olympic infrastructure. When completed, the OV will affect not only the surrounding areas but also broader urban development patterns related to housing supply, the creation of new retail centres, employment shifts, and new transport mobility trends. The site is located in the northern outskirts of the conurbation in an economically and socially highly polarized area that is characterized by high density, a predominance of low income housing (but with some high income enclaves), deprived migrant population zones, indus- trial estates, and generally low value uses. It falls under the jurisdictions of the municipality of Acharanai and the local community of Thakomakedones (Fig. 4.1). It has to be designed to meet the needs of 16,000 athletes and dele- gates and will, after the Olympics, be converted to a regular housing area (for about 10,000 inhabitants) and potentially to a tertiary service centre.

The actual outcome of this urban redevelopment project, currently under construction, is still unknown but there are still challenging questions that arise. How will the localities be affected by this major urban redevelopment scheme, given the actual time and financial constraints? Could there still be any mechanism which can guarantee that part of this collective investment 'can be returned to the collective purse' (Edwards 2000) and especially to the local community? Finally, could the OV act as a paradigmatic case that brings with it changes in urban policy? In other words, might the planning and

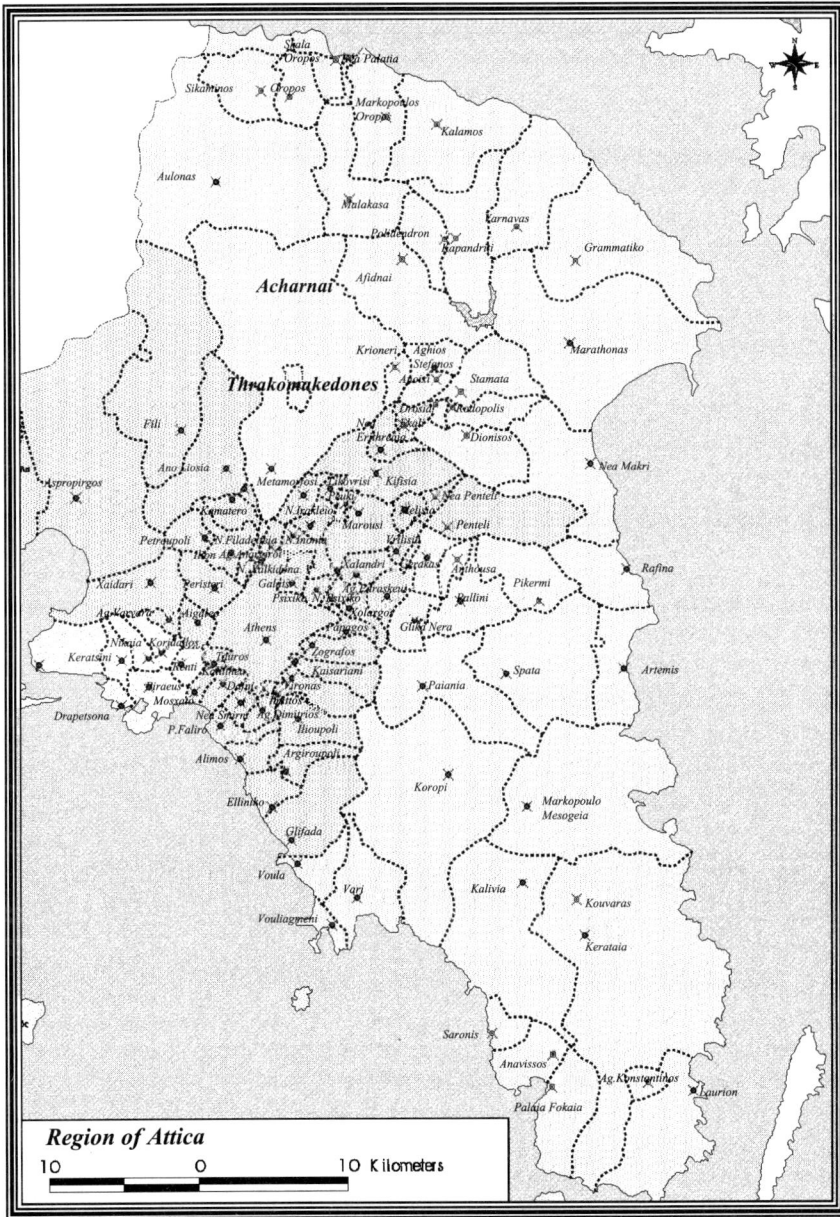

Fig. 4.1. Region of Attica municipalities and study areas

Source: Ministry of the Interior, Public Administration and Decentralization, 2000.

implementation of the OV lead to a much-needed new developmental rationale for the city as a whole?

4.2. Institutional Framework and the Changing System of Government/Governance

The OV redevelopment scheme is a hybrid that fuses together two systems of government/governance, which in theory are supposed to act in a complementary manner through mutual programming agreements. These two systems of government/governance can be defined respectively as the 'normal' and the 'exceptional'. The 'normal' system deals with regular policy, developmental and control issues (planning, development control, service provision, etc.) as codified in the established legal framework. The 'exceptional' system has been specifically created for the preparation and administration of the Olympiad. The competencies of both systems extend to all tiers of government, although the 'exceptional' system is characterized essentially by its central and semi-autonomous statute.

4.2.1. The 'normal' system of government

The 'normal' government/governance system operating within the case-study area involves state departments and central state institutions (especially the Ministry of the Environment, Planning, and Public Works and its affiliated Organization for the Implementation of the Athens Regulatory Plan, the Ministry of the Interior, and affiliated central institutions such as the (public) Workers Housing Organization that falls under the Ministry of Labour), the Periphery of Attica (a centrally controlled regional institution that controls major investment flows and, above all, the Community Support Framework funds), the General Prefecture of Attica, and the Prefecture of East Attica (these are respectively intermediate regional and sub-regional level democratically elected institutions). Ultimately, at the local level, there are two main institutions involved, the municipality of Acharnai and the local community of Thrakomakedones. This array of institutions that are 'normally' involved in planning and development suggests a confusing and complex decision-making process. The situation is further complicated by the weaknesses of the mid-1990s administrative reform (Law 2218/1994) that did not provide sufficient transparency in the allocation of new competencies and funds, especially with respect to the position of the prefectures. Broadly speaking, under the existing state of affairs local authority statutory competencies evolve within a conventional sphere of service provision and policy (Getimis 1990: 307–33; EU 1997); any positive local developmental initiative is in principle of a non-statutory character.

The principal policy tools of the 'normal' system that are adopted and exert a certain influence on the local setting are the Regulatory or Master Plan for Athens (now revised in compliance to demands posed by the Olympic Games, see below) and the local land use plans of the respective local authorities. The Athens Regulatory Plan (Law 1515/85) designates the Acharnai area as of 'supra-local importance'. It provides for the development of a 'metropolitan nodal transportation centre' as well as a regional wholesale/industrial centre within the municipal boundaries. The local land use plan of Acharnai (approved in 1989, amended in 1990 and 1995) places emphasis on land use control (assigning land use, building heights, plot surface coverage, and floor space indices) and on the designation of urban expansion zones. The local community plan of Thrakomakedones is simply a layout plan of residential and limited retail uses. Other physical policies adopted locally involve zoning projects in specific areas of the municipality and regulations concerning forests and natural heritage protection. The local land use plan of Acharnai is currently amended through the insertion of measures to deal with the new conditions posed by the OV and to improve the areas adjacent to the site.

Local economic development policy initiatives arise mainly in order to comply with non-statutory central government action plans that are produced in direct association with EU funding such as the Strategic Development Programmes (SPA) and the so-called operational programmes (the Community Support Framework and the Peripheral Operational Programmes). In addition, some disjointed municipal actions have been occasionally taken as attempts to promote economic development. The municipality of Acharnai in particular has launched a number of projects like job creation schemes and local development programmes (Municipality of Acharanai 1993; Municipality of Acharanai and NTUA 2001). Their implementation, however, remains scattered and limited. The same holds for a number of initiatives developed in compliance with the European Union's URBAN programme and the Special Development Programme for Local Authorities (EPTA), which has been funded and administered by the Ministry of the Interior. Inherently, most local developmental efforts target the securing of steady financial flows for the implementation of basic infrastructure projects. On the whole the normal system proves to be rather too weak to deal with and promote local development initiatives. Moreover, it seems unable to construct strong negotiating institutions and/or empower the locality to integrate exceptional investments, such as the Olympic Village redevelopment, into a long-term local policy perspective.

4.2.2. The 'exceptional' system of governance

The Olympic Games can also be seen as an 'exceptional' institutional action, which significantly affects all aspects of planning, development, and related policy. Hence, a top-down decision-making system has been introduced, which does not incorporate statutory mechanisms that permit a systematic consultation with local authorities and population groups implicated in the numerous areas that host Olympic infrastructures. Planning for the Games has been accompanied by the creation of major new institutions designed to operate autonomously or in parallel with existing public agencies at all spatial scales. Law 2598/24 Mar.1998 provided for the establishment of two key new bodies: the National Committee for the Olympic Games and the Organizing Committee of the Olympic Games. The National Committee for the Olympic Games 2004 has supreme control over the design and organization of the Games. To our reading, nowadays, most of the National Committee's competencies and responsibilities are being carried out by inter-ministerial commissions. The Organizing Committee (Athens 2004 SA) is a corporate body with the legal status of a private company that can operate according to market criteria. It has the right to set up affiliated companies that can take full responsibility for the construction and management of all major projects. The main aim of the company is to organize the 2004 Olympic Games and to undertake all necessary infrastructure works. The company is equipped with exceptional implementation powers and is in a position to accumulate resources autonomously and to control statutory policy practices. By definition, Athens 2004 SA assumes a supra-national outlook and can make decisions that surpass formal state jurisdictions. Moreover, it acts as a privileged interlocutor with international financing organizations (such as the International Olympic Committee, the European Union, and the European Investment Bank) and private capital. Athens 2004 SA has established working relationships and signed 'mutual programming agreements' with state institutions, local authorities, and professional chambers.

Moreover, in 1999 an 'extraordinary' law for the Olympic works was enacted in Parliament (Law 2730/25 June 1999: Planning, Integrated Development and Implementation of Olympic Works). The law introduces special planning provisions for the host areas of Olympic infrastructure, extraordinary acquisition procedures for private and public land, and new organizational-administrative arrangements. Evidently, this legislative action also denotes a rupture with normal policy procedures and practices at all spatial administrative levels of the Athens metropolitan area. More specifically, according to the law, at the higher (metropolitan) spatial level, the outstanding importance of the Olympic Works in terms of public interest implies the imposition of essential modifications to the Athens Master Plan. In addition, this exceptional legal framework enables the Minister of Planning to establish a common procedure for granting the necessary building permits for all host sites in the agglomeration. The purpose is to contain the process at the central state level in order to achieve uniform and comprehensive building permit delivery and safety enforcement procedures and to guarantee the deployment of the necessary administrative actions within the appropriate time limits. The same lineage of power applies to policy issues such as development control and the delineation of urban expansion zones.

This 'exceptionality' therefore also affects lower administrative and policy-making levels. Hence, for every host locality of Olympic infrastructure (such as the ones of the study area), the Ministers of Planning and Cultural Affairs, in consultation with the Organization of the Athens Regulatory Plan and the local and regional authorities have to formulate a 'Special Integrated Plan' (Article 3) that must be approved by Presidential Decree. These 'Special Plans' contain all necessary planning, building, and environmental considerations that will enhance the spatial organization of the host areas. They also provide for the acceleration of decision-making and for the procedural efficiency of the implementation process (Greek Parliament Bulletin 1999). The role, however, of the local authorities is noticeably curtailed, involving the assumption of a purely advisory role in the process. More specifically, the local authorities must express their observations and objections to the Organization of the Athens Regulatory Plan within a month from the date they receive the plan proposals. If the local authorities do not meet these time constraints, a Presidential Decree will enact the plan regardless of their views. By and large, 'Special Plans' have institutional supremacy over local planning documents. Within this policy rationale, Law 2730/25 June 1999 has also defined the framework for the Olympic Village scheme both in technical and institutional terms. It enables the Organizing Committee (Athens 2004 SA) or a subsidiary company to implement the OV land-use plan and, together with other parties, assume responsibility to develop and exploit its assets in the future (Article 4).

Even greater indications of the exceptional modalities introduced by the law are given by the enforced acquisition procedures for private and public land and, in particular, the compulsory purchase orders for assets required in the context of the Olympic works (price determination, acceleration of court decisions, identification of landowners, compensation terms, etc.). Other exceptional provisions of the Olympics Law relate to the provisional use of assets (Article 11), the transfer of properties (Articles 11, 12, 13), and the use of coastal areas (Article 14). Due to the delays to the implementation of the purchase orders that were caused by landowners, these exceptionality measures have been further strengthened, leading to the introduction of a stricter Compulsory Purchase Code. Furthermore, in the attempt to tackle the trivialities and bottlenecks that have emerged in the implementation process of the Olympic works, another general Law was enacted (Law 228/9 Oct. 2001, 'Issues on Olympic Hospitality, Olympic Works Infrastructure and other matters'). Broadly speaking, this new law marks a further 'exceptionality' boost in the Olympic Games redevelopment process.

Set within this exceptional system that explicitly curtails local involvement, there is very little room for manoeuvring by the local institutions in order to deal systematically with such a major redevelopment programme. This mixed rationale of exceptional and normal provisions stipulates the formation of a closed development model that pays little attention to the social and economic environment in which it has to operate. The local authorities maintain a distant acceptance of the Olympic Village (based on vague expectations of benefits that might arise from infrastructure provisions and the real estate market) with no inherent commitment to getting actively involved in the process. In fact, from the very beginning of the consultation period, the municipality of Acharnai has taken a positive stand concerning the OV redevelopment in its jurisdiction. Occasionally, though, it has affirmed some claims or planning gains that it seeks to obtain from this project (Municipality of Acharnai 1999). These claims, however, have been drafted more systematically in a Co-operation Protocol (2000), which has not yet been signed, with the Workers Housing Organization (the institution in charge of the OV redevelopment (see below)). The protocol, however, does not foresee any major local involvement and participation in the overall structure of the OV scheme. On the whole, the local authority appears to be reluctant to formulate a detailed and integrated proposition. Emphasis is placed on potential gains in technical infrastructure and far less on the social and economic aspects. The claims made by the local community of Thrakomakedones in relation to the scheme replicate more or less the same logic: they have been limited to road improvement proposals, the upgrading of the forested land adjacent to the site, the construction of water treatment plants, and other minor works such as forest fire protection infrastructure.

4.3. The Olympic Village in Urban Development Strategies

4.3.1. The broader strategy

The Olympic Games Redevelopment programme is structured around ten major nodal developments of sports and other service installations that are interconnected via the Olympic Ring Road, with the Olympic Village as an integral component. The aim is to permit accessibility between the different installations and services within a 20 minutes average time-distance radius (Fig. 4.2). The prevailing policy rationale of the programme is closely linked to a conventional physical land use policy plan and has no strategic development component. In other words, although the Olympic works could have acted as a catalyst for fostering a wider strategic policy response to the city's growing needs (Committee for the Athens 2004 Candidacy and University of Thessaly 1997), this was not considered to be feasible, despite the fact that the development of such a strategic vision was part of the discourse by which the bid was legitimized. Furthermore, it is clear that the general Olympic redevelopment programme has not given any consideration to identifying common local goals and complementary areas of action with existing local development strategies. For example, no systematic consideration has been given to the implementation of locally defined goals that are linked to Olympic infrastructures, to potential post-Olympic uses, or to developing joint financial programmes. To

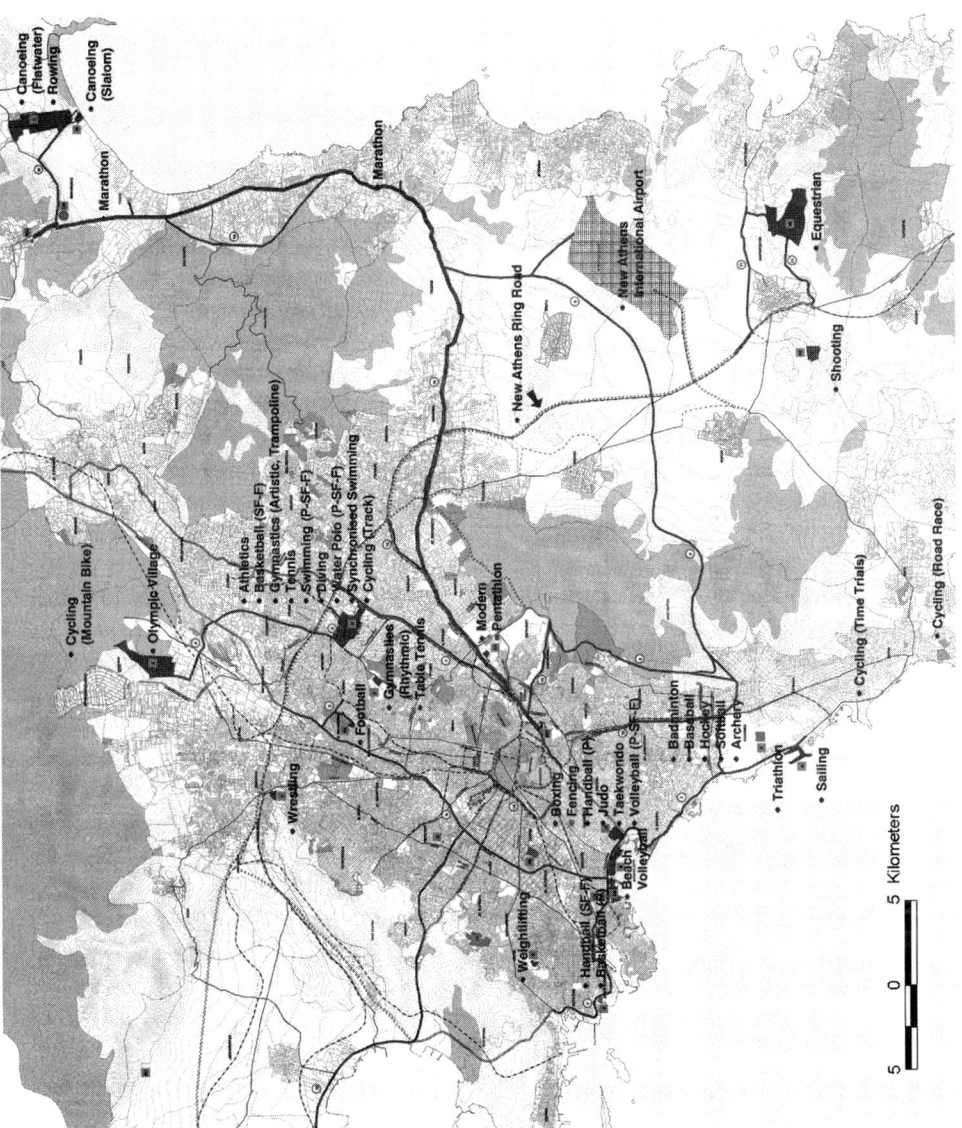

Fig. 4.2. The Olympic Games planning and design principles

Source: Athens 2004 SA, 1998.

our understanding, the Olympic Village also remains simply a nodal development within the Olympic programme and is not a part of any other consistent broader development strategy.

4.3.2. The history of the site and the project

The OV site is situated at the northern outskirts of the conurbation, in the location called Lekanes Acharnon, at the foot of Mount Parnitha. The Parnitha Mountain in the east and the plains in the south shape the morphology of the area. The remains of the ancient Roman Adrian Aqueduct are also to be found there. The site predominately consisted of private agricultural land that has since been acquired through compulsory purchase orders.

The wider area in which the Olympic Village is being constructed has been a long-standing feature of the planning debate for Athens. It has been subject to two non-implemented redevelopment proposals, put forward respectively by the planners Sokos in 1956 and Doxiades in 1960. The proposals shared the idea of creating a node for metropolitan decentralization in this location (DEPOS 1997; Synadinos *et al.* 1999). In 1972, during the dictatorial regime, a pilot housing estate for 5,000 inhabitants in Acharnai was designed by EKTENEPOL (a property development company affiliated to the former Mortgage Bank of Greece). In 1995, the Workers Housing Organization (OEK), the core public housing institution in Greece, became involved in a project proposal for the construction of 3,000 housing units in the area. The decision to create the Olympic Village in Acharnai, more or less at the current site, dates from 1990 and was adopted in the context of the (unsuccessful) 1996 Olympic Games bid. In the subsequent, and winning, 2004 Olympics proposal, the use of this site for the OV was maintained. This time, however, the selection procedure was supported by environmental sustainability criteria (Location Study and Olympic Village Master Plan, 1998).

The quasi-unconditional preference for this area has been the end product of consecutive planning proposals that viewed the Acharnai district as a decentralization node for the conurbation. This sets the scheme within a 1960s expansionist planning philosophy. Yet, in the present-day context, the OV redevelopment represents a major contradiction in terms of metropolitan priorities. More specifically, one of the core problems of contemporary Athens is that of urban sprawl. Nevertheless, the OV scheme serves an objective of decentralization and expansion rather than containment; although the latter is a principal sustainability objective. In this regard the decision in favour of the Acharnai area has triggered a debate about its suitability for hosting a redevelopment initiative of this magnitude. Official documents, of course, developed arguments in support of the selection of the area, for example that the Olympic Village can act as a connecting-transition zone from the built to the non-built environment in the Athenian suburban setting and, therefore, protect more effectively the vulnerable environment of Mount Parnitha (Location Study and Olympic Village Master Plan 1998). The counter-arguments, voiced even in an early stage (Technical Chamber of Greece 1990) raised doubts concerning the suitability of Acharnai. An inner-city location was considered to be better equipped to accommodate such a scheme and to create greater benefits for the city. Later concerns were focused on environmental land use issues. The area has been considered to be inappropriate (Mavridou 1998) as it is an integral part of the precious suburban open space—a highly vulnerable asset in the agglomeration of Athens. Furthermore, the emphasis placed on physical–environmental criteria already suggests that local social and economic parameters remained outside the field of vision. In turn, the conflicting nature of the adopted criteria and the associated economic and social vacuum in which procedures were carried out created an atmosphere of uncertainty. The OV location choice has been constantly debated throughout the preparatory process. Even a few months before the enactment of the law (2730/25 June 1999) that officially finalized the designation of the OV site, there were still voices (Tzanavara and Vassiliadi 1999: 48) that pressed for the need to consider changing the chosen location.

4.3.3. The surrounding localities and their dynamics

Perhaps the most essential feature to examine is the socio-economic dynamics of the localities (Acharnai and Thrakomakedones) that host the OV redevelopment scheme and how these could affect or be affected by the scheme. As mentioned above, this is a feature that has been seriously neglected by the policy-makers involved in the redevelopment programme. The municipality of Acharnai is one of the largest municipalities of the Attica Prefecture (Athens Greater Region) and is portrayed by many as the 'dustbin' of Athens, because of the predominantly deprived population living in the area, a serious lack of technical and social infrastructure, and the concentration of functions and activities that are considered undesirable for a dense urban fabric (such as military installations, the water-treatment station of the Metropolitan Water Authority, the Police School, the Flower Market, storage facilities for major public companies, and such like). The community of Thrakomakedones is a small, high-income suburban area, formally developed and well laid out; it is essentially a wealthy enclave within the deprived surroundings of Acharnai. What is more, both localities were dramatically affected by the catastrophic earthquake of 7 September 1999, which has radically changed social, economic, and physical conditions. The earthquake affected the whole of the Attica Basin, causing the death of 143 people. The two case-study areas were close to the epicentre and were among the most seriously affected zones. In the municipality of Acharnai, thirty-six people died, 13.2 per cent of the housing stock was completely destroyed, 37.2 per cent of buildings suffered damages requiring repair, and 48.3 per cent showed minor damages; 10,000 people were registered as homeless. In addition, social infrastructure (twenty-nine school

Table 4.1. Population in the study area, 1971–1991

	1971	1981	1991
Prefecture of Attica	2,303,051	3,369,443	3,523,407
Acharnai Municipality	28,096	41,039	61,352
Thrakomakedones local community	304	1,101	3,135

buildings), productive industrial installations, and technical infrastructure suffered severe damages. Thrakomakedones was also heavily affected: approximately 275 buildings were destroyed and 489 suffered extensive damages. Needless to say, this had severe negative repercussions on the housing stock, the employment levels, and out-migration flows (University of the Aegean 2002).

From a long-term perspective, the socio-economic dynamics of the study area have been significantly affected by population growth through in-migration. Acharnai has been a prime host zone for migrants and refugees, especially since the end of the Second World War. This was due to its location as an entry district of the agglomeration, the local forging of social-family-ethnic networks and the employment opportunities in the surrounding industrial area. Waves of incoming population have shaped the developmental patterns of the area, leading to consecutive changes in its physical, social, and economic structure. Since the 1960s, as a consequence of population growth, the area's economic base changed from agricultural production and husbandry to activities in manufacturing and construction employing non-qualified labour. Immigration trends can be broken down into two major ethnic groups: (*a*) the so-called new refugees (*neo-prosfyges*) or returnees (migrants of Greek ethnic origin from former Soviet Union states and in particular from the Black Sea area) and (*b*) gypsies. Between 1971 and 1981, the municipality experienced a population increase of 49.8 per cent, with a further 45.8 per cent rise between 1981 and 1991 (Table 4.1). According to estimates by the municipality, the current population is more than 120,000. There are severe discrepancies between available labour supply and employment demand, and between social needs and availability of technical and social infrastructure (e.g. schools). Discrepancies are especially acute for the younger age groups, which are over-represented in Acharnai (Table 4.2). The prevailing job profile is that of the non-skilled industrial and construction labourer. The economically active people in Acharnai represent 38.6 per cent of the total population (1991 Census); 'technicians', 'manual labourers', and 'transportation personnel' are still the dominant categories (48.7 per cent of the economically active population), while 'scientists' and 'higher administrative personnel' are under-represented (6.7 per cent and 0.8 per cent respectively). Part of the employment potential depends on informal subcontracting relations and on locally operating Small

Table 4.2. Population age groups in the study area and adjoining municipalities, 1991

	0–4	5–9	10–14	15–19	20–24	25–29	30–34	35–39	40–44	45–49	50–54	55–59	60+
Municipality Acharanai	4,224	5,087	5,685	5,723	5,267	4,770	4,826	4,449	4,178	3,265	3,545	3,001	7,332
Thrakomakedones	102	200	326	254	209	159	156	217	257	258	246	184	567

Source: National Statistical Service of Greece (Census).

Table 4.3. The sectoral composition in Acharnai municipality according to enterprises and turnover

Sector	E	T
00 Miscellaneous	14	2.367
15 Food and drink industry	86	18.361
17 Production of textile fibres	88	7.430
18 Clothing and fur elaboration and painting	74	1.869
19 Leather industry and related products	19	24.171
20 Furniture industry and wooden and cork products	68	3.245
21 Paper industry	30	5.179
22 Publications, printing, sound and visualization, information means	34	6.045
24 Production of chemical substances and products	22	5.952
25 Elastic products and plastic materials	40	11.186
26 Non-metal mineral products	48	4.486
27 Basic metal products	6	988
28 Metal products (except machines and equipment)	117	8.557
29 Construction of machines and appliances	25	3.484
31 Construction of electric machinery and equipment	11	638
33 Construction of medical tools, accuracy tools, and time meters	4	249
34 Car building and trailers	6	260
35 Building of other transport equipment	6	2.699
36 Furniture and related industries	115	6.387
41 Water collection, purification, and distribution	5	42
45 Building construction	282	4.211
50 Auto vehicle sale, maintenance, and repair	122	7.714
51 Wholesale and commission trade (except cars and motorcycles)	208	43.289
52 Retail, except car and motorcycle dealers, utensil repair	816	24.208
53 Hotels and restaurants	178	2.931
60 Land transportation through pipelines and related means	92	1.112
63 Auxiliary to transport services, travel offices	22	201
67 Relative to auxiliary to banking intermediaries services	5	15
74 Other entrepreneurial activities	172	1.815
80 Education	9	38
85 Health care	5	69
92 Recreation, cultural, and sport activities	23	360
93 Other service activities	58	469

Source: National Statistical Service of Greece (Census), 1994.

and Medium Sized Enterprises. Income levels in the Acharnai area are among the lowest in the agglomeration (see Table 4.3.), as are educational levels, with illiteracy as high as 9.2 per cent. Thakomakedones portrays a contrasting picture. With a total population of approximately 3,000 inhabitants, high income and qualified professional strata are over-represented. Although the economically active population in Thrakomakedones is similar to that of Acharnai (36.8 per cent of the total), it consists mainly of 'scientists' (30.9 per cent) and 'retailers and sellers' (25.1 per cent).

The socio-economic dynamics of the study area have also been shaped by the operation of a particular land development pattern. Above all, it has the potential to provide cheap land. Escalating demand for predominantly cheap land by the incoming population has thus sparked three complementary processes that have, in turn, generated a particular local land development pattern: land acquisition for owner occupation; property fragmentation; and urban sprawl.

The post-war land development in Acharnai has followed an expanding land acquisition process for owner occupation, producing a parallel reduction of agricultural holdings and a gradual growth of speculative housing and other uses. A second process has been property fragmentation. This has been a very intense phenomenon; today more than 60 per cent of plots are of an average size of 150–200 m^2 in Acharnai, compared to 500 m^2 in Thrakomakedones. Thirdly, land development in the area has resulted in extended urban sprawl. Built-up urban land amounted to a modest 1,500 acres in 1961, but reached 12,000 acres in 1971, 26,400 acres in 1981, and 29,300 acres in 1991. Over the past fifteen years, 15,000 acres of land have been urbanized or incorporated in formal town plan boundaries. Construction rates in terms of granted building permits in the municipality of Acharnai have been among the highest in the conurbation and are clearly exceeding those granted for neighbouring municipalities. From 1981 to 1997, 8,544 building permits have been granted, 52 per cent of which concerned construction of new buildings, and 32.5 per cent were extensions to the existing fabric, such as additions of new floors or horizontal expansion of buildings. The end of the 1990s marked a peak period in construction activity; although a downward trend manifested itself after the 1997 earthquake (Fig. 4.3).

In sum, on the one hand, there is predominantly low value land and property demand (associated primarily with the migrant population), land fragmentation, self-financed construction, and weak (or non-existent) building/development control. On the other hand, high income suburbanization demand is also present, expressed by formally designed layout plans, by fairly large plot sizes, and by high land values. Nevertheless, the operation of the local land system is presently facing some inherent problems that are affecting the preservation of the fragile social and economic equilibrium that the area has thus far sustained. There is, above all, a problem related to land value increases that hampers the preservation of cheap assets, deriving primarily from the reduction of the supply of land. In other words, the consecutive urban expansion phases, the (remaining) high valued agricultural sites, the growing presence of high income housing areas (which do not lend themselves to intensive fragmentation), and the location of numerous industrial establishments in the non-urbanized setting have led to a constant reduction in the supply of land and, in turn, relative increases in land values.

The enforced planning legislation is another factor that has affected land values. Planning provisions that incorporate properties into the town plan automatically lead to an increase in land values. Historically, increases in land value were counterbalanced by new waves of private property acquisitions, urban sprawl, and land fragmentation, although this safety valve to keep land

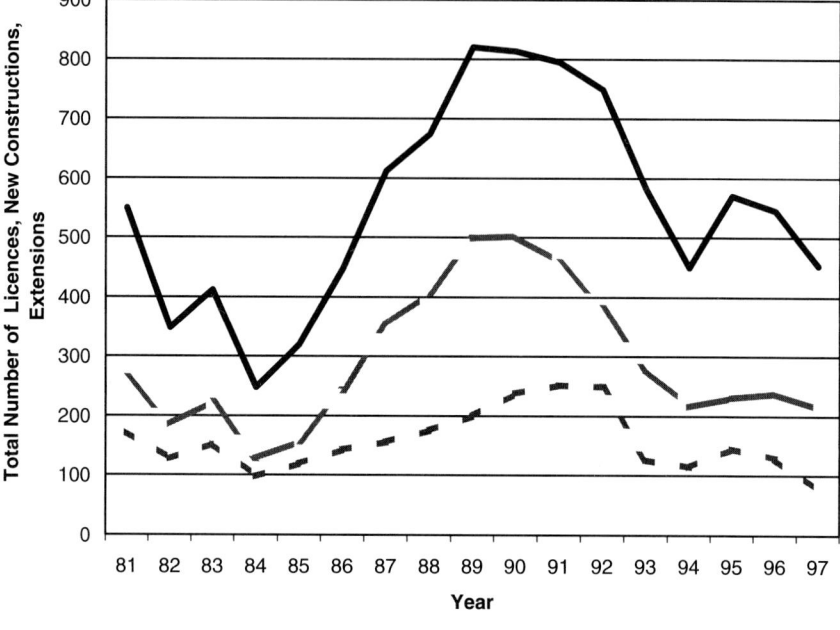

Fig. 4.3. Aggregate building activity in Acharnai and Thrakomakedones

values in check is now disappearing. In addition, the earthquake produced an unprecedented crisis in the housing and rental sectors, with rents increasing by 40–50 per cent between 1999 and 2001 (University of the Aegean 2002). A new investment like the Olympic Village will further unbalance the critical socio-economic equilibrium of this land development (Fig. 4.4).

4.4. The Olympic Village Plan

The design procedures for the OV were subjected to a merry-go-round of delays and changes before the project was eventually finalized, because of interlinked location, institutional, and financial complexities. The first Olympic Village Plan was prepared by the architect-planner Kandylis in 1989 as part of the 1996 Olympic Games bid. The Kandylis Plan was later revised

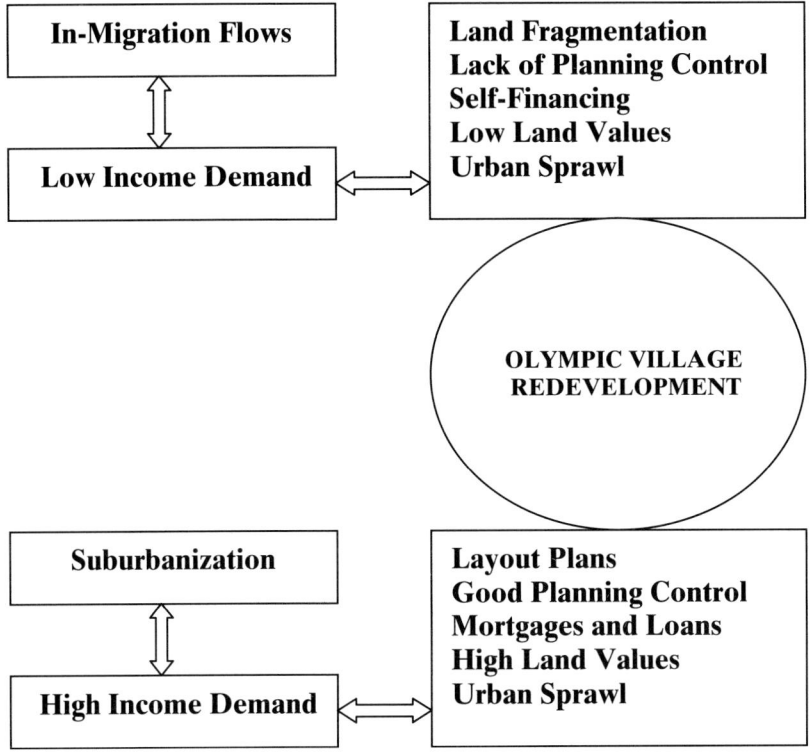

Fig. 4.4. Dominant patterns and the Olympic Village redevelopment

and integrated into the application for the 2004 Olympics bid. In 1998, a revised proposal was drafted and the final Olympic Village plan was subsequently approved. Despite this, the Olympic Committee (Athens 2004 SA) asked for a radical revision of the plan, and in September 1999 launched a tender for an architectural-planning design competition. Five planning groups were selected, but the tender was unexpectedly cancelled. The official explanation for this abrupt change referred to the need to establish a 'more objective selection process' and a new international tender was organized. This time, twenty-six candidates participated and three first awards were given. However, none of the winning designs was used; instead they served as a blueprint for drafting the final plan. This lengthy procedure meant that, for two years, there was neither a plan nor a detailed implementation programme. Needless to say, the final plan produced by the Workers Housing Organization bears little resemblance to the winning designs from the competition or, for that matter, to any other previous plan. The final plan was endorsed by Presidential Decree on

13 March 2001 ('Plan Approval of the Olympic Village Area in Acharnai Municipality').

The total OV area is 1,240,821 m^2, and is designed to serve the needs of approximately 16,000 athletes and delegates during the Games. The proposed Olympic land use plan consists of three zones: the International Zone-Olympic Village Centre; the Residential Zone; and the Olympic Park (Athens 2004 SA 1999: 29; OEK, 2000: 6). The Residential Zone covers 255,400,000 m^2 (with 86,800 m^2 built-up area), public utilities occupy 151,000 m^2, the Park (or Green Zone) takes 236,000 m^2, and the road and related infrastructure 236,000 m^2. Evidently all the proposed buildings and infrastructures imply a wide range of different conversion costs for the post-Olympic era. After the Games, each zone must be redeveloped in compliance with the 'normal' planning system. The Olympic residential zone will become a 'general residential area', whilst the international zone will be developed as an 'urban centre' with considerable commercial, retail, and service functions.

4.5. Financing and Implementing the Olympic Village

The OV plan has followed a path of trial and error with respect to implementation and funding mechanisms. The post-Olympic development of the Olympic Village was initially seen as 'an opportunity for the private sector to develop the area and to meet Athens's growing urban needs' (Committee for the Athens 2004 Candidacy 1997). The OV concept has been dominated by positive expectations for launching a 'contractor-based' redevelopment through the adoption of a quid pro quo system (Epilogi 1997: 58–60; Athens 2004 SA and Synadinos and Associates 1998*b*). The anticipated developer's profile was that of international financial–real estate institutions. Strangely enough, the numerous feasibility studies (focusing mostly on the viability of the scheme as private investment) that have accompanied the OV development in its various stages share two common arguments: the necessity of involving the public sector in the development process; and the difficulty of defining the role of the private sector in the redevelopment process (ORCO 1990; Committee for the Athens 2000 Candidacy 1990; DEPOS 1997; DEPOS 1999; Price Waterhouse Coopers 1999).

It soon became obvious that this philosophy based on private development did not create a feasible pathway for implementation, and the initial enthusiasm for the project soon waned. The OV development was significantly more complex than the development of single-function infrastructure such as highways, bridges, or airports, where a 'monopoly condition' exists for the exploitation of the asset. This renders profitable exploitation difficult, as has also been demonstrated by other cases in Europe (see Newman and Thornley 1996: 250–51). In addition, the state has been slow to invest locally in infrastructure, environmental improvements, or urban renewal schemes, with a consequent absence of positive external effects on land rents. Not surprisingly, this has failed to attract private investors to the area, and so far they have shown little interest in investing.

Under these conditions, in which private investment is limited or absent, the government has appointed the Workers Housing Organization as the core implementation and funding institution in charge of the OV development. This means that over a very short period of time—even before the beginning of the actual construction process—a marked shift has taken place from an initially purely private development rationale to a predominantly public one. The Workers Housing Organization (OEK) is a public institution that operates as an autonomous legal entity (under the control of the Ministry of Labour) and owns its capital assets, with a mission to provide housing for wageworkers. In February 2001, the establishment of a private statute company (controlled by OEK) to undertake the implementation of the OV was approved (Ministerial Decision, Ministry of Labour no. 190259/21 Feb. 2001, 'Approval of the Organizational Structure and Functioning of Olympic Village SA'), followed by the setting up of the Olympic Village SA company (Law 2819/15 Mar. 2001, 'Establishment of Olympic Village SA'). The main functions of the company involve project formulation, the administration of architectural and construction bids, and the management of construction assignments through self-financing or co-funding schemes. It can create, affiliate with, or participate in other companies as and when the need arises to facilitate the development process. The Olympic Village SA will also be in charge of the post-Olympic management of the project until 2006.

4.6. The Olympic Village's Impact on the Localities

4.6.1. Policy reports and projections

By and large, the potential impact of the redevelopment programme on the Athens agglomeration has not been widely examined, and no attention was paid to the impact on the adjoining localities. The official reports and policy documents (Committee for the Athens 2000 Candidacy 1996; 1997) portray 'in principle' a positive perspective in terms of economic gains, an improved 'physical infrastructure', and an expected amelioration of environmental conditions (Athens 2004 SA, and Synodinos and Associates 1998a). No attempt has been made to view the project in relation to socio-economic dynamics, existing local needs (e.g. housing or social infrastructure, etc.), or employment, and virtually nothing has been said with respect to local economic sectors such as retail and the manufacturing industry.

The feasibility studies (ORCO 1990; Committee for the Athens 2000 Candidacy 1990; DEPOS 1997; DEPOS 1999; Price Waterhouse Coopers

Table 4.4. The phasing of the Olympic Village development process: anticipated activities and areas of potential employment demand

Phases	Duration	Anticipated activities	Employment demand
Preliminary-preparatory	2 years	Architectural building tenders Finalization of decisions Expropriation and acquisition of sites	Engineering consulting Architectural consulting Management expertise consulting Specialized knowledge Public sector involvement
Construction	3 years	Site clearance Soil removal—excavations Foundation construction Fixed equipment Mobile equipment Surrounding open spaces works	Engineering expertise Architectural expertise Management expertise Qualified construction employment Non-qualified construction labour Technical support services Commercial services
Olympic Games	1 month	Administration Maintenance Catering Transport Information communication Medical health care Security General services	Provisional employment Maintenance services Subcontracting services Contract-based employment Voluntary services
Post-Olympic		Administration Maintenance Transport Medical health care Commerce, Retail Other services Recreation	Commercial retail employment Employment in administration Employment in recreation activities Maintenance services

1999; OEK 1999; Lambert Smith Hampton 2001) have only indirectly addressed the issue of local impact. In their attempt to identify potential demand for post-Olympic use, these reports have only taken into consideration the general demand trends for the Athens agglomeration as a whole and have ignored local dynamics. In addition, no particular suggestions have been made to link the redevelopment programme systematically with the development of other uses and with demand trends in retail and services in the area.

4.6.2. The socio-economic impact

It is difficult to produce any concrete appraisal of the impact of the OV development on the localities and especially on the local socio-economic dynamics, as the project is still in the construction process. Potential effects could be approached in relation to the phasing of the redevelopment process and the post-Olympic uses. Table 4.4 sketches one possible relationship between the four major redevelopment phases and local employment. These phases are the preliminary-preparatory period, the building period, the Olympic Games period, and the Post-Olympic era. Presumably, most benefits to local employment will be generated during the building phase (now in progress) due to the inherent potential of the building activities to absorb local labour and the central role of the construction sector in the district.

This potential does not appear to have been systematically exploited in spite of the fact that the possibility of generating construction sector employment through the scheme was acknowledged in the drafted protocol between the municipality and the Workers Housing Organization. More specifically, the municipality listed the following demands to be considered in the redevelopment programme: the adoption of a positive discrimination rationale favouring the local unemployed and population affected by the earthquake; the imposition of a minimum share of local labour for all construction firms engaged in the project; and the participation, through programming agreements, of a municipal 'construction enterprise' in building works associated with the scheme. Little has been said about the involvement of the local manufacturing sector in the redevelopment process of both SMEs and major industries, in leading sectors such as wood, furniture and metal, and transport.

With respect to the Olympic Games period itself, a core area of concern could be the insertion of local population in lower-end services at the OV. The potential local gains during the post-Olympic era have not been considered at all. The magnitude and type of employment generation will depend heavily on the uses that will be allocated to the International Zone of the OV (commercial, retail, and service uses), but nothing is yet clear about the post-Games redevelopment plans. The municipality, however, in the aforementioned protocol seeks to obtain an active role in the definition of the post-Olympic uses through the application of a 'pre-emption right' or through the allocation of a considerable part of the International Zone to community uses.

4.6.3. *The impact on land development*

The impact of the OV redevelopment on local land development will depend on the type of demand that the scheme will seek to satisfy during the post-Olympic era. The scale of the OV has been such that expectations were raised and local market trends affected long before its implementation. These high expectations were tightly linked to the anticipated arrival of 'big international developers'. A survey carried out between 1997 and 1999, and addressed at local major real state firms in Athens (Delladetsima, 1999), has identified significant increases in land prices in the areas directly adjacent to the OV (266 per cent for urbanized sites, 312 per cent for sites outside the town plan boundaries, and 157 per cent in the Thrakomakedones area). The project's funding mechanism is of critical importance since it defines the type of valorization that the OV assets will be given in the future. The funding philosophy, however, has already shifted from a self-financed private sector-led system (quid pro quo) to a full public redevelopment programme (leaving only the International Zone with the potential to be a privately run development). If a full private sector system had been adopted that targeted high standard housing (and other related uses), it might have had severe repercussions for the low income local market. A high income redevelopment process, combined with the existing suburbanization process, would have led to additional increases in land values. Clearly, the response from the low value sectors would have been pressure for further land fragmentation and urban sprawl.

The endorsed model based on public housing development—with the possibility of privately financed development of the International Zone—has the inherent risk of dragging the market downwards. The construction of an extensive public housing area also means the maintenance of a highly rigid social composition that excludes local demand for middle-class housing and related uses. For the time being, any possible flexibility to provide uses more adjusted to other housing demand segments and to create employment-generating activities is tightly linked to faith in the International Zone. In this regard, another round of debate concerning the future of the International Zone is starting. The initial question about whether the entire OV would be a private self-financed scheme of a publicly funded operation is now being raised for the far smaller area of the International Zone. Yet another feasibility study has been commissioned to seek the most appropriate solution (Lambert Smith Hampton 2001).

Set in such a fluid context, faced with such numerous delays, and given the anxiety to meet the deadlines, it seems that everything is dealt with as a mere engineering and infrastructure project. In any case, construction capital seems to be the winner. The central government has been swift enough to allocate (after the necessary tender) the construction of the housing part of the OV area to four major building consortia (who will carry out most of the Olympic Games works). These are contractors that could comply with the 'exceptionally introduced rules' for speeding up the process and make the best use of the budget—approximately 130 million Euro—but would leave aside qualitative parameters, integrative actions with local municipalities, and concerns over the local impact and future maintenance costs of the scheme. It is, for example, not yet known if the local authorities will be responsible for carrying the maintenance burden of the infrastructure after the Games.

4.7. Conclusions

The analysis shows that the Olympic Village as a novel redevelopment scheme has introduced a set of totally new conditions in the system of government/governance. These include new institutions, new planning modalities, land use changes, and financing mechanisms; with still different forms of institutional requirements expected to emerge during the post-Olympic era. The participation of private capital in the process has not been realized, and the optimism of the early period concerning the role of private self-financing has been seriously rolled back. As a consequence, the OV project has shifted from a self-financed private sector to an entirely public sector development. A highly complex design and implementation process, characterized by slow progress and numerous delays, has accompanied this shift. However, the effects at the local level are already felt in terms of changing socio-economic parameters and related real estate market dynamics.

It is also evident that the construction of the OV has been seen as purely a legal, institutional, and engineering matter. Expected returns from rent yielding activities have not been evaluated and no longer-term investment mechanism has been identified. Similarly, local employment, social, and infrastructure needs have been largely ignored. No attempt has been made to define a 'role' for the 'Village' (the town) in the 'post-Olympic' conurbation.

Nevertheless, even in its current incomplete state, and despite the negative practices that have been observed until now, the OV constitutes a unique vantage point from which to observe the making of contemporary Athens. This new development is designed to serve different short- and long-term needs, and is to be implemented in an area that reflects an array of acute unemployment, housing, and environmental problems. It is a microcosm of issues that are prevalent throughout the Athens agglomeration. Clearly, this has only been a beginning. There is plenty more to come and to evaluate. The experience may ultimately prove to be an exceedingly fruitful learning process.

References

Athens 2004 SA (1999). *Conceptual Design Competition for the Olympic Village*. In Greek. Volume 8/12. Athens: Athens 2004 SA.

——and Synadinos and Associates (1998*a*). *Plan and Location Study for the Olympic Village*. In Greek. Athens: Athens 2004 SA.

——and——(1998*b*). *Technical Report for the Co-financing Application for the Olympic Village Construction*. In Greek. Athens: Athens 2004 SA.

Committee for the Athens 2000 Candidacy (1990). *Olympic Village Feasibility Study*. In Greek. Athens: Committee for the Athens 2000 Candidacy.

——(1996). *Candidacy Files*. Vol. I-I-II. Athens: Committee for the Athens 2000 Candidacy.

Committee for the Athens 2004 Candidacy (1997). *The Athens 2004 Candidacy File*. Vol. I-I-II. Athens: Committee for the Athens 2004 Candidacy.

——and Kyriopoulou, A. (1997). *Planning Approach for the Olympic Village and its Broader Surrounding Area*. In Greek. Athens: Committee for the Athens 2004 Candidacy.

Committee for the Athens 2004 Candidacy and University of Thessaly (1997). *Spatial Effects of the Olympic Games and Integration with a Programming Framework*. In Greek. Athens: Committee for the Athens 2004 Candidacy.

DELLADETSIMA, P. M. (1999). 'Survey on the Real-estate Market in the Acharnai-Thrakomakedones Area, in the context of URSPIC'. Unpublished report. Athens.

——(2001). 'Urban Development in Greece and Landed Assets'. *Proceedings, Economic History of Thessaloniki*. In Greek. Thessaloniki: Ministry of Macedonia Thrace—University of Macedonia.

DEPOS (Public Corporation for Housing and Urban Development) (1997). *The Olympic Village: Feasibility Study-Economic Projections*. In Greek. Preliminary Report. Athens: Committee for the Athens 2004 Candidacy.

——and——(1999). *Demand Housing Types and Prices in the Olympic Village— Tendencies in the Real Estate Market in Greater Athens: Sample Survey*. In Greek. 1/99. Athens: DEPOS.

EDWARDS, M. (2000). 'Property Markets and the Production of Inequality', in S. Watson and G. Bridge (eds.), *A Companion to the City*. Oxford and Malden, Mass.: Blackwell, 599–608

Epilogi (1997). 'The First B.O.O.T. Experiment for Greek Construction Enterprises'. In Greek. *I Epilogi, 6/7*: 58–60.

European Union (1997). *The EU Compendium of Spatial Planning Systems and Policies*. Brussels: CEC.

GETIMIS, P. (1990). 'Urban Development and Policy', in P. Getimis *et al.* (eds.), *Urban and Regional Development*. In Greek. Athens: Themelio, 307–33.

Greek Parliament Bulletin (1999). *Report of the Continuous Committees on Cultural and Economic Affairs on the Legislative Plan of the Ministry of Cultural Affairs/Planning and Integrated Development of the Olympic Games Areas*. In Greek. Athens: Greek Parliament Bulletin.

Jones Lang Lassale (2001), 'Reaching Beyond the Gold: The impact of the Olympic Games on the Real Estate Market, Athens: *JLL*, Issue 1.

Lambert Smith Hampton (2001). 'Survey and Analysis Report on the Potential Exploitation of the Olympic Village International Zone'. Report. In Greek. Athens: Lambert Smith Hampton.

MAVRIDOU, M. (1998). 'The Location of The Olympic Games Works and the Urban Environment: The Olympic Village Impact on the Suburban Green Space of Athens'. In Greek. Unpublished report. Athens: NTUA Research Group.

Ministry of Planning Housing and Environment (1985). *Acharnai General Land-Use Plan*. In Greek. Athens: Ministry of Planning Housing and Environment.

——and Ministry of Cultural Affairs (1999). *The Planning Integrated Development and Implementation of the Olympic Games Works and Other Issues Law*. In Greek. Athens: Government Gazette 4.

Municipality of Acharnai (1993). *Acharnai Local Development Programme*. Athens: Municipality of Acharnai.

——(1999). 'Report on the Olympic Village'. In Greek. Unpublished. Athens: Municipality of Acharnai.

——and OEK (2000). 'Cooperation Protocol'. In Greek. Draft report unpublished. Athens.

——and National Technical University of Athens (2001). *Survey on Planning and Social Parameters in the Municipality of Acharnai: Determination of Strategic Planning Guidelines for Sustainable Development*. Athens: NTUA.

NEWMAN, P., and THORNLEY, A. (1996). *Urban Planning in Europe: International Competition, National Systems and Planning Projects*. London and New York: Routledge, 250–1.

OEK (Workers Housing Organization) (1999). *Integrated Proposal for the Operational Plan of the Olympic Village Construction with the participation of OEK*. Report. In Greek. Athens: OEK.

——(2000). *The First Steps for the Olympic Village*. In Greek. Information Bulletin 18/8. Athens: OEK.

ORCO SA (1990). *Olympic Village Feasibility Study*. Report. Athens.

PEIROUNAKIS, N. (1997). 'Exaggerated Expectations for Real Estate Price Increases'. In Greek. *O Ikonomikos Tachidromos*, 2/10.

Price Waterhouse Coopers (1999). 'Draft Stage One Report: Section 4/The Olympic Village'. Report. Athens, 1–31.

SIOMOPOULOS, K. (2001). 'The Real-Estate Market in the Context of New Major Works', *Akinita*, 4/01.

STAVRINOU, C. (1999). 'The Impact of the Olympic Games 2004 on the Greek Property Markets: Current Experience and Some Forecasts for Future Effects'. In *ERES 6th European Conference*. Athens: ERES.

SYNADINOS, P., et al. (1999). 'The Athens Olympic Village—The Settlement/Olympic Village in 2005'. In Greek *Technical Chamber of Greece Bulletin*, 2061: 26–7.

Technical Chamber of Greece, ARAVANTINOS, A., FRAGOULI, D., POLYZOS, J., and MANTOUVALLOU, M. (1990). *The Effects of the OG Works on the Athenian Urban Agglomeration*. In Greek. Athens: Technical Chamber of Greece/NTUA.

University of the Aegean, (2002 in progress) and DELLADETSIMA, P. M. (co-ordinator). *Creation of a Data Base and Decision Support System for the Reconstruction of the Acharnai-Thrakomakedones Area*. Research programme. Athens: University of the Aegean/EPPO.

TZANAVARA, H., and VASSILIADI, N. (1999), 'New Plans for 2004 for the Saronikos Coastal Front'. In Greek. *I Eleftherotypia*, 30/4: 48.

5

Gambling Politics or Successful Entrepreneurialism? The Orestad Project in Copenhagen

John Andersen

5.1. Introduction

Denmark is commonly regarded as a relatively egalitarian society. Although at the national level the relative strength of the Danish welfare regime serves to explain why the thesis of a general social polarization cannot be supported, there are important pockets of deprivation at the local level. In the Greater Copenhagen area, the inequality between affluent neighbourhoods dominated by owner-occupants and those with a high concentration of social housing units has grown in recent decades. The metropolis has been suffering from budget deficits for decades due to a relatively shrinking tax base. The districts outside Copenhagen have benefited most by the growth in high-paid service sector jobs. Since the early 1990s, these structural problems have prompted an aggressive entrepreneurial strategy of revitalization. The most relevant aspect of this new city entrepreneurialism is the Orestad Urban Development Plan (UDP) for the Oresund region.

The neo-corporatist style of state-led governance that characterizes the Orestad UDP contrasts sharply with the dominant participative tradition characterizing the Danish planning system. In part, this has been the result of the outdated political-administrative structures prevailing in the capital. While at the national level empowerment-oriented and bottom-up urban programmes are in operation, which include some deprived districts of Copenhagen, the Orestad UDP represents a completely different model. However, although in the original plan the project was conceived as a market-funded UDP, private investors have thus far been reluctant to participate and the project has been financed with state and municipal loans. In sum, the Copenhagen case demonstrates the dualistic character of Danish urban policy and governance: on the one hand the emergence of new élite-oriented revitalization projects embodied in the development strategy for the Oresund Region, and on the other the persistence of social action programmes for the most deprived districts.

5.2. The Orestad Project

The Orestad project is located south-east of the city centre on Western Amager between the historic centre of Copenhagen and the International Airport, near the new Oresund bridge to Sweden. The overall plan provides for the development of a new urban district, called Orestaden, over a period of thirty years. The new district is to act as a modern equivalent of the old centre (Fig. 5.1 and Plate 5.1).

The area has a total surface of 310 ha, which are situated in a 2,600 ha green area previously used for military purposes. It is, therefore, somewhat physically detached from the rest of the city. An integrated part of the overall project is the construction of a new Metro, which links the Airport, Orestad, and the centre of the city. The Metro became operational in 2002 and this in combination with the improved highway and railway system, provides Orestad with top quality transport facilities. The Orestad project envisages the integration of both sides of the Swedish–Danish fixed link in the Euro region (Oresund). The UDP is the critical node in the promotion of the cross-border Oeresund Region and is linked to an explicit regional recovery and internationalization strategy. Planning and development is being carried out by the Orestad Development

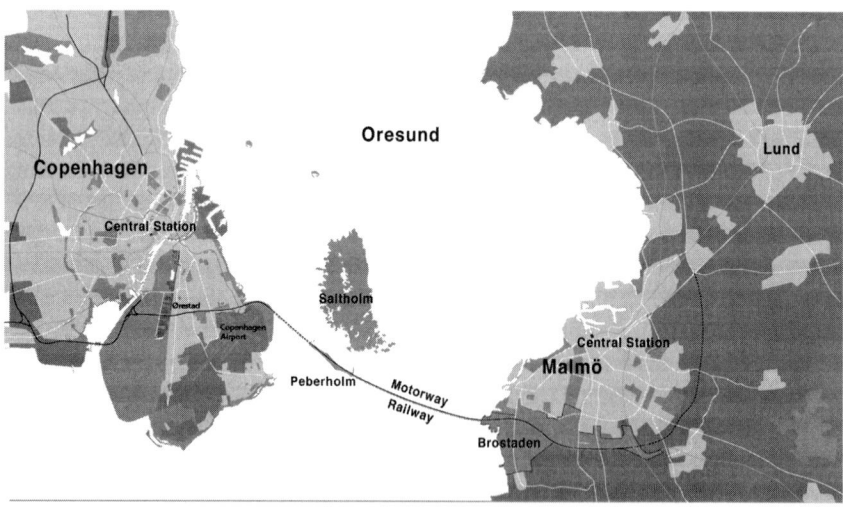

Fig. 5.1. Location of Orestad and Oresund region
Source: The Orestad Development Company.

Plate 5.1. The imagined Orestad City in 2025 (Source: The Orestad Development Company)

Corporation (ODC), which is an independent organization owned by the state (the Ministry of Finance and the Ministry of Transport (45 per cent) and the city of Copenhagen (55 per cent).

When fully developed, the new district of Copenhagen is planned to consist of:

1. 60 per cent business area: including industry (mainly knowledge based), business and financial services, and headquarters for multinational companies, providing 50,000 jobs (estimated by the ODC).
2. 20 per cent housing: 8,000 housing units (both rental flats and condominiums) are planned, with an estimated population of 25,000.

3. 20 per cent higher education, public and private research facilities, cultural amenities, official agencies, and commercial activities. These facilities will serve an estimated 22,000 students.

5.3. Institutional Framework and Urban Governance Conflicts in the Copenhagen Region

Until the 1970s, urban policy was characterized by top-down rational planning processes and procedures. The post-war 'golden age of the Welfare City' rested on a strong centralized City Hall administration in the hands of a powerful social democratic leadership that had been in power since the beginning of the nineteenth century. During the 1970s, the efficiency and legitimacy of the regime was challenged by a weakened tax base as a result of industrial decline and demographic changes, as well as by successful critical mobilization by new urban movements. The latter challenged the top-down style of planning and governance and mobilized for community-based participatory urban regeneration. At the start of the 1980s, the political and institutional dislocation of this regime fused with a deep financial crisis in the city. This in turn increased the conflicts over additional grants at a national state level, which was, from 1982 until 1992, under the political control of a liberal–conservative coalition.

From the late 1980s onwards, the national state exerted increasing pressure on the local government to initiate a metropolitan strategic growth policy. A gradual shift towards an 'Entrepreneurial City' strategy, linked to the emerging cross-border regional strategy, became the new orientation of the 1990s. In this strategy, Orestad became the flagship project for the Oresund's regional integration and development process. The Danish UDP began to embody a strategic 'revitalization partnership' between the state and the capital city.

5.4. Political and Economic Changes in the 1970s and 1980s: Contextualizing the Shift to City Entrepreneurialism in the 1990s

During the 1970s the hegemonic social democratic urban regime which had dominated City Hall since the beginning of the century was strongly challenged by the growing power of new urban movements and the New Left (Socialist Left Party and the Socialist People's Party), which together held between 30 per cent and 40 per cent of the seats in the City Council. The New Left forces heavily criticized the Social Democrats for a top-down authoritarian urban renewal policy, which did not take the social and cultural diversity of the new urban space into account. The visions of these new urban movements were shaped by a criticism of rational planning paradigms practised through rigid bureaucratic forms and procedures, and pursuing the interests of an (imagined and imaginary) standard working- and middle-class family.

The tensions between City Hall and the new urban movements became manifest around 1980, and reached a peak with a week-long fight between locals and the police in the streets of Noerrebro in that year. The event was provoked by the city government's decision to remove a popular playground (Byggeren) from the area, although in reality it was also about the authoritarian and non-participatory style of implementing urban renewal schemes. After this episode, the political climate deteriorated even more, and, at the national political level, the municipality of Copenhagen became labelled as partly 'ungovernable'. The municipal department for urban planning had since 1977 been headed by the popular Villo Sigurdson from the Left Socialist Party. However, after the election in 1981 where Sigurdson and his party again improved their position, the social democratic Mayor decided to remove authority for the department for urban planning from him and it was put under direct Mayoral control. The left claimed that this removal was illegal and a year-long court battle ensued. The conflict paralysed the Copenhagen urban planning system completely, as this political polarization and institutional dislocation fused with deep financial problems.

Copenhagen was hit much harder than the rest of Denmark by the unemployment crisis that struck from the mid-1970s onwards, and this was combined with a long-term trend, apparent from the 1960s, of a massive loss of manual industrial jobs. The level of public investment in Copenhagen also shrank compared to the rest of Denmark. This was due in part to a national decentralization policy, which was the dominant spatial policy paradigm until the late 1980s. Furthermore, the municipalities outside Copenhagen benefited from a significant growth in high paid service sector jobs. The strength of the left-wing parties and the Social Democratic Party prevented drastic cuts in welfare services as a means of solving these financial problems, but in a context of shrinking revenue this led to the accumulation of public debts and to lower levels of public investments. In 2001, the debt stood at approximately 1.6 billion Euro and is still a major burden on the municipal budget.

During the 1980s, there were three main policy responses to this fiscal crisis. Firstly, until the mid-1980s, political pressure was exercised to obtain additional state grants. The social democratic national government, which was in office until 1982, had recognized the need for serious negotiations with the municipality of Copenhagen. When the conservative–liberal government came to power in 1982 after decades of social democratic rule, an expert commission to assess the condition of Copenhagen was created. The commission pointed towards two negative self-perpetuating mechanisms of the socio-economic crisis: industrial decline, lack of new growth, and unemployment; and an expensive demographic composition, with many elderly and young, and an

Table 5.1. Income, workforce, and social assistance in the Copenhagen region

Geo-administrative unit	Workforce as percentage of population	Blue-collar workers as percentage of workforce	Unemployed as percentage of employed	Average gross income, 15–66 years (CPH = 100)	Families on social assistance as percentage of population
Copenhagen	53	18	14	100	12
Greater Copenhagen region	56	15	10	125	9
Denmark	56	22	12	108	6

Source: Munk 1998.

increasing concentration of other low income groups and the socially excluded (Andersen *et al.* 1984). Despite considerable political pressure, however, the system of municipal reimbursement and state grants remained almost unchanged. Rising municipal debts were the inevitable result.

Secondly, housing policy gradually changed in favour of middle and high income households. Social housing in Denmark dates back to the beginning of the twentieth century when the first social democratic-controlled municipalities supported housing co-operatives that were closely linked to the labour movement (Kolstrup 1996), and since then this has been an important part of social democratic housing policy. The democratic tradition of self-governance in the housing co-operatives is regarded as unique 'social capital' which constitutes one of the often-overlooked strengths of the Danish welfare regime. The number of newly built social housing estates decreased during the 1980s, and has stopped completely since the late 1990s. Furthermore, the municipally owned houses were sold off and privatized in the mid-1990s. This change in housing policy towards privatization, aimed primarily at attracting higher income groups and improving the tax base of the city, was gradually accepted by the social democratic leadership during a ground-breaking coalition government with the strengthened liberal and conservative members of the City Council. The social housing associations, which traditionally held a strong position in the social democratic networks of governance, have therefore been relegated to a much more peripheral position. These political changes fused with economic changes as the combination of inflation with tax reductions for private ownership from the 1960s onwards made the purchase of property very advantageous for upper working-class and middle-class households. This led to the beginning of a continuous process of housing segregation, because as middle income residents left the social housing sector the share of low income residents increased. The combined result of these changes was that the social geography in the metropolitan region became more polarized (Thor-Andersen 1999).

After the battle for full employment was lost in the late 1970s, the growing group of people suffering from long-term labour market exclusion gradually concentrated in distinct urban districts. Whilst some Copenhagen neighbourhoods, such as the inner city and Christianshavn, experienced a rise in private ownership and private co-operative housing associated with gentrification, others with a larger share of social housing, like Bispebjerg and Kongens Enghave, have moved from the middle to the bottom of the urban social hierarchy (Munk 1998).

Thirdly, attempts were made to develop a coherent regional strategy for employment and infrastructure development within the framework of the Greater Copenhagen Council (GCC), the regional authority.

The task of the GCC as a regional political authority was to ensure infrastructure development and to undertake growth-stimulating initiatives. From its very beginning, in 1974, the GCC suffered from a functional and financial crisis, partly because of its ill-defined legal status. Furthermore, the GCC was paralysed by internal struggles between the poor social democratic and leftist councils that governed Copenhagen and the richer conservative–liberal municipalities outside Copenhagen. The conservative–liberal government finally closed down the GCC in 1987 (in parallel to the abolishing of the Greater London Council in the United Kingdom by the Thatcher government), and the metropolitan region was left without a political authority. Of course, the closure of the GCC only increased the problems of governing Copenhagen and the surrounding region.

In the face of a long lasting municipal budget deficit and political administrative dislocation at the regional level, in the late 1980s the conservative–liberal government held a very strong bargaining position *vis-à-vis* the municipality of Copenhagen. Most observers claim that the city of Copenhagen has been under *de facto* national state administration since the late 1980s. As will be shown below, it was in this economic, institutional, and political context that the Danish UDP, the Orestad project, was born.

5.5. The Orestad UDP and the New Urban Strategy

A new urban regime of 'state led city entrepreneurialism' (Harvey 1989) emerged in the late 1980s. The new, pragmatic, social democratic leadership in Copenhagen gave up its former policy of confronting the national state head on, and became less committed to taking the interests of low income groups into account in its housing policy. In the field of urban renewal, a more open and pluralistic style of governance emerged, followed by a more participatory orientation based on ideas of communicative and incremental planning

(Sehested 1999) in the 1990s. The large-scale urban renewal programme on Vesterbro is the flagship example of this trend that integrated ecological and aesthetic experimentations into ongoing programmes. However, the most ground-breaking change, from the late 1980s onwards, was the linkage of the urban regeneration strategy to a metropolitan regional growth strategy. A relatively stable state–metropolis growth alliance emerged at the beginning of the 1990s and this continued after the Social Democratic Party returned to national power in 1992.

The case study UDP, the Orestad project, became the flagship project for the implementation of this new strategy. It should, however, be emphasized that the 'Schumpetarian/entrepreneurial' orientation was to some extent still immersed in basic social democratic values, including the maintenance of a strong public sector in the field of social services, welfare provision, and the inclusion of the trade union leadership in the policy networks. Hence, from the outset, Danish urban Schumpeterianism had some social democratic or 'nego-tiated economy' foundations unlike, for example, the United Kingdom, where Schumpeterianism was linked to an aggressive neo-liberal strategy which was not socially mediated. The most important change was the introduction of an emphasis on urban development as a strategic tool in order to achieve a better competitive position *vis-à-vis* other European city regions for investments that would facilitate a desired transition towards a service-based post-industrial economy and urban form (Anderson and Matthiessen 1993). Copenhagen was now to act as a dynamo for regional and national growth. This was a significant shift away from previous Danish regional policy, which had emphasized inter-regional equalization, and therefore treated the capital unfavourably in the ongoing struggles over the allocation of public infrastructure development and other investments. In particular, the cross-border Oresund region, made up of five administrative units on Zealand (Frederiksborg, Roskilde, and Copen-hagen county, and the municipalities of Copenhagen and Frederiksberg) and the southern part of Sweden, Skaane, re-entered the discourse as the preferred site to develop as a potential growth engine, with Copenhagen as its pivotal point. The Oeresund bridge between Denmark and Sweden had been discussed since the powerful European Union (EU) lobby, the 'Round Table of European Industrialists', suggested it in 1983 (Lemberg 1999). From 1989 onwards, the comprehensive visioning of Copenhagen as the centre of a competitive region emerged in official city Master Plans and was backed up by influential parts of the academic community. In this discourse and policy orientation, both the Oresund bridge and, later, the Orestad project, became powerful symbols of, and for, a future competitive, creative, learning, and knowledge-based region.

In 1990, a Metropolitan committee on traffic investments, the Würtzen Committee, suggested the establishment of a Copenhagen Metro system and the development of the Orestad area as a new urban district for Copenhagen. The special feature of this UDP in terms of its organizational and financial construction was the combination of two different projects: the construction of the new Orestad city district; and a huge expansion of the transport infrastructure, which would connect Amager with Frederiksberg by means of a new Metro system with its nexus in central Copenhagen. The Metro investment was linked to supplementary investments in highways linking central Copenhagen with the Greater Copenhagen area, and railways connecting Orestad and Amager with the existing Danish and Swedish railway systems. The land for this project had been earmarked since the idea of creating a new city district was first suggested in 1963, and was jointly owned by the state (45 per cent) and the municipality (55 per cent). At that time, however, the plan was driven by the need for additional social housing in the Copenhagen area, and was met with scepticism due to the dominant national orientation in regional planning which emphasized expansion to the west of the capital. The plan was put aside after the oil crisis and sharp economic decline in 1973, but was revived almost twenty years later in a new context and with decidedly new content, linked with the emerging regional and urban entrepreneurial strategy (Anderson and Matthiessen 1993).

The crux of the plan was that it suggested step by step incremental planning within an overall master plan. The proceeds from the selling of land would be used to finance the Metro, and when the latter project was completed (scheduled for 2003) the proceeds would be channelled back to cover outstanding liabilities from the urban development project. This stretched the original mandate given to the Committee, as the original remit was to plan for future traffic investments in the capital (Andersen 1998).

However, since the suggested Copenhagen Metro system was part of the package, the Committee argued that the conditions of the mandate had not been transgressed. Because of the pragmatic perspective of the initial planning, the project offered to solve pressing problems for a range of different sectors and at a variety of different scales. From the perspective of growth machine theory (Harding 1994), neo-Marxist regulation theoretical approaches (Jessop 1998), or regime theory (Stones 1993), such design process could be seen as a step in the formation of a neo-corporatist growth regime. Following Stones, a regime can be defined as a relatively stable group with access to institutional resources that enable it to have a sustained role in making governing decisions. The 'iron law' of regimes is that they must be able to mobilize resources suitable for the political agenda at a given time and place (Stones 1993: 21).

An important tactical strength of the project was its capability to overcome the strong scepticism of the national politicians who represented the interests of the province. The informal but powerful Jutland lobby, which included politicians in both the opposition and the government, had effectively blocked previous large Copenhagen infrastructure investments. With the proposed new financing scheme, the Copenhagen infrastructure and regional growth package could be presented as being basically neutral to the state budget. For the liberal–conservative government, the institutional form of the Orestad Development Corporation (ODC) had a national political rationality. The use of hybrid organizations in urban development as well as in other areas of policy (Sehested 1999) was in line with the government's general new public management orientation and attempts to introduce more business-like *modus operandi* in public affairs and planning (Andersen 1998).

In the design phase of the UDP, at the beginning of the 1990s, a coalition of the Conservative and Liberal Parties controlled the national level, while the Social Democratic Party was the largest party in Parliament and the dominant party in the Copenhagen City Council. At the political level, the key actors in the new ground-breaking state–capital growth coalition were the leaders of the Social Democratic and Conservative Parties. When the plans leaked to the public, they stirred considerable criticism for their democratic short cuts and unrealistic financial foundations. Existing statutory planning guidelines had been completely overruled—a fact that all professors of Urban Planning in Denmark emphasized in their remarkably sharp criticism of the proposal (Larsen and Paludan 2000). Influential professionals in urban planning and critics within the public domain described the plans using unsavoury terms such as 'Elitist Corporate Planning' and 'Politics of Illusionism' (Lemberg 1999). The social democratic–conservative and state–municipal/capital 'City Entrepreneurial Coalition' unanimously rejected the criticism, and was powerful enough to speed up the process of implementation. The agreed law to initiate the process also stated that the ODC would be established to manage the development and selling of land and the construction of the Metro.

5.6. Lack of Democratic and Financial Transparency

The primacy of market-led redevelopment over comprehensive planning and existing procedures was very manifest in the design phase. The Danish UDP represents a clear case of 'exceptionality' (Moulaert, Swyngedouw, and Rodriguez 1999) in relation to existing planning instruments—a controversial feature of the project from the beginning. The new solution was criticized for being a hybrid: on the one hand, an autonomous private shareholder company was established; while, on the other, a public/private partnership with financial means was underwritten by a state-guaranteed credit line of 850 million Euros. The project's proponents argued that the ODC combined the best of two worlds: it was publicly controlled but with sufficient autonomy to operate efficiently in market terms. The critics argued that the project combined the worst of two worlds: lack of both effective democratic control and transparent economic management. This enduring criticism resulted in a modification of the 'exceptionality' status and, when it came to implementation, the master plan and the subsequent series of subplans were passed through the City Council in accordance with existing planning procedures.

The first step in the implementation of the project involved the organization of an architectural competition. Twenty-one leading Danish architects argued that the project was not embedded in a coherent vision of a sustainable city for the future, or the needs of deprived neighbourhoods, and insisted that the whole idea of a 'compact hyper-growth district' was not sufficiently substantiated (Larsen and Paludan 2000). The master plan of the Orestad project incorporated some of these criticisms and amended some of the architectural and aesthetic aspects of the project. However, the core idea of the creation of a 'hyper-growth district', combined with an 'élitist image' (in terms of the planned housing provision) of the new city district remained unchanged.

5.7. A Hesitating Market

The main problem, which became evident around 1996/7, was the disappointingly low level of private investment. The mobilization of (semi-)public partners to invest in the project thus became crucial for the survival of the ODC. Ironically, the project was originally presented as being more or less cost neutral for public budgets, as urban rent (after closing the rent gap through developing the area) was expected to finance the investments. However, thus far in the implementation there has been a massive increase in the use of public loans and costly (re)orientations of public investments to the UDP. Public criticism of the project's financial reliability was articulated in 1997 by the United Left Party and was later picked up by the influential business magazine *Monday Morning*. Their analysis estimated that the project was likely to cost the taxpayers between 1 and 2 billion Euro.

Although the project was less than halfway through its implementation phase, the ruling growth coalition argued that it had already passed its 'point of no return' as the then social democratic Minister of Traffic labelled it during a parliamentary debate. Despite extensive overspending, the growth coalition was still characterized by a 'Spirit of the Three Musketeers', who invested their political prestige in confirming their belief in offensive entrepreneurialism. The rationale seemed to be that the political and economic costs of accepting increased public investments would be lower than those associated with opening up a debate to revise fundamentally the economic and legal organization of the UDP. Throughout the implementation of the project, however, the original calculations have proven to be far too optimistic. The level of debt continuously increased and the planned repayment period was extended from around ten years to between twenty and thirty years. In 1999, the revenue from land already sold was only 3.3 per cent of the total initial calculated revenue (Andersen, Hougaard, and Jensen 1999). The critics argue that a large part of

Table 5.2. Public investments in the Orestad

Project	Public investments in Euro
Copenhagen University	228,000,000
IT University and Research Park	48,000,000
Research Park	46,000,000
The National Archive and the Royal Library	202,000,000
Danish Broadcasting Corporation (DR)	269,000,000
Copenhagen Hospital Corporation (HS)	5,000,000
Opera House	40,000,000
Total	838,000,000

Source: Andersen, Hougaard, and Jensen 1999.

the stated income is speculative because of the restrictive conditionality clauses stipulated in the contracts signed with some of the larger private investors, and that the other part of the 'revenue' is really derived from public investments (and hence from the taxpayer), including pure 'gifts' from the state. The dominant actor in the efforts to reallocate (semi-)public institutions to Orestad was the Ministry of Finance. During 1998, this Ministry encouraged public institutions to consider the Orestad building sites if they were planning to move their offices and promised to be 'helpful' in finding additional resources, since the price of building sites in Orestad were among the highest in the Region. The results of all these efforts are summarised in Table 5.2.

In addition to the public investments, state lending to the project passed the 1 billion Euro mark in 1999, with an extra 200 million Euro added to the original state loan of 850 million Euro. One major problem in the implementation of large-scale UDPs is that the point of no return makes it difficult to redirect UDPs once they are set in motion. UDPs have a very strong element of the politics of gambling, which tends to follow a logic of irreversibility. The critics of the ODC claim that the presentation and calculation of benefits and risks was over-optimistic, yet it was clearly seductive. The growth coalition and the ODC argue that the bridge to Sweden will boost the real estate market in the area and that the ODC will be able to increase its income from land sale substantially. In so far as this strategy will work, the progressive element in the Danish UDP package is the plan of investing the urban rent in a public good: a new Metro. In City Hall, the project's critics have calculated that the price for paying back the debts of the ODC will amount to an additional tax burden of 0.7 per cent for twenty years.

Should the project be successful, Orestad will add up to 50,000 new jobs and 10,000 new high income households to the area. The project might be able to attract high income citizens to live in Orestad instead of, for example, in the richer northern municipalities outside Copenhagen, with a positive impact on the municipal budget. In terms of the social geography, a successfully developed Orestad is supposed to be an internationally 'exclusive' district. The possible negative side effect could be increased polarization, rather than bridging the social, cultural, and economic forces of the affluent and the less affluent in a transition towards the post-industrial city.

In the final implementation phase, there are still possibilities for housing other than high income residents to encourage a more socially and economically mixed population. Furthermore, some room for manoeuvre might exist to stimulate synergistic effects between the Orestad development and strategies for socio-economic improvements benefiting the inhabitants of the deprived neighbourhoods—for example, development of service sector jobs, social economy initiatives, etc. However, for the moment there are no signs from the growth coalition behind the project that point to a change in the élitist profile of the project. Yet it is not inconceivable that, depending on future economic and political dynamics, this discussion might begin to figure in future decisions on possible redirections of the project. This is not least due to the new orientations in national urban policy, which emphasize the problem of segregation and the need for a new holistically oriented urban policy (Ministry of Housing and Urban Affairs 1999). This is the theme we shall turn to in the next section.

5.8. Between Neo-élitist Growth Policy and Empowerment of Deprived Districts

The present situation is characterized by ambivalence and conflicting agendas. The present urban policy regime consists of two contrasting programmes: a Schumpeterian strategic growth policy, based at the state, regional, and municipal level on the one hand; and a decentralization programme of elected district councils in Copenhagen with reinvented participatory planning instruments supported by nationally funded social action programmes for deprived urban areas on the other. The missing links between the UDP and the programmes for social renewal concerned with social sustainability, local creativity, and empowerment in the deprived urban areas and the avoidance of socio-spatial polarization constitute the most striking paradox in the ongoing dispute over Danish and EU urban policy.

Looking back from the present, it is obvious that the urban movements were excluded from the new powerful growth policy networks. However, it should be noted that the voice of community activists has re-entered the urban scene since the mid-1990s, not least because of the state's implementation of area-based social action programmes in deprived districts, inspired by former social renewal projects and by the EU's anti-poverty programmes. However, their localist and socio-cultural orientation have limited these actions. Structural socio-economic issues have not been addressed, and the articulation of these initiatives with a broader revitalization strategy has been almost non-existent, despite the fact that the national programme rhetorically stresses the necessity of such linkages. Hence, an ambiguous duality can be identified between the strategy for economic revitalization dominated by neo-corporatist, élitist governance and the area-based programmes for deprived districts influenced by planning ideas based on social mobilization (Friedmann 1987) and community empowerment (Craig and Mayo 1995). This dualism is also manifested at the state level, where a growing tension can be identified between the Ministry of Financial Affairs, which emphasizes the entrepreneurial aspect of urban governance and the Ministry of Urban Affairs and Housing, which emphasizes the need for comprehensive urban policy.

The present urban policy framework in Denmark can, consequently, best be described as being ambivalent, but now that the aim of linking social, ecological, and economic objectives has been more clearly articulated, it can perhaps also be described as being innovative.

5.9. Conclusion

The absence of collective action from the bottom is a serious problem for social polarization. Socially productive, transformative conflicts encourage the mutual understanding and social learning of collective and individual actors and hence reduce transaction costs and enhance social capital, the norms and networks which facilitate collective action for mutual benefit (Andersen 1999). From the social polarization angle, which has been the leitmotif of the entire URSPIC project, the analysis leads us to identify the challenges as the development of holistic policy objectives (taking social, ecological, aesthetic, and economic considerations into account), where UDPs are part of a coherent regional socio-economic strategy, and the (re)development of participatory planning and policy instruments, which stimulate local participation/community empowerment and transparency of good practice and learning across the local, regional, national, and transnational levels. In terms of governance this includes efforts to include partners usually excluded from the growth policy network, such as the third sector, social housing associations, and agencies representing deprived neighbourhoods.

The challenge of the New Inclusion Policy is to integrate actors representing interests at the bottom of the social ladder and foster coalitions between excluded groups and sections of working and middle classes, and to enable the actors to operate across different spatial levels. The forces of social polarization operate at a variety of scales, and the forces of inclusion must aim to do likewise.

In the design phase, and at least in the first part of the implementation phase, the growth coalition and the UDP leaderzhip mobilized a strong discursive power due to their offensive construction of the agenda for future social, aesthetic, and economic development. Unlike the 'New Developers'—capable of leading the city into the post-modern world—the critics were associated with old-fashioned 'politics of resistance' or labelled as 'idealistic radical democrats' and thus in part excluded from influential policy networks. This situation of asymmetrical power relations in the public discourse created difficult conditions for the linkage of urban (re)development with notions of inclusion and social justice.

The new urban governance, where decision-making power is transferred to relatively autonomous agencies, raises questions about the need for institutionalized alternative expertise in the design and implementation process. If 'Entrepreneurial Governance' cannot be avoided, then access to alternative knowledge networks as well as representation and voices for actors outside the neo-élitist governance networks becomes crucial in order to avoid extremely asymmetrical power relations in the policy process. This problematic also relates to the well-known problem of subsidiarity—the division of tasks and competencies between local, city, region, state, and EU levels.

In Copenhagen, the politically created absence of a regional level of government was one of many factors that produced dislocation with regard to adequate democratic regulations for urban redevelopment. Technocratic actors in the professional planning complex took power through policy-making and corporate networks, and succeeded in opening the strategic terrain of a new metropolitan growth regime. The Danish case, therefore, suggests two lessons: the importance of the political and institutional empowerment of deprived districts, which need their own political and institutional platform in order to articulate their demands: and the importance of an elected regional government to open up and challenge the power of autonomous closed élitist policy networks operating on the regional scale. The old conflict between politics and the market is thus becoming increasingly crucial in this new age of globalization.

Acknowledgements

Thanks to Trine Fotel, Roskilde University, for useful comments.

References

ANDERSEN, B. R., *et. al.* (1984). *The Copenhagen Report*. Research Institute of Municipalities and Counties in Denmark. Copenhagen: AKF.

ANDERSEN, JAKOB (1998). *Fra folkestyre til fællesstyre*. Copenhagen: Gyldendal.

ANDERSEN, JAKOB, HOUGAARD, G., and JENSEN, S. H. (1999). *Second Annual Report for the U.R.S.P.I.C. Project*. Roskilde: Roskilde University, Department of Social Sciences.

ANDERSEN, J. (1999). 'Post-industrial Meritocracy or Solidarity'. *Acta Sociologica*, 42/4.

ANDERSON, Aa., and MATTHIESSEN, C. W. (1993). *Oeresundsregionen: kreativitet, integration, vækst*. Copenhagen: Munksgaard.

CRAIG, G., and MAYO, M. (1995) (eds). *Community Empowerment*. London: ZED Books.

FRIEDMAN, J. (1987). *Planning in the Public Domain: From Knowledge to Action*. Princeton: Princeton University Press.

HARDING, A. (1994). 'Urban Regimes and Growth Machines Towards a Cross-national Research Agenda'. *Urban Affairs Quarterly*, 29/3: 356–82.

HARVEY, D. (1989). *From Managerialism to Entrepreneurialism: The Transformation of Urban Governance in Late Capitalism. Geografiska Annaler, Series B: Human Geography*, 17 B: 1–30.

JESSOP, B. (1998). 'Globalisation, Entrepreneurial Cities and the Social Economy', in P. Hamel, L. T. Lustiger-Thaler, and M. Mayer (eds.), *Urban Movements in a Global Environment*. Urban Studies Yearbook. Sage.

KOLSTRUP, S. (1996). *The Origins of the Welfare State (Velfaerdstatens roedder)*. Viborg: SFAH.

LARSEN, J. L., and PALUDAN, E. H. (2000). *Omkring Orestaden*. Copenhagen: Centre for Interdisciplinary Urban Studies.

LEMBERG, K. (1999). 'Kan fysisk planlægning, miljø og økonomi enes?'. Research Report 119. Roskilde University: Department of Geography.

Metropolitan Commission (1989). *What Do We Want to Do with the Capital? (Hovedstaden—Hvad vil vi med den?.)* Copenhagen: Ministry of State.

Ministry of Housing and Urban Affairs (1999). *The Future of the City (Fremtidens By)*. Copenhagen: Ministry of Housing and Urban Affairs.

MOULAERT, F., SWYNGEDOUW, E., and RODRIGUEZ, A. (1999). *Rapport Final: Urban Redevelopment and Social Polarisation in the City. U.R.S.P.I.C.* Lille: CNRS.

MUNK, A. (1998). *Succession and Gentrification Processes in Older Neighbourhoods*. Hoersholm: The Danish Building Research Institute.

SEHESTED, K. (1999). 'Investigating Urban Governance—From the Perspectives of Organisation, democracy and planning'. Paper for the Nopsa Conference, Uppsala. Roskilde: Roskilde University.

STONES, C. (1993). 'Urban Regimes and the Capacity to Govern: A Political Economy Approach'. *Journal of Urban Affairs*, 15/1: 1–28.

THOR-ANDERSEN, H. (1999). 'Urban Restructuring—Towards a New Urban Form?' Paper for ENHR-MRI Conference, Hungary. Copenhagen: Department of Geography.

6

Facing Fiscal Crisis: Urban Flagship Projects in Berlin

Hartmut Häußermann and Katja Simons

6.1. Introduction

Great changes have taken place in Berlin since 1990. Reunification brought about a profound transformation of the political and socio-economic life of the city, as well as transforming its spatial structure. Several interrelated processes shape this dynamic urban redevelopment: the transformation from a socialist to a capitalist order in the East, spatial changes as a consequence of reunification, and the restructuring of the urban economy. A major change has been the post-socialist transition of the Eastern part of the city, which has altered all conditions for urban development (Häußermann 1997). Private ownership, the introduction of a market economy, and new planning laws were all (re)introduced in this area. This has resulted in a re-evaluation of the city centre through the introduction of new planning schemes and the development of a real estate market in an area where for forty years no land value or market had existed. Because of this, new structural concepts have had to be developed for the city as a whole.

The breaching of the wall also brought an end to the anomalous status of West Berlin as a 'white dot in a sea of red', located in the heart of a social-ist country. In political terms, it signalled the end of an occupied city-state and its full integration into the legal, socio-economic, and political system of a unified Germany. With the end of this extraordinary political situa-tion, all past subsidies that had been provided as part of securing its role as the 'outpost of the free world' were quickly discontinued. Until 1989, there were scarcely any economic activities taking place in Berlin without public funding: 50 per cent of the local budget was derived from federal transfers, and many jobs existed in the civil service, because the private economy would not employ as many people as was deemed politically necessary for the exposed city. The loss of subsidies for industrial activities and for public administration during the period 1990–92 immediately led to a rapid decline in the number of jobs. Furthermore, these processes were embedded in the dynamics of socio-economic restructuring induced by major sectoral shifts.

Economic structural change has brought radical changes to the labour market, since both parts of the city had been isolated from international competition, and—during a period when globalization shaped urban economies all over the world—from international economic development. Between 1989 and 1997, Berlin underwent a rapid process of deindustrialization as the number of manufacturing jobs declined in the Eastern part by nearly 80 per cent, and in the Western part by 30 per cent (Häußermann and Kapphan 2000: 106).

The 1991 decision to move the seat of national government from Bonn to Berlin represented efforts to shape and create a new national government centre. Capital functions were housed within the former Eastern city centre, and, alongside this, many new jobs in the service sector have been created over the last decade. Berlin's reinstatement as the national capital raised great expectations with respect to its potential transformation into an internationally competitive city. There were many illusionary growth scenarios in the early reunification phase—very welcome in a city in which economic dynamism had been absent for so many years. The population was estimated to grow by millions, and consequently the demand for housing and office space was expected to explode. These expectations were supported by forecasts of dynamic growth for the reunited city. The lost identities of East and West Berlin were to be replaced by a vision of Berlin as an international metropolis, based on its innovative potential in science, research, and culture, and on its geopolitical position between the Western and transforming Eastern part of Europe's new political and economic landscape. Berlin was expected to catch up with structural changes, leading to the making of a post-industrial city, and it was expected to take up a leading role in the European urban hierarchy. However, the actual development of the city differed from these visions. Stagnating population growth, economic decline, high levels of unemployment, fiscal crisis, and state retrenchment became the key phrases of the 1990s. Unemployment in the city has doubled since 1990, and, because of very low tax income and growing expenditures on the reorganization of the urban infrastructure (and also growing social problems), a serious fiscal crisis occurred. In the early period of transformation, many 'big projects' were planned in addition to the construction of a new government district. Nodes for a new traffic system, the expansion of housing provision, the redevelopment of derelict areas after the process of deindustrialization, and the construction of new facilities for cultural activities and sporting events—all needed urgent implementation.

Our case study of Berlin-Adlershof—'the city of science, technology, and media'—may be used as a lens through which the transformation process of the city, its deficiencies and problems, may be viewed. This project aims to establish a High-Tech and Science Park on the former site of the East German Academy of Sciences and German Broadcasting Station, located at the southeast edge of Berlin (see Fig. 6.1). The project intends to regenerate this urban

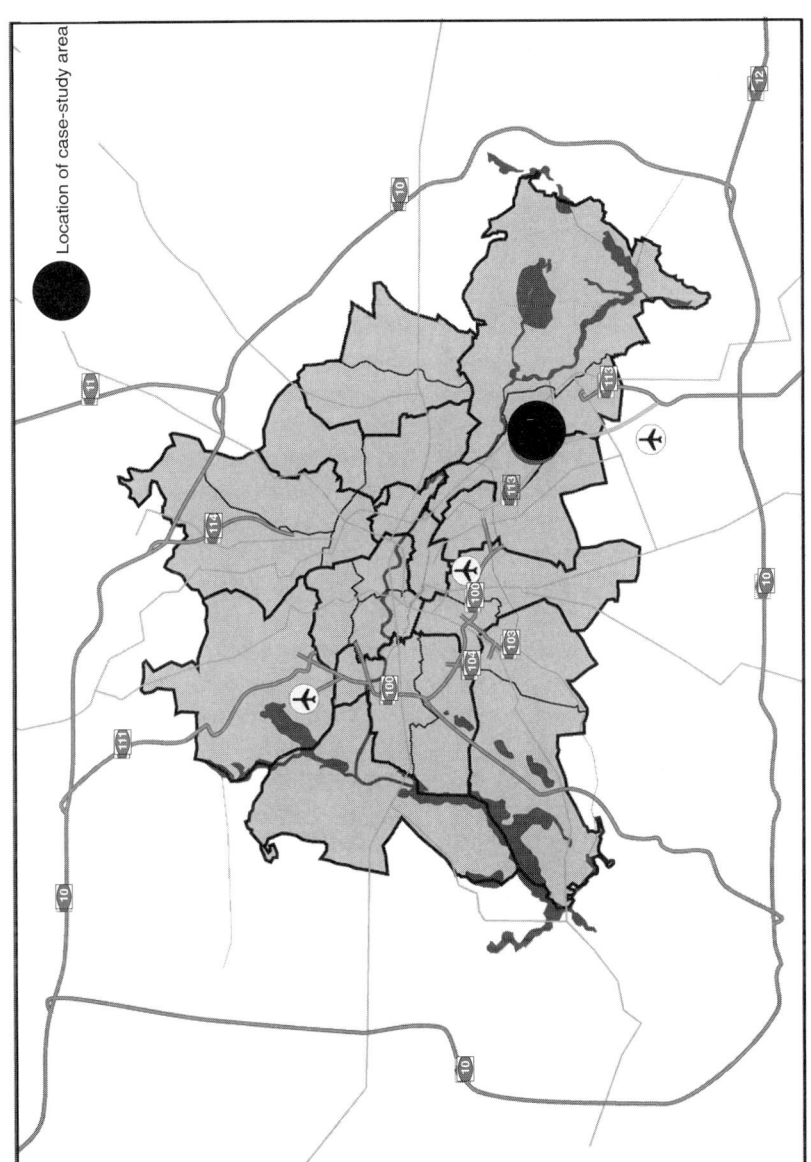

Fig. 6.1. Location of Adlershof Project, Berlin

area and to play a catalytic role in economic development, especially in providing new opportunities for employment. The main objective is to create a 'new city' on a 420 ha site with an expected 20,000–30,000 new jobs and housing for 10,000 people. The core will be a landscape park, surrounded by a Science and Business Park (WISTA), a university campus, a media and communication centre (MediaCity), as well as commercial and housing areas. The faculty of mathematics and of natural sciences (Humboldt University) has already started to move from the city centre to Adlershof. The key concept is to facilitate co-operation between research and high-tech enterprises. The resulting synergy is supposed to catalyse cycles of innovation that can be converted into commercial products. Adlershof is promoted as the biggest and most important project for Berlin's economic future.

This chapter will first discuss the institutional framework for urban development policy. We shall then sketch the starting-point for redevelopment activities after reunification and highlight the place of big projects therein. In the first half of the 1990s, several large-scale office, housing, and urban regeneration projects were initiated. This boom in the number of projects put an increased financial burden on the investment budget of the city. However, the public administration did not succeed in keeping a lid on the proliferation of projects. The subsequent section is followed by an analytical account of the case-study findings on Berlin-Adlershof. We shall discuss the strategies of the public and semi-public actors and the financial flows involved. This will illuminate the city's emerging post-Fordist governance structures as well as the impact on public budgets, and will lead into a discussion of the political efforts to steer and control development activities. Finally, the effects on employment are presented. In sum, we shall show that large-scale projects bring several opportunities with them, but, more importantly, they come with procedural difficulties, have a negative impact on democratic control, and are exposed to unforeseen financial risks when faced with slower than expected growth or even a downturn in demand.

6.2. Berlin's Governance Institutions for Urban Development Policy

Berlin is one of the sixteen states (*Länder*) in Germany. Along with Hamburg and Bremen, Berlin is a city-state. These cities are treated as *Länder* and have powers and responsibilities that other cities must share with their state governments. The unified city is a decentralized body divided into city boroughs (*Bezirke*)—administrative subunits comparable to municipalities, but lacking fiscal autonomy. Typical responsibilities of these boroughs are public health, social services, and the maintenance of green areas, playgrounds, and streets.

They are also in charge of urban planning and development. Lacking most of the basic competencies for local self-government, such as legislative powers or the right to raise taxes (Rytlewski 1999), the boroughs are not autonomous. In Berlin, all building plans must be submitted to *Bezirk* planning officials for approval, unless a project is removed from borough competence (Strom 2001). For example, this is the case whenever a project involves more than one *Bezirk* or has an 'extraordinary political impact', meaning an impact on the city as a whole. Examples of this are the redevelopment of Potsdamer Platz, plans for the traffic system, the planning of the national capital, or the transformation of Berlin-Adlershof. For these projects, there is a built-in competition between central and borough authorities.

Berlin's governing mayor (*Regierender Bürgermeister*) serves both as the city's head and as prime minister of the state of Berlin. The senators are both state ministers and heads of different local departments. They constitute the cabinet (*Senat*), the executive decision-making authority. According to the city-state constitution, governing mayors do not have the authority to determine the *Senat* programme: they are only *primus inter pares* and thus have no direct control over the senators who run the different departments (Grunert 1992). Each department is hierarchically organized, with the senators occupying the highest position and state secretaries being responsible for the internal operation. Members of the *Senat* are responsible for their own portfolios. Senators often use this independence to act according to the special interests of their administration or department. The departments are relatively independent from each other: their competencies are clearly defined and organized in a top-down fashion. Hierarchical organization and strict delimitations have proven to be counter-productive when tasks need to be assigned or projects decided through co-operation between different departments. A key feature of the political system in Berlin is a strong, but fragmented, administrative state. Evidence for the still oversized public sector—a result of the bureaucratic socialist administration as well as of state public employment in West Berlin— is that usually several agencies are responsible for one task. 'For example, although the sale of public land is technically the responsibility of the Finance Department, in fact the Urban Development, Construction, and Commerce departments as well as each *Bezirk* all have sections concerned with public real estate' (Strom 2001: 26).

The division between functional agencies has even been reinforced during the past decade of coalition governments when different departments have been left in the hands of different parties (Strom 2001). During recent parliamentary terms, there has been a 'great coalition' between the Christian Democratic Union and the Social Democratic Party; accordingly the *Senat* positions were divided between these two governing parties. For instance, the responsibility for planning and development has been split up and, consequently, several *Senat* authorities shared these tasks. The Department for Urban Development elaborated the development plans and determined the guidelines, while the Department for Construction was responsible for the realization of project planning and building supervision. As members of different parties held these two *Senat* positions, policy-making became a field for acting out partisan conflicts within the government. Since the parliamentary term of 1999, these two departments have been fused into one single agency, thereby enhancing the capability to shape urban development policy.

In addition to these state agencies, there are a number of new actors and initiatives that have entered the arena of urban development policy. One example is the *Stadtforum*, a broad planning commission in which representatives of the city administration, associations, and independent experts regularly and publicly debate central issues of urban development. Also, in 1993, the private sector created the initiative 'Partner for Berlin—Association for Capital City Marketing', promoting Berlin and trying to improve the standing of the city.

In general, a restructuring of the interrelation between the public and the private sector has taken place. While there used to be a clear distinction between private clients and the city authorities in West Berlin and public–private partnerships existed simply through public incentives (tax-deductible investment and construction loans, significant tax reductions, etc.) to promote private investment (Leue 1997), the private sector and intermediate organizations have become increasingly involved in recent years in urban planning matters. This has led some to consider this a 'revolutionary experience' for planning procedures in Berlin (Lütke-Daldrup 1992: 201).

6.2.1. *Urban planning and legal processes*

Planning systems can be differentiated by national variations in legal and constitutional structures as well as by administrative and professional cultures (Newman and Thornley 1996). A feature of the German system is the importance given to the written Constitution. This sets out the responsibilities of the different levels of government. The central state shares much of its power with the *Länder,* which have their own constitution and representatives taking part in national decision-making. The two key features of this approach are a strong legal framework and a decentralized decision-making structure. The implication for the planning system is that plans and planning permissions have legal backing, but there exists considerable variation in planning practice across the different states. The planning system generally operates at, or below, the level of the *Länder*. The Federal level basically lays out a framework of regulations to ensure basic consistency in the planning legislation of each *Land*.

There is a great variety of planning tools contained in the Federal Building Code that regulates the implementation of land use and building activities (Schmidt-Eichstaedt 1998). These regulations assign the responsibility for control to the municipal level and make provisions for two further types of plan. First, the 'preparatory land use plan' provides a general spatial framework and criteria for the regulation of land use in local authority areas. This plan is binding for public authorities but not for private landowners. Secondly, there is a 'building plan', which has to conform to the land use plan and is legally binding, providing specific information to would-be developers about precise building regulations.

Since the early 1990s, flexibility has been introduced in the planning system through certain tools, which come into effect when no binding plan has been prepared. Several private projects in the centre of Berlin have been initiated without the procedures stipulated in the 'building plan' legislation (Häußermann 1995). A new instrument has been in operation, called the 'project plan' (*Vorhaben- und Erschließungsplan*), which was originally devised for use in the new *Länder*. Since 1993, however, this has been extended to cover the whole country. In this case planning permission can be given without a local plan, if a developer guarantees to take over the financial responsibility for the planning and implementation of the project. Investors are thus integrated into the planning and financing of a project at an early stage. The influence of private actors on urban planning has also increased through the introduction of 'urban design contracts' (*städtebaulicher Vertrag*). In the case of these, the city and a private investor agree on and sign a contract on a specific project. The municipality forgoes its power to develop vacant land in exchange for a planning and financial commitment on the part of the investors.

These new tools have introduced a stronger project-led policy as well as a form of co-operation between public and private actors in urban planning. Through the integration of private investors in the planning process, project realization is more likely to proceed compared with 'traditional' models, in which the role of the public sector was mainly restricted to planning activities. Urban regeneration tasks are no longer solely pursued by traditional state intervention and agencies. The new public–private partnerships empower cities to carry development projects through to their full implementation. However, this privatization of planning raises further issues of legitimacy and accountability.

6.2.2. Public planning authority in Development Areas

Whilst the projects in the city centre, at Potsdamer Platz and at Friedrichstraße, are classic examples of private urban development, there are also several examples in Berlin of state-led project planning. In the beginning of the 1990s, several Development Areas were designated with a total area of 900 ha. Amongst them are two waterfront developments—Rummelsburger Bucht and Wasserstadt Oberhavel; Eldenaer Straße, where an old slaughter-house is to be converted into a trade and service centre; Biesdorf Süd; and Adlershof. Since the growth expectations for Berlin had been very high, the construction of about 30,000 new apartments and 75,000 jobs were planned. In these Development Areas, a planning instrument has been applied that involves strong public intervention. Although a private development agency is commissioned to implement the development tasks, the main responsibilities for management and financing remain with the public sector. This 'urban development measure' was (re)introduced in the national building law in 1990. It is mobilized to redevelop derelict areas and to meet an increased demand for housing and new places of work (Bunzel and Lunebach 1994). With the help of this instrument, a coherent plan is to be realized in a designated area, within a specified time frame. It is said to be the 'sharpest sword' among all tools for urban development, since the main idea is to accelerate the planning process by facilitating the state's access to land. The law permits the expropriation of land in the case of landowners being unwilling to co-operate or sell.

These legal powers offer the public sector greater planning authority *vis-à-vis* private owners. Property values are frozen for a set number of years and a portion of profits is recaptured by the city when the land is sold to investors. The cost for the development measures is supposed to be refinanced through the development value—that is, the difference between the purchase price of the property before development of the area and its post-development sale price. The goal of these measures is to increase the public's leverage in shaping an area that will play a key role in future development, and prevent private owners from gaining speculative profits as a result of these public measures (Lemmen 1997; Häußermann and Strom 1994). This legal tool and the success of its self-financing philosophy is highly dependent on increasing land value levels. It is, therefore, vulnerable to changes in the real estate market.

6.2.3. The project boom in the early 1990s—strategic planning or 'muddling through'?

In the first half of the 1990s, urban development policy in the reunited Berlin was almost exclusively concerned with improving the physical environment and with reorganizing space for real estate development. The project boom that hit Berlin is an excellent example of the hopes pinned on big projects as driving forces in urban revitalization. This project-led urban development policy emerged as the main strategy in Berlin to stimulate economic growth and to organize innovation. Large projects have now become the most visible redevelopment strategy pursued by the city in its search for growth and competitiveness. Projects enable policy-makers to show visibly their capacity to act and to demonstrate dynamic changes in the city. They facilitate targeted actions and a flexible response to urgent urban problems. By the mid-1990s, roughly one hundred urban redevelopment projects of various sizes were in the planning or implementation stage (SenStadtUm 1995). At the same time, there were warning signs suggesting that the anticipated growth scenarios on which these projects were based were overblown. For example, an effect in the development of the real estate market was that supply-side reserves increased and tenancies were slow to be concluded. As the Department for Urban Development realized, 'These projects bind the spending of Berlin's budget and the capacities of its administration' (SenStadtUm 1995: 82). The state authorities understood that too many projects had been initiated at the same time. It was at this point that 'strategic planning' got a place on the agenda in Berlin, as an instrument to control processes of urban development and to set priorities.

A new strategy had therefore become necessary. In February 1994, the committee 'Berlin 2000'—a gathering of all state secretaries—instructed the Department for Urban Development to set out priorities for urban development policy. Expert reports were carried out, in order to gain a better insight into the planning activities and their financial requirements. In order to set priorities, each project had to be evaluated. Development Areas, urban renewal areas, housing and mixed-use projects were included in the evaluation list (Prognos 1994). First-level priority was given to the Eastern inner city, with the task of establishing capital functions and developing the city centre. Meanwhile the Western inner city was considered to be the least important in terms of project development. The south-east, where Adlershof is located, was considered to have great potential for redevelopment and also scored highly. On the basis of these priority areas, the projects were then evaluated according to their contribution to housing, to local economic development, to improvement in infrastructure provision, and so on. Another criterion was the contribution to crucial developmental objectives (seat of the government, metropolitan service activities, science, culture, and fairs). Berlin-Adlershof ranked highly and was assigned fourth place following projects of a similarly high priority, such as the national government district and Potsdamer Platz (Prognos 1994: appendix p. 1). The findings of the expert report showed that Berlin would not be able to carry through all the projects. The report stressed that the financial requirements would go well beyond the available budgets and lead to a critical explosion of expenditure by 1999 at the latest. There would, therefore, be no scope for initiating new projects or for coping with risks related to the existing projects.

In spite of these warnings, 'strategic planning' and the effort to control urban development activities failed because of the entrenched 'administrative egoism' in Berlin's bureaucratic system. According to members of the urban development department, there was a lack of willingness in the different state agencies to co-operate in urban development policy and to co-ordinate the projects. All departments stuck, instead, to their own projects, i.e. large-scale projects for business or for housing. Secondly, disapproval of subordinating sectoral interests and priorities to overriding objectives of urban development was expressed. Finally, the issue of strategic planning was gradually submerged in the course of the election campaign of 1995 and during the construction of the new *Senat* in January 1996.

In conclusion, the debate on priorities and on the financing of large-scale urban development projects and the intention to plan strategically was an attempt on the part of the city authorities to re-establish control over urban planning procedures in the city. This testifies to a lack of a co-ordinated urban development planning in Berlin and of the inability to govern a big city rationally.

6.3. Case Study: Berlin-Adlershof—The City of Science, Technology, and Media

6.3.1. The beginnings

Berlin Adlershof is located at the south-east edge of Berlin in an outer borough (Treptow) and is the former site of the East German Academy of Sciences and of the German Broadcasting Station (see Fig. 6.1). Nearby is an old airfield, parts of which were turned into a training ground by the national army of the German Democratic Republic. At that time, the whole area was a 'secret island', closed to the public. Before reunification, about 5,500 scientists, technicians, and other employees worked in the various natural science and technical institutions or service centres of the Academy. The fall of the wall resulted in sudden changes—the closure of the Academy of Sciences and the Broadcasting Station; the incorporation of some institutes into West German research structures; the establishment of private company structures; and the dismissal of a large number of the employees.

In 1991, a management company—the Entwicklungsgesellschaft Adlershof mbH (EGA) (now WISTA Management)—was established by the Department for the Economy and was instructed by the government to develop and implement a concept for the scientific and economic future functions of the area. In spring 1992, the state secretary of the Department for Urban Development presented the first version of a framework plan for a 'new generation' of science and technology parks, with an emphasis on the development of an urban network of mixed uses (SenStadtUm 1994). To protect their own claims, the Department for the Economy and Department for Science reacted with different proposals. Thus, whilst the project required a co-ordinated process, several state agencies continued to pursue their own interests. On the basis of a joint bill, however, the *Senat* decided, on 16 February 1993, to choose a private development corporation and to review the framework plan through a co-operative planning procedure. The result of the planning workshops was a 'plan of consent' that was presented to the press by three state secretaries—the Secretaries for Urban Development, for Science, and for the Economy respectively. This symbolized a closing of ranks.

6.3.2. A web of actors

Large-scale projects generate an interactive system in which different interests are negotiated and a common objective created. The project is co-ordinated through an exchange of resources (Cattacin 1994). The integrative approach of Adlershof is to combine several policy fields, which is quite an exceptional urban development strategy in Berlin. On top of this, the project is tied to a great variety of public, semi-public, and private agents. The challenge, therefore, is to balance the different policy interests (economic, scientific, urban, cultural, etc.) and to reach a compromise on a common development model. The label 'city of science, technology, and media' symbolizes this willingness to integrate such a variety of policy fields. Big projects like Adlershof also create new modes of institutional relations, as there is a critical shift to a more pluralistic policy style, redefining the roles played by local authorities. New structures have been created that lead to a stronger fragmentation of responsibility. This can also be detected in the planning stage and the realization of the project in Adlershof. In the name of flexibility and efficiency, a private organization has supplanted local authorities and incorporated policy-making powers and competencies. The development corporation (BAAG) has been created for the specific purpose of managing the project. It has been constructed as an intermediate organization, operating between the public administration and private investors. The developer is a trustee that uses financial means from a trust fund, guaranteed by the state.

To preserve state control, a steering group was established, made up of seven state secretaries of the *Senat* and an official of the borough of Treptow. This committee decides on the development and economic plan as well as the schedule and financing of the development measure. The steering group has to agree on important decisions such as the purchase of land in the development area. This is a significant political body, established to channel the conflicting views, and to co-ordinate the competencies of all the departments involved in the project and maintain Berlin's influence over the decision-making process.

Apart from the *Senat* of Berlin, there is no control or advisory committee responsible for the whole project and able to co-ordinate the activities of the development corporation, the management company (BAAG, WISTA MG), and the actors connected to the various parts of the project (MediaCity, University, Science and Business Park, etc.). As an official report states, 'Most decisions up to now have been prepared in bilateral talks or in multilateral, varied and non-binding agreements' (SenWFK 1998: 10). As a consequence, the planning process loses transparency, limiting the possibilities for parliamentary control. Because of this lack of transparency, the Green Party filed a demand to submit the current plans to the Berlin parliament in March 1996. They argued that up-to-date data on the development and changes in the cost of the projects were considered necessary in order to enable parliamentary control and to evaluate the projects. Meanwhile, the economic plans of the development corporations have been submitted to the property committee of the parliament.

6.3.3. *Financial flows and pressures on public budgets*

The great variety of actors permits a bringing together of skill from different agents and the ability to mobilize their financial resources. The development corporation BAAG estimates that, up to the year 2010, private and public investment will amount to 2.81 billion Euro (5.5 billion DM) in Adlershof. Of that total, 2.19 billion Euro (4.3 billion DM) is estimated to come from private sources, while 610 million Euro (1.2 billion DM) will be public investment. By 2001, only 23.1 per cent of these resources had been committed (either contractually or having already been spent) (SenStadt 2000: 7): 560 million Euro (1.1 billion DM) has already been invested in Adlershof, of which 189.17 million Euro (370 million DM) comes from private investors; 214.74 million Euro (420 million DM) has been invested on the WISTA science and technology site, and 176.39 million Euro (345 million DM) in science facilities and the university campus (SenStadt 2000: 7). The realization of Adlershof is mainly based on public funding. Regional and national financial support has been combined with money from the European Structural Fund to support the infrastructure in the Science and Business Park (WISTA). With respect to investment, there is clearly still a deep gap between rhetoric and reality.

The central idea behind the planning instrument used in Adlershof is to use means from the trust fund to develop the area and to prepare it for construction. Thus, the tasks that are financed with the trust fund are the planning and management activities of the development corporation and measures for preparing the area. The cost of these activities is then supposed to be recuperated by selling building sites that are ready for development. This means that the financial feasibility of the project depends on the difference in land value before and after preparation. Since not all expenditures can be recuperated in this way, the *Senat* decided in 1996 that 'traditional' public tasks will be financed by the state budget. This includes the acquisition of land for public infrastructure, external development tasks, public facilities, and the removal of dangerous waste from previously state-owned property.

When Berlin-Adlershof, Wasserstadt Oberhavel, Eldenaer Strasse, Rummelsburger Bucht, and Biesdorf Süd were designated as Development Areas in the early 1990s, it was expected that these projects could be part-financed by selling the land available for building at the development value. However, land prices have been declining since 1994 in both Berlin and the Development Areas (SenBWV 1998). Land turnover is lower than expected, and the income from selling the land is too low for the original plan to be successful. As a consequence, development corporations receive credit in order to prefinance development measures. These bank loans are supposed to be paid off through income at a later stage. If this leads to a deficit in the trust fund, Berlin has to cover the difference from the state budget.

Concerned by this significant burden to the public budget and rising debts, the political opposition has started to question the necessity for, and financing of, the Development Areas. Because of this, the financial committee of the parliament agreed in June 1998 to invite the Auditor-General's Office to inspect the financial situation in each Development Area. This office's mission was to report on the possibilities for reducing costs and terminating loss-making activities. Lastly, the parliament decided in November 1998 to stop borrowing (except for existing contractual obligations), until the results of such examinations have been made available. The development corporations did not understand this decision, since interrupting the projects temporarily reduced their scope of action, questioned their reliability vis-à-vis potential investors, and undermined their credibility. However, the rising mountain of debts in the Development Areas made the members of parliament put on the 'emergency brake'. Debts from the trust funds in the Development Areas, for which the state is liable, had risen to 650 million Euro (1.29 billion DM) in December 1999. In September 2000, the level of indebtedness stood at 680 million Euro (1.34 billion DM) (SenStadt 2000: 15). This explains why the parliamentary opposition have increasingly criticized the financial negligence of those in charge of these large-scale projects.

6.4. Employment Effects

One of the main strategies used to justify public investment in the Science Park is to invoke its contribution to research in the key technologies of the twenty-first century and its associated job creation in these fields. The stated goal is to achieve an acceleration of the innovation cycle of trade and industry in Berlin, by means of close co-operation between scientific institutes, the university, and technology-related companies. New innovation centres are supposed to attract small and medium-sized companies and to offer infrastructure and fiscal incentives. As part of this 'high-tech fantasy', Adlershof joins the science and technology scene of the metropolitan area.

The closure of the Academy of Sciences was part of the reunification contract, in order to adapt the existing potential of the West German science structure. The science institutes established in the past years have either been newly founded or moved from West Germany to Adlershof. Some East German scientists took part in 'integration programmes' or in job creation measures in R. & D.-related activities. In 1991–2, 1,300 short-term jobs in research projects were created. In the course of this, the *Senat* instructed a consultancy company to carry out a labour market programme. In addition, a company was set up to co-ordinate these job-creating measures. However, the number of employees in job creation programmes has gradually decreased and most of these short-term jobs have ended. Unfortunately, these have almost entirely failed in building bridges to the higher-level labour market.

According to annual surveys of the managing company (WISTA MG), the number of companies has grown from 237 in December 1998 to 357 in December 2000, with a total employment of 3,600; 49 (15 per cent) companies are spin-offs from the former Academy of Science, 135 (40 per cent) are new start-ups, and 181 (45 per cent) are relocations or satellites of existing companies. The 13 non-university research institutes employ approximately 1,600 employees, including 800 scientists.

There are several labour market mechanisms at work in order to attract companies to Adlershof, such as innovation centres within specific technology fields and business-incubator centres that support small and medium-sized enterprises (SME). Only some of the firms that use these centres are in their start-up phase. Some have moved from other locations on the project site or from other parts of the city to profit from the available services and low rents (Wilmes *et al.* 1997). The lack of a coherent and polished concept for the Science and Business Park has proven a barrier to attracting SMEs with a distinct profile to Adlershof. This is why the 'existing mix' in Adlershof has been described as 'a matter of coincidence' (Dörhage 1999: 402).

MediaCity—the media site in Adlershof—is the largest site for film and television production in Berlin with independent SMEs (with ten employees each on average) for pre-production, production, equipment, and post-production. There are about 115 companies with 913 permanently employed and 964 freelance staff. The industrial estate comprises 56 companies with approximately 650 staff.

On the whole, employment in Adlershof has been affected by two major developments. First, reunification caused radical changes through winding-down the Academy of Sciences and restructuring the media site. Secondly, it has been affected by new opportunities resulting from the urban development project. On the one hand, former employment structures have been transformed and employment drastically reduced, whilst, on the other hand, the development of a new science, technology, and media centre is creating new jobs in these fields. The general objective of the local government is to foster and encourage local development and employment growth. Urban politics has thereby taken an entrepreneurial stance to economic development through the promotion of local areas to attract new businesses and support for small firms. Sites like Adlershof have been opened up, and substantial packages of aid and assistance are offered as inducements to SMEs, in order to improve the competitiveness of the city.

6.5. Conclusion

Inter-urban competition has made cities reorganize urban space around areas for new technologies, high level services, leisure activities, and attractive housing. Derelict places are renewed, in order to convey new post-industrial images and to attract investments and jobs. The planning vision in Adlershof takes urban regeneration much further than merely improving the built environment. The concept is based on an integrated project programme with a focus on scientific and economic development. Compared to large-scale projects with a strong physical bias, Adlershof has a more ambitious objective of fostering strategic redevelopment.

This chapter has shown that a strong regulatory framework is present in Adlershof. The 'urban development measure' is used to implement a coherent development plan within a particular time frame. As a state-led development scheme, there is strong public sector involvement in all stages of the project, from planning to implementation. The planning scheme has incorporated the practice of public–private partnerships. This implies a transfer of planning powers to the private sector and the strengthening of market-led approaches. A private development corporation (BAAG) has been created which manages the project. Limited entrepreneurial flexibility is, nevertheless, guaranteed, as a result of strong state regulation and the fact that the state carries the financial risks. Anticipated profitability is supposed to make the project economically feasible. However, returns are highly dependent on increases in land value, which would permit the siphoning off of surplus value and the recuperation of the cost of development activities. Since this is not happening in practice, procedural difficulties ensue and financial burdens are imposed on the public sector.

Today, Berlin's financial situation is a cause for great concern. The current fiscal crisis has both economic and political roots. An effect of the recession has been fiscal stress—tax revenues have not increased sufficiently to compensate for lost subsidies or to keep pace with the demands of unification and the exigencies of dealing with unemployment. Public expenditure has increased tremendously as a result of redevelopment activities, the upkeep and expansion of urban infrastructure, the renovation of public buildings, etc. Increasing expenditure and decreasing income have led to a growing budget deficit. Subsequent fiscal retrenchment and reductions in expenditure negatively affect education, culture, and social services.

The high number of large urban development projects constitutes a long-term drain on public finances. This is especially the case in the five Development Areas, where deficits have been rising continuously. The obligations associated with the long-term financial scheme of these big projects are not paralleled by the expected growth in tax income or by the sale of public land. These projects absorb financial resources that could be used for much-needed improvements in other areas. The pending fiscal stress was discussed at the beginning of the 1990s, but policy-makers failed to reduce projects to a reasonable number and size. Finally, after the collapse of the 'great coalition' between the conservatives and the social democrats—because of the crash of the state-owned bank (Bankgesellschaft) in the early summer of 2001—the government is now seriously considering cutting back the number of Development Areas to four.

When large-scale projects have been put on track and face changed conditions, they are not easily remodelled or terminated. The plan has been presented to the public, contracts signed, and money spent. In addition, different parts of the project are often interdependent, making it difficult to abandon parts without negatively affecting others. Even if the project turns out to be unrealistic with regard to actual demand, the state and investors are already often in too deep to be able to back out. As large projects gain their own specific momentum, they become highly risky endeavours. When the state 'goes to the market', it is exposed to the risks of market processes. In addition, UDPs of this kind conflict with demands for democratic control, shown by the fact that, as soon as such entrepreneurial investment is started, public authorities (the parliament included) have to behave like private economic actors. If expected returns are not met, the state has to re-capitalize the project, and this usually implies cuts in other areas of public expenditure. Therefore, terminating the project does not imply a loss of private capital, but the increase of public debt. No democratic body can prevent this infernal logic.

In the case of Adlershof, there was an urgent need for action in the early 1990s, in order to find new employment opportunities—not only for the former employees of the Academy of Sciences and the German Broadcasting Station, but also for other qualified workers, who had lost their jobs in the process of transformation and economic restructuring. The plan to create more than just a 'standard' science park and to include different uses in an ambitious vision ('new city') goes back to the growth scenarios and a supposed incessant demand for housing and office/commercial space in Berlin. Yet, the socio-economic context and the real estate development turned out to be less dynamic than expected, thus impeding the progress of the project. As other examples have shown, the world is littered with the ruins of many such dreams that have failed, or have yielded insufficient results at far too high a cost (Castells and Hall 1994). Nobody can estimate the effects an alternative path of investment in local development would have had but the failure of an entrepreneurial strategy is obvious. What is also clear is that citizens will have to pay for the failure for many years through large deficits in the public budget.

References

BUNZEL, A., and LUNEBACH, J. (1994). *Städtebauliche Entwicklungsmaßnahmen— ein Handbuch*. Berlin: Difu-Beiträge zur Stadtforschung.

CASTELLS, M., and HALL, P. (1994). *Technopoles of the World: The Making of the 21st Century Industrial Complexes*. London and New York: Routledge.

CATTACIN, S. (1994). *Stadtentwicklungspolitik zwischen Demokratie und Komplexität— Zur politischen Organisation der Stadtentwicklung: Florenz, Wien und Zürich im Vergleich*. Frankfurt and New York: Campus Verlag.

DÖRHAGE, W. (1999). 'Wissenschaftsstandort und Industrielle Forschung. Defizite und Chancen Berliner Forschungs- und Innovationspolitik am Beispiel des Technologieparks Adlershof', in W. Momper *et al.* (ed.), *Berlins Zweite Zukunft, Aufbruch in das 21. Jahrhundert*. Berlin: Ed. Sigma, 391–413.

GRUNERT, B. (1992). 'Politisches System,' in Presse- und Informationsamt des Landes Berlin (ed.), *Berlin Handbuch—Das Lexikon der Bundeshauptstadt*. Berlin: FAB Verlag, 961–71.

HÄUßERMANN, H. (1995). 'Stadtentwicklung im Labor, Berlin-Mitte,' in M. Wentz, *Stadtentwicklung*. Frankfurt and New York: Campus Verlag, 76–89.

——(1997). 'Social Transformation of Urban Space in Berlin since 1990,' in O. Källtorp *et al.* (ed.), *Cities in Transformation—Transformation of Cities: Social and Symbolic Change of Urban Space*. Aldershot: Avebury, 80–97.

——and STROM, E. (1994). 'Berlin: The Once and Future Capital.' *International Journal of Urban and Regional Research*, 18/2: 335–46.

——and KAPPHAN, A. (2000). *Berlin: von der geteilten zur gespaltenen Stadt?* Opladen: Leske and Budrich.

LEMMEN, F. J. (1997). 'Die städtebauliche Entwicklungsmaßnahme als Regelinstrument der Baulandbereitstellung,' in B. and H. Dietrich (eds.), *Boden—wem nützt er?, wen stützt er? Neue Perspektiven des Bodenrechts*. Braunschweig and Wiesbaden, 220–9.

LEUE, G. (1997). 'Partnerschaft der Privatisierung der Planung? Public-Private-Partnership in Berlin nach '90,' in U. Altrock (ed.), *Plansoll erfüllen—5 Jahre Planung im vereinigten Berlin*, Diskussionsbeitrag No. 49, Institut für Stadt- und Regionalplanung, TU Berlin, Aug. 1997, Berlin, 32–42.

LÜTKE-DALDRUP, E. (1992). 'Planungsboom in Berlin.' *RaumPlanung*, 59: 193–202.

NEWMAN, P., and THORNLEY, A. (1996). *Urban Planning in Europe: International Competition, National Systems & Planning Projects*. London and New York: Routledge.

PROGNOS (1994). *Prioritätensetzung der Planungsvorhaben in Berlin*, Tischvorlage für die Staatssekretärs-Runde am 19 Dec. 1994, Berlin.

RYTLEWSKI, R. (1999). 'Berliner Politik: Zwischen Kiez und Stadtstaat,' in W. Süß and R. Rytlewski (eds.), *Berlin. Die Hauptstadt. Vergangenheit und Zukunft einer europäischen Metropole*. Bonn: Bundeszentrale für politische Bildung, 295–329.

SCHMIDT-EICHSTAEDT, G. (1998). *Städtebaurecht—Einführung und Handbuch*. Stuttgart, Berlin, and Cologne: Kohlhammer.

SenBWV (Senatsverwaltung für Bauen, Wohnen und Verkehr) (1998). *5. Bericht zu den städtebaulichen Entwicklungsmaßnahmen an den Vorsitzenden des Hauptausschusses*, 12 June 1998.

SenStadt (Senatsverwatlung für Stadtentwicklung) (2000). *7. Bericht zu den städtebaulichen Entwicklungsmaßnahmen an den Vorsitzenden des Hauptausschusses*, 24 Oct. 2000.

SenStadtUm (Senatsverwaltung für Stadtentwicklung und Umweltschutz) (1994). *Johannisthal—Adlershof Technologie- und Wissenschaftsstadt*. Berlin: Kulturbuchverlag.

——(1995). *Projekte der räumlichen Planung—Fortschreibung*. Berlin: Kulturbuchverlag.

SenWFK (Senator für Wissenschaft, Forschung und Kultur) (1998). *Ein Konzept für den Wissenschafts- und Wirtschaftsstandort Berlin-Adlershof (WISTA) Bestandsaufnahme und Empfehlungen zur gegenwärtigen Entwicklung des WISTA*. Berlin.

STROM, E. A. (2001). *Building the New Berlin: The Politics of Urban Development in Germany's Capital City*. Lanham, Md., Boulder, Col., New York, and Oxford: Lexington Books.

WILMES, M., KEIL, I., and SCHROEDER, K. (1997). *Der Forschungs- und Technologiepark Berlin-Adlershof—Modell einer neuen Form regionaler Kooperation zwischen Wirtschaft*, Wissenschaft und Politik, apt-papers 4, Arbeitsstelle Politik und Technik, Berlin.

7

Old Élites in a New City: Restructuring the Leopold Quarter and the Europeanization of Brussels

Guy Baeten

7.1. Introduction

Europeanization has triggered substantial economic, political, and cultural change in the city of Brussels. It has evolved from a relatively unimportant national capital to one of the most multicultural and cosmopolitan cities in the world, exerting substantial political and economic power in Europe and the rest of the world. More than one-third of Brussels's inhabitants are now of foreign origin. In this chapter, I will argue that, in spite of this dramatic post-war socio-economic and demographic change and this new cosmopolitan reality, Brussels is still governed by traditional political and economic élites operating within well-tested formats of urban governance and urban planning. Drawing upon a case study of the Leopold Quarter (or EU district), I will demonstrate how the city continues to be shaped through the hegemonic power of existing financial-economic élites. Underneath the layers of cultural change and the city's shifting position within global politics, urban planning in the EU district is still firmly in the hands of office developers. Urban geographers seem to have shifted their attention somewhat away from the analysis of 'traditional' political-economic relations of power as the base for understanding change and continuity in the city. This contribution seeks to demonstrate the persisting importance of those power relations in shaping the fate of the contemporary city.

The first section of this chapter will briefly describe socio-spatial polarization in Brussels and analyse the extent to which the Europeanization of Brussels is playing a role in this. Secondly, the history of urban planning in the EU district will be reconstructed. Thirdly, the impact of the transformations taking place in the EU district and of the wider Europeanization of Brussels on the city and its residents will be investigated. The final section deals with changes and continuities in the governance of Brussels.

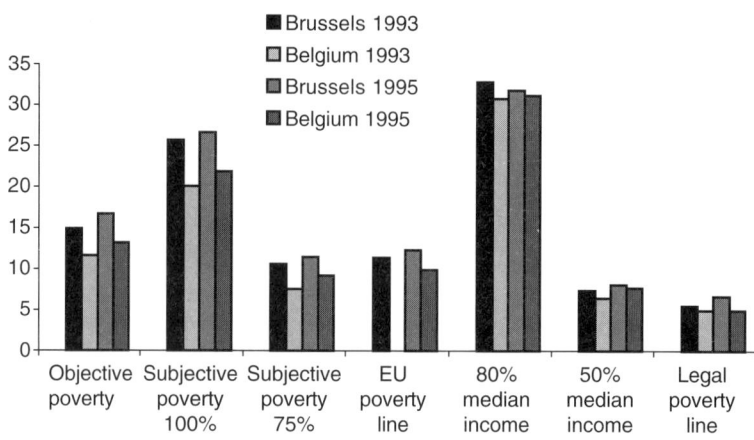

Fig. 7.1. Measuring poverty in Brussels and Belgium, 1993 and 1995

7.2. Socio-Economic Crisis, Spatial Segmentation, and Urban Restructuring

The World Exhibition opened in Brussels in 1958, with the city and the rest of the nation celebrating the virtues of modernity and progress. On the same day that it opened, Abbé Froidure released the results of the first major post-war poverty study in Belgium in order to turn some attention to the flipside of increasing welfare levels. In the midst of growing affluence and prosperity for most people, the total earnings of more than 10 per cent of the Belgian population were below the official minimum income level (KB-Stichting 1987). The Belgian welfare society has never managed to eradicate poverty completely: depending on the type of measurement, contemporary poverty figures for Brussels and Belgium seem to have risen slightly. Of course, percentages vary according to the type of measurement and fluctuate between 5 and more than 30 per cent of the total population. However, regardless of measurement, poverty figures for Brussels tend to be systematically higher than for the rest of Belgium (De Keersmaecker 1997 and 1998) (see Fig. 7.1). Paradoxically, the Brussels region is, in terms of Gross Regional Product per capita, the second richest region in Europe, preceded only by Inner London and leaving city regions such as Paris and Hamburg behind (Eurostat 2002) (Table 7.1).

Brussels has faced increasing socio-spatial polarization, although the supporting evidence is somewhat ambiguous, and it is not clear to what extent the EU presence is contributing to this. The Gini-coefficient, expressing overall income inequality in Brussels, increased from 0.378 in 1982 to 0.391 in 1991 (Mens en Ruimte 1994). However, simple statistical inequality indicators show

Table 7.1. Gross regional product per capita for the top ten European regions

Region	GDP per capita 1997–1999 EU15 = 100
Inner London (UK)	246
Brussels Capital Region (B)	223
Hamburg (G)	183
Luxembourg (L)	180
Ile de France (F)	154
Vienna (A)	151
Oberbayern (G)	150
Darmstadt (G)	148
Utrecht (N)	144
Bremen (G)	142
Flanders (B)	108
Wallonia (B)	80

Source: Eurostat 2002.

that spatial differences in income, unemployment, employment, and population composition have, in general, actually *decreased* or increased only slightly in recent years (Schupp 1995). Nevertheless, socio-economic conditions in particular neighbourhoods are seriously deteriorating (see Martens 1996; Lievens *et al.* 1975; Kesteloot 1996; 1997; Kesteloot *et al.* 1996; 1998; De Corte 1996; De Decker 1994). In addition, youth unemployment has become a serious problem in various municipalities of the metropolitan area and is, in fact, the only indicator of spatial inequality in Brussels that has really increased (Schupp 1995).

Furthermore, the number of people entitled to minimum income support in Brussels has almost doubled from 6,890 in 1990 to 13,074 in 1996 (Fig. 7.2). This does not mean, of course, that poverty has doubled in half a decade (it is as much an indicator of poor people asserting their rights as of actual poverty levels), but it nevertheless illustrates the growing degree of acute poverty in Brussels. Furthermore, poverty is more and more concentrated in inner-city zones, while suburban areas are witnessing increasing levels of prosperity. The agglomeration of Brussels now hosts both the richest Belgian municipality (Lasnes) as well as the poorest (St-Joost-ten-Node) (Kesteloot *et al.* 1998).

There is considerable debate over the role of Brussels's functional transformation from national to European capital in these processes of spatial segmentation and inner-city impoverishment. For some, the presence of the European Union is polarizing the Leopold Quarter, the city, and its suburban fringe into a very wealthy class of 'internationals' on the one hand, and a domestic workforce whose comfortable place in the city is increasingly under siege on the other. From this vantage point, the rapid post-war

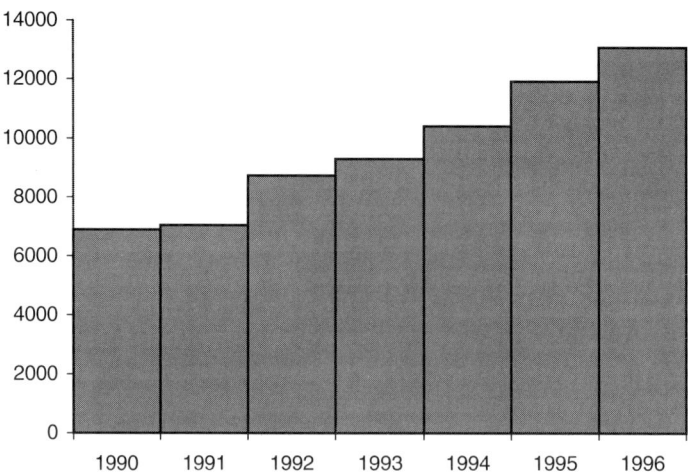

Fig. 7.2. Number of people entitled to minimum income support in Brussels (1990–1996)

internationalization of Brussels is actually threatening the viability of large inner-city residential areas. Access to affordable housing in certain municipalities, including some municipalities on the fringes of Brussels, has become increasingly difficult as housing prices have more than doubled in a decade (Baeten 1998). In addition, the international organizations' constant need for additional office floor space in places like the Leopold Quarter has legitimized the ruthless and restless expansion of offices into adjacent residential areas, leading to the (forced or voluntary) displacement of thousands of inner-city dwellers. Income inequalities have been sharpened in a country where these have traditionally been small, at least partially because the average EU employee's income is three times as high as the average Brussels income (Mens en Ruimte 1994). The process of Europeanization has contributed to the further marginalization of an already less powerful Flemish-speaking minority in Brussels, since the majority of the European immigrants speak French as their first or second language. The rapid inflow of temporary élite migrants (EU bureaucrats) has created a new class of urban nomads whose geographical reach is seemingly transnational, if not global, and their command over urban space is apparently beyond the reach of the local population. Over time, the city was forced to invest in expensive urban transport infrastructure in the Leopold Quarter in order to meet the requirements of the new urban nomads' extensive geography of everyday life.

Others have welcomed this post-war internationalization process as a necessary catalyst to revive a slackening, de-industrializing urban economy. The EU presence has rapidly transformed a formerly lethargic national capital into arguably the most cosmopolitan city in Europe. It has continuously fuelled vast parts of the economy, including construction industries, real estate agencies, catering, hotels, the tourism and transport sector, conferencing, and the media. The multiplier effect of total EU-related spending in Brussels is as high as 2.3 (Iris Consulting 1998). The benefits of Brussels's internationalized economy have been reaped not only by a narrowly defined (and stereotyped) class of well-paid, highly educated 'internationals' and office developers, but also by large parts of the unskilled, poorly educated, often immigrant, urban residents, whose employment is directly or indirectly dependent on this globalized economy. This development has substantially contributed to the successful conversion from an industrial economy to a prosperous internationalized service economy. The impact of de-industrialization on the socio-economic fabric of Brussels would have been substantially worse without these new types of service employment.

The reconstruction of the history of the Leopold Quarter will enable us to provide a more balanced view somewhere between these two polarized opinions. I shall demonstrate how the transformation of this neighbourhood has continuously and restlessly contributed to complex and intertwined processes of exclusion *and* inclusion, to processes of both polarization *and* integration, and to the creation of both poverty *and* prosperity.

7.3. Restructuring the Leopold Quarter: The Europeanization of Brussels

7.3.1. The Leopold Quarter and development plans for Brussels before the EU

The Société Civile pour l'Agrandissement de la Capitale de Belgique started to built the first extension of Brussels outside its medieval walls in 1837. The so-called Leopold Quarter (see Fig. 7.3) was meant to be the new residential space for the aristocracy of Brussels who wished to escape the problems of disease and social unrest in the city centre. In spite of all the planned *grandeur* in the neighbourhood, the aristocracy did not out-migrate to the Leopold Quarter before new infrastructure such as the Rue de la Loi (1852) and the Leopold railway station (1855) was fully in place, and until the toll ring that separated the area from the city was abolished in 1860. The Leopold Quarter remained an aristocratic neighbourhood until the mid-twentieth century, although modest office development had been taking place since the beginning of that century and parts of the upper class had already started to out-migrate towards green, suburban villages from the 1920s onwards. The area effectively started to depopulate from the early 1930s.

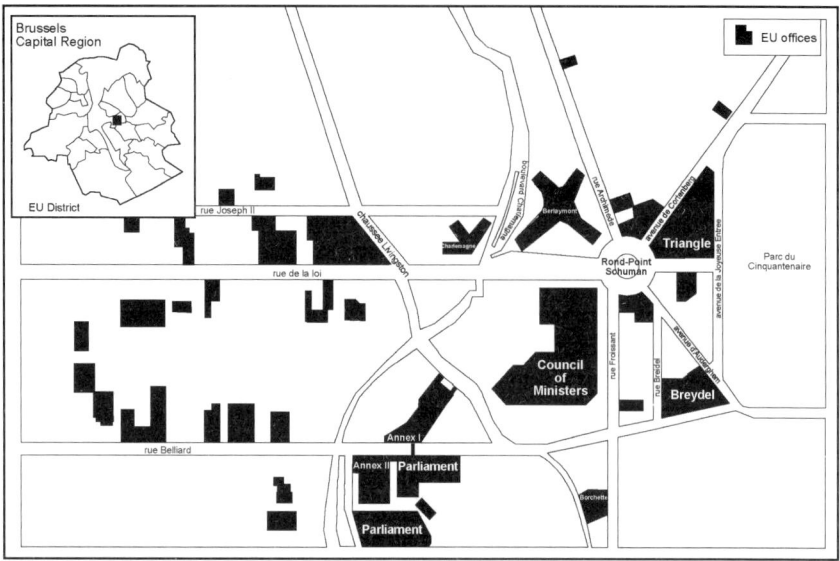

Fig. 7.3. The Leopold Quarter in Brussels: outline map

From the 1950s onwards, this élite neighbourhood was gradually taken over by office developers. The 1958 World Exhibition, most famously known for the remaining *Atomium*, signalled the Belgian culmination of the celebration of 'modernity'. A strong belief that demolishing old neighbourhoods and replacing them with modern buildings and infrastructure was the only solution to inner-city problems fuelled the destruction of vast parts of pre-war Brussels, including the Leopold Quarter, while urban highways, tunnels, and underground car parks brought the car to the city. Several post-war plans contributed to the deterioration of inner-city milieus and the promotion of office development and easy car-based accessibility. The emblematic Techné Plan of 1962, for example, which strongly advocated inner-city highways and inner ring roads, was written by ex-colonial urban planners who had returned from the former Belgian colony of Congo (which became independent in 1960), and who then became the leading urban planners for, and administrators of, Brussels. They surely considered Brussels to be in urgent need of a new 'colonization' by means of rational, orderly, and disciplinary urban design, and declared three-quarters of the inner city to be 'slum neighbourhoods'. The plan has never been fully implemented, but it nevertheless inspired a plethora of development plans for particular neighbourhoods between 1962 and 1975 (see Lagrou 1989).

7.3.2. Current plans

The Leopold Quarter is subject to various spatial plans, which in name protect its residential character, but in reality do not exert a decisive influence on the development of the area. These plans include the Regional Plan of 1979, the Space Brussels-Europe Study of 1988, the Structure Plan of 1995, and various detailed municipal plans.

The 1979 Regional Plan is a legally binding physical land use plan that mainly aims to preserve residential areas, green spaces, and historical buildings from further deterioration and destruction. The post-war modernization efforts, particularly those preceding the 1958 World Exhibition, had a devastating effect on the pre-war urban structure and caused the demolition of many architecturally splendid buildings (Martens 1996; Lievens, Brasseur, and Martens 1975). However, the Regional Plan could not prevent ten street blocks in the Leopold Quarter, which were zoned for residential or mixed use, from being effectively absorbed by EU-related building projects (Papadopoulos 1996). The 1988 Space Brussels-Europe Study, commissioned by the then Brussels Minister for Spatial Planning, delineated nine Primary Intervention Zones in the area. Like the Regional Plan, this study was full of good intentions in terms of protecting remaining residential blocks, but, with hindsight, it appears to have mainly served as a legitimization for the construction of the European Parliament in two of the Primary Intervention Zones while the destruction of residential areas continued. The 1995 Structure Plan is the most recent and most promising spatial plan that has so far been produced for Brussels, but it shows all the weaknesses that are typical for spatial plans that do not strictly define binding land use but provide only vague objectives that are open to a multitude of interpretations. The Structure Plan delineates particular areas in the city for different uses. The Leopold Quarter is earmarked partly as a housing conservation area and as a site for metropolitan service activities, which coincides largely with the 1979 land use zones. The main change is the *de facto* incorporation of the European Parliament area into the zoning for offices.

It is unlikely that the Structure Plan, in contrast with earlier plans, will enable the preservation of the remaining housing blocks in the area. Anecdotal evidence from visual observation in the area suggests that speculation by developers in residential blocks adjacent to the existing office areas continues, and the Plan does not prevent the continuation of semi-legal or illegal strategies by growth coalitions of developers, investors, and politicians, which have dominated and organized the development of the Leopold Quarter in previous decades.

7.3.3. Locating the EU headquarters

The reason why the Leopold Quarter is now hosting most of the European institutions is rather accidental. Discussions about which city should become the venue for one or more European institutions started soon after the war, with the foundation of the European Community of Coal and Steel (ECSC) in 1950. The cities of The Hague, Strasbourg, Luxembourg, and Liège in Belgium were competing candidates to host the headquarters of the ECSC. In 1952 a temporary agreement was reached which was hugely influential in creating the current sprawl of different EU institutions throughout Europe. It was agreed that Luxembourg would 'temporarily' host the seat of the ECSC, but the French city of Strasbourg would be the venue for its General Meetings. The initial idea to bring all European institutions together in one city as a symbol of Europe's post-war unification efforts had failed. The signing of the Treaty of Rome in 1958 revived the discussion about venue cities. The idea of a single venue city was taken up again, but the six founding Member States were not able to agree until 1965. Meanwhile, a revised temporary agreement stipulated that Luxembourg and Strasbourg would maintain their respective functions, but the European administration would reside in Brussels (a compromise reached between the three 'big' players: France, Germany, and Italy). A Belgian insurance company was willing to let one of its offices in the Leopold Quarter to the European Economic Council (EEC) administration. Strasbourg and Luxembourg, however, were not prepared to agree with this decision without some kind of compensation.

The idea of a single venue city was finally abandoned in 1965, with the Council of Ministers reaching a compromise in which the European Parliament would meet in Strasbourg, while the Parliamentary Secretariat, European Court of Justice, and the European Investment Bank would remain in Luxembourg. Brussels would be the seat of the European Commission, the Economic and Social Committee, and some parts of the Parliamentary Secretariat. The Council of Ministers would be 'mainly working in Brussels'. The European Parliament (EP) in particular disagreed with this decision, since its activities remained spread over three cities, and its members had to commute between Brussels, where the Parliamentarians worked, and Strasbourg, where plenary sessions were held. The European Parliament, which was able to decide autonomously about its internal organization, including its location, decided in 1981 no longer to meet in Luxembourg, and in 1985 agreed to build a suitable venue centre in Brussels. The question of the location of the activities of the EP remained unresolved until a compromise agreement was reached in Edinburgh in 1993. The European Parliament's twelve annual plenary sessions would be held in Strasbourg, while Brussels would host all other meetings, including those of the Parliamentary Commissions. Brussels would from now onwards also be the seat of the Committee of the Regions.

The cost of this uneasy compromise after forty years of inter-urban competition is considerable. It is estimated that the cost of moving people and documents between the European Parliament's venues in Brussels and Strasbourg amounts to 60 or 70 million Euro per year. Moreover, the Parliament occupies expensive buildings in each city to hold its various meetings (the value of the buildings of the Brussels 'European Parliament', although initially called 'International Congress Centre' in order not to provoke Strasbourg, is estimated by one interlocutor to be between 1 and 1.5 billion Euro).

7.3.4. *Extending European office floor space*

By 1968, the European institutions rented about 200,000 m² (of which the Berlaymont building is the most famous—see Fig. 7.3) around the Schuman Square (Rond Point Schuman), which was at that time still surrounded by residential housing, some of unique architectural value. However, the Secretariat of the Council of Ministers, the Economic and Social Committee, and Euratom were at the time still spread around the city. The Belgian government decided to concentrate all European offices in the Leopold Quarter area, despite the important presence of residential functions. Moreover, at that time there was no planning document and policy-makers did not anticipate the vast expansion of the European institutions that was soon to follow. The demand for offices by the European institutions was such that it put high pressure on the surrounding residential areas: this demand called for large, mono-functional, monolithic blocks which would guarantee a certain degree of safety and function as representational cultural capital. The absence of an explicit spatial strategy would soon lead to urban planning chaos. Throughout the 1970s and 1980s, local and national governments and the private sector had their own preferences and plans, leading to successive waves of compulsory purchases by the government, land speculation, displacement of local residents and destruction of entire housing blocks, and construction of new buildings around the Schuman Square. All of this happened in the absence of any long-term vision.

In contrast to previous state-led office developments for local and national service activities, EU office expansion was mainly developed by private investment consortia, which let their office blocks to the European organizations via real estate agents. At the time, European institutions were not able to buy offices because of the absence of a final decision on the question of venue. Buying offices in Brussels would have been considered a proactive strategy on the part of European bureaucrats to force a decision in favour of their preferred location, and would have antagonized other venue cities. Until 1993, the location and construction of European offices was therefore entirely dependent on decision-making by concealed alliances between private developers and investors, who effectively decided where to build offices through land purchases, demolition, and speculation, and public institutions that basically limited their role to providing *ex post* legal permission or shaping the planning framework in support of the private developers' hidden development agenda.

The Berlaymont building (130,000 m²), completed in 1968 and still the main landmark EU building, was built on the original site of the nineteenth-century Berlaymont cloister which had been demolished in 1962. Next to the Berlaymont building, forty-four nineteenth-century stately houses gave way to the 1967 Karel de Grote or Charlemagne building ($35,000\,m^2$). The developers' image of further expansion of EU offices north of the Schuman Square led to compulsory purchases and the displacement of 300 inhabitants. Several housing blocks were torn down, but because effective office demand ran behind the developers' imagination these sites remained empty and were used temporarily as car parks. Moreover, the permanent threat of new development plans ensured that many of the remaining housing blocks were gradually abandoned by the residents and began to deteriorate. The 1976 preliminary Regional Plan for Brussels, for example, declared that the area north of the Schuman Square was 'to be developed through concerted negotiation'. This simply meant that the area would remain open to any kind of development proposed by the developers.

From the early 1980s onwards, however, the idea of expanding north of the Schuman Square was abandoned and the government decided—as stipulated in the new Regional Plan of 1979—to extend the European zone south of the Square (see Fig. 7.3). The reason for this shift perfectly illustrates the hegemonic power of private capital in Brussels's urban development. A Belgian bank (BAC, now BACOB) had acquired land south of the Schuman Square and considerable profits were lurking around the corner if the potential value of this land could be realized by means of office development. The BAC, closely associated with the Christian Democratic Party, used all its political influence to become one of the leading financial institutions in the further development of the Leopold Quarter. Again, hundreds of people had to be displaced to make place for the successive southern extension of office space for the EU (Brukselbinnenstebuiten 1993).

7.3.5. *Current use and future pressures*

The Leopold Quarter now has around 2 million m^2 of office floor space, most of which is used by national and international public institutions; 89 per cent of the previous building stock has been demolished. Thirty of the remaining houses are now legally protected (Baeten 1998). Although the massive office blocks of the EU (European Parliament, Council of Ministers Building, and Berlaymont) certainly dominate the area, there is still about $650,000\,m^2$ of residential space. Approximately 26,000 people still live in the area and 80,000 commuters move in daily (Mens en Ruimte 1994; Brussels Capital Region 1993). The Leopold Quarter is one of the most expensive office areas in Brussels, with rents of more than 200 Euro/m^2. In comparison with most other leading European cities, however, office rent levels remain relatively low in Brussels (Mens en Ruimte 1994).

A systematic survey (Brussels Capital Region 1993) shows that, by the end of 1992, the office surface in the Leopold Quarter totalled $1,742,000\,m^2$, more than half of which was built during the 1960s and 1970s. The EU occupies one-third of this, while private sector companies occupy another third. Private

Table 7.2. Date of construction, type of occupancy, and occupancy by office block size (end of 1992)

Period	Square metres built		
	Absolute	Relative (%)	Cumulative percentage
Before 1960	191,620	11	
1960–9	452,920	26	37
1970–9	487,760	28	55
1980–9	278,720	16	81
1990–5*	330,980	19	100
Total 1992	1,742,000	100	

* including buildings under construction.

Occupant	Office space		Size of buildings			Total buildings	
	Absolute ×1,000 m²	Relative %	<500 m²	500–4,999 m²	>5,000 m²	Absolute	Relative %
European Union	627	36	3	15	41	59	8
International Public Sector	105	6	27	34	5	66	9
National Public Sector	401	23	10	48	21	79	11
Banking and Insurance	296	17	41	70	15	126	17
Other private sectors	313	18	307	97	9	413	55
Total	1,742	100	388	264	91	743	100

Source: Brussels Capital Region 1993.

companies in Brussels, with the notable exception of banking and insurance companies, tend to rent offices at more peripheral locations with easy car accessibility and plenty of opportunity to build brand new office blocks. The EU currently has fifty-nine office buildings in Brussels, most of which are larger than 5,000 m², and is by far the most visible office user in the area. The European Parliament (371,000 m²) is not even included in these figures. The private companies in the area typically occupy smaller office blocks (see Table 7.2).

The expansion of EU offices seems likely to continue in the near future. The EU estimated its own new office demand between 1997 and 2005 at 772,500 m². This includes an office reserve of 5 per cent, but it does not include additional demand for offices by potential new EU Member States, each of which would typically occupy an additional 50,000 m². Of this additional EU demand 485,000 m² can be met within the Leopold Quarter; 137,000 to 185,000 m² can be met by renovating and extending existing buildings, but 100,000 to 150,000 m² new office space has to be found in other areas of Brussels. It was also suggested by one interlocutor that the EU wants to halve the current

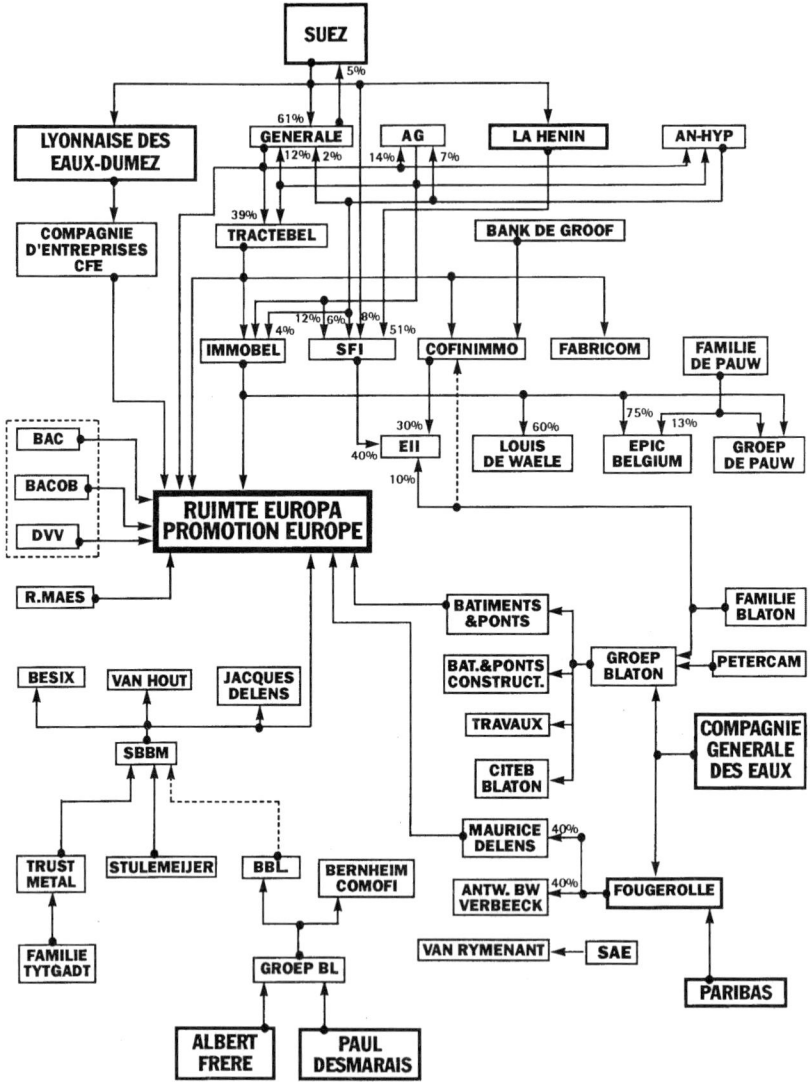

Fig. 7.4. The financial networks of developers' capital in the Leopold Quarter

number of office buildings it uses (from sixty to thirty). This concentration would enable the EU to occupy fewer but more 'representative' buildings, and facilitate better communication among its employees. Most importantly for Brussels, it would also set off a new wave of office construction and office renewal in the Leopold Quarter.

7.4. The Impact of Restructuring on the Leopold Quarter

7.4.1. Employment

In 1994, there were approximately 16,000 employees working for EU institutions, with total EU-related employment totalling more than 53,000, two-thirds of whom reside in Brussels. It is estimated that these figures will increase to 26,000 and 83,000 respectively by 2005 (Iris Consulting 1998). Whilst it is evident that the EU presence contributes significantly to local employment creation in Brussels, it has also accentuated income polarization in the city. Estimates show that, in 1994, the average net income of EU employees was approximately 150,000 Belgian francs per month (3,750 Euro), while the average income in the city is *c*.50,000 Belgian francs (1,250 Euro) (Mens en Ruimte 1994). Moreover, these figures do not reveal the discrepancy between the high salaries and comfortable working conditions within the EU institutions, and the working conditions and wage levels in EU-related industries, such as catering, security, hotel services, and the like, or on EU office construction sites where sizeable numbers of (European) immigrant workers are employed. The EU has not only initiated the in-migration of wealthy, well-educated EU officials, but also the (occasionally illegal) in-migration of poor, non-educated Europeans and Africans working in downstream sectors.

7.4.2. Creation of urban wealth

The European institutions together spent 1.3 billion Euro in Brussels in 1991, 1.7 billion Euro in 1994, and plan to spend 2.7 billion Euro in 2005. Together with expenditures by institutions that are directly or indirectly related to the EU institutions, these figures amount to 3 billion Euro, 3.9 billion Euro, and 6 billion Euro respectively (Iris Consulting 1998). It is important to note, however, that not all these expenditures imply local consumption, as EU salaries, for instance, are only partly spent locally. Furthermore, while these figures show that the overall net monetary economic gain from the EU presence in Brussels is high, the Brussels region also faces a range of both monetary and non-monetary costs (social, environmental, infrastructural, etc.), which are of course not included in the above figures.

7.4.3. Residents and housing

The 1991 Census shows that about 26,000 people still live in the Leopold Quarter and the adjacent statistical sectors (comparable to enumeration districts in the British Census). Almost half of them (11,072) are non-Belgians, with large Moroccan (1,884), Italian (1,271), and French (1,163) communities. It has an active population of 8,887 (33 per cent of total population) and a low unemployment figure (2.9 per cent of total population), compared to 7 per cent for the city as a whole (Bres 1997). While population numbers in inner Brussels have been stagnant in recent years, inner-city residents find it increasingly difficult to obtain affordable accommodation. Exact figures are not available, but evidence from interviews suggests that prices for dwellings in the Leopold Quarter tripled or even quadrupled during the first half of the 1990s. The housing market in the Leopold Quarter is under particularly high pressure, not only because of office demand, but also because of the growing numbers of temporary residents who are working for the EU or EU-related institutions. Their significantly higher purchasing power and willingness to pay high rents for local accommodation have forced substantial numbers of low-income inner-city residents to out-migrate.

7.5. Governing Socio-Spatial Polarization

Brussels has an astonishingly high level of office development. In the early 1990s, it had $7\,m^2$ of office space per inhabitant, more than twice the per capita area of Paris or London (which at that time had a ration of around $3\,m^2$/ inhabitant) (Brukselbinnenstebuiten 1993). By the end of 1996, this ratio had risen to 9.6 (Bres 1997), with an additional 1.2 million m^2 of office space located in residential buildings (Beeckman 1997). This means that a total of almost 11 million m^2 office floor space is now available in a city of 945,000 in habitants. In 1997, an additional $680,000\,m^2$ were completed, and another $500,000\,m^2$ in 1998. Estimates by Jones Lang Wootton (Het Nieuwsblad, 9 Sept. 1998) suggest that a further $150,000\,m^2$ was completed by the end of 1999, and another $380,000\,m^2$ in 2000. It is clear that such a demand for office space puts strong pressure on inner-city residential areas and creates considerable speculative fervour. Yet, tax revenues from office blocks do not contribute in important ways to municipal budgets, representing only about 3 per cent of the city's total budget.

The development and consolidation of the international, if not global, role of the city is not only partly responsible for these skyrocketing levels of office demand, but has also generated a peculiar socio-economic dynamic. Brussels is not only the capital of Belgium and Flanders, but is now also hosting most of the institutions of the European Union (EU), the NATO headquarters, the West-European Union (WEU), and the Benelux offices, along with many other lesser known ones. In the wake of these leading international institutions, other international institutions and companies have arrived in the city: diplomats, lobbyists, NGOs, company headquarters, legal and consultancy services, financial institutions, international schools, etc. Brussels hosts more international organizations than any other city in Europe, and is third in the world (after Paris and Vienna) in the number of international conferences organized (with more conferences than London or New York). This results in a rapidly expanding international élite of well-to-do urban dwellers who have (unwittingly) contributed to heighten socio-spatial and language polarization in the city. Moreover, their 'effect' is not measured in official statistics as most of these 'internationals' have their home addresses elsewhere.

In addition, the rising number of European civil servants has intensified the division between poor Brussels and the wealthy suburbs in Flanders and Wallonia. After working hours, more than half of Brussels's workforce (54 per cent) retreat to these areas and therefore do not contribute to the eroding tax base of the city—a major problem as income tax represents more than half of the revenue for the Brussels region. Incorporating these wealthy communities into the administrative borders of the Brussels region is politically unacceptable for most Flemish political parties, since it would involve Flemish suburban communities receiving bilingual status. Most Flemish political parties already see the officially bilingual region of Brussels as an 'oil stain' that spreads French-speaking populations to the neighbouring Flemish-speaking municipalities, and strongly object to this 'Romanization' of 'their' space. The peculiar language geopolitics of Belgium—bilingual Brussels, Flemish-speaking Flanders, French-speaking Wallonia, and a German-speaking minority—no longer fits, as the Brussels metropolitan region has morphologically expanded into Flanders and Wallonia since the current geo-linguistic boundaries were agreed on in 1963.

What are the political conclusions to be drawn from the above? Brussels's lamentable financial situation, resulting from the mismatch between its administrative and socio-economic borders, has been and is still invoked to justify urban policies that attempt to replace low income groups with high income residents. It goes without saying that income divides correlate strongly with ethnic divides. The replacement of 'low income groups' with 'high income groups', and, in its wake, the silent and remarkably unchallenged replacement of non-whites with whites, has become one of the central tenets of contemporary urban policies in Brussels.

Alternative policies to raise the city's budget have never been fully considered, let alone effectively implemented. One alternative could be to incorporate some 50,000 high income employees of various international organizations, two-thirds of whom are effectively living in Brussels, into the local tax base, since these 'internationals' currently benefit from complete tax exemption (see Evans 1994). It is estimated that because of this tax exemption the municipalities of the Brussels region annually forgo 1.2 billion Euro of tax revenues, a figure corresponding to 10 per cent of their total tax income. In some municipalities with many 'internationals', like Etterbeek, Sint-Pieters-Woluwe, and Sint-Lambrechts-Woluwe, this figure is as high as 20 per cent (Baeten 1998). The provision of sufficient financial transfers from the rest of the country to Brussels, so that the city can fully fulfil its national, European, and global central role without being obsessed by its own local tax base, could be another alternative. However, none of these alternatives is high on the political agenda.

Firstly, Brussels has always maintained a very permissive attitude towards international institutions (such as NATO, the EU, and the WEU) that could theoretically move to another city, in order to avoid provoking them. Secondly, interregional financial transfers in Belgium have the potential to be politically explosive due to their peculiar implications for language politics. Financial transfers from Flanders, Belgium's richest region, to the poorer regions of Brussels and Wallonia, would involve a money transfer from Flemish-speaking to (mainly) French-speaking Belgium, which is difficult to accept for most Flemish political parties. Hence, politicians generally agree on the idea that Brussels is in urgent need of a more wealthy population in order to widen its tax base. To put it more frankly, the acute problematic of poverty is translated into a fiscally inspired policy to 'get the right people in and kick the wrong people out'.

7.6. Conclusion

Since 1945, Brussels has evolved from a 'sleepy' national capital to a truly international city, which is now host to more foreigners and more international organizations (relative to its population size) than probably any other European capital (Mens en Ruimte 1994; Dendauw and Van Den Panhuyzen 1995). Although it has become one of the wealthiest city regions in Europe, poverty and social polarization remain major features of the city, although it is not entirely clear to what extent the Europeanization of Brussels has played a decisive role in these processes. The formation of a new class of 'internationals' has undoubtedly contributed to growing income polarization, and housing prices in certain parts of the wider Brussels region have risen sharply. At the same time, the international organizations and dependent service industries are now crucial to the city's economy and have created considerable wealth and employment opportunities in a de-industrializing city. The arrival of the new subclass of 'internationals' is highly welcomed by the élites of Brussels, since they consider this new form of wealthy in-migration as a key instrument to foster a socio-demographic transformation of an increasingly impoverished inner city. The Europeanization of Brussels has been inserted into a politics of 'poor-cleansing'.

Against the backdrop of these socio-economic changes, the city has adopted a *laissez-faire* attitude towards office development in the EU district. The absence of a political regime that is willing to deal effectively with the major political, economic, and cultural transformations currently occurring in Brussels has enabled powerful, but non-elected, actors, such as private office developers, financiers, and speculators, to continue to play a hegemonic role in the city's development. Brussels's post-war land use policies have always had an 'anarchist bent', and some of the more colourful post-war city 'builders', like

Charlie De Pauw, have become part of local heroic imagery, and are almost as well known by the public as local politicians. The fragmentation of political power in Brussels, combined with a more general crisis of legitimacy of state institutions throughout the country, has increased the power of private investment companies, which can create and destroy neighbourhoods at whim. The history of the Leopold Quarter, once the first suburban setting for the out-migrating upper class and now a virtual mono-functional office zone, is certainly no exception to this. In fact, Brussels has evolved from a relatively unimportant national capital to one of Europe's leading cities *in spite of* Belgian and Brussels politics (see Demey 1992; Swyngedouw and Baeten 2001). The example of the Leopold Quarter in Brussels serves to demonstrate the continued dominance of the financial and economic élites in shaping the outlook of the city.

The new Brussels—cosmopolitan, multicultural, and of international political importance—is ruled by old élites that have successfully inserted Brussels's dramatic post-war transformation into well-established forms of governance that serve the interests of traditional élites (see Baeten 2001*a*; 2000*b*; Swyngedouw and Baeten 2001). The main polarization in Brussels is now between the growing numbers of inhabitants that increasingly shape its cultural and social life but are deprived of any meaningful access to the centres of political power, and the traditional political, financial, and economic élites who continue to dominate the city's political agenda.

References

ALCOCK, P. (1997). *Understanding Poverty*. London: Macmillan.

BAETEN, G. (1998). *Brussels*. Leuven: Institute for Urban and Regional Planning, University of Leuven.

——(2001*a*). 'The Europeanization of Brussels and the Urbanization of "Europe": Hybridizing the City, Empowerment and Disempowerment in the EU District.' *European Urban and Regional Studies*, 8/2: 117–30.

——(2001*b*). 'Clichés of Urban Doom: The Dystopian Politics of Metaphors for the Unequal City—A View from Brussels.' *International Journal of Urban and Regional Research*, 25/1: 55–69.

BEECKMAN, H. (1997). 'Het stedelijk beleid van de Europese Unie versus Brussel. Een paradox?'. M. Sc. diss. Leuven: Institute for Urban and Regional Planning, University of Leuven.

Bres (1997). *Brusselse statistische indicatoren*. Brussels: Bres.

Brukselbinnenstebuiten (1993). Eurotaurus. Brussels: Brukselbinnenstebuiten.

Brussels Capital Region, *Review of Office Property* (various years).

Brussels Government (1995). *Gewestelijk Ontwikkelingsplan*. Brussels.

DE CORTE, S. (1996). 'Wijkontwikkeling met wijkcontracten? Stadsvernieuwing in

Brussel,' in P. De Decker, B. Hubeau, and S. Nieuwinckel (eds.), *In de ban van stad en wijk*. Antwerp: EPO, 209–18.

DE DECKER, P. (1994). 'Onzichtbare muren. Over leven in achtergestelde buurten en de reproductie van sociale uitsluiting.' *Planologisch Nieuws*, 14/4: 341–66.

DE KEERSMAECKER, M.-L. (1997). *Vierde Rapport over de Staat van de Armoede in het Brussels Hoofdstedelijk Gewest (Fourth Report about the State of Poverty in the Brussels Capital Region)*. Brussels: Gemeenschappelijke Gemeenschapscommissie van Brussel-Hoofdstad.

——(1998).'Staat van de Armoede in het Brussels Hoofdstedelijk Gewest. De Opbouw van Sociale Indicatoren,' in J. Vranken, B. Vanhercke, and G. Van Menxel (eds.), *20 Jaar OCMW. Naar een Actualisering van het Maatschappijproject*. Leuven: ACCO, 79–102.

DEMEY, Th. (1992). *Bruxelles. Chronique d'une capitale en chantier. 2 vols.* Brussels: Paul Legrain.

DENDAUW, S., and VAN DEN PANHUYZEN, W. (1995). *De Congresfunctie van Brussel*. Brussels: Bres.

EUROSTAT (1996). *Concurrentievermogen en Cohesie: Tendensen in de Regio's. Vijfde periodiek Verslag over de sociaal-economische Situatie en Ontwikkeling van de Regio's in de Gemeenschap*. Brussels.

EVANS, R. (1994). 'Brussels,' in A. Harding (ed.), *European Cities towards 2000: Profiles, Policies and Prospects*. Manchester: Manchester University Press, 2–67.

Iris Consulting (1998). *De Sociaal-Ekonomische Impact van de Europese en Internationale Instellingen in het Brussels Hoofdstedelÿk Gewest. Verleden en Toekomst*. Brussels: KPMG.

KB-Stichting (1987). *Armoede en Bestaansonzekerheid. Het Armoededebat. Benaderingen, Begrippen, Metingen*. Brussels: KB-Stichting.

KESTELOOT, C. (1994). 'Three Levels of Socio-spatial Polarization in Brussels.' *Built Environment*, 20/3: 204–17.

——(1996). 'De verwaarlozing voorbij? Achtergestelde buurten en hun ontwikkelingskansen,' in P. De Decker, B. Hubeau, and S Nieuwinckel (eds.), *In de ban van stad en wijk*. Antwerp: EPO, 25–62.

——(1997). *De geografische dimensie van de dualisering in de maatschappij*. Leuven: Institute for Social and Economic Geography, University of Leuven.

——*et al.* (1996). *Atlas van achtergestelde Buurten in Vlaanderen en Brussel*. Brussels: Ministerie van de Vlaamse Gemeenschap.

——and VANDENBROECKE, H. (1997). 'Achtergestelde buurten en stedelijk beleid in Vlaanderen.' *Planologisch Nieuws*, 17/2: 100–23.

——MISTIAEN, P., and DECROLY, J.-M. (1998). 'De Ruimtelijke Dimensie van de Armoede in Brussel. Indicatoren, Oorzaken en buurtgebonden Bestrijdingsstrategieën', in J. Vranken, B. Vanhercke, and G. Van Menxel (eds.), *Armoede en Sociale Uitsluiting. Jaarboek 1997*. Leuven: ACCO, 125–55.

LAGROU, E. (1989). *Welke Stedebouw voor Brussel, Hoofdstad van Europa?* Brussels: St-Lukaswerkgemeenschap.

LIEVENS, J., BRASSEUR, N., and MARTENS, A. (1975). *De grote stad: een geplande chaos? De Noordwijk van krot tot Manhattan*. Leuven: Davidsfonds.

MARTENS, A. (1996). 'Hier leven wij! Bewonersparticipatie in de Brusselse Noordwijk (1968–1995)', in P. De Decker, B. Hubeau, and S. Nieuwinckel (eds.), *In de ban van stad en wijk*. Antwerp: EPO, 193–207.

Mens en Ruimte (1994). *De sociaal-economische impact van de Europese en internationale instellingen te Brussel.* Brussels.

MINGIONE, E. (1996). 'Urban Poverty in the Advanced Industrial World: Concepts, Analysis and Debates,' in E. Mingione (ed.), *Urban Poverty and the Underclass: A Reader.* Oxford: Blackwell, 3–40.

NIS (National Institute for Statistics). *Bevolkingsstatistieken* (various years). Brussels.

PAPADOPOULOS, A. (1996). *Urban Regimes and Strategies: Building Europe's Central Executive District in Brussels.* Chicago: Chicago University Press.

SCHUPP, C. (1995). *Ongelijkheidsindicatoren in het Brusselse hoofdstedelijke gewest.* Brussels: Bres.

SWYNGEDOUW, E., and BAETEN, G. (2001). 'Scaling the City: The Political Economy of "Glocal" Development—Brussels' Conundrum.' *European Planning Studies,* 9/7: 827–49.

VRANKEN, J., GELDOF, D., and VAN MENXEL, G. (1997) (eds.). *Armoede en Sociale Uitsluiting. Jaarboek 1997.* Leuven: ACCO.

8

Competitive City: Governance and the Changing Dynamics of Urban Regeneration in Dublin

Brendan Bartley and Kasey Treadwell Shine

8.1. Introduction: Globalization, Europeanization, and Changing Irish Politics

In Ireland, as elsewhere in the developed world, national and municipal governments have adopted entrepreneurial practices such as place promotion, flagship projects, image boosterism, and urban regeneration schemes in order to promote competitive advantage on the international and global stage (Bartley and Saris 1999; Hall and Hubbard 1998). These practices are associated with new economic and social policies that coincide with a transformation of urban politics. An increasing stress is placed on facilitating market operations, through a new business-oriented management ethos within local and central government. In the mid-1980s, for example, the Irish government adopted a new business-friendly, macro-economic strategy and associated promotional policies to achieve urban renaissance in Dublin, the main growth centre and capital city of the Republic of Ireland. Dublin accounts for almost one-third of the national population of approximately 4 million people. Since the adoption of the new policies, Dublin, with the rest of Ireland, has experienced an unprecedented economic boom. The economic growth is long-standing but has been spectacular for the last seven to ten years. The high and sustained economic growth rates have led many commentators to compare Ireland's recent economic performance to that of the dynamic 'tiger' economies of East Asia—hence the application to Ireland of the titles 'Celtic tiger' and 'Emerald tiger' (Breathnach 1998; Sweeney 1999). However, the 'success strategy' deployed in Ireland is a hybrid approach to policy and practice based on a mix of American economics and EU principles of social democracy. In summary, the Irish national government adopted American-style *economic policies*, with an emphasis on a cheap and flexible labour force and competitive, entrepreneurial governance practices. At the same time, EU initiatives in the domain of social affairs have been mirrored in Irish policy. In particular, the principle of alleviating 'social exclusion' has been adopted from Europe as a means of ameliorating the social polarization trends that have accompanied the boom in Ireland (Bartley and Treadwell Shine 1999).

At the municipal level, the Irish national government responded to the latest pressures of globalization and intensified city competition by adopting adventurous entrepreneurial practices and regeneration policies designed to modernize or 're-image' the capital city. It sought to boost Dublin's competitive advantage and to obtain a high ranking in the new urban order emerging from the consolidation of the EU as a world super-region. The government consciously experimented with new 'flagship' projects and new implementation arrangements in the race to 'avoid being left behind' in the scramble for places in the nascent European city hierarchy (Bartley 2000). The new entrepreneurial policies and practices have led to new 'visions' and re-imag(in)ings of Dublin city including the use of urban regeneration projects to increase the attractiveness of the city for national and global investment. While the Urban Development Project (UDP) in Dublin docklands has been acknowledged as an economic success, it has also contributed to social polarization effects. The precise impacts of the UDP on social polarization are obscured by the 1990s economic boom in Ireland and cannot be clearly extricated from other boom effects throughout Dublin city and Ireland. However, it is clear that reactions against the local exclusion and democratic deficits aspects of the Docklands UDP have provided an impetus for the promotion of anti-exclusionary 'social models' of urban renewal, and for a seeming move towards inclusive partnership approaches to urban regeneration. This can be most clearly seen in the evolution of urban regeneration policy in Ireland from the inception of the docklands (physical/economic) model in 1986 to the most recent Integrated Area Plans (IAPs) which have a strong community participation and social benefits emphasis.

8.2. From Isolation to Globalization: Three Phases of Economic Policy

The evolution of macroeconomic strategy and associated physical planning in modern Ireland can be divided into three distinct phases (see Table 8.1). The first phase, which stretched from national independence in 1921 to the late 1950s, was the pre-modernization era of national isolationism in Ireland. The Irish government, dominated by large centre populist political parties, pursued closed-market protectionist economic policies based on the ultimately

Table 8.1. Economic policy phases and related trends in Ireland

	Phase 1 1921 to 1960	Phase 2 1960 to 1986	Phase 3 1986 to 2001
Economic policy	Economic isolationism: sustainable indigenous development ('Sinn Fein')	Industrialization and integration into world economy: strategy to attract inward investment	Post-industrial strategy to attract only high growth, hi-tech industries and services
Governance	Centre populist party dominance of central government: weak local government	Centre populist party dominance of central government and emergence of coalition governments: weak local government	Coalition governments and proliferation of partnerships: relaxation of central government controls over local government
Urban planning	Minimal (*ad hoc*): main focus on housing provision	Local government urban planning introduced but authoritarian control maintained by central government	Adaptive entrepreneurialism: targeted regeneration and flexible planning
Landscape	Rural / agricultural landscape and society: compact cities and towns	Urbanization: low density suburbanization model and inner city decline	Urban reassertion and revitalization: polymorphic inner city renewal and suburbanization and commuterization
Docklands site	Busy docklands area	Decline and dereliction of up-river docks	From (*a*) single focus 'exclusive' economic/physical regeneration of the city to (*b*) Integrated Area Development and social inclusion community focus

unsuccessful aim of achieving national self-reliance through the cultivation of indigenous industries. During phase 1, Ireland was a predominantly rural country and urban centres experienced little or no growth due to emigration. The second phase stretched from 1960 to the mid-1980s and is characterized as the era of internationalism and early modernization. During this period open trading on the international markets was embraced in conjunction with policies to attract international companies into the country as a source of employment and prosperity. A modern land use planning system was introduced by the Irish national government in 1963 for the purpose of assisting and regulating the anticipated industrialization, and associated urbanization trends (Bartley 1998).

The third phase of macroeconomic policy, which began in the mid-1980s and extends to the present, is the period of advanced modernization and consolidated international integration. An open market economic model of global trading and targeted inward investment in selected leading-edge international business sectors was combined with a minimalist social democratic model of state expenditure and a national partnership approach to planning and managing the economy. During this period, a sequence of national coalition governments engaged increasingly with both the private business sector and community interest groups in the third sector as part of a new mode of flexible governance. Many legal constraints on local authorities were removed to enable them to become more involved in proactive development strategies. It was also during this phase that the modern urban regeneration era effectively got under way when, in 1986, blighted urban zones were officially designated for renewal by central government. These targeted areas were provided with tax exemption status and other incentives to stimulate private investment in the city. It is this third phase that coincides with the pressures of intensified city competition associated with accelerating European integration and globalization trends. During this period, Dublin, like many other cities, became a laboratory for testing the potential of new urban regeneration initiatives.

8.3. Planning Failure—the Decline and Renewal of Dublin

The emphasis on urban regeneration during phase 3 is a by-product of the unsuccessful experience of modern planning in Ireland during phase 2. Like the United Kingdom (of which it was a colony until the formation of the Irish State in 1921), Ireland does not have a statutory level of regional government. It has instead a dual political system comprised of two levels of government—local and national (Newman and Thornley 1996). The country-wide planning system introduced in 1963 was assigned to the local authorities. However, central government retained most of the control over economic promotion and development in Ireland and this severely restricted the planning autonomy of the local authorities. Although they had been delegated responsibility for urban planning, local authorities were also decisively constrained, in this period, by the Irish legal framework and operated effectively as an executive arm of national government. Under this planning regime, the local authority for the municipality of Dublin pursued a central government endorsed development strategy of urban decentralization that permitted a pattern of low-rise, low-density 'new town' suburban expansion to occur in the surrounding local authority areas at the expense of the city. This produced a long-standing relocation trend that contributed to a rapid decline of the inner city. This trajectory persisted until the mid-1980s when serious concerns were expressed about the decay of the inner city and the ever-widening commuter belts that were resulting from the relocation of residents and industry to the urban fringe (Bartley 2000).

In the mid-1980s, a new settlement strategy was commissioned by central government, to look specifically at the future needs of the Dublin region. Highlighting the weakness of the planning system and the absence of any commitment from central government to funding an alternative urban policy, this report sought to be 'realistic' by producing a 'trend' plan that recommended a continuation of the prevailing decentralization (Bartley 2000). The publication of this report coincided with the advent of the new (phase 3) national economic development strategy designed to boost the Irish economy by employing neo-liberal, targeted approaches to public and private sector spending and investment. Within this context, reaction against the proposed plan led to arguments about how to 'save' Dublin, and the inner city in particular. In the ensuing debates about the prospective shape of the city, the decline of the city centre was viewed as a problem but also as an opportunity for fresh initiatives and experiments that could draw on similar experiences abroad. Central government adopted a focused model based on designating specific areas for renewal. Other, more comprehensive, city-wide planning strategies suggested at the time as alternative approaches to the revitalization of Dublin were ignored. The targeted urban development project (UDP) approach drew upon the experience of the London Docklands and similar experiments with urban regeneration in Britain and America. The introduction of an extremely low Corporation Tax rate (10 per cent) was a particular Irish twist to the UDP approach (Sharry 1999). The flagship area selected for renewal in Dublin was in a derelict part of the Dublin docklands close to the city centre (see Fig. 8.1). This move was controversial in Ireland, in particular because the creation of an unelected executive organization to manage the project (the Docklands UDC) usurped the planning powers and responsibilities of the municipal government in Dublin. The establishment by central government of the UDC led to a fightback by local government against its exclusion from the docklands site. This involved the local authority developing its own distinct models of urban regeneration, and proclaiming itself to be a competitive, competent, and democratically accountable agency capable of achieving successful entrepreneurial regeneration in the city.

8.4. The Dublin Docklands Story: Part One. The UDP and its Impacts

The initial Docklands UDP area, known as the Custom House Docks area (CHDA), comprised 11 ha which was expanded to 29 ha in 1987, when the site

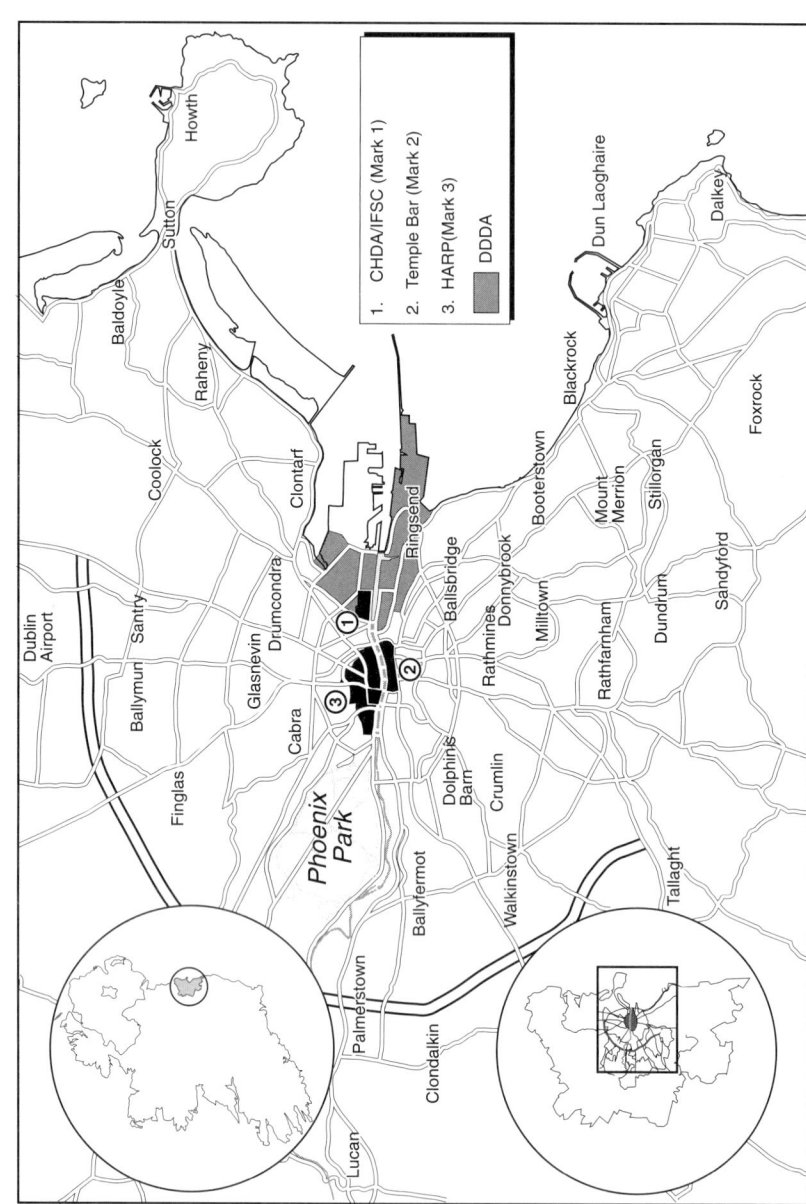

Fig. 8.1. Dublin: city and urban regeneration locations

was also designated by central government as the primary location for an International Financial Services Centre (IFSC) (see Fig. 8.2). The project has been hailed as a major economic success story. However, the social, political, and, to a lesser extent, physical aspects of the scheme received widespread criticism. In the context of growing public concerns about the democratic deficits and exclusionary features of the project, the subsequent 'fight-back' by the 'enfeebled' local authority contributed to the complex conditions in which new urban governance arrangements and alternative models of urban regeneration have emerged in Dublin. One outcome of this ongoing confrontation between the local authority and the Docklands UDC is that urban regeneration policies have changed considerably. The initial concern with securing property-led economic objectives through a technocratic style of management has given way to approaches based upon broad partnership schemes that seek to achieve a wider mix of economic and social objectives for targeted areas. This new strategy and implementation regime is also being pursued and mediated by new urban governance networks. The quest for urban renaissance in Ireland through flagship development projects (UDPs) is no longer viewed as a matter for government or its subordinate agencies alone. It is increasingly seen as a collaborative effort involving new and flexible political, administrative, and participatory arrangements encompassing a range of options such as special purpose regeneration agencies (UDCs), public–private partnerships (PPPs) and, more recently, tripartite (public–private–community and other third sector) partnerships.

It is difficult to disaggregate the effects of the UDP project in this initial docklands site from the multitude of activities and influences associated with the economic boom but some immediate impacts are discernible across the physical, commercial, social, and political spectra. The CHDA has been physically renewed and is now described as a new urban precinct (see Plate 8.1). The UDP has thus extended and relocated the centre of gravity of the Central Business District (CBD) in Dublin. The site has been 'successfully' transformed but not in accordance with the original plan for the area. The absence of a vibrant mix of uses and the predominance of office development differentiates the regenerated UDP area from the typical CBD land use profile. The UDP in its original planning scheme (published in 1987) proposed the transformation of the derelict CHDA into a vibrant area with a wide range of uses, including offices, residential, retail, hotels, restaurants, and tourist facilities. The international recessions in the late 1980s resulted in a slowdown in the Irish economy. The focus on establishing the IFSC at the site led to a predominance of office activities and a limited amount of residential development on the site. The resulting mono-functional landscape of the UDP site has also isolated it from surrounding communities and from Dublin city as a whole. This isolation is reinforced by the presence of security guards and by the perpetual monitoring of the area through Closed Circuit Television (CCTV). Electronic security gates, a moat, and a wall several metres in height (referred to by the local

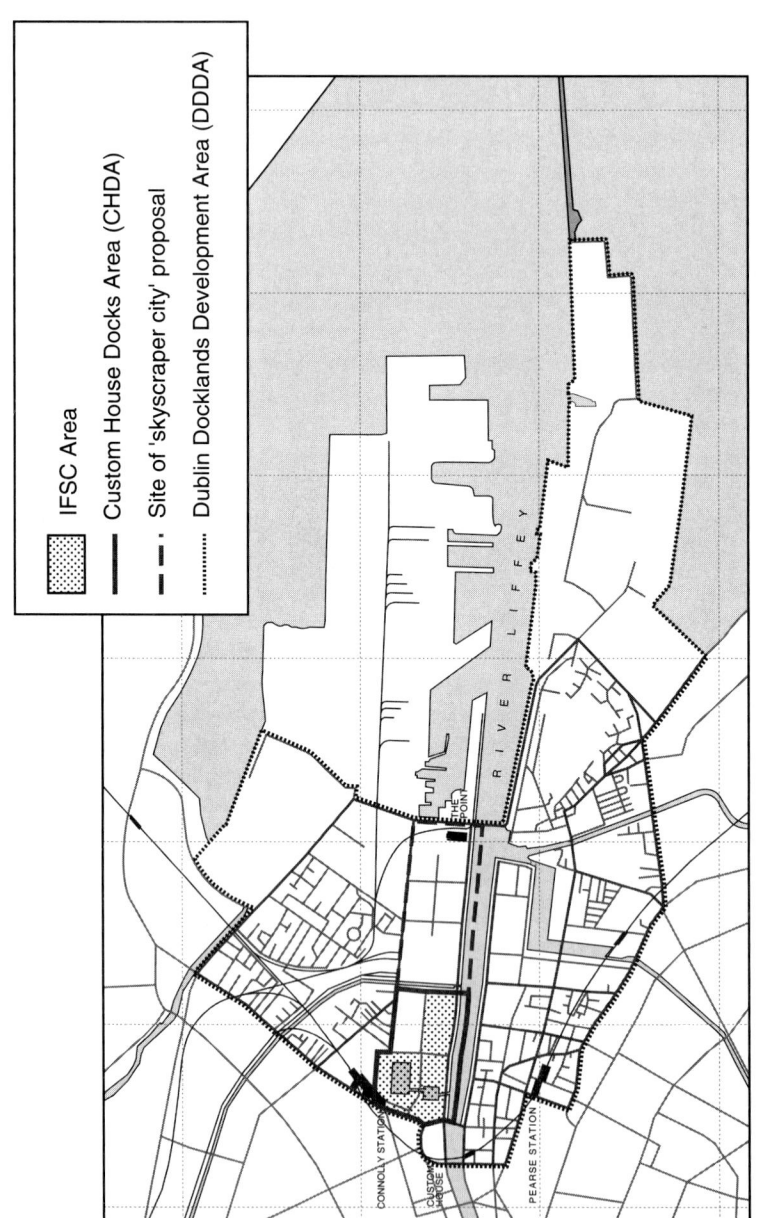

Fig. 8.2. Dublin Docklands regeneration sites

Reproduced by permission of DDDA

Plate 8.1. Dublin Docklands (CHDA/IFSC) site before (*above*) and after (*below*) regeneration

communities as 'The Berlin Wall') segregate the indigenous communities from the 'new' communities established after the CHDA regeneration.

Private investment has been successfully attracted to the UDP, and the UDP is being hailed as a commercial success, due to the high demand for office space within the IFSC, the significant employment generated on site, and the high tax returns accruing to the state. Over 2 billion Euro tax revenue per annum is generated by the on site activities and Dublin city is now viewed as a modest but fast growing International Financial Services Centre (McDonnell 1999; Murphy 1998). Over 14,500 people were employed in the extended IFSC site in early 2001 (Durney 2001). However, despite the physical and economic success of the UDP in regenerating the Customs House Docks site, the lack of trickle-down benefits for the local indigenous communities has been strongly criti-cized (DOELG 1996a: 91). For example, local communities have not benefited as much from the new middle and high grade jobs provided within the site, although they have gained a number of lower-paid service jobs.

The UDP has also had significant impact upon the property markets, both within the CHDA and in the surrounding neighbourhoods. There is a growing shortfall in the availability of social and affordable housing to local people in the docklands area. Residential development in the CHDA accounted for only 5 per cent of total development on the site whilst office space accounted for 83 per cent of all development in the IFSC in 1996 (DOELG 1996a: 88). As the economy boomed in the 1990s, Dublin experienced an acute shortage of office space. With companies now queuing to get into the successful IFSC site, the intense demand for office space squeezed other real estate markets, most notably the provision of social and affordable housing within and around the UDP. The housing sector crisis is exacerbated by immigration and by official housing policy. The provision of social housing has been reduced throughout Ireland, due to the post-1986 retrenchment of public sector welfare spending. For example, the state provided approximately 8 per cent only of the total new houses built in the country in 1998 as against 27 per cent in 1985. In the regen-erated inner-city areas, local communities that traditionally would have been at the bottom of the housing market now find themselves with diminishing levels of housing provision and increased competition from incoming residents for the limited stock of available residential units. The situation is particularly acute in the Docklands UDP and neighbouring areas. Local residents can-not compete with investors or owner-occupancy purchasers for the limited supply of private residential units available in the area. The result has been gentrification of the initial UDC site and the exclusion from the life of the area, through the housing market, of many of the latest generation of the indigenous population.

The high degree of central government involvement in, and promotion of, the initial docklands regeneration ensured that from the very beginning the CHDA/IFSC was presented as a national political success story. Until recently, the interests and concerns of local communities were not so visible.

In fact, local communities and activists were initially excluded from political involvement in the UDP. However, a coalition of local communities and organizations was established to combat the exclusion of local issues and people from the UDP. This coalition succeeded in raising the profile of the local communities in the national media and successfully lobbied government and other agencies for support during major confrontations with the UDP. The coalition was also instrumental in securing the election of a local community activist to the national parliament. These achievements, together with a series of successful resistance campaigns, provided the coalition with sufficient leverage to ensure that the UDC acknowledged local community interests in the later stages of the UDP (Rafferty 1998). When its ten-year life span expired in 1996 the Docklands UDC was re-established by government and legal provision was made for direct representation of the local communities on the Board of the reconstituted UDC.

8.5. Reactions to the UDP: Four Models of Urban Regeneration

The impact of the UDP project, and in particular its perceived successes and failures, have stimulated reactions to urban regeneration policy that have resulted in the emergence of new models of urban regeneration in Ireland (see Table 8.2). These changes involved both targeted competitive economic policies and new urban and social policy dimensions, and thus reflected a general trend towards urban entrepreneurialism. The trends suggest that while Dublin is becoming an entrepreneurial city, it is selectively adapting entrepreneurial practices and policies in order to fit the Irish context. Indeed, Dublin can be perceived as an unusual hybrid of American economics with a very strongly mediated EU social dimension. A growing awareness of the problems faced by other entrepreneurial cities, has led many at the helm of entrepreneurial changes within Dublin city to take special notice of the effects of market forces and especially market failures on competitive cities (Gough 1999). In particular, the negative social impacts of the early UDP projects produced a heightened awareness in local and central government of the risks of social polarization inherent in entrepreneurial approaches. Finally, many of the recent entrepreneurial changes observed in Ireland and in Dublin are attempts to ameliorate the specific bureaucratic and centralized political structure of Irish government.

If the first (Mark 1) model of urban regeneration in Dublin is the autonomous UDC approach represented by the CHDA/IFSC site, the second urban regeneration model (Mark 2) is exemplified by the Temple Bar regeneration project (see Fig. 8.1). When financial office complexes went out of favour as the bottom fell out of the stock exchange and property markets in the late

1980s, heritage related tourism projects quickly became the prevailing fashion in urban renewal for most 'competitive cities'. Temple Bar is a typical example of the new fashion that emerged at that time. This second model used financial incentives and a new UDC (Temple Bar Properties) to manage the project. Private sector businesses were invited to participate in the regeneration process in partnership with Temple Bar Properties. However, the local authority retained planning control in Temple Bar, and worked in conjunction with the Temple Bar UDC to develop a Framework Plan for the site. The local authority was back in the picture as a key player, albeit not in the leading role. However, the local authority and the designated UDC worked together to draw up an Architectural Framework Plan. Unlike the IFSC site, the Temple Bar Plan proposed a people-oriented site with a permeable urban fabric and high quality open spaces.

The third urban regeneration model (Mark 3), formalized in 1994, is typified by the Historic Area Rejuvenation Project (HARP) (see Fig. 8.1). Here, the local authority took the lead in choosing the designated area for regeneration and retained planning control over the site. This approach allowed for considerable involvement by local community representatives and others interested in the development of the area. In this model the local authority leads the potential public–private sector partnerships but the community and other elements of 'civil society' are actively drawn into the partnership arrangements.

In 1996 the International Management Consultancy firm KPMG was commissioned by central government to review the first decade of Urban Renewal Schemes in Ireland. The findings of the KPMG report echoed the results of a similar KPMG study carried out in the UK for the British government. The Irish report concluded that the Mark 1 model was a success in economic and physical terms. However, it criticized the democratic and community deficits associated with the Docklands UDC project due to (*a*) the exclusion of local government from the project, and (*b*) the lack of regeneration benefits accruing to local residents. The report recommended that subsequent urban regeneration schemes should be based on a partnership social model similar to the Mark 3 approach sponsored by the local authority, which was considered to be a more 'democratic' model than its predecessors. The report also explicitly recommended the introduction of a more clearly defined and integrated area-based approach to urban regeneration (KPMG's Mark 4 model).

The Mark 4 model was embraced by the local authority when the Integrated Area Plan (IAP) approach to urban regeneration was introduced by central government in 1998. In this Mark 4 approach, local government, or another management agency, is responsible for the designation and planning for each IAP. In order to obtain designated status as an urban regeneration zone from central government, IAPs were required to demonstrate their social need and other credentials in competition with other potential IAPs. These IAPs were also expected to adopt clear, comprehensive goals for the total regeneration of the area and local participation through partnerships. In summary, the latest

Table 8.2. Four models of urban regeneration in Dublin

Model	Mark 1	Mark 2	Mark 3	Mark 4
Representative project (inception)	CHDA UDC (1986)	Temple Bar (1991)	HARP Site (1995)	Integrated Area Plans (IAPs) (1998)
Changing governance / planning procedures	Local authorities by-passed by independent executive agency (UDC) which produces Master Plan for designated area	Local authority included in negotiated framework plan by dominant UDC	Local authority leads project and prepares planning scheme for site; local authority also retains planning control over site	Central government selects IAPs via competitive bidding contest; local authority, UDC, or other agencies can lead project
Partnership	Public–private partnership (PPP) only	Public–private partnership (PPP); some formal co-operation between UDC and local authority	Early tripartite partnership approaches. Liaison between local authorities, community, private sector	Intensified and more diverse partnership approaches (including tripartite stakeholder partnerships between state agencies, communities, businesses, etc.)
Social housing component	None	Minimal	Significant housing dimension—mixed tenures	Major focus on social benefits including local housing needs

Mark 4 model combines many of the practices seen in other entrepreneurial cities (Hall and Hubbard 1998). It involves new forms of governance to support and target regeneration in a designated area. It also requires local authorities to engage in competitive bidding in order to get central government funding for these areas, a significant difference from the Mark 3 model.

8.6. The Docklands Story: Part Two. An Ironic Twist

The remit of the Docklands UDC was renewed in 1996 at the end of its ten-year term of office and its area of jurisdiction was expanded to 526 hectares (see Fig. 8.1). Following on from the KPMG report recommendations, the UDC for the extended docklands regeneration area, the Dublin Docklands Development Authority (DDDA), embraced the Mark 4 (partnership) model in 1997. The reconstituted UDC's new Master Plan includes proposals for the social, economic, and holistic regeneration of the docklands area. Moreover, there appears to be a move towards more flexible and accountable forms of governance on the part of the UDC, through the establishment of a Consultative Council to liaise with local communities who are also represented on the governing Board of the UDC.

However, the 'fight-back' mentality of the local authority continues to create friction between it and the UDC, and this is particularly evident in controversies associated with recent development project proposals for the extended docklands. The political and community involvement dimensions of the recent confrontations produce an even more complex picture of the governance landscape in Dublin. Fifteen years after the establishment of the initial Docklands UDP, the UDC and the local authority for Dublin are still locked in a struggle for control of the docklands area and central government appears to have endorsed the involvement of both agencies in urban regeneration. The local authority in its public advertisement and visual display literature describes itself with the slogan 'leading change in the city'. However, the Docklands UDP continues to be a major competitor with the local authority. The economic and physical success of the initial CHDA/IFSC project ensures that the UDP model is still held in high regard by central government. However, the traditional planning control remit for the docklands area has been returned to the local authority and coexists alongside the legal powers granted to the UDC by the urban regeneration legislation.

The replacement, through revised legislation, of the old CHDA/IFSC model by the new social and community-oriented DDDA model has created a confused and paradoxical situation in relation to urban planning policy and practice in Dublin. The DDDA can fast-track development schemes in the extended area under its legal jurisdiction. However, the local authority now has power to receive and approve planning applications for the same docklands area should private developers choose to by-pass the DDDA's fast-track route. In short, two separate planning routes are available to developers of sites in the extended docklands regeneration zone: (*a*) a fast-track, guaranteed 'partnership collaboration' route through the UDC using the provisions of the special legislation but requiring adherence to the new Mark 4 style principles, including commitments to community gain and other social benefits, in particular the provision of a significant percentage of social housing; and (*b*) a slower and less secure route through the local authority using the traditional planning application process which allows for subsequent appeal against the decision of the planning authority but with no obligations on the part of the planning authority or developers to deliver community gain because the area has not been specifically designated as an IAP by the local authority.

The contradictions inherent in this dualistic planning system were thrown into relief when a major development consortium, following consultations with the local authority, opted in 1999 to apply to the local authority for planning permission for a huge high-rise development scheme in the extended docklands area. The footprint of the proposed scheme was similar in scale to the London docklands project at Canary Wharf and would have created the first Manhattan-style skyscraper cityscape in Dublin. It became evident that one of the main reasons that the consortium chose to by-pass the UDC collaboration route was to avoid the Mark 4 style community-gain provisions of the UDC's new Master Plan. It also became clear that in the prevailing economic climate of rapid economic growth in Dublin, private developers could secure a ready demand for office and other commercial space. They were, accordingly, reluctant to forfeit a significant portion of the project profits to community gains such as social housing. Faced with the hard-line commitment of the UDC to securing community gain as part of its new social remit, the private development consortium opted for the traditional planning route as offering the best opportunity to avoid the community gain demands.

Ironically, the UDC is now allied to the local communities in opposition to the local authority, which appears to be willing to grant such planning permissions for the docklands area in the face of this opposition. Thus, a strange situation has developed. In an ironic turnaround, the 'hero–demon' roles of the local authority and UDC have been reversed in the perception of the local and wider public. The UDC, previously criticized for its lack of community consultation and once seen by many in the docklands area as a virtual enemy of local communities, is now portrayed as their main ally. Meanwhile, the local authority seems to have adopted a strong pro-development stance in relation to the docklands area and turned away from the community-oriented position it claimed to adopt in its earlier confrontations with the UDC. The planning authority's decision to grant permission for the proposal was ultimately overturned by an independent planning appeals board which arbitrates on objections to decisions made by the planning authorities in Ireland. The planning system has become more flexible and fragmented but also more contradictory and confused.

8.7. Towards Stakeholder Governance:
Indigenous Change and External Influences

The move towards entrepreneurialism presented above appears to suggest that pressures for change are purely indigenous, relating especially to the structure of Irish government and the confrontation occasioned by the establishment of the UDC. Most of the local authority officials that we interviewed in the course of our research believed that this was the case and insisted that they were leading change in response to challenges in the local milieu. However, our research reveals definite external influences, especially from America via New Zealand. For example, many of the management changes in the local authority can be traced back to a central government report on strategic management. This report was drawn up by a high-ranking group of civil servants and drew heavily on neo-liberal management changes in New Zealand's government to make similar recommendation for Irish national government. While local authority officials could point to this report as an influence for change, few could trace the link back to New Zealand. The New Zealand approach was heavily influenced by North American management theories from the mid-1980s and found its way on to the Irish agenda through a special management training module provided by the University of Dublin for senior Irish government officials. Thus, despite the apparent autonomy of the local authority in developing an indigenous strategy to the UDC model of urban regeneration, external influences are clearly discernible. Local government is still reacting to central government direction and control, whilst central government is itself reacting to outside influences that reflect competition-oriented economic and governance policies emanating from the leading American business management schools.

The original UDP project in Dublin contributed to the growing social polarization trends observed in Ireland since the mid-1980s. The changes in urban regeneration policy implemented in Dublin after the inception of the UDP incorporated new competitive economic policies. However, they have also included a move towards social policies aimed at tackling social polarization and social exclusion. The social polarization effects observed within the UDP were partly responsible for the new emphasis on social inclusion. However, greater contributions to these social policy changes have come through other socio-political influences including EU social policy. EU policies to promote economic integration and competitiveness have been accompanied by the development of parallel social inclusion initiatives designed to maintain social cohesion and mitigating the potential negative consequences of economic restructuring. Irish policy changes have mirrored EU policy changes closely, to a large extent because of the need to maximize grant funding from Europe, particularly for welfare spending purposes. A series of formal national partnership programmes designed to stimulate employment and address social exclusion directly parallel other social partnership programmes in Europe. These partnerships pursue social inclusion in its own right as a strategic objective and as an integral part of the partnerships themselves.

Despite the congruence between Irish policy initiatives for tackling poverty and employment and EU policy initiatives on these issues, local community involvement in local development in Ireland has, until recently, been minimal. Thus in the early 1990s, the EU 'went in the back door' and set up funding for new pilot programmes, aimed at addressing social inclusion, poverty, and local development issues, with social inclusion as its *raison d'être* (Turnbull 1999). The most significant of these alternative socio-political programmes in Dublin is the Area Development Management (ADM) Ltd. ADM is an independent partnership company established by the EU, in agreement with the Irish government in 1994, to co-ordinate and support the activities of thirty-eight local 'area partnership' companies in Ireland. These local partnership companies prepare action plans to address issues of unemployment, training, enterprise, community development, and the environment in the partnership areas. While these are not specifically physical regeneration plans, the link between poverty and poor environments is obvious, and by tackling these issues the plans seek to assist the economic *and* social regeneration of poor communities. They are complementary to traditional urban regeneration schemes in so far as the latter usually seek physical transformation while the former are more concerned with social and economic transformation. Thus, the goal of these partnership companies is to produce local development plans that 'bend urban development towards social inclusion' (Turnbull 1999). In other words, these partnership companies complement the new urban regeneration policies promoted by government by targeting directly the potentially negative impacts for local communities of competitive economic and urban policies. These area partnerships have demonstrated a new way of working, providing important networking links between statutory agencies, local businesses, and local communities.

The establishment of ADM constituted an important commitment to using an area-based partnership approach to addressing poverty and exclusion in Ireland. It has been increasingly employed as a flexible, new management addition to the armoury of Irish welfare intervention mechanisms. As such, it is intended to bridge the gap between perceived bureaucratic state inertia (especially at local government level) and the potential of private sector company models for achieving economic and social development at a local level. However, ADM is not completely independent of government. ADM liaised closely with the local authority in the preparation of the Mark 3 renewal schemes. It was also represented on the committee established to develop what became the IAP (Mark 4) approach. This representation reflects the new forms of governance that are emerging in Dublin city, and illustrates that such forms of governance need not be confined to local versus central government tensions or revolve only around business interests and new economic policies. ADM contends that it was its influence that pushed Irish government towards the adoption of social inclusion issues and towards embracing the social models of urban regeneration; that more holistic urban regeneration policy includes moves towards new social as well as economic policies. Of course, the ADM is itself being directly funded by the EU, and hence guided at least in part by EU policies promoting social inclusion. Once again, the proclaimed autonomy of the various parties is based on a failure to recognize outside influences. It is evident that the local authority is following models similar to the ADM, which is itself following EU models.

8.8. Flexible Fragments: Inadequacies of Current Approaches to Regeneration

The most recent urban regeneration (Mark 4) model is employed both by the local authority and the Docklands UDC. However, this IAP model, while stressing more flexible and purportedly inclusive forms of governance, also stresses entrepreneurial practices that do not always sit easily with these new forms of governance. The IAP approach seeks to bring multi-sectoral, but potentially exclusive interests, to the table in order to accomplish integrated and holistic local urban regeneration. Thus, while there is a stated commitment to integrated development by all actors involved in the potential regeneration of the city, there are nevertheless serious problems that need to be addressed. The most relevant of these is how to balance the deployment of competitive economic policies with the social concerns and needs of local communities. Despite the seeming successes of bringing together American-style economic policies with EU-style social policies to shape the urban environment of Dublin, there still is no comprehensive or coherent national urban policy for either the country or its metropolitan capital.

The IAP approach may have the potential to become a useful tool in the armoury of urban regeneration policy in Dublin. However, the approach constitutes a piecemeal, selective approach to planning rather than a universal, comprehensive approach. IAPs are clearly not an alternative to wider, long-term planning strategies. Targeted approaches necessarily entail competition between communities in an effort to draw down resources for one or a few specific areas. Where the 'losers' in this scenario are left with virtually no safety net, they run the risk of becoming completely excluded from, and invisible within, the regenerated patchwork urban landscape. As the current housing crisis in Dublin illustrates, piecemeal urban regeneration cannot compensate for the absence of comprehensive housing and settlement policies. Wider urban policies are still essential. Without comprehensive metropolitan or regional planning strategies, serious doubts remain about the effectiveness of the targeted, *ad hoc* (and fragmented) approach to planning associated with even the Mark 4 model of urban regeneration.

8.9. Conclusions

The emergence of Dublin as an 'entrepreneurial city' has been illustrated here by the Docklands UDC flagship project, which became both a marker and catalyst for emerging entrepreneurial practices in Dublin. This chapter focused on the governance implications of the Docklands UDP and its impact upon subsequent changes in urban regeneration policy. Urban regeneration strategy in Dublin has evolved as a combined result of reactions to the initial UDP model of regeneration and the changing dynamics of Irish politics, which have in turn been influenced by changes in the European and global contexts. The original UDP approach to urban regeneration, which placed exclusive emphasis on physical-economic renewal, has been supplanted by a more democratic model, which lays considerable stress upon social and political accountability to the local community. In Ireland, the quest for urban renaissance through flagship urban development projects (UDPs) is no longer viewed as a matter for government or its subordinate agencies alone. It is increasingly seen as a collaborative effort involving new and flexible political, administrative, and participatory arrangements involving a range of options such as special purpose regeneration agencies (UDCs), public–private partnerships (PPPs), and, more recently, tripartite (public–private–community) partnerships. In this sense, Dublin is now pursuing a more mixed and 'adaptive' entrepreneurial approach to metropolitan development. This approach is a hybrid of (*a*) American neo-liberal economic promotion policies, and (*b*) EU social partnership policies designed to promote social inclusion and common standards of welfare provision. This 'adaptive entrepreneurial' approach seems to avoid the worst excesses of American-style 'boosterism' approaches to achieving economic growth by addressing aspects of social polarization and poverty while at the same time promoting entrepreneurial practices.

Dublin has moved away from the initial single issue UDC/UDP approach to urban regeneration. The most recent model of urban regeneration in Ireland, the IAP (Mark 4) approach, already incorporates many recommendations that flowed from evaluation of the CHDA/IFSC project. This UDC (Mark 1) model was just one of many potential approaches to urban regeneration within Dublin. The fact that it was rejected can be interpreted as a sign of failure. However, it could equally be argued that the UDC has not been rejected but modified and socialized. The perceived successes and failures of the earlier model have led to it being updated with a seemingly more positive, wider ranging, and inclusive array of policies for urban regeneration in Dublin. Thus, the 'evolving' UDPs may become a useful tool for assisting local communities rather than a vehicle of oppression. However, selective targeting is a potentially exclusionary approach in its own right which, carried to its logical extremes, could be construed as a neo-liberal style retrenchment of welfare spending. Partnership approaches must be monitored to ensure that they do not become a vehicle for more subtle forms of social exclusion and social control. A restrictive focus on poor places, instead of poor people, may suit administrators of welfare funds because such targeting is a convenient and cost effective way of spending money from welfare budgets. On the other hand, the moves towards collaborative market facilitation have created space for new coalitions and partnerships. While these coalitions and partnerships can be élite and exclusionary, this has not necessarily been the case in Ireland to date, as illustrated by the case study of the proposal to create a 'Manhattan landscape' in the extended Dublin docklands. The contributions of social policy initiatives to tackling social exclusion in general and more specifically in UDP schemes cannot be ignored. Urban regeneration policy in Dublin has been marked by attempts to address social issues and to increase democratic accountability, even as more competitive and entrepreneurial practices are simultaneously being implemented.

The regulatory role of city planners has been supplemented by a refashioned emphasis on planning as a flexible and proactive entrepreneurial function. However, planning has also become more fragmented and selective in focus. City-wide planning is being supplanted by a patchwork of targeted (area-based) urban regeneration, stakeholder-style planning projects. The Mark 4 IAPs are the latest incarnation of the urban entrepreneurial approach that evolved after the inception of the initial Dublin docklands flagship project. Recent evidence suggests that IAPs may have the potential to contribute to urban regeneration in Dublin, but they are not an alternative to wider, comprehensive planning strategies. The current housing crisis in the city provides a clear illustration that piecemeal urban regeneration cannot compensate for the absence of comprehensive housing and settlement policies. Competitive place-based approaches to planning have not eliminated the need for strategic government and planning to secure integration and avoid fragmentation. Coherent urban policies and long-term integrated planning are necessary to avoid potentially wasteful contradictions and harmful inconsistencies.

References

Area Development Management Ltd. (1995). *Integrated Local Development Handbook*. Dublin: Government Stationery Office.

——(1998). *Annual Report 1997*. Dublin: Government Stationery Office.

BANNON, M., *et al.* (1989). *Planning the Irish Experience 1920–1988*. Dublin: Wolfhound Press.

BARTLEY, B. (1998). 'Exclusion, Invisibility, and the Neighbourhood in West Dublin', in A. Madanipour, G. Cars, and J. Allen (eds.), *Social Exclusion and the Neighbourhood in European Cities*. London: Regional Studies Association and Jessica Kingsley Publishers.

——(2000). 'Four Models of Urban Regeneration in Dublin', *Construction Concepts*, May–June: 28–33.

——and SARIS, A. J. (1999). 'Social Exclusion and Cherry Orchard: A Hidden Side of Suburban Dublin', in J. Killen and A. MacLaran (eds.), *Dublin: Contemporary Trends and Issues for the Twenty-First Century*. Dublin: Geographical Society of Ireland, 81–92.

——and TREADWELL SHINE, K. (1999). 'Promoting Economic and Social Gains—The Emergence of Dublin as an Adaptive Entrepreneurial City'. *Insite*, Journal of the Royal Town Planning Insitute (Irish Branch, Southern Section), Autumn–Winter: 20–3.

BREATHNACH, P. (1998). 'Exploring the "Celtic Tiger" Phenomenon: Causes and Consequences of Ireland's Economic Miracle'. *European Urban and Regional Studies*, 5/4: 305–16.

CAREY, S. (1999). Interview. Assistant City Manager for Planning and Economic Development, Dublin Corporation, and Board Member, DDDA.

COLLINS, C. J. (1986). 'Largescale Urban Renewal: A Developer's Viewpoint'. *Built Environment*, 12/4: 208–15.

COLLINS, M., and O'CONNOR, R. (1996). *Dublin Docklands Area Master Plan: The Socio-Economic and Employment Structure of the Dublin Docklands Area*. Dublin: Economic and Social Research Institute.

CRAIG, S. (1994). *Progress though Partnership*. Dublin: Combat Poverty Agency.

Department of the Environment and Local Government (DOELG) (1994). *Urban Renewal Programme: New Life in Your Town 1994*. Dublin: Government Stationery Office.

——(1995). *Guidelines on Residential Development in Urban Renewal Designated Tax Incentive Areas*. Dublin: Government Stationery Office.

——(1996a). KPMG consultants, with Murray O'Laoire Associates and Northern Ireland Economic Research Centre. *Study on the Urban Renewal Schemes*. Dublin: Government Stationery Office.

——(1996b). *Better Local Government: A Programme for Change (BLG)*. Dublin: Government Stationery Office.

——(1997). *1998 Urban Renewal Scheme: Guidelines*. Dublin: Government Stationery Office.

——(1998). *Urban Renewal Schemes Guidelines*. Dublin: Government Stationery Office.

Department of the Taoiseach (Prime Minister) (1996). *Second Report to Government of the Co-ordinating Group of Secretaries: Delivering Better Government: Strategic Management Initiative: A Programme of Change for the Irish Civil Service*. Dublin: Government Stationery Office.

Dublin Corporation (1991). *Dublin City Development Plan 1991*. Dublin: Civic Offices.

——(1996). *HARP Plan*. Dublin: Civic Offices.

Dublin Corporation (1998). *Modernising Dublin Corporation*. Dublin: Civic Offices.

Dublin Docklands Development Authority (1997). *Dublin Docklands Area Master Plan 1997*. Dublin: Government Stationery Office.

DURNEY, T. (2001). Interview. Development Director, Dublin Docklands Development Authority, DDDA Offices, Dublin.

FITZGERALD, J. (1999). Interview. City Manager, Dublin Corporation, Dublin.

GOUGH, M. (1999). Interview. Senior Planner, Corporate Planning Unit, Dublin Corporation, Dublin.

HALL, T., and HUBBARD, P. (1998). 'The Entrepreneurial City and the New Urban Politics', in T. Hall and P. Hubbard (eds.), *The Entrepreneurial City: Geographies of Politics, Regime, and Representation*. Chichester: John Wiley and Sons, 1–23.

MACAMHLAIGH, A. (1999). Interview. Executive Board Member Dublin Docklands Development Authority and former Chief Executive of the Custom House Docks Development Authority (CHDDA). Custom House Docks, Dublin.

MCDONNELL, P. (1999). Interview. Planning Officer, Planning Department, Dublin Corporation, Dublin.

MCGUIRK, P. (1995). 'Power and Influence in Urban Planning: Community and Property Interests in Dublin's Planning System'. *Irish Geography*, 28/1.

MACLARAN, A. (1993). *Dublin: The Shaping of a Capital*. London: Belhaven.

MARTIN, J. (1999). Interview. Deputy Planning Officer, Planning Department, Dublin Corporation, Dublin.

MURPHY, L. (1998). 'Financial Engine or Glorified Back Office? Dublin's International Financial Services Centre Going Global'. *Area*, 30/2: 157–65.

NEWMAN, P., and THORNLEY, A. (1996) (eds.). *Urban Planning in Europe: International Competition, National Systems and Planning Projects*. London: Routledge.

NOLAN, B., WHELAN, C. T., and WILLIAMS, J. (1998). *Where are Poor Households*. Dublin: Oak Tree Press and Combat Poverty Agency.

OATLEY, N. (1998). 'Cities, Economic Competition, and Urban Policy', in N. Oatley (ed.), *Cities, Economic Competition, and Urban Policy*. London: Paul Chapman Publishing, 3–21.

PARKINSON, M. (1998). *Combating Social Exclusion: Lessons from Area-based Programmes in Europe*. London: The Policy Press.

RAFFERTY, M. (1998). Interview. Manager, Community Technical Aid, Dublin.

SHARRY, C. (1999). Interview. Co-ordinator of Urban Renewal Schemes, Department of the Environment and Local Government, Dublin.

SMITH, C. (1999). Interview. Marketing Assistant, Dublin Docklands Development Authority, Dublin.

SWEENEY, P. (1999). *The Celtic Tiger: Ireland's Continuing Economic Miracle*. Dublin: Oak Tree Press.

TAYLOR, A. (1999). Interview. Member, Economic Development Unit, Dublin Corporation, Dublin.

TURNBULL, S. (1999). Interview. Policy Co-ordinator, Area Development Management Ltd., Dublin.

9

Modernizing or Polarizing Vienna?

Vanessa Redak, Andreas Novy, and Joachim Becker

9.1. Introduction

It is commonly accepted that the 1990s brought modernization to Vienna. The spatial organization of the city was transformed, with the emergence of new actors, new planning philosophies, and a new urban landscape. Skyscrapers replaced churches as the dominant feature of the townscape, real estate agents were canvassed as the harbingers of progress, and city marketing of large-scale projects was substituted for statutory planning. All these changes were crystallized in the new Urban Development Projects (UDPs), which were implemented in the city during that decade. In the eyes of the experts and the public alike, Vienna is being finally 'modernized'.

This chapter reflects on the contradictory nature of this modernization process, by illustrating the dramatic changes which Vienna has been experiencing in recent years, interrupting a decades-long tradition of specific homogenizing and inclusive policies. The aim of this contribution is to excavate the historical roots underlying this apparent modernization and to embed the analysis of Viennese urban processes into a broader political-economic multi-scale analysis. The first section paints a broad picture of the socio-spatial structure of contemporary Vienna, while the second section describes the political and economic restructuring of Vienna against the backdrop of changes in national and global political-economic regimes. In the third section, the large UDPs of Donau City and Nordbahnhof are discussed, and their strategic role as main sites for enacting new social-liberal policies is demonstrated. In a dialectial process, these UDPs are both a response to global changes as well as part of the process of urbanizing globalization. This process is analysed in greater detail in the next section, which details the specific effects of the UDP on the local scale.

9.2. The Viennese Model of Inclusive, but Conservative Urban Policies

Vienna is a contradictory city. On the one hand, social scientists routinely refer to 'Red Vienna' because of the social democratic history of inclusive welfare policies on a local level. For almost a century, social democratic reformism organized the municipal delivery of high quality public services, including transport, education, and housing. Even leisure facilities are more or less evenly distributed and are affordable for the whole population, with large public spaces and green areas and a wide variety of subsidized sporting and recreational services. This public strategy of service delivery 'from the cradle to the grave' resulted in a relatively homogeneous socio-spatial structure, characterized by the absence of no-go areas and deliberate policies of privileging working-class neighbourhoods. On the other hand, despite being governed by social democracy, Vienna can be characterized as a conservative city. Over a period of several decades, the city has implemented social service policies, which were defined, designed, and financed at the national level. The Austrian welfare regime itself can be characterized as conservative (Esping-Andersen 1997), as social citizenship is based on employment and national citizenship. A number of social groups, such as, among others, migrants,[1] have always been disadvantaged and have remained at the margins of the inclusive Austrian-style post-war Fordist welfare strategies.

From a socio-spatial perspective, the Viennese townscape has changed little since the Second World War. Restrictive rent controls, implemented after the First World War, strongly limited the housing market and guaranteed generally affordable housing, and private real estate capital has not been important as a local actor. Housing was provided by the municipality, financed with funds from the central government (Novy *et al.* 2001). Planning was the executive domain of social democratic experts, mainly trained at technical universities. The hegemonic planning philosophy, however, was based on the principle of 'soft' urban renewal and went against large-scale modernization projects. Until the 1990s, the construction of buildings more than six storeys high was permitted only under exceptional circumstances. However, planning strategies changed after 1989, and the development and construction of large UDPs started. Skyscrapers and new urban micro-milieus for the upper-middle class emerged, new planning bodies were created, and a new image of the city was born. At the same time, the city administration decided to create a second city centre on the bank of the river Danube, the UDP Donau City.

We shall analyse this UDP and its related changes in urban planning from both micro- and macro-perspectives. The micro-perspective will show how the development projects led to social polarization in one of the areas (Stuwerviertel) neighbouring the UDP. The macro-perspective will take the UDP as a hallmark for the political and economic restructuring of Vienna, expressing the emergence of a new liberal urban regime in Vienna. This model relies on market mechanisms and locational competition. Inscribed as it is in the structures of the Viennese political economy, it constitutes a social-liberalism as it still relies—at least rhetorically—on a commitment to a municipal welfare state and is still largely implemented by the Social Democratic Party.

9.3. From Fordist National Centre to Semi-peripheral Entrepôt

Compared with other European cities, both the urban landscape and the political economy of Vienna experienced relatively little change until recently. In the Viennese context, globalization should not be understood as an undifferentiated internationalization process. Although liberal, market-led restructuring in the last decade resulted in the denationalization of the Austrian economy, it became integrated into the German, or more precisely Bavarian, productive system rather than becoming tied to global, footloose, capital.

Austria continued to pursue a supply-side Fordism well into the 1970s. This implied a Fordism that was well aware of the small national market and therefore tried, from the very beginning, to capitalize on a relatively cheap and docile labour-force and on promoting exports, especially to Germany (Becker and Novy 1999). The 1970s saw ever-greater economic integration with the Federal Republic of Germany (FRG), including an increase in foreign direct investment from this source, and a considerable increase in exports, particularly from assembly-line industries. At the same time, the government stabilized the domestic market by means of Keynesian fiscal policies. However, the latter had to be abandoned in the early 1980s after the USA brought about a steep rise in international interest rates, thereby contributing to increasing the cost of public debt in many countries. Since then, Austria's regime of accumulation has become more extensive and has been integrated ever more closely into the German regime. Also, since 1989, companies based in Austria have established new ties with East European neighbour states. An increasingly social-liberal type of regulation at the national and European level, which has deeply affected Vienna's local economy, has cemented these changes.

One aspect of these changes has been the partial de-industrialization of the Viennese economy. Between 1981 and 1994, Vienna lost about one-quarter of its industrial plants and 35 per cent of its industrial employment although the development of value-added manufacturing has fared much better (Mayerhofer 1999: 41 ff.). Some standardized consumer good industries experienced a decline in both employment and value-added, and most experienced intensive de-industrialization. These industries had been orientated towards the domestic market during Fordism and suffered from enhanced international competition. The service sector was generally more dynamic than manufacturing, and business services have experienced the strongest growth. The share of property (including real estate) and business-related services in Vienna's gross regional product rose dramatically from 22.8 per cent in 1980 to 35.9 per cent in 1994 (Eigner and Resch 1999: 70, table 8). Space-intensive services like trade and transport have hardly expanded their employment base in Vienna itself, but have grown in the metropolitan area around the city (Mayerhofer 2000: 43 ff.). Public services have continued to be a main pillar of the Viennese economy, but have suffered from restrictive budget policies.

From the late 1940s until the 1960s, Vienna was the control centre of the Austrian economy (Tödtling 1984: 404), although some industrial subsectors, like the electro-technical industry, have a long history of German control. This control function was partially exercised by banks that held capital shares in other sectors, along the lines of the classic German 'holding-company' model. Since the 1970s, the expansion of German capital into Austria has eroded this control function, with many of the larger manufacturing companies being controlled by German capital. By 1996, German companies held shares in all but one of the major food retailers, and they are traditionally well represented in the insurance business. In 2000, the bavarian HypoVereinsbank took a controlling share in Austria's largest bank, Bank Austria, from the Vienna Communal Holding Company (Grubelnik 2000: ch. 2 and statistical appendix). In sum, German influence has now extended to the strategic heights of Austria's economy. In a parallel development, companies located in Austria have rapidly stepped up their direct investment in neighbouring East European states since 1990. This trend has been particularly pronounced in trade and in the financial sector (Höbinger 2001: 85, table 5.9), which tend to have their Austrian headquarters in Vienna. In a somewhat contrasting development, the share of the neighbouring East European states and Poland in Vienna's exports has declined from 20 per cent in 1997 to 13.9 per cent in 1999 (Höbinger 2001: 60). It could be argued that—in terms of control over companies and investment decisions—Vienna has been downgraded to a semi-peripheral position between German cities (particularly Munich) and the central-east European space-economy. In a way this is reminiscent of Vienna's international position in the 1920s.

Socio-economic change in Vienna, the right-wing turn in national politics, and Austria's entry into the European Union (EU) have had a major impact on local regulation, which, in turn, has helped to stabilize the structural changes in the local economy. Keynesianism has eroded more slowly at the local scale than at the national level. It was only with Austria's entry into the EU and the concomitant budgetary restrictions agreed in the Maastricht treaty that fiscal Keynesianism was finally abandoned after 1995. Abandoning local Keynesianism has brought with it a slow erosion of the local welfare state.

The switch from attracting manufacturing companies to wooing service-based capital and real estate companies was much more gradual. The Donau City and Nordbahnhof UDPs were among its early expressions. This shift was accompanied by a discursive switch to the rhetoric of 'city competition', which turned into the leitmotif of the process of establishing a new strategic plan in the late 1990s, when the conservative People's Party became part of the local governing coalition (Novy *et al.* 2001). Strategic planning, however, did not deal with the reverse side of 'city competition', in particular the growth of a low wage sector composed primarily of migrant labour. Spatially, this sector clustered in a few run-down quarters around the city centre.

9.4. Donau City and Nordbahnhof UDPs

In many of the advertising and promotion campaigns for Vienna in the 1990s, the Donau City UDP played a significant role, because it was the one and only large-scale project capable of attracting the interest of international developers (DIFU 1995: 4). The development plan for the UDP coincided with the idea of hosting the Expo 1995. As Budapest, the Hungarian capital, also wished to become the Expo city for 1995, politicians from both cities agreed to initiate the so-called 'Twin City Expo', which enabled both Vienna and Budapest to become Expo sites. This campaign was conduced under the motto 'Bridges into the Future', which also signalled a new orientation in Vienna's economic policy. Vienna was to be promoted as a 'Gateway to the East', with international companies choosing the city as the base for expanding their services into Eastern Europe. However, the plan never aimed to build bridges over the social divide between Austrian citizens and the generally poorly housed migrants and their descendants, originating from the East and working in Vienna.

With the Expo plan, city officials intended to create the conditions deemed necessary for Vienna to become an international finance and service centre, a pivotal trading centre for western exporters, and a preferred location for new trade and services-related investments. As the public debate about the Expo 95 started shortly after the opening of the Eastern European countries in 1989, xenophobic fears of migrants 'flooding' Vienna spread quickly. The extreme right-wing Freedom Party (FPÖ) exploited the political situation by cashing in on boiling racist resentment (Becker 2000). Greens and alternatives also opposed Expo 95, because of fears of further skyrocketing of housing rents (SRF 2000), and wasteful spending of public money. In line with a deeply rooted tradition of opposing large-scale projects, the fear of increased competition in the labour and housing markets due to a shift in national policies towards economic liberalism was a decisive factor in the referendum that was held in May 1991, in which a large majority of the Viennese population voted against Expo 95. Although the outcome of the referendum was not legally binding, the Viennese government decided to withdraw from the project to avoid the emergence of deeper-seated conflicts. However, the democratic outcome was interpreted minimalistically as, in the words of a high planning official, 'the Expo was a means, not the objective' (Steiner 1991: 19). Indeed, planners had strong arguments in their favour: creating a second city centre on fallow land with good access by means of public and private transportation would improve the attraction of Vienna. Since the local government had already put a considerable amount of money and effort into the development of this particular area, it did not want to retire completely from the project. The city administration decided to establish the WED (Wiener Entwicklungsgesellschaft für den Donauraum AG), the Viennese development society for the Danubian micro-region, to act as the general developer for Donau City. WED was in charge of preparing a Master Plan, for designing a tenant-settlement policy, for building the infrastructure of the site, and for co-ordinating its commercial exploitation. The project—an expansion of the municipally owned Vienna International Centre (VIC)—covers a total area of 17.4 ha., which once served as a waste disposal site. The total investment cost was estimated at 1.1 billion Euros.

Donau City covers a subcentre of the urban area of Vienna near the Danube, consisting of the 'UNO-City' (a basically ex-territorial complex completed around 1980), the Austrian Conference Centre, and the area of the UDP—a large multifunctional project. On this site, more than 1,500 subsidized flats, offices, shopping, leisure, and cultural facilities were built. By 2001, the Twin Tower (in 1998, Vienna's highest office building), the Ares Tower (40,000 m^2 of office space), the Saturn Tower (31,500 m^2 of office space), Tech Gate—a public private partnership offering research and conference facilities—a primary school, two kindergartens (one English-speaking), a bilingual primary school, a Roman Catholic church, and a Cineplex-Centre had been or were at the stage of being completed. Further projects are planned.

The whole Donau City project is supposed to be a flagship for Vienna, in particular strengthening its role as an international meeting-place. With regard to city planning, it serves as a bridge connecting the city centre and the fast growing residential areas in the north. The area is connected to the city via the development axis Lasallestraße, which links the 'old' city centre with the new one, and with the former railway station Nordbahnhof. The development project Nordbahnhof (approx. 74.5 ha) is a result of a competition workshop held in 1991/2. This site was to be developed as a 'town in the town', consisting of multifunctional elements: flats, offices, leisure facilities, etc. The owner of the Nordbahnhof is the ÖBB (the Austrian railway company), which sells the land to interested developers.

9.4. Urbanizing Globalization: Polarization in Stuwerviertel

In close proximity to the Nordbahnhof development area lies the popular quarter of the so-called Stuwerviertel. The consequences of the new planning strategies can be observed at a micro-level in this particular neighbourhood. This quarter has a high proportion of low income inhabitants, and is mainly populated by old age pensioners and migrants. Stuwerviertel is also known as a 'red light' zone with mostly illegal prostitution. Serious conflicts have emerged in this area in recent years, with frequent reports in the tabloid press of problems with illegal prostitution and the tensions between the domestic and migrant population. It is therefore interesting to know if and how the new development area Nordbahnhof has affected life in the rather run-down Stuwerviertel. As migration has been one of the most prominent topics in the political life of Vienna and Austria during recent years, we shall focus our survey on migrants in the UDP area, starting with a general assessment of migration in Vienna.

9.4.1. Migration in Vienna

Due to the local welfare state and the relative strength of the social security system, social exclusion is less pronounced in Vienna than in other European cities (Becker and Novy 1999). There is, however, one group that is visibly hit by social exclusion: migrant workers. Migrants are both socially and politically excluded, lacking representation in both the larger neo-corporatist interest groups and the political parties. In Vienna, the political discourse of the right-wing Freedom Party (FPÖ), a general liberal political trend, and growing social disintegration tendencies have established a discursive field in which migration was easily cast as conflictual and problematic. Migration has become associated with crisis and conflict and has become an object for political intervention.

During the 1960s and 1970s, the Viennese population was characterized by a high proportion of old people and a declining birth rate. The resultant labour shortfall was partially addressed by domestic migration, as citizens from the periphery of Austria moved to the city. Although, initially, there were few foreign migrants, this situation began to change in the mid-1970s. The economic crisis and the trend towards tertiarization increased the demand for flexible labour, Austrian companies started to employ migrant workers, and the rate of foreign immigration increased rapidly. The so-called *Ostöffnung* (the opening-up of borders with neighbouring countries to the east of Austria) created a new reservoir of cheap labour. Moreover, migrant workers no longer considered their stay in Austria as temporary but rather as permanent. As a result, family members of many migrant workers moved to Austria in the context of family reunification. Between 1981 and 2000, the share of foreign citizens in the Viennese population increased from 7.4 per cent to 18.1 per cent (Kaufmann 1995; Wiener Integrationsfonds 2000).

On the other hand, Vienna showed strong tendencies towards suburbanization, with a significant part of the domestic Viennese population moving to suburbs beyond the Viennese borders. As a result of these two trends, the migration balance to the city (*Wanderungsbilanz*) at the end of the 1970s showed a positive surplus of about 6,000 people (Kaufmann 1995: 152). Immigration of foreigners therefore filled the gap created by the exodus of some segments of the domestic population from Vienna, a general trend that continued until the 1990s. During that decade, Vienna registered an increase in population of 9,808 people (MA 66).

Foreign migration to Vienna reached its peak during the period 1992/3. Afterwards, the share of migrants in the local population remained stable as a result of tougher legal regulations which restricted immigration into Austria. The two largest groups of foreigners in Vienna are migrants from the former Yugoslavia (Croats, Serbs, Bosnians) and from Turkey. The migrant community also tends to be younger than the domestic population, with 16.3 per cent being aged under 15 (compared to 14.3 per cent for the domestic population), and only 7.3 per cent being aged over 60 (compared to 24.5 per cent of Austrian citizens in Vienna) (Wiener Integrationsfonds 2000: 72); 60 per cent of the migrants belong to lower income groups and are employed in unskilled jobs (compared to only 18 per cent of the domestic population). Even in comparison with Germany, Yugoslav and Turkish workers are extremely concentrated in unskilled jobs and display little upward mobility (Fassmann *et al.* 1999).

9.4.2. Housing policy in Vienna

Of particular importance in terms of exclusion and/or polarization is the housing situation of migrants. Most live in so-called *Gründerzeit* areas, dominated by houses built before 1919. They are privately owned, consist of small flats, and have a substandard infrastructure (no toilets inside the flats, no hot water, no bathrooms or comparable facilities). Another characteristic of *Gründerzeit* buildings is the rather small courtyards, which offer neither green spaces nor places for children to play. Recreation and leisure facilities are rare and have to be found elsewhere, for example in public parks (Rotenberg 1995: 27). Although only one-third of the domestic population live in houses constructed before 1919, approximately 85 per cent of migrants live in houses of this age (see Wiener Integrationsfonds 2000: 47).

With respect to the demographic structure, *Gründerzeit* areas are dominated by two population groups: migrants and elderly Austrians. Both groups share some problems: they are counted among the lower income groups, and limited purchasing power and other financial restrictions constrain their access to the Viennese housing market (see Kaufmann 1999). Furthermore, migrants are refused access to social/public housing (so-called *Gemeindebauten*) as tenancy is restricted to Austrian and EU citizens (see Giffinger 1998). In general, migrants are confronted with a worse quality/price ratio for flats than the Austrian population. In 1993, Turkish and ex-Yugoslavian tenants had to pay, on average, 0.73 Euro more per square metre than Austrian citizens. The status of their contracts is also legally less secure (Kaufmann 1995: 155).

9.4.3. Polarization in the UDP area: the case of Stuwerviertel

Stuwerviertel is one of these *Gründerzeit* areas and is adjacent to the Nordbahnhof UDP. The 1991 Census shows a significant concentration of migrants in the quarters near the Nordbahnhof. In Stuwerviertel itself the pro-portion of foreign citizens is about 30 per cent, whereas the Viennese average is 18.1 per cent (Wiener Integrationsfonds 2000: 70). The area is both socially and geographically isolated—it is encircled by several multi-lane roads, and con-nected to only one other residential area. The other surrounding areas consist of either the recreation zone of the Wiener Prater or the newly built offices in front of the Nordbahnhof. This image of a contained space is reflected in the perceptions of the inhabitants of the district Leopoldstadt (Ifes 1997) of which Stuwerviertel is a part: in their eyes Stuwerviertel represents an 'island on the island'.[2]

None the less, Stuwerviertel and its surrounding areas enjoy a relatively good infrastructure (Redak and Schwaiger 1999). There are many schools of all kinds, a kindergarten, and even a public swimming pool for children in the neighbourhood. It is close to an underground line and to a major public trans-port junction. Public transport is efficient, and the streets are lined with trees. There are three parks within a small area of Stuwerviertel (Max Winter-Platz, Venediger Au, Mexikopark) and the recreation zone of the Wiener Prater is nearby.

However, there are almost no connections between the Nordbahnhof UDP and the neighbouring quarter of Stuwerviertel, with newly built office blocks on one side, and run-down residential buildings on the other. Stuwerviertel is still considered to be an 'island on the island', whose in-habitants relate closely to each other (according to their ethnic backgrounds or their social status), but do not have any contact with the 'office people' of the Nordbahnhof. The street between the two areas (Lassallestrasse) still functions as a socio-spatial divide. This suggests that the new developments did indeed have an impact on social polarization in this area. An area which was formerly relatively homogeneous is now divided: low income groups on the one hand are juxtaposed with business people and élites on the other. The UDP had no integrative effect or dynamism, and can in no way be considered an example of integrated area development (Moulaert *et al.* 2000). On the contrary, the UDP as a whole was never aimed at alleviating social polarization or improving the poor housing conditions of migrants or other less-privileged people. All the projects have been planned and executed with hardly any regard to the resident population.

As yet, the processes of gentrification and socio-spatial displacement have not been observed, although it remains to be seen whether such developments will occur in the future. There are already some signs of change in the quarter: in recent years, a number of 'lofts' in Stuwerviertel have been renovated and transformed into habitable flats. New traffic regulations have been imple-mented and illegal prostitution has been made more difficult. With these new 'lofts' and the construction of more expensive, well-equipped flats, the supply of housing for higher income groups in the area is expanding. As we know from the literature, this could be a first step on the ladder leading to future full-scale gentrification (Dangschat 1999; Friedrichs 1995; Hamnett 2000). The recent process of upgrading substandard housing might result in the gentrification of the whole neighbourhood at the expense of displacing migrants. Although the substandard *Gründerzeit* buildings are not very desirable living spaces, they still represent an affordable home for low income groups. The disappearance of this segment of the housing sector would hit the migrant population of Vienna particularly hard. Whereas Austrians can opt for public housing, this is not possible for migrants. As there are no alternative solutions, the housing situation of migrants will deteriorate, primarily because the density of occupancy in the still existing *Gründerzeit* flats will increase. The socio-spatial polarization in Vienna will therefore be closely linked to the future position of migrants and the methods of 'solving' their housing problems.

9.5. Conclusion and Outlook

The continuing liberal political reforms are part of a more global hegemonic project of deliberate exclusion of some social groups from both decision-making and access to (parts of) the city. In this chapter, we did not discuss access to decision-making power (see Novy *et al.* 2001), but focused on the issue of socio-spatial exclusion. While post-war statutory planning and Fordist-style urban policies aimed at homogenization, the contemporary liberal urban strategies, in contrast, foster fragmentation in the name of pluralism and diversity. In the case of Vienna, these strategies deliberately ignore the two most important forms of social exclusion: the lack of social and political citizenship for migrants and the relative absence of affordable living space for low income groups. The social exclusion of migrants in Vienna is not really part of the concern of the new development projects. This is even more worrying as one of the UDP projects—the Nordbahnhof—is located immediately adjacent to an area with a high proportion of migrants and characterized by continuous tensions between 'Austrians' and 'foreigners'. The public rhetoric about Vienna as an open, international, and cosmopolitan city, building bridges towards Eastern European neighbours, neither corresponds with the everyday Viennese urban experience and Austrian immigration policies nor with the increasingly xenophobic tendencies among the Viennese population (Kohlbacher and Reeger 1999). Racism is deeply rooted in Viennese political culture, dating back at least as far as the anti-Semitism of the Christian-Social Party at the turn of the twentieth century. With emerging new social-liberal modernization policies, aimed at creating an increasingly competitive society, large parts of the population switched to the competition ideology they felt closest to: racism (Becker 2000). The fact that migrants do not have political or social citizenship rights constitutes the very foundation for their socio-spatial segregation. Racism, however, prevents this problem from being tackled at either the national or the local level.

In sum, urban politics in Vienna are experiencing a shift from social democratic strategies based on welfare provision, to social-liberal strategies based on large-scale projects and aimed at favouring the upper-middle classes on the one hand and defensive strategies of preserving the welfare state on the other hand. This shift carries important implications for spatial configurations. While the latter stimulates homogenizing tendencies, the other leads to a fragmented and disjointed urban space. Public funds are no longer evenly distributed over the whole urban territory or focused on disadvantaged areas. They are deliberately invested in the winning parts of the city, the 'flagship' UDPs. Urban policy, thereby, fosters polarization instead of integration. This process may result in more severe social and political struggles about the distribution of the gains of urban development. Struggles over the allocation of public funds and the form of public investment are likely to become more intense in the future. Furthermore, massive changes in the political configuration of the ruling power bloc took place during the 1990s, combined with changes in the degree of access different social actors have to the state. The losers are obviously the working class and low income households. The neo-corporatist and clientelist access to the state is weakened, further eroding access to direct decision-making that was already difficult under social democratic hegemony. Migrants do not partake in political decision-making and have almost no access to public housing. It is particularly ironic that public housing is often actually constructed by migrant workers who are legally excluded from renting the finished product. During the 1990s, only superficial attention was paid to strategies of so-called integrated area development (IAD) that care about winning and losing neighbourhoods at the same time. Neighbourhood management focuses on the poor quarters, in our case study Stuwerviertel, without any concern for integrating these areas with the more upmarket neighbourhoods on the other side of the Lassallestraße.

The chief beneficiary of liberal urban restructuring is real estate capital. At a national level, it pushes for housing rent deregulation, while at the same time calling on the state to upgrade certain local areas within the city to the detriment of other areas. Although it has not yet succeeded in the Nordbahnhof, co-ordinated infrastructure provisioning was successfully implemented in Donau City and the Lassallestraße, and is of crucial importance for real estate capital. New models of governance, as proposed by URBAN, which bring together EU funding with a local public–private partnership might turn out to be an efficient instrument for implementing gentrification in Vienna's downgraded *Gründerzeitvierteln*. Whether or not they will succeed depends primarily on national housing rent regulation. Current national housing regulations make it difficult to evict tenants, thereby empowering the residents to the detriment of real estate capital's interest in substituting more affluent tenants for current ones, in the process of local upgrading and gentrification.

The Urban Development Projects in Vienna have so far fostered the modernization of certain parts of the city and facilitated the incorporation of the city into new transnational productive systems. At the local level, however, this has resulted in polarization in some areas.

The global–local interplay, as popularized by Borja and Castells, tries to capture the process of urbanizing globalization as a deliberate strategy of de-legitimizing the nation state. Our case study does not support the euphoric view that 'it is now local government . . . that . . . can most effectively contribute to improving productive and competitive conditions for the companies on which, in the last analysis, the welfare of the local society depends' (Borja and Castells 1997: 3). The Viennese case study gives clear evidence that decision-making at the *national* level with respect to housing tenure law and to citizenship rights continues to be of utmost importance for the inhabitants of downgraded quarters in Vienna. A new progressive politics of scale must, therefore, link the global and the local to the national. Progressive urban policies must not be manipulated by populist retaliation measures against the nation state (Borja and Castells 1997: 4 ff.). Therefore, 'glocalization' as defined by Swyngedouw is a more analytical concept that emphasizes the struggle over territorial configurations at different spatial scales. 'The struggle over scale and its substantive definition works itself out as a struggle over the command over space and territory' (Swyngedouw 1992: 61). Local politics complement, but cannot replace, supra-local regulations. Following Swyngedouw, the final outcome of liberal urban restructuring in Vienna will depend on the outcome of social and political struggles. It will depend on the concrete form of local strategies for integrated area development as well as on the design of national and EU regulations in the areas of housing, land rents, the welfare state, and citizenship.

Notes

1. As the term 'immigrant' (like 'foreigner') has a very negative connotation in many countries, we prefer to use the term 'migrant' as it is very often used in anti-racist debates and literature.
2. The district Leopoldstadt forms, together with the district Brigittenau, a sort of urban 'island' because the Danube and the Danube canal encircle it on all sides.

References

BARTL-FANNINGER, R. (1994). 'Städtische Freiräume und Migrationen am Beispiel des Max Winter Platzes im 2. Wiener Gemeindebezirk'. Diplomarbeit (Master's thesis). Wirtschaftsuniversität Vienna.
BECKER, J. (2000). 'Der aufhaltsame Aufstieg der FPÖ'. *Das Argument*, 237: 247–57.

——and NOVY, A. (1999). 'Divergence and Convergence of National and Local Regulation: The Case of Austria and Vienna'. *European Urban and Regional Studies*, 7/2: 127–43.

BORJA, J., and CASTELLS, M. (1997). *Local and Global: The Management of Cities in the Information Age.* London: Earthscan.

DANGSCHAT, J. (1999). *Modernisierte Stadt. Gespaltene Gesellschaft. Ursachen von Armut und sozialer Ausgrenzung.* Opladen: Leske and Budrich.

DIFU (Deutsches Institut für Urbanistik) (1995). *Bedeutung weicher Standortfaktoren—Fallstudie Wien.* 2nd draft, Jan. 1995. Berlin.

EIGNER, P., and RESCH, A. (1999). 'Wirtschaft und Stadt. Entwicklungsprozesse in Wien seit 1945'. Manuscript. Vienna.

ESPING-ANDERSEN, G. (1997). *The Three Worlds of Welfare Capitalism.* Cambridge: Polity Press.

FASSMANN, H., *et al.* (1999). 'Ausländische Arbeitskräfte in Deutschland und Österreich', in H. Fassmann *et al.* (eds.), *Abgrenzen—ausgrenzen—aufnehmen. Empirische Befunde zu Fremdenfeindlichkeit in Österreich.* Klagenfurt: Drava Verlag, 95–114.

FRIEDRICHS, J. (1995). *Theorie der Stadtentwicklung.* Opladen: Leske and Budrich.

GIFFINGER, R. (1998). 'Segregation in Vienna: Impacts of Market Barriers and Rent Regulations'. *Urban Studies*, 10/35: 1791–1812.

GÖRG, B. (1999). 'Best of European Cities. Ein intelligenter Stadtvergleich'. *Rathauskorrespondenz*, 9: 1–3.

GRUBELNIK, K. (2000). *Der zweite Anschluss. Deutschlands Griff nach Österreichs Wirtschaft.* Vienna: Molden.

HAMNETT, C. (2000). 'Gentrification, Postindustrialism, and Industrial Occupational Restructuring in Global Cities', in G. Bridge and S. Watson (eds.), *A Companion to the City.* Oxford: Blackwell, 331–41.

HÖBINGER, A. (2001). 'Wirtschaftliche Konsequenzen der EU-Erweiterung für Österreich. Eine Analyse der Auswirkungen auf den Dienstleistungssektor und die Metropole Wien unter besonderer Berücksichtigung des Bankensektors. Ph.D. diss. Wirtschaftsuniversität Vienna.

Ifes (1997). *Stuwerviertel. Bevölkerungsbefragung im Stuwerviertel und in der restlichen Leopoldstadt.* Report. Vienna.

KAUFMANN, A. (1995). 'Wohnsituation und räumliche Verteilung von Zuwanderern im Wiener Stadtgebiet'. *Statistisches Jahrbuch für die Republik Österreich*, Vienna.

——(1999). 'Wohnversorgung und räumliche Verteilung von Zuwanderern im Wiener Stadtgebiet'. *Kurswechsel*, 2: 76–91.

KOHLBACHER, J., and REEGER, U. (1999). 'Wohnnachbarschaft und Ausländerfeindlichkeit', in H. Fassmann *et al.* (eds.), *Abgrenzen-ausgrenzen-aufnehmen. Emprirische Befunde zu Fremdenfeindlichkeit und Integration.* Klagenfurt: Drava Verlag, 115–28.

MA 14 (Magistrat der Stadt Wien) (1999). Bestandsstatistik, at *http://www. magwien.gv.at/VTS/?SEITE=percent2Fma66percent2Fwienzahlpercent2Fi302.htm&S0 =auslper centE4nder#P0*

MA 66 (Magistrat der Stadt Wien). *Statistische Mitteilungen der Stadt Wien,* various issues.

MAYERHOFER, P. (1999). 'Wien ist anders. Spezialisierung und Entwicklungschancen einer nun "internationalen" Stadtregion', in J. Schmee and A. Weigl (eds.), *Wiener*

Wirtschaft 1945–1998. Geschichte—Entwicklungslininen—Perspektiven. Frankfurt-on-Main: Peter Lang Verlag, 39–70.

MAYERHOFER, P. (2000). 'Regionale Effekte der Tertiärisierung in Österreich. Wachstumsgewinne vor allem für die Zentren?', in J. Schmee and M. Mesch (eds.), *Dienstleistungsstandort Wien. Beschäftigung, Innovation, Wettbewerbsfähigkeit.* Frankfurt-on-M.: Peter Lang Verlag, 39–68.

MOULAERT, F., DELVAINQUIÈRE, J. C., and DEMAZIÈRE, C. (2000) (eds.). *Integrated Area Development in European Cities.* London: Oxford University Press.

NOVY, A., REDAK, V., JÄGER, J., HAMEDINGER, A. (2001). 'The End of Red Vienna— Recent Ruptures and Continuities in Urban Governance'. *European Journal of Urban and Regional Studies,* 8/2: 131–44.

REDAK, V., and SCHWAIGER, E. (1999). 'Stadtentwicklung und Segregation. Das Stuwerviertel'. *Kurswechsel,* 2: 69–75.

ROTENBERG, R. (1995). *Landscape and Power in Vienna.* London: John Hopkins.

SCHRÖDER, U. (1993). 'Welt-Stadt. Zum veränderten Verhältnis von Weltausstellung und Stadtentwicklung'. *Leviathan,* 13: 71–88.

SRF (2000). *Immobilienpreisspiegel, www.srf-tuwien.co.at/index/index,* 30 Oct. 2000.

STEINER, K. (1991). 'Das Leitprogramm für den donaunahen Entwicklungsraum'. *Perspektiven,* 6/7: 17–19.

SWYNGEDOUW, E. (1992). 'The Mammon Quest. 'Glocalisation', Interspatial Competition and the Monetary Order: The Construction of New Scales', in M. Dunford and G. Kafkalas (eds.), *Cities and Regions in the New Europe: The Global-Local Interplay and Spatial Development Strategies.* London: Bellhaven Press, 39–67.

TÖDTLING, F. (1984). 'Organisational Characteristics of Plants in Core and Peripheral Regions in Austria'. *Regional Studies,* 18/5: 397–412.

WIENER Integrationsfonds (1996). *Bericht über das Jahr 1996.* Vienna.

——(2000). *Bericht über das Jahr 2000.* Vienna.

10

Restructuring Cities: Miracles and Mirages in Urban Revitalization in Bilbao

Arantxa Rodríguez and Elena Martínez

10.1. Introduction

After two decades of uninterrupted decline, metropolitan Bilbao is experiencing an extraordinary 'urban renaissance'. The basis for this transformation has been the setting up during the 1990s of a myriad of initiatives and projects aimed at reorganizing the physical and socio-economic profile of the city and launching a process of revitalization. Urban policy has played a crucial role in this process, heavily supported by strategic investments in large transport and infrastructure projects that have paved the road to metropolitan regeneration. As a result, in less than a decade, Bilbao has jumped from being an archetype of a declining industrial city to become the new 'Mecca of urbanism' (Masboungi 2001), the flagship of which is the Guggenheim Museum.

At an international level, the recipe of Bilbao's revitalization is widely marketed as an extraordinary success, a unique example of best practice in urban regeneration and a model for any other metropolis similarly plagued by problems of de-industrialization and decline. However, Bilbao's regeneration strategy is far from innovative. On the contrary, Bilbao is something of a latecomer in the adventure of revitalization and has followed closely on the tracks of other old manufacturing cities adopting a revitalization strategy focused around large-scale and emblematic projects.

In this chapter we analyse changes in urban policy formulation and implementation in Bilbao during the 1990s, focusing on urban revitalization strategies. The first section of the chapter presents an analysis of socio-economic restructuring in metropolitan Bilbao. The second section discusses the rise of urban regeneration strategies through a series of key instruments and schemes. The third section focuses on implementation dynamics and changing governance structures. Finally, section 10.4 examines project-led regeneration in

Bilbao through an analysis of a large emblematic urban renewal project, Abandoibarra.

10.2. Restructuring the Manufacturing City

During the last two decades, the dynamics of socio-economic restructuring have radically transformed the urban economy and environment in metropolitan Bilbao. The remaking of the city has followed two distinct stages. From the mid-1970s until the late 1980s, urban change was driven primarily by de-industrialization and productive reorganization processes. Gradually this long phase of economic and urban decline came to a halt at the turn of the decade, as a new cycle of urban development was ushered in by a wide array of urban regeneration initiatives and strategies.

Like so many other old industrial agglomerations in western Europe (Cheshire *et al.* 1988; OECD 1983, 1987), as a leading manufacturing centre and primary port city within Spain, Bilbao suffered intensely from the consequences of restructuring and industrial decline. The crisis of manufacturing hit the city's industrial base particularly hard, due to its specialization in traditional sectors and heavy industry, being thus dominated by so-called mature technologies and being very exposed to international competition (Escudero 1985). Between 1975 and 1996, metropolitan Bilbao lost almost half (47 per cent) of its manufacturing jobs and the share of industrial employment dropped from 46 per cent to 23 per cent. Most of these losses took place in heavy industries such as steel, shipbuilding, machinery, and electrical equipment, concentrated in large Fordist firms with a significant proportion of public ownership.[1] Likewise, the contribution of manufacturing production to the area's gross output[2] fell from 43 per cent to 28 per cent during this period (Eustat 1986; 1991; 1996).

The collapse of manufacturing was somewhat mediated by the slow but continuous growth of services that since the mid-1980s provided practically all net job growth in the metropolitan area. By 1999, this sector accounted for half of total employment and contributed over 55 per cent of the county's gross output. Although the increase in service sector employment has only partly compensated for the loss of manufacturing jobs, this trend reveals a fundamental shift in the urban specialization base, away from manufacturing and towards services. Tertiarization dynamics have also been accompanied by changes in the city's occupational structure, involving a significant fall in the share of manual labour and a rising proportion of technical and managerial occupations[3] throughout the metropolitan area (Rodríguez *et al.* 2001). None the less, the structure of this sector remains closely linked to manufacturing demand maintaining a structural deficit of advanced and specialized services compared to other large metropolitan areas in Spain. This bears critically upon the capacity of Bilbao to retain its traditional role as a directional centre of the Atlantic region.

Manufacturing decline and changes in the hierarchy of sectors have gone hand in hand with a profound reorganization of labour market and income opportunities. Unemployment grew uninterruptedly from 1975, remaining at an alarming 27 per cent in the mid-1990s before the return of economic dynamism pushed this rate down to 16 per cent in 2000 (Eustat 2001). However, falling unemployment rates have been accompanied by an increasing casualization of the urban labour market and industrial relations that have led to growing vulnerability and disadvantage. These factors have also increased the risks of exclusion for large segments of the metropolitan area's population (Rodríguez *et al*. 2001). The extent to which this trend permeates the reorganization of the urban labour market is the rising proportion of non-tenured contracts that in 1998 reached 40 per cent of all contracts (Egailan 1999).

The uneven spatial distribution of industrial job losses, service sector developments, and occupational shifts has played a critical role in reshaping and intensifying the social, economic, and functional divisions of Bilbao's metropolitan space. Municipalities on the left bank of the river, where the mines, port facilities, and large manufacturing plants were located, have accounted for an inordinate proportion (two-thirds) of total job losses and plant closures. They also, consequently, suffer the highest rates of unemployment and socio-economic deprivation. In contrast, the initial concentration in the right bank municipalities of residential and tertiary act functions has been strengthened both by residential transfers from the left bank as well as by the decentralization of new services from the city itself (Martínez and Vicario 1997).[4] Contrasting metropolitan dynamics have led to a pattern of increasing poverty and deprivation within the left bank and the municipality of Bilbao and a widening per capita income gap between metropolitan municipalities and social segments (Rodríguez *et al*. 2001; Martínez and Vicario 1997).

De-industrialization processes have not only left behind a trail of economic decline, unemployment, and rising poverty and deprivation but have also produced a landscape of massive physical and environmental destruction throughout the metropolitan area. The physical consequences of industrial decline are most visible along the riverbanks, the privileged location, for more than a century, of port facilities and heavy industry—notably steel and shipbuilding—highly dependent on the economic and transport functions of the river. The concentrated, exclusive, and high land consumption model associated with these activities displaced other urban functions away from the riverfront and shaped in very fundamental ways the urban structure of metropolitan Bilbao. Since the late 1980s, industrial decline and the transfer of port activity outwards to the seaside have rendered these locations obsolete, transforming them into an extended waterfront of decay and dereliction (see DOTVMA 1993; 1998). A measure of this physical decline is provided by the accumulation of so-called industrial ruins throughout the metropolitan area.

In 1991, a Basque government study identified 158 derelict industrial sites in the metropolitan area of Bilbao, occupying close to 450 ha, and over 3,500 ha of excavated mining grounds (DOTVMA 1993). A decade later, an update inventory still registered more than 330 ha of derelict industrial sites within the metropolitan area (DOTVMA 1998). A large proportion of these sites were located on the riverfront especially along the left bank of the river Nervión, the manufacturing heart of the city, where close to two-thirds of the classified industrial land was derelict (DUVMA 1994).

By the early 1990s, after almost two decades of continuing economic, functional, and physical disintegration, the profile of Bilbao had become decidedly that of a declining industrial city (DEP 1989). This trend was further aggravated by an absolute disregard, on the part of policy-makers, of the urban/ metropolitan scale as a relevant sphere of intervention and the absence of any strategy to reverse urban decline. Thus, while a number of metropolitan areas in Spain—notably Barcelona and Seville but also others—were taking advantage of the economic recovery of the late 1980s to launch massive urban redevelopment schemes and projects (MOPU 1990; Arias 2001), Bilbao seemed hopelessly trapped in a spiral of endless decline.

However, the beginning of the 1990s marked a turning-point in the city's evolution as the active search for new sources of growth and advantage opened up a new phase of urban restructuring in Bilbao. This shift was supported, first, by growing awareness of the distinct urban dimensions of decline and of the need to move beyond sector policies towards more territorially targeted and more integrated policies. Second, this awareness went hand in hand with increasing recognition of the links between urban/metropolitan dynamics and regional development that placed Bilbao at the centre of a strategic debate on the region's future prospects and development policies (DEP 1989).[5] And third, the return of economic growth in the late 1980s also gave a new impetus to urban redevelopment initiatives, geared to take advantage of expansive conditions. In this context, the search for urban regeneration became the basis for a new consensus on the need to intervene actively and strategically in the metropolitan area.

10.3. Urban Regeneration Policies in Bilbao: From Spatial and Strategic Planning to Project-led Revitalization

After years of prolonged socio-economic and physical decline and of startling passivity on the part of institutional and political agents, urban regeneration jumped to centre stage in Bilbao at the turn of the 1990s. All of a sudden, the city, or rather the metropolitan area, was rediscovered as a privileged site of intervention, as a myriad of projects, plans, and revitalization schemes were put forward. The turn to regeneration was accompanied by critical innovations in urban policy formulation and implementation, including the development of new planning instruments and governance institutions (Rodríguez 1995; Esteban 2000). These innovations were largely a response to shifting priorities, notably the emphasis on promoting urban competitiveness and growth. But policy innovations were also precipitated by the continuing challenges to planning and the search for more (so-called) effective means of improving urban performance. In the process, regulatory procedures gave way to more active and targeted forms of intervention (Rodríguez and Martínez 2001). Thus, as in other metropolitan areas throughout Europe (Hall 1996), urban regeneration strategies in Bilbao spearheaded the emergence of a new mode of intervention in the city. This new model was structured around three main axes: (*a*) a proactive approach to spatial planning, (*b*) the adoption of strategic planning, and (*c*) large-scale urban projects and infrastructure.

10.3.1. Spatial planning for economic regeneration

The 1990s began with an extraordinary mobilization of planning initiatives in Bilbao that put an end to a prolonged period of passivity and stagnation in urban policy-making. In contrast to other large cities in Spain where the return to democratic rule had been followed by the production of very innovative urban development plans and statutory norms (Terán 1996; Alonso 1999), Bilbao was surprisingly diffident in making use of its newly restored planning powers. The abrogation in December 1980 of the Greater Bilbao Corporation (the metropolitan authority set up during Francoist times) did not lead to an immediate updating of spatial planning at a municipal level and the Metropolitan Plan of 1963 remained in force for almost another decade. Finally, after a long impasse, the presentation of the Draft of the new Bilbao Master Plan in May 1989 signalled a turning-point and the beginning of a new phase of urban development policy in the city.

The starting-point of Bilbao's Master Plan was the process of decline and the loss of the centrality experienced by the city since the mid-1970s. Consequently, the primary objective of the Plan was to reverse urban decline and re-establish the position of the city as the dynamic financial and service centre for the so-called Atlantic Arch region (AB 1989: 19). In order to do so, the Plan focused on a number of key renewal operations of brownfield areas left behind by plant closures or relocation of manufacturing activity and infrastructure such as obsolete railway and port facilities. These derelict sites were seen as providing critical redevelopment opportunities for the location of new residential and economic functions, as well as the production of emblematic areas and infrastructures related to centrality and capital city functions. Specifically, the Master Plan draft defined four so-called 'opportunity areas': (*a*) Abandoibarra, a 35 ha industrial and inner-port enclave in the downtown area, to be transformed into the new business and symbolic centre of the city; (*b*) Zorrozaurre, a large badly degraded inner-city industrial area, projected as a new mixed residential and tertiary waterfront sequel to Abandoibarra; (*c*) Ametzola/Eskurtze, a 22 ha site occupied by a railyard and freight stations to be converted to passenger traffic and reclaimed for residential uses; and (*d*) the abandoned mining sites of Miribilla and El Morro, comprising more than 90 ha designated for residential development.

The redevelopment of derelict sites was the leitmotif of the Plan's proposals, as well as its primary means for urban regeneration. In particular, Abandoibarra and Zorrozaurre played a strategic role, since their renewal was tied to the production of highly qualified spaces for the location of dynamic tertiary activities and capital city functions. These 'new centrality' areas were planned to become directional business centres on a regional scale, contributing to enhancing the city's competitive position in the changing urban hierarchy. Emblematic renewal operations were, therefore, the fundamental instrument for urban regeneration, providing the physical conditions necessary to transform Bilbao into a new post-industrial capital of the Atlantic region.

Urban regeneration was also the driving force of a metropolitan-level planning scheme that started to be drafted, almost in parallel with the new Bilbao Master Plan. The guidelines for this metropolitan plan emphasized the need for physical and spatial restructuring as a necessary—although not sufficient—condition for metropolitan regeneration. Spatial restructuring rested, fundamentally, on taking advantage of the new development opportunities offered by derelict sites left behind by productive reorganization and plant closures. The proposal identified seven 'opportunity sites' along the banks of the river, occupying an area of around 600 ha. The recovery of these sites was perceived as a historic opportunity for realizing the potential for tertiarization of the regional and metropolitan economy and for relaunching a new urban development phase in exactly the same locations that earlier had led the process of industrialization (Leira and Quero 1992).

The first draft of the metropolitan planning directive (*Plan Territorial Parcial*), presented in 1994, put forward a scheme based on the removal of obsolete industrial and infrastructure facilities and substandard housing located on both sides of the riverbank, releasing that land for alternative productive and residential uses (DUVMA 1994). The proposal centred on the redevelopment of key opportunity sites for tertiary and leisure-related activities structured around a metropolitan road axis that acted as the organizing as well as the catalysing element of metropolitan change. This initial proposal was subject to numerous amendments before a final draft was presented in 1997. However, lack of consensus among political groups and among the different institutions involved, combined with considerable financing difficulties, led to the withdrawal of the draft and the commissioning of a new proposal that remains under preparation.

10.3.2. In search of a strategy: the Strategic Plan for Metropolitan Revitalization

One of the first initiatives to focus on metropolitan decline was the strategic debate on the future of the Basque Country launched by the Basque government at the end of 1988. The 'economic revitalization of metropolitan Bilbao' was at the centre of these debates. The result was a series of proposals for promoting economic recovery including the need to develop new territorial planning and policy tools to guide the process of revitalization. In particular, the recommendations pointed to the adoption of strategic planning to fix a coherent set of short- and medium-term objectives that could provide a framework of consensus, co-ordination between public institutions, and partnership with the private sector for carrying out different initiatives and projects (DEP 1989). The outcome of this process was the drafting, three years later, of the Strategic Plan for the Revitalization of Metropolitan Bilbao. At the same time, a public–private partnership, Bilbao Metropoli-30, was set up to implement and give continuity to the process of strategic planning (Martínez 1993).

The revitalization strategy put forward in the Strategic Plan was structured around eight 'critical issues' or policy areas, reflecting the metropolitan economy's strengths and weaknesses: investment in human resources, development of advanced services, mobility and accessibility, urban and environmental regeneration, cultural centrality, co-ordinated management of public and private sectors and social action. For each of these areas, the Plan defined specific goals and targets and means and strategies that were then transformed into a series of action Plans to be developed by the relevant public and private actors. Thus, the Plan projected an integrated vision of problems and actions to be carried out in a co-ordinated manner by the different public and private agents. In this way, strategic planning provided for a model of intervention based on an active, integrating, and co-operative strategy on a metropolitan scale (Esteban 2000).

Ten years after the launching of the strategic planning process, in April 2001, Metropoli-30 presented the new strategic guidelines for a second wave of revitalization. The new proposal, 'Strategy 2010', focuses around capitalizing on the socio-economic and urban regeneration achievements of the previous phase of revitalization that had placed Bilbao 'amongst the most modern and vanguard European cities today' to transform it over the next decade into—nothing less than—a 'global city' (Metropoli-30 2001). This rather overstated vision reveals the extent to which strategic planning has been stripped of any pretension of playing a substantive role in the process of metropolitan regeneration and remains more and more at the level of idealized modelling.

However, regardless of the concrete material effects on Bilbao's regeneration process, territorial strategic planning has made a significant contribution to urban policy formulation. First, it has helped decisively in the creation of an integrated framework for discussing and defining policy initiatives and projects at the metropolitan scale, validating this level as the functional and relevant unit for territorial intervention and regeneration strategies. Second, strategic planning has contributed critically to generating a dynamic of collaboration, consensus formation, and co-operation among different institutional and private agents. Nevertheless, despite these critical contributions, strategic planning has not succeeded in becoming an effective instrument for guiding and supporting integrated urban policies in Bilbao. The lack of a clear demarcation of planning capacities and of an organic linking of the promoting institutions, combined with limited institutional and political involvement, have eroded drastically the potential of the Strategic Plan to play a propulsive role and act as the articulating force for decisions and initiatives.

10.3.3. Large-scale infrastructures and project-led regeneration

The third linchpin of urban regeneration strategies in Bilbao has been massive investment in large transport and infrastructure projects. These projects have played a fundamental role in urban regeneration acting as catalysers of change and creating the conditions for site redevelopment at numerous locations. Besides, transport and infrastructure investments have also paved the way for a new model of intervention in the city, based on large-scale urban projects that are commonly developed on derelict industrial sites and obsolete infrastructure. These large-scale redevelopment operations had already become an important urban policy tool in other cities in Spain in the second half of the 1980s (MOPU 1990); they included a variety of schemes, from the building or remodelling of large-scale transport infrastructure in cities (ports, airports, railways, or urban roadways), to the development of large-scale service infrastructures, land redevelopment for economic activities, large international events, and rehabilitation projects (Arias 2001). The paradigm for this large project-led urban redevelopment model was the urban operations carried out in Barcelona and Seville in 1992.

In Bilbao, project-led redevelopment was spearheaded by investments in key transport infrastructures: (*a*) the building of the Metro and the reorganization of the metropolitan railway system; (*b*) the expansion of the port and its connected railway operations; and (*c*) the construction of the new airport terminal. These projects were rounded off by important investments in other infrastructure, notably the Guggenheim Museum.

The building of the new underground system, the Metro, was a first sign of the changing urban development context in Bilbao. After fifteen years of debate, the construction of this began in 1989 and provided the city with significantly more than a new mode of transport; the Metro became a symbol of the new dynamism driving public intervention in the city and of Bilbao's evolving image bolstered by the effective aesthetic content of Norman Foster's design. The opening of Line 1 in 1995, after an investment of almost 500 million Euro—co-financed by the Basque government and the Bizkaia County

Council—became a milestone for the change of direction. Work on Line 2, along the Left Bank, began two years later, at an estimated cost of close to 240 million Euro.

The construction of the Metro coincided with the plans for extending the Port of Bilbao, an operation promoted by the Basque government and the Port Authority within the framework of the Infrastructure Agreement signed by the Basque and Central administrations in February 1989. This Agreement included extending the outer port surface area as well as significant restructuring of railway and road infrastructures to improve the port's communications. Work on the port extension began in 1993 and the first phase finished six years later, after an investment of 210.4 million Euro. The second phase, with an estimated cost of 390.7 million Euro, is already under way and will be completed by 2005.

As in many other port and manufacturing cities, the releasing of inner-port areas has supplied important redevelopment opportunities in metropolitan Bilbao. But these opportunities have been sustained by massive investments in new facilities elsewhere. Therefore, the modernization of the port has played a critical part in urban redevelopment, allowing for the transfer of dock and warehousing activity out of inner-port areas and liberating them for new urban uses and functions. Two of the most emblematic urban renewal operations developed during the 1990s in Bilbao, Abandoibarra and Ametzola, were dependent upon relocation of activity to new outer port facilities.

The remodelling of Bilbao Airport was also part of the transport and infrastructure investments included in the Infrastructure Agreement signed by the Basque and central administrations in 1989. After numerous delays and adjustments in the original project, work on the airport extension began at the end of 1995 with the construction of the new passenger terminal, designed by Santiago Calatrava. The terminal, the cost of which reached 60.1 million Euro, was opened in November 2000, improving not only accessibility and external communications but also contributing decisively to promoting a new image of Bilbao as an innovative and dynamic city.

Finally, project-led regeneration achieved its ultimate expression in the most emblematic initiative of the early 1990s: the location of a Guggenheim Museum in Bilbao. Negotiations on the building of a branch of the Museum started in the middle of 1991 between the Basque administration and the Guggenheim Foundation. Held in extreme secrecy, negotiations progressed rapidly to such concrete matters as the financing of the project, the choice of architect, and the location of the Museum within the city, leading to the signing of a preliminary agreement in December of that year. The basis for agreement was a timely convergence of interests between the Guggenheim Foundation, actively engaged in a strategy of internationalization as a means to overcome severe financial difficulties, and the Basque authorities desperately in search of an emblem that could transform, if not the city's productive base, at least Bilbao's image as a declining industrial centre. However, the agreement was critically backed up by the Basque institutions' fiscal autonomy, which guaranteed 100 per cent of the financing of the project that reached almost 144 million Euro. In the absence of more traditional sources of foreign investment, the location of the Guggenheim Museum branch contributed effectively in raising Bilbao's international profile while placing it among cities that incorporated cultural initiatives as a key instrument of urban regeneration (see Bianchini and Parkinson 1993; Kearns and Philo 1993; for the case of Bilbao see Gómez 1998).

In any event, the signing of a preliminary agreement for the location of a branch of the Guggenheim Museum in Bilbao was soon followed by the City Council's approval of the project and allocation of land in Abandoibarra—before a detailed plan for this area had begun to be drafted. Construction work on the Museum started in October 1993, only a few months after the proposal of Cesar Pelli and Associates for the planning of Abandoibarra had been selected in the second International Competition of Ideas. The opportunity opened up by Frank Gehry's design allowed a highly risky project whose success many still find surprising. Nevertheless, the situating of the Museum in Abandoibarra strengthened Abandoibarra's emblematic character and contributed decisively to valorizing the site, thus guaranteeing the financial viability of the Abandoibarra operation.

To sum up, the 1990s opened with the development of a number of large-scale transport and infrastructure projects that provided the basis of a new model of intervention in the city. In Bilbao, this type of project-driven urbanism was particularly tied to the exploitation and valorization of redevelopment opportunities generated by the dismantling of (heavy) industry and the reform of railway and port infrastructure to launch a process of metropolitan regeneration. Bilbao thus followed in the wake of numerous European and North American cities that had made large-scale urban projects the paradigmatic instrument of planning for regeneration.

10.4. Implementing Urban Regeneration: Consensus Planning, Competitive Management, and New Governance Structures

The shift towards a project-led approach to urban redevelopment has been accompanied by very fundamental changes in policy implementation in the city and the emergence of new governance structures (Rodríguez 1995; Esteban 2000; Rodríguez and Martínez 2001). Paradoxically, focused and fragmented projects have come hand in hand with a renewed emphasis on consensus building and collaboration between different institutional levels and cooperation and partnership between the private and public sectors, as being crucial for guaranteeing their success. The complex nature of these urban operations, the scale of intervention, the interdependence of institutional levels, the high financing costs, their integrated character, etc., are seen to require new management schemes in order to enhance flexible responses, to adapt rapidly to changing circumstances, and to facilitate co-ordination among the different agents (Borja and Castells 1997). 'Collaborative advantage' (Font 1997) takes on a full strategic meaning within the management of large-scale urban projects, as the dynamics of collaboration, partnership, and consensus building are defining elements of these schemes.

In Bilbao, as in other cities in Spain, the setting up of large urban redevelopment projects and integrated transport–urbanism–environment operations has been tied, since the mid-1980s, to the spread of concerted action (Arias 1999; MOPT 1993). The search for consensus rested initially on the inter-institutional agreement on infrastructure signed by the central and Basque administrations in 1989, in which such initiatives as the airport extension and the remodelling of the airport terminal were defined. Later, following the strategic operations in Seville, Barcelona, and Madrid in response to the international events of 1992 (Universal Exhibition, the Olympic Games, and the Cultural Capital of Europe, respectively), the Ministry of Public Works, Transport and the Environment (MOPTMA) launched a new policy for cities based on concerted schemes for developing integrated transport, urbanism, and environmental operations. This initiative aimed at spreading the logic of large-scale urban development operations, as applied in Seville and Barcelona, to other cities. Bilbao was singled out as one of the first candidates for carrying out these concerted operations (Arias 1999).

Within this framework of co-ordinated strategic actions, the regeneration of metropolitan Bilbao was considered a 'State operation'. This priority status responded, first, to the alarming economic and functional decline of the area and the concentration of derelict industrial land and obsolete transport facilities belonging to the central administration. Second, this status was also justified by the key strategic position of Bilbao as an economic and functional pole within the Atlantic region. In the context of this new policy for cities launched by MOPTMA, in November 1991 the Basque and central administrations signed an agreement to set up a consortium to carry out integrated transport, urban development, and environmental projects within the metropolitan area of Bilbao. The setting up of Bilbao Ría 2000 in November 1992 gave a fundamental push to the new urban policy model and opened up a new phase in the revitalization of metropolitan Bilbao.

The creation of Ría 2000 can be explained by a combination of three critical factors. First, there was the emerging consensus on the need to concentrate efforts and carry out co-ordinated actions for the revitalization of Bilbao. Co-operation, partnership, and collaborative advantage became synonyms of good governance. A second factor was the recognition of extraordinary land management difficulties related to the landownership structure of derelict sites that required *concertación*, that is, agreement among the different agents involved. And a third factor was the extremely high costs of renewal operations and the imperative of financial self-sufficiency as a condition for urban renovation initiatives—a factor that called for more entrepreneurial forms of management. The three factors converge in the complex distribution of competencies, powers, and funds created by the decentralization of the Spanish state during the transition to democracy. Far from settled, the administrative/political division of labour creates a constant arena of conflict and negotiation. In the case of urban regeneration in Abandoibarra, this dynamic is further complicated by the location of urban planning powers at the local level and fiscal powers at the regional one, while landownership is overwhelmingly held by public firms and institutions of the central administration.

In the context of the budgetary austerity following the large-scale events of 1992, plans for developing co-ordinated strategic actions were based on self-financing. Urban operations had to be managed in a way that minimized any contribution of public capital from the ordinary budget, so that formulas for financing from outside the budget had to be found. The financial commitment of the central government was limited to the handing over of land owned by state companies in the city and the capital gains that these might generate in the property market. The relinquishing of this income by the Port Authority was compensated for by the newly equipped installations which form part of the port extension; as far as the railway companies are concerned, FEVE and RENFE surrendered their land to Ría 2000 in exchange for the work carried out on the railway infrastructure. The system of financing was based on the surrender of some of the land held by state companies (industrial or infrastructures) which the City Council then proceeded to re-qualify for new urban use, thus allowing, after the necessary investment for re-urbanization, the revaluation of the land and the generation of capital gains on their sale; these profits financed the re-urbanization work and the provision of the necessary infrastructure. The imperative of financial self-sufficiency enforced a rationale of financial balance, in which the viability of operations was guaranteed by the fact that the costs of urbanization and of reinvestment in infrastructure were met by the sales prices of the land.

Bilbao Ría 2000 began operations with two outstanding projects in Bilbao that were outlined in the Master Plan: Abandoibarra and Ametzola. The central location of Abandoibarra and the fact that most of the land (almost 95 per cent) belonged to public companies and bodies (RENFE, INI, Port Authority, and Bilbao Council) were decisive factors in the choice of this area as the launch pad for Ría 2000's intervention. The transformation of this old industrial–port area (35 ha) into the new directional centre of the city made it the emblematic project par excellence. This operation was linked to the construction of the southern rail bypass, mentioned above, in line with the reorganization of the railway system for passengers and goods, scrapping the

Olabeaga–La Naja section which passed through Abandoibarra separating it from the Ensanche, diverting the local train service to the southern rail bypass, and extending and covering over the railway cutting as far as Ametzola. This operation has made it possible to cover the railway sidings of three goods stations and logistic areas in Ametzola (11 ha), allowing the land to be redeveloped for residential use. Ría 2000 later went on to include action in Barakaldo on the banks of the river Galindo on lands previously belonging to Altos Hornos de Vizcaya, which had been turned over to Bizkaia County Council because of tax debts. This operation, aimed at recovering an area of 50 ha for productive, residential, and leisure use, was linked to an urban regeneration project in the adjacent neighbourhood. In the year 2000, the society widened its area of intervention to Bilbao La Vieja, where it participated in the financing of some actions within the integrated regeneration plan.

The development of the Abandoibarra–southern rail bypass–Ametzola operation marks the beginning of a new stage in the management of city planning in Bilbao and the metropolitan area based on co-ordinated, integrated, and focused actions aimed at improving the flexibility and efficiency of intervention. The transfer of planning and executive powers to Ría 2000 shifts the traditional structures out of the hard core of strategic action management. This is not immune to conflict and polemic. On the one hand, despite its status as a private company with public capital and its basically executive allotted role, Ría 2000 acts, in fact, as a public agency with significant capacity to determine planning functions, since it takes decisions over priorities for intervention, use of land and other properties, and management of public funds to develop initiatives. And, although traditional regulating instruments are still the legal reference, the new dynamics of application, execution, and management have had the effect of reducing the importance of these as mechanisms for city planning. In this way, Ría 2000 has gradually relegated the traditional planning departments to a subordinate level, taking over an increasing number of powers related to urban revitalization, including the management of the most emblematic operations and projects in the city and the metropolitan area.

A key feature of Ría 2000 is that it acts as a form of public–public partnership to deal with operations in cases where the property or the decision-making capacity is shared among several institutional bodies. It manages the concerted decisions for strategic intervention. Although these operations are determined through standard planning procedures, Ría 2000 retains considerable planning powers regarding priorities for intervention, disposal of land and other property, building characteristics, and the management of public funds for redevelopment. And, while regulatory planning instruments are still the legal reference, the dynamics of implementation and their relevance as guiding tools has diminished considerably.

On the other hand, the status of Ría 2000 as a private management company poses urgent questions about the relative weight granted to objectives of financial viability and the profitability of actions, objectives characteristic of a company that has to maintain financial balance and remain self-financing, and those that fitted with its strategic and social actions, regeneration, improvement in quality of life, etc., which do not meet these criteria. The demands of self-financing can also drastically condition the ability of this structure to carry out other regeneration initiatives in run-down areas or in projects where financial profitability cannot be guaranteed. This type of budget restriction could lead to the exclusion of less profitable projects: those that are not located in central areas where property development offers lower returns. In this sense, for the sake of greater technical efficiency, this town-planning company leaves its social and political legitimacy open to question.

In sum, the significance of Ría 2000 lies in its considerable potential as a co-ordinating and executive agency and its capacity to act as a unified body in urban redevelopment schemes in metropolitan Bilbao, thus vastly improving the prospects of implementation. However, Ría 2000's status as a private firm poses critical questions regarding the 'privatization' of planning and the lack of political accountability. Moreover, the self-financing restrictions imposed upon Ría 2000 may drastically limit its capacity to carry out other regeneration initiatives in derelict areas outside of central locations. In fact, the overwhelming concern with financial feasibility, as a guiding principle for intervention, may well prove this model to be inapplicable to sites other than central areas of high commercial potential. In this sense, the social and political legitimization of quasi-privatized planning, on the grounds of superior technical efficiency, may be jeopardized. Moreover, the imperative of short-term profit logic introduces a speculative bend to the agency's operation, which severely undermines its regeneration objectives. If urban regeneration means something more than physical renewal, then equity and redistribution considerations must mediate efficiency.

10.5. Abandoibarra: Project-led Regeneration in Bilbao

In Bilbao, project-led urban regeneration was most clearly expressed in Abandoibarra, a 35 ha manufacturing and port enclave on the left bank waterfront, in the residential and tertiary heart of the city. Physically cut off from the surrounding residential areas by a railway track and a 10 m level difference, the economic functions of this area contributed to reinforcing its segregated and residual quality. During the 1970s, Abandoibarra suffered steady decline as a result of the transfer of dock activity to outer port locations and the crisis of manufacturing that reached its zenith after the closure of the Euskalduna shipyards in the mid-1980s. However, the privileged location of this enclave within the central district allowed for this decay to be interpreted as a unique opportunity to eliminate obsolete uses and functions and transform it into the flagship of a new post-industrial urban model. The demolition in 1992 of the shipyards marks the turning-point for Abandoibarra and its transformation

Table 10.1. Abandoibarra's chronology

Data	Quest
1989	
May	Closure of Euskalduna shipyards
	Draft of new Bilbao Master Plan (PGOU)
1991	
May	The association Bilbao Metropoli-30 is set up
July	Competition of Ideas for the Bilbao Guggenheim Museum. Frank Gehry's design selected
December	Signing of the agreement between the Guggenheim Foundation and the Basque government to set up a branch of the Guggenheim Museum in Bilbao
December	The Bilbao City Council allocates land for the location of the Bilbao Guggenheim Museum in Abandoibarra
December	Competition of Ideas for the Congress and Concert Hall to be sited in Abandoibarra. The project by F. Soriano and D. Palacios chosen
1992	
May	Competition of Ideas for redevelopment of Abandoibarra
June	Metropoli-30 presents the Strategic Plan for the Revitalization of Metropolitan Bilbao
November	Bilbao Ría 2000, a limited company, is set up to manage urban redevelopment schemes in metropolitan Bilbao
1993	
February	II International competition for Abandoibarra's redevelopment where Cesar Pelli's proposal is selected
October	Work on the Guggenheim Museum starts
1994	
December	The City Council votes the final approval of Bilbao Master Plan (27 Dec. 94)
1995	
March	Work on the Southern Railway Pass begins
April	Municipality planners present the detail plan (PERI) for Abandoibarra
1996	
	Work on the Euskalduna Congress and Concert Hall starts
1997	
February	Abandoibarra's redevelopment work begins
March	The Architects Professional Association presents its alternative for Abandoibarra. This is dismissed by Ría 2000 and the Bilbao City Council
	The City Council of Bilbao asks Cesar Pelli to draft a new detail plan for Abandoibarra
October	The Bilbao Guggenheim Museum starts operating
1998	
July	Pelli presents a new redevelopment scheme for Abandoibarra
October	The County Council of Bizkaia (Diputación) approves the transfer of its administrative offices to Abandoibarra's emblematic tower (55.000 m²)
1999	
February	The Euskalduna Congress and Concert Hall is inaugurated
April	Pelli's new detail plan (PERI) is approved by Bilbao City Council
April	Ría 2000 starts selling the first residential land lots in Abandoibarra
2000	
March	Work on the building of the Sheraton Hotel begins
May	Work on the Ribera Park starts
May	Building of Abandoibarra's new pedestrian bridge begins
October	Work begins on the Zubiarte shopping mall

into a so-called 'new centrality area' at the metropolitan as well as the regional level.

10.5.1. Abandoibarra: a new directional centre?

The regeneration of Abandoibarra took off with the presentation, in May 1989, of the draft of the new Bilbao Master Plan in which Abandoibarra was identified as one of the most emblematic spaces within the city and an area of extraordinary urban potential. The Plan assigned Abandoibarra a strategic role, proposing its conversion into a new business centre, a specialized area for the location of advanced services and complementary retail and leisure facili-ties, including a number of emblematic infrastructures—originally a science and technology museum and a conference hall. Thus, while the Plan cancelled the site's industrial designation, it still retained its fundamental productive character, projecting it as a new directional area capable of driving the process of metropolitan regeneration and articulating a leadership position for Bilbao in the Atlantic Arch (AB 1989). Moreover, the draft proposal excluded, explic-itly, any residential development in Abandoibarra thus emphasizing its stra-tegic and directional profile.

The production of a detailed plan for Abandoibarra has followed a long and difficult process. Formally, this process began with the call for a competition of ideas in May 1992 and concluded in April 1999 when the City Council approved the detailed plan (Plan Especial de Reforma Interior, PERI) for Abandoibarra. In the process, Cesar Pelli's original design, selected in the com-petition, has been subject to continuous changes in order to accommodate shifting priorities and real estate market conditions.

Following the Master Plan's guidelines, Pelli projected Abandoibarra as an extension of the central district towards the riverfront, adopting a standard waterfront layout with a strong symbolic content. Pelli's proposal fixed the directional and strategic character of the area by designating over 200,000 m^2 of 'high level' tertiary space and key infrastructures including an international congress and concert hall and the Guggenheim Museum, for which land had already been designated. This scheme was almost immediately modified to take into account the Council's request to minimize any risks involved in the real estate operation by dividing up the large office tower planned by Pelli into two or more smaller buildings. Subsequently, uncertainty about the capacity of the local real estate market to absorb the projected supply of office space continued to encourage a shift in balance towards a higher proportion of residential and retail uses that are seen as being much more profitable and secure (Esteban 2000).[6] By the time the first draft of the detailed plan was approved, in 1995, the tertiary and strategic focus of the Abandoibarra operation had been severely undermined by predominantly short-term financial feasibility logic.

However, the new design for Abandoibarra failed to obtain the necessary political support and was fiercely contested by different social groups. A coalition of neighbourhood organizations, mobilized against the high density and speculative bias of the operation, and retail associations, alarmed by the location of a large shopping centre in Abandoibarra, was backed up by the local architects' professional society, which felt marginalized from the design of the city's most emblematic redevelopment scheme. And, while the institutions in charge quickly dismissed an alternative design presented by this coalition in 1997, it added to a sense of uncertainty and lack of definition in the project. To break this impasse, the City Council decided to revoke the plan and commissioned Pelli to draft a new detailed plan according to its original design but adapting it to the new socio-economic and real estate market context. The new PERI concentrated tertiary spaces in a single emblematic tower allocated to the Diputación, the county-level government, and two small adjacent buildings; limited residential use to four blocks; and increased the total area assigned to green and open spaces. It also modified significantly the design and size of the shopping mall, as well as the road infrastructure—incorporating a new tramway access. In sum, it envisaged a building area of 211,000 m^2 with 74,000 m^2 for office space, 700 housing units—25,000 m^2, 30,000 m^2 of culture and higher education infrastructures, and 170,000 m^2 of green and open spaces. This detailed plan was finally approved by the City Council in April 1999, six years after the first proposal had been presented and after four years of constant changes and uncertainty. By then, the two emblematic infrastructures, the Guggenheim Museum and the Euskalduna Congress and Concert Hall, were already in operation, the shopping centre had been allocated, and the first housing lots had been sold (see Plate 10.1).

Plate 10.1. Cesar Pelli's Plan for the redevelopment of Abandoibarra

Thus, the regeneration of Abandoibarra has followed a long and very complex evolution. In the process, the project has shifted its original productive and directional focus towards residential and consumption-oriented functions. This shift has been encouraged by the difficulties perceived by the managing institutions in valorizing Abandoibarra's land on the basis of strategic office developments and the greater financial opportunities offered by the residential real estate market. Given the constraints on financial self-sufficiency, the feasibility of the project was then secured by the speculative increase in housing prices, tagged to the expansion of demand in luxury housing in the city and the effect of the real estate boom of the mid-1990s. The decision adopted by the county government in the summer of 1997, to relocate all its offices to Abandoibarra, contributed to further undermining of the strategic pull of the area, conceived initially as attracting private capital investment in advanced services. Thus, the public rather than the private sector, and the local rather than the international initiative, continued to secure the impetus for the development of the area.

10.5.2. *Lights and shadows of success in Abandoibarra*

The Abandoibarra operation is widely presented as a success story of urban regeneration. This assessment rests predominantly on the perceived impact of this development on the physical renovation, functional reorganization, and image transformation of the metropolis. However, a detailed analysis of the initiative suggests reasons for a more sober evaluation.

At the level of the city as a whole, the impact of the Abandoibarra operation should be measured against its capacity to achieve its original strategic objectives: to enhance the competitiveness of the city: to attract international investments; to acquire key command functions and high level producer services; and to diversify its productive base. Since the project is still in its implementation phase, a whole assessment in these terms will have to wait. None the less, some patterns of change can already be distinguished by looking at the impact of Abandoibarra's regeneration scheme on real estate markets and on the development of new functions in the city.

- **Speculative renewal and the impact on the real estate market:** The impact of the project on real estate markets concerns mostly Abandoibarra's neighbouring districts. The overriding tendency in the last four years has been towards reinforcing price increase tensions in the adjoining areas, especially in the most expensive neighbourhoods, Abando-Indautxu but also the Campo Volantín and Deusto, on the opposite side of the river and facing the project. This perception is supported by evidence from the dynamics of the housing sector during 1998 and 1999; while housing prices in the city increased by an average of 10 to 15 per cent,[7] in the Abando district the increase was 30 to 40 per cent, thus reflecting a tendency towards increasing price differentials within the city. A highly contained supply relative to demand, limited land availability for construction, and the high expectations created by the Abandoibarra project are considered to account for this differential rise. Already, the estimated price for these units has more than tripled the initial valuation of Ría 2000 from 810 Euro/m^2 in 1995 to 2,810 Euro/m^2 in 1999. The diffusion of this increase in the housing market to surrounding neighbourhoods is already under way. At the same time, the transfer of the required legal quota of lower income housing initially located in Abandoibarra to another urban operation in Ametzola has formidably enhanced the luxury and élitist character of this development.

The market for office space will also be strongly affected by the development of almost 90,000 m^2 in Abandoibarra. A large share of this supply, almost 60 per cent, is already allocated to the Diputación, the provincial-level government. The transfer of all the Diputación's departments and services to Abandoibarra's singular skyrise will liberate over 40,000 m^2 of prime office space in the centre of the city. The selling of that stock to one or more promoters is a precondition to financing the cost of transferring its facilities to Abandoibarra. The release and placing into circulation of that stock is considered to be the 'most important real estate market operation in the history of Bilbao' for which the Diputación actively seeks the engagement of international promoters. This is a risky operation because of the potential saturating impact of the market, especially if developments in alternative locations, currently under way, prosper. Alternatively, this effect could be somewhat compensated by reallocating part of the central district's housing stock currently being used for office purposes to residential use as a result of the transfer of service firms to the new facilities in Abandoibarra. The market for retail space is also being affected by the allocation of over 30,000 m^2 in Abandoibarra. Local retail associations have stressed the threat that the shopping mall poses to traditional commercial areas of the city centre, notably Casco Viejo, Abando, and Indautxu. However, it is too early to anticipate the potential shifts and displacements in this market. So far, the most visible outcome is an increase of close to 30 per cent in the price of retail space in the area next to the Guggenheim, as well as the opening up of fast food places and tourist-oriented shops.

Finally, the spill-over effects of Abandoibarra on the real estate market would depend very much on the price-setting dynamics of the final products of the site itself. However, escalating reference prices last year provide some preliminary signs to this effect.

- **The Guggenheim 'effect':** Alternatively, the impact of the Abandoibarra development operation can be considered in relation to the effects of the location of one of its most emblematic projects: the Guggenheim Bilbao Museum (GBM). This project was born in the early part of the 1990s, at a time when the whole scheme for Abandoibarra was still being drafted. And, while the decision to locate the Museum in the Abandoibarra site was made a posteriori, the initiative was clearly in tune with the strategic objectives of

Plate 10.2. Abandoibarra site, 2002

the urban regeneration operation. In both cases, the search for alternative economic activities capable of replacing manufacturing as the engine of economic and urban growth was part of the general philosophy of the project.

The so-called 'Guggenheim effect' operates, firstly, in the realm of the symbolic. Already before its opening date in October 1997, the GBM had become the outstanding icon for the revitalization of metropolitan Bilbao. Designed by Frank Gehry, this $24,000\,m^2$ museum was soon recognized as an architectural landmark and the new emblem of the city. The parallels between the original, innovative, and highly seductive design of the building and the city itself have been purposefully underlined as part of an image reconstruction operation and a city marketing strategy. And, indeed, from this perspective, the GBM can be considered a complete success.

However, both the marketing and the image reconstruction aspects were initially conceived as mediated objectives of a strategy aimed at enhancing the city's capacity to compete for international capital investments, the acquisition of key command functions, and high level producer services as well as visitors. And, from this point of view, the 'Guggenheim effect' is still to be shown. So far, the most important positive impact has been the spectacular increase in the number of visitors to the museum and city, exceeding even the most optimistic expectations. For a city that has traditionally been 'out of the tourist track', the attraction of almost 1,400,000 visitors during the first year of operation of the museum is doubltess a big success. The international dimension of the museum is highlighted by the fact that almost 30 per cent of the visitors came from abroad; 32 per cent came from the rest of Spain and 40 per cent from the Basque Country.

On the other hand, a recent evaluation carried out by the international consulting firm KPMG Peat Marwick (1999) estimates that direct expenditures made by visitors to the GBM during the first year of operation amount to 194 million Euro, that is almost 180 Euro per visitor. The sectors that have benefited most are hotels, transport, restaurants, bars and coffee shops, and retail establishments. According to the study, the expenses associated to the operation of the museum during the first twelve months of activity have generated a value added of more than 150 million Euro, that amounts to approximately 0.47 per cent of the gross regional product. This value is considered to contribute to the maintenance of around 3,800 jobs in the mentioned sectors. At the same time, the value added generated has produced an increase in local fiscal capacity and tax revenues (value added taxes, capital taxes, and income tax) estimated to be close to 28.1 million Euro. Thus, in financial terms, the operation can so far be considered rather successful as the initial investment has been fully recovered.

In view of these results, local and regional authorities have emphasized the strategic significance of the museum for the city's (and the region's) development of a cultural tourist industry contributing not only to revitalization but also to the diversification of the area's economic base. Yet, in this respect, the possibility that the GBM could act as the trigger for the development of a cultural sector remains rather remote. The reasons for scepticism lay at several levels. First, the lack of a coherent strategy and the *ad hoc* way in which decisions have been made without a clear strategic framework. A second factor relates to the narrow focus on consumption-oriented aspects and the disregard for the production-related aspects of the GBM operation. A production-based strategy would require a more proactive policy of support for local firms and investment in the sector which until now has been missing. Third, the determining role of the GBM would depend largely on its capacity to create local upstream and downstream linkages. But, in order for these linkages to develop, a much more targeted strategy and also a greater degree of autonomy for the Bilbao Museum *vis-à-vis* the New York office is required. So far, the Bilbao Museum operates very much as a franchise, a factor that severely undermines its potential multiplier effects. And fourth, the regeneration potential of this project may also be impaired by the internationalization strategy of the Guggenheim Foundation as the serial production of new branches throughout the global urban landscape erodes the uniqueness of the Bilbao branch. The recent decision reached by the Foundation to build a new Guggenheim in Manhattan in the image of the Bilbao Museum is the first in a potentially long list of cities ready to host another branch. Thus, unless the Bilbao Museum is integrated into a wider socio-economic and urban strategy, there is a high risk that the attraction capacity of the city might soon be rendered ephemeral as the novelty effect wears off.

Finally, in terms of attracting international capital investment and key command functions into the city, the impact of the Guggenheim Museum has proved to be manifestly limited. So far, all direct investment associated with the setting up of the GBM has come from the Basque public administration, an act made possible by the special fiscal autonomy status of the Basque region. However, the original expectations regarding the attraction of direct foreign investment and command functions to the city have not been met. Until now, the undeniably strong advertising capacity of the GBM has had little impact in attracting international capital investment for Abandoibarra's regeneration process itself. So far, foreign investment is limited to the luxury hotel that will be developed by the Starwood holding that operates the Sheraton Hotels worldwide. Aside from this, only the shopping centre, Ría 21, incorporates, to a limited extent, the presence of international capital. More significantly, the attraction of command functions or headquarters to the site seems by now highly improbable and, in any event, has disappeared entirely from this policy agenda.

In sum, a preliminary analysis of the impact of Abandoibarra's redevelopment scheme suggests that its success lie predominantly in the realms consumption and circulation. The production side of this project, its directional and strategic quality, has all but disappeared under the dominance of a short-term return maximization logic that has weakened the strategic component of the scheme and heightened its speculative dimension. Socio-spatial considerations have been gradually removed from the debate, while diffused growth and trickle-down income effects are projected at an even more ephemeral level. This is highly relevant in the context of the socio-spatial polarization dynamics identified above.

10.6. Conclusions

During the last decade, large-scale urban redevelopment projects have emerged as the fundamental tool for urban revitalization strategies in metropolitan Bilbao. On the one hand, these projects are conceived as strategic operations that link the renewal of derelict sites and obsolete infrastructures to the production of the conditions necessary to launch a new phase of urban development. From this perspective, large-scale urban redevelopment projects can be considered a central component of the life of the city. On the other hand, the managing and financing of large urban projects are evidence of critical shifts in public intervention in the city and an ongoing renegotiation of the role of public and private actors in urban regeneration schemes and policy in general. These shifts include the subordination of statutory planning to the needs of large-scale emblematic projects in which focused and fragmented intervention operates as a laboratory for urban policy innovations. The setting up of mixed managing structures and quasi-private institutions is also an important element of a changing governance system that is drastically altering traditional planning modes and procedures.

Abandoibarra provides an excellent lens through which to analyse these trends in Bilbao. As in other redevelopment schemes, the Abandoibarra project is originally presented as an emblematic intervention firmly anchored in a strategic framework whose final objective is to provide the physical and functional conditions for competitive restructuring in the urban economy. However, the overwhelming emphasis on efficiency and financial feasibility has left the project the captive of a short-term return maximization logic that subordinates the strategic component to the requirements of speculative redevelopment. This shift is all too evident in Abandoibarra's turn from a production-oriented development to a consumption-based renovated space catering to the demands of the urban élite.

The weakening of the strategic component of Abandoibarra impinges upon the economic objectives of the project and its capacity to lead a process of competitive restructuring of the urban economy. And, while there is some evidence of economic recovery in metropolitan Bilbao, the question remains as to whether property-led redevelopment schemes such as this provide a sound base for urban revitalization. This is a critical issue since this scheme is presented as a test case of a policy to be generalized to the whole urban region.

The speculative character and the potentially regressive consequences of narrow short-term feasibility also challenge the financial sustainability of this model. Thus, the speculative bias introduced by the diffusion of a financial maximizing logic can have extremely negative consequences as speculative increases filter through the metropolitan land market. Needless to say, the consequences on access to housing for less favoured income groups can be totally devastating. Notwithstanding trickle-down effects, the new urban policies epitomized by Abandoibarra's redevelopment scheme incorporate a not insignificant risk of social and spatial exclusion, as uneven redevelopment may exacerbate existing social and functional divisions of space within the metropolitan area.

Finally, improvements in urban policy in metropolitan Bilbao would require overcoming the limits imposed by the overriding emphasis on economic feasibility and short-term maximization and acknowledging the need for a more integrated socio-economic strategy. This means the need to re-focus in a more direct way on the consequences of both economic decline as well as uneven redevelopment; that is, to incorporate both an economic and social strategy for integrated development in the new urban agenda.

Notes

1. In 1975 basic industries and metal manufacture constituated more than 70 per cent of total manufacturing employment in metropolitan Bilbao. A decade later, in 1986, these activities still accounted for 68 per cent of industrial employment, but their share of total employment had dropped from 22 per cent to 12 per cent. Nevertheless, while the destruction of industrial jobs took place fundamentally during the first half of the 1980s (1981–85), some manufacturing branches (notably Basic Metal production) continued to lose employment up to the late 1990s.
2. The data correspond to the administrative boundary of Bizkaia, the county equivalent, and an area where the metropolitan area of Bilbao represents close to 75 per cent of population and employment. There are no production estimates below this administrative level.
3. Between 1986 and 1996, the percentage of technical and managerial occupations has grown both in absolute as well as relative terms in metropolitan employment; during this decade, the proportion of managers almost tripled while technical occupations increased by one-third. This growing professionalization runs parallel to a reduction in the proportion (and absolute numbers) of manual labour in metropolitan Bilbao (see Rodríguez *et al.* 2001).
4. Between 1981 and 1986, the proportion of metropolitan service sector employment located within the municipality of Bilbao fell from 52 per cent in 1981 to 44 per cent in 1996. During the same period, the share of services employment doubled in the Right Bank area: from 10.4 per cent to 21 per cent (see Rodríguez *et al.* 2001).
5. Not surprisingly given the fact that metropolitan Bilbao represents around 45 per cent of the population and approximately 50 per cent of the region's GDP (Metropoli-30 1997).
6. In 1995, PERI estimated that land prices for office development were about one-third of land prices for the housing market. This price differential contributed to a redistribution of land uses towards residential and retail functions. Thus, the area assigned by the 1995 PERI to residential ($72,450\,m^2$) and retail ($28,000\,m^2$) uses almost doubled the area allocated for tertiary uses ($57,290\,m^2$) (Bilbao Ría 2000 (1998), Informe de Gestión).
7. General factors have contributed to this increase, notably changes in the mortgage loan market associated to falling interest rates, the process of European monetary integration, and the introduction of the single currency that is forcing the emergence of black money and undeclared savings. In the case of Bilbao, there is also the prospect of economic regeneration and urban growth.

References

ABRAMO, P. (2001) (ed.). *Cidades em Transformação: Entre o Plano e o Mercado. Experiências Internacionais de Gestão do Solo Urbano.* Rio de Janeiro: Observátorio Imobiliário e de Políticas do Solo.

ALONSO, L. (1999). 'Modelos de crecimiento y cambios espaciales recientes en las ciudades españolas. Un panorama desde el fin de siglo.' *Papeles de Economía Española*, 80: 249–65.

ARIAS, F. (1999). 'La regeneración de la ría de Bilbao: más allá del Guggenheim'. Paper presented at the 'Seminario sobre experiencias en ambientes urbanos históricos', Conference Málaga.

——(2001). 'Concertações e operações urbanas: a experiência espanhols', in P. Abramo (ed.), *Cidades em Transformação: Entre o Plano e o Mercado. Experiências Internacionais de Gestão do solo Urbano.* Rio de Janeiro: Observátorio Imobiliário e de Políticas do Solo.

ASHWORTH, G. J., and VOOGD, H. (1990). *Selling the City*. London: Belhaven Press.

ATIENZA, L. (1991). 'Un proyecto estratégico para la revitalización del Bilbao Metropolitano', in A. Rodríguez, *et al.* (eds.), *Las Grandes Ciudades: debates y propuestas.* Madrid: Economistas.

Ayuntamiento de Bilbao (AB) (1989), *Avance del Plan General de Ordenación Urbana de Bilbao. Criterios, objetivos y soluciones generales de Planeamiento.*

——(2000*a*). *Texto refundido de la Modificación del Plan Especial de Reforma Interior de Abandoibarra. Pleno 13 Apr. 1999. Aprobación definitiva.* Dec. 2000.

——(2000*b*). *Plan General de Ordenación Urbana de Bilbao. Aprobación del Texto Refundido 27 Dec. 94.* Dec. 2000.

BIANCHINI, F., and PARKINSON, M. (1993). *Cultural Policy and Urban Regeneration: The West European Experience.* Manchester: Manchester University Press.

Bilbao Metropoil-30 (2001). *Bilbao 2010. Reflexión Estratégica.* Bilbao.

Bilbao Ría 2000 (1998), *Memoria.* Bilbao.

——(2000), *Memoria.* Bilbao.

BORJA, J., *et al.* (1985). *Teoría e intervención en la ciudad.* Madrid: Fundación de Investigaciones Marxistas.

——and Y CASTELLS, M. (1997). *Local y Global. La gestión de las ciudades en la era de la información.* Madrid: Taurus.

BUSQUETS, J. (1993). 'Perspectiva desde las ciudades'. *Ciudad y Territorio Estudios Territoriales* (95–96), 1: 163–74.

CALVO, L. (1990). 'El control del crecimiento urbano', in MOPU (ed.), *10 años de planeamiento urbanístico en España.* Madrid: MOPU.

CASTELLS, M. (1990). 'Estrategias de desarrollo metropolitano en las grandes ciudades españolas: la articulación entre crecimiento económico y calidad de vida', in J. Borja *et al.* (eds.), *Las grandes ciudades en la década de los noventa.* Madrid: Sistema.

CASTILLO, J., DÍAZ, M., and GÓMEZ-LARRAÑAGA, P. (1993). 'Bilbao Metrópoli 30 en el contexto de los cambios comarcales en el País Vasco'. *Boletín de Estudios Económicos*, 48/148: 81–96.

CHESHIRE, P., HAY, D., CARBONARO, G., and BEVAN, N. (1988). *Urban Problems and Regional Policy in the European Community.* Luxembourg: Office for Official Publications of the European Communities.

Departamento de Economía y Planificación-Gobierno Vasco (DEP) (1989). 'Bases para la revitalización económica del Bilbao Metropolitano'. *Ekonomiaz*, 15: 58–76.

Departamento de Ordenación del Territorio, Vivienda y Medio Ambiente-Gobierno Vasco (DOTVMA) (1993). *Programa de Demolición de Ruimas Industriales en la Comunidad Autónoma de Euskadi.* Gasteiz: Servicio Central de Publicaciones del Gobierno Vasco.

——(1998). *Actuaciones del Programa de Demolición de Ruinas Industriales en la Comunidad Autónoma de Euskadi.* Gasteiz: Servicio Central de Publicaciones del Gobierno Vasco.

Departamento de Ordenación del Territorio, Vivienda y Medio Ambiente-Gobierno Vasco (DOTVMA) (2000). *Actuaciones del Programa de Demolición de Ruinas Industriales en la Comunidad Autónoma de Euskadi*. Gasteiz: Servicio Central de Publicaciones del Gobierno Vasco.

Departamento de Urbanismo, Vivienda y Medio Ambiente-Gobierno Vasco (DUVMA) (1994). *Plan Territorial Parcial Bilbao Metropolitano*. Gasteiz: Servicio Central de Publicaciones del Gobierno Vasco.

DUMONT, G. F. (1995). 'La competencia entre las ciudades'. *Situación*, 3: 55–68.

Egailan (1999). *Censo del Mercado de Trabajo, 1998*. Gasteiz.

ESCUDERO, M. (1985). 'Esplendor y caída del Gran Bilbao'. *Ciudad y Territorio Estudios Territoriales*, 82: 113–31.

ESTEBAN, M. (2000). *Bilbao, Luces y Sombras del Titanio. El Proceso de Regeneración del Bilbao Metropolitano*. Bilbao: Universidad del País Vasco.

Eustat (1986). *Censo de Población y Vivienda 1986*. Gasteiz: Servicio Central de Publicaciones del Gobierno Vasco.

——(1991). *Censo de Población y Vivienda 1991*. Gasteiz: Servicio Central de Publicaciones del Gobierno Vasco.

——(1996). *Censo de Población y Vivienda 1996*. Gasteiz: Servicio Central de Publicaciones del Gobierno Vasco.

——(2001). *Anuario Estadístico Vasco 2002*. Gasteiz: Servicio Central de Publicaciones del Gobierno Vasco.

EZQUIAGA, J. M. (2001). 'Projetos de transformacao urbana na Madri do fim do sculo', in P. Abramo (ed.), *Cidades em Transformação: Entre o Plano e o Mercado. Experiencias Internacionais de Gestão do Solo Urbano*. Rio de Janeiros Observótorio Imobilário e de Politicas do Solo.

FONT, J. (1997). 'Civil Society Reinventing Metropolitan Administration: Recent Iberian and Latin American experiences'. Paper presented at IV Table Ronde de l'Institut International des Sciences Administratives. Québec, 14–17 July 1997.

FOX-PRZEWORSKI, J., GODDARD, J., and DE JONG, M. (1991) (eds.). *Urban Regeneration in a Changing Economy*. Oxford: Clarendon Press.

GÓMEZ, M. V. (1998). 'Reflective Images: The Case of Urban Regeneration in Glasgow and Bilbao'. *International Journal of Urban and Regional Research*, 22/1: 106–21.

HALL, P. (1996). *Cities of Tomorrow*. Oxford: Blackwell.

KEARNS, G., and PHILO, C. (1993) (eds.). *Selling Places: The City as Cultural Capital, Past and Present*. Oxford: Pergamon Press.

KPMG Peat Marwick (1999). *Impacto de las actividades de la Guggenheim Bilbao Museoaren Fundazioa en Euskadi*. Conclusions document.

LEIRA, E., and QUERO, D. (1992). 'Bilbao. Territorio y regeneración productiva'. *Ciudad y Territorio Estudios Territoriales*, 39: 117–31.

MARTÍNEZ, A. (1993). 'La revitalización de areas metropolitanas. El caso del Bilbao Metropolitano'. *Boletín de Estudios Económicos*, 48/148: 63–71.

MARTÍNEZ, M., and VICARIO, L. (1997). 'Polarización socio-espacial en el Area Metropolitana de Bilbao'. *Inguruak*, 17: 163–92.

MASBOUNGI, A. (2001). 'La nueva Meca del urbanismo'. *Projet Urbain*, 23: 17–21.

Ministerio de Obras Públicas y Transportes (MOPT) (1993). *Plan Director de Infraestructuras 1993–2007*. Madrid: Secretaría General de Planificación y Concertación Territorial.

Ministerio de Obras Públicas y Urbanismo (MOPU) (1990). *10 Años de Planeamiento Urbanístico en España.* Madrid: Instituto del Territorio y el Urbanismo, Ministerio de Obras Públicas y Urbanismo.

Nieva, A. (2001). 'En Nombre de la Ciudad'. *Projet Urbain*, 23: 8–9.

OECD (1983). *Las Ciudades en Transformación.* Madrid: MOPU.

——(1987). *Revitalización de las Economías Urbanas.* Madrid: MOPU.

Otaola, P. (2001). 'Un ambicioso proceso de transformación'. *Projet Urbain*, 23: 48–55.

Precedo, A. (1993). 'Las políticas de desarrollo y renovación urbana en Europa'. *Ciudad y Territorio Estudios Territoriales*, 1/98: 579–95.

Projet Urbain (2001). 'Bilbao, la culture comme projet de ville/La cultura como proyecto de ciudad'. Projet Urbain 23, Direction Générale de l'Urbanisme de l'Habitat et de la Construction. Sept. 2001

Ravetz, A. (1980). *Remaking Cities: Contradictions of the Recent Urban Environment.* London: Croom Helm.

Rodríguez, A. (1995). 'Planning the Revitalisation of an Old Industrial City: Urban Policy Innovations in Metropolitan Bilbao', in C. Demazière and P. Wilson (eds.), *Local Economic Development in Europe and the Americas.* London: Mansell.

——and Martínez, E. (2001). 'Del declive a la revitalización: oportunidades y límites de las nuevas políticas urbanas en Bilbao'. *Ciudad y Territorio Estudios Territoriales*, 131: 441–59.

——————and Guenaga, G. (2001). 'Uneven Redevelopment: New Urban Policies and Socio-Spatial Fragmentation in Metropolitan Bilbao'. *European Urban and Regional Studies*, 8/2: 161–78.

Terán, F. (1996). 'Evolución del Planeamiento Urbanístico (1846–1996)'. *Ciudad y Territorio Estudios Territoriales*, 28: 107–8.

Urrutia, V., Areilza, G., and Ureta, J. (2000). *Planes con incidencia urbanístico-territorial en la margen izquierda.* Final Report.

Van den Berg, A., and Van Klink, A. (1995). 'Planificación estratégica y marketing urbano'. *Situación*, 3: 25–37.

Vazquez Barquero, A. (1995). 'Los planes estratégicos para el desarrollo urbano'. *Situación*, 3: 11–24.

website *http://www.ifresi.univ-lille1.fr/PagesHTML/URSPIC/URSPIC*, 2001.

11

Urban Development for Competitiveness and Cohesion: The Expo 98 Urban Project in Lisbon

João Cabral and Berta Rato

11.1. Introduction

The Expo 98 urban project on the east side of Lisbon started as an event to celebrate Portuguese discoveries. The promotion of, and justification for, the location of the Expo in the old industrial eastern part of Lisbon was that the implementation of this Urban Development Plan (UDP) would contribute to the regeneration of a derelict and neglected part of the city. The financial and institutional investment necessary for putting together this enterprise was also justified as a key element of the national strategy to assert the position of Lisbon as a capital city in the European Union. The marketing of the project was built around an attractive scenario—the creation of 18,000 jobs and housing for 25,000 people, in an exclusive riverfront environment. The location of prime facilities and infrastructure (museums and theatres, an oceanarium, a trade fair, and a large multi-purpose sports hall) and the political and financial commitment of the state provided a good incentive for capital investment and for ensuring adequate returns.

In order to ensure adequate and fast access to the area, massive investments were made in the road system, in a new Metro line and in the construction of a modern inter-modal station. For the administration of the project a special company, Parque Expo 98 SA, was created and granted extensive development powers. The financing of the project was achieved primarily through the sale of the land for property development, but also through the exposition itself (tickets and sponsorship) and the European Regional Development Fund.

The objective of this chapter is to present an empirical analysis of the Expo 98 urban project in the context of the theoretical perspectives outlined in Chapters 1 to 3.[1] In the process of implementing this urban project, two critical issues motivated the debate. Firstly, the Expo project was seen as a competitive asset in affirming the position of Lisbon in the context of greater competition between cities due to the dynamics of European integration and globalization. Secondly, it raised questions about the integration of such large investment and land use alterations with the long-term planning objectives for Lisbon and its metropolitan area. In addition, this concern was linked to other critical issues such as promoting social cohesion in the face of rising problems of social exclusion, and implementing an adequate system of governance for the Lisbon metropolitan area.

The chapter is divided into four main parts. The first part describes the development of the Lisbon urban agglomeration under a variety of political and economic regimes influenced by different sets of urban policies and systems of government, and locates the Expo urban project within the development of the old industrial eastern zone and the Lisbon Metropolitan Area (LMA). The second part describes the process of design and implementation of Expo 98 and the urban development project associated with it. The third part assesses the particular conditions under which the Expo 98 urban project was created as part of an explicit strategy for urban competitiveness with consequences for the policy objective of promoting cohesion. The conditions for combining objectives of competitiveness and cohesion were determined by the particular financial model applied, the strategy for spatial integration, an ambitious project of real estate development and economic restructuring, and an ambiguous plan for integrating the residential areas and the local community. The conclusions are summarized in a table that lists the main features of the Expo 98 urban project according to criteria of competitiveness and cohesion (Table 11.2).

11.2. Lisbon—Urban Agglomeration and Capital City under Different Regimes

11.2.1. A restructuring metropolis

In 1991, the LMA was home to 2.5 million people in eighteen municipalities, or approximately a quarter of the total population of Portugal. The Lisbon municipality, the capital city (26 per cent of the population in 2.7 per cent of the area of the LMA), exhibits all the symptoms of many old, dominant, urban centres—an excessive concentration of economic, administrative, and cultural power (54 per cent of total jobs, 40 per cent of which are located in the central part of the city), a declining population (−4 per cent, −5 per cent, and −17.9 per cent for each of the last three decades respectively[2]), poor quality of urban life (serious pollution and traffic congestion), and inner-city problems of rehabilitation (particularly in the old historic quarters) and rehousing (34 per cent of the total number of people of the LMA living in illegal slum areas and 37,000 of a total of 110,000 are registered for rehousing).

Through successive phases of economic and demographic expansion, the growth of the capital city had both a positive and a negative effect on the surrounding municipalities (population growth was 21 per cent, 36 per cent, and 1.3 per cent in the LMA during respectively 1960/70, 1970/81, and 1981/91[3]). The surrounding localities benefited from relocation of economic activities and experienced intensification of urban land use and of urbanization (between 1981 and 1991, the built-up environment increased by 20 per cent). As a result, the Lisbon population represented 26 per cent of the total population of the LMA in 1991 compared to 41 per cent in 1970. The 312,800 ha of the LMA are a highly differentiated space, combining a network of historic and new cities and dense urban areas with municipalities strongly linked with rural activities, two large natural parks, beach and tourist resorts, extended new and old industrial areas, and two estuaries with important port infrastructures. The resulting 'internal reorganization' of the LMA combined, as Portas *et al.* (1998: 298) put it, with forms of 'social dualisation and segregation': 'This situation has led families in the middle income groups to leave the capital city; those who remain are the better-off section of the population, which stimulates the supply of luxury housing; the poorer strata of the population (precarious accommodation and public housing); and an undifferentiated sector that pays old rents.'

In the late 1990s, the development of the city of Lisbon was still an expression of the main transformations occurring in the LMA. Patterns of deindustrialization and gentrification combined in its highly urbanized and dense space, reflecting the process of social and economic integration into the larger metropolitan area. At the same time, the primary role of the city was sustained by its increasing administrative and economic importance, raising land use values in ways which had implications for the co-ordination and efficacy of urban development policies. Conditions for such co-ordination did not exist as the planning and the government of the LMA was spread over different administrations and different municipalities and political parties pursued their own particular strategies.

A history of a centralized political and administrative power that did not create conditions for regional economic and social development underlines the continuing dominance of Lisbon. The industrial growth and the spatial development that occurred after the 1960s was characterized by a continuation of the process of capital concentration and the urbanization of society. In the absence of spatial policies promoting decentralization, capital was allowed to take full advantage of economies of agglomeration without having to relocate production. This also confirmed the leading position of the Lisbon Metropolitan Area.

11.2.2. The changing urban policy in Lisbon and the eastern zone

Until 1990, the city of Lisbon had two sets of Master Plans, the Plano Geral de Urbanização (1948) and the Plano Director de Lisboa (produced in 1967 and only officially approved in 1977). Throughout the 1960s (a period of rapid industrialization), the 1970s and 1980s (a period characterized by the increasing tertiarization of the city economy and by urban sprawl into the northern and southern areas of the LMA), and up until the 1990s, the urban government of Lisbon municipality and of the adjacent municipalities was mainly dictated by short-term management criteria. Projects and pressure for property and speculative development were dealt with on a contingent basis, while sectoral projects and plans for critical areas (roads and transport, infrastructure, social housing, control of illegal settlements) were produced to respond to political pressures and to avoid social conflicts.

Most of the social housing schemes were implemented on land expropriated by the state in the 1930s under the interventionist government of Duarte Pacheco, public works minister and head of Lisbon municipality. His rule was marked by a strong intervention in land development, combining objectives for asserting fascist ideology with major public infrastructure works and housing projects. The eastern part of the city offered the best score for those schemes for which special plans were designed. The particular features of a planned urban landscape (expressing modern movement trends) and social composition (mostly working class), combined with the industrial buildings and infrastructure of the port area, marked the characteristics of the eastern zone.

In 1990, the governing socialist/communist coalition in the Lisbon municipality proposed the launch of a set of planning instruments to replace the outdated urban plans. Both a Strategic Plan and a Master Plan were initiated in 1990. The Strategic Plan was published in 1992 and the Master Plan, the Plano Director Municipal, was approved in 1994. The future of the riverfront and the harbour, and the integration of the eastern part of the city were critical aspects of both these plans. The strategic plan singled out the Riverside Arc as one of the four structural areas of the city and identified the area of the eastern riverfront as a 'Logistic Platform' of the city and the metropolitan region, strengthened by its position as a 'City Port' (Soares 1996).

A key element of the strategy for the eastern zone was the implementation of adequate transport and road infrastructure in order to make the area more open and accessible to the road network of the LMA and to the riverfront. Another key factor was the creation of conditions to modernize the existing industrial areas, and the decision to locate and build important public infrastructures and facilities with regional significance (a multi-purpose Pavilion and the Lisbon International Trade Fair). In sum, the urban development project created for implementing the world exposition in 1998 was going to promote the necessary conditions for rapid changes in parts of the urban area. This was to be made possible through the creation of special planning and

financial conditions that represented new forms of urban governance with contradictory results.

11.3. The Expo 98 Urban Project in the Eastern Zone of Lisbon—Formulation, Design, and Implementation

The chosen site for the exposition was 350 ha of riverfront land around the
Olivais Dock built for hydroplanes in the 1930s (Plate 11.1). The concept of
modern infrastructure promoted by an event with national and international
prestige was seen as the driving force for the rehabilitation of this disused part
of the city. This also fitted well within the objectives of the regional plan for the
metropolitan area (PROTAML) and of the Lisbon Strategic and Master Plans,
which both aimed at a better integration of the port areas into the spatial and
economic development of the city. It also complemented and enhanced the
opportunities created by projects already programmed under the national and
regional investment plans, financed by the European Regional Development
Fund (ERDF), for transport and infrastructure, most notably the construction
of a new bridge over the river Tagus, the construction of a new motorway, and
the extension of the railway line and train system. Finally, the idea of an integrated public investment scheme was seen as the solution to the long-term
problems of this abandoned port area and a way to expedite the closure or
relocation of hazardous, polluted, and environmentally dangerous industrial
installations (an oil refinery and fuel tanks, an abattoir, a sewage treatment
plant, and a landfill dump site).

The position of the newly elected socialist/communist local authority in
Lisbon was instrumental in the choice of the eastern zone. The area had
already been considered for redevelopment in previous plans, and the Expo
development became integrated within these by means of new zoning regulations and planning objectives. The issue of promoting 'nationality' and party
ideals, linking the celebration of the Portuguese discoveries with the theme of
the Oceans, appealed to the social democrats in the government. In addition, in
Lisbon and Loures (the adjacent municipality) the socialists and communists
in power saw an opportunity for attracting investment and generating inflow of
capital. The task of creating and implementing, within just five years, a high-
tech and marketable environment on a site with so many problems was both a
challenge and a means of providing a justification for the mobilization of significant financial resources. The fact that the project started 'from the end', to
be completed for the opening of Expo in May 1998, represented a factor external to the normal running of the social and planning procedures which characterize 'non-exceptional' transformation processes in the built environment.
It also justified the adoption of discretionary and authoritarian forms of management, which opened up channels for forms of clientelism.

Plates 11.1*a* and 11.1*b*. The Expo 98 site in Lisbon (Source: Parque Expo SA)

Once the site was chosen, the work developed simultaneously in different directions. Four of these were critical to the success of the project: (i) the construction of an adequate administrative and legal framework; (ii) the production of an urban and exposition plan with an appealing design, an adequate

Table 11.1. The Urbanization Plan for the Intervention Zone of Expo 98

Total area of the Intervention Zone	350 hectares (100 per cent)
Total area of land for construction	125 hectares (36 per cent)
Total area of land not for construction	225 hectares (64 per cent)
(railways and roads, pedestrian circulation, public	
spaces, green areas and parks, docks, quayside bridge)	
Total paved area for construction	2,460,000 square metres
Index of global utilization	0.70
Index of net utilization (total area minus the urban park)	0.92

Source: Parque Expo S.A. 1996.

planning framework, and a feasible financial programme; (iii) land expropriation and site preparation; and (iv) functional integration into the wider urban fabric through extending the road and transport system.

In March 1993, the Portuguese government established a special 'company', Parque Expo 98 SA to co-ordinate and implement the project. The social capital of Parque Expo 98 was entirely public, the main shareholders being the state and the Lisbon and Loures municipalities. Parque Expo 98 was the main shareholder of six other companies that were set up to run the real estate project, the exposition itself, and some of the facilities that would continue after the exposition. The government granted Parque Expo full and exclusive planning and licensing powers within the whole of the Expo development area, the so-called Intervention Zone (IZ). Agreements were reached with the two municipalities to assure the swift handling and approval of planning permissions and for issuing construction permits without delays. Special tax exemption facilities were also granted to Parque Expo, which, moreover, was given powers to acquire land through expropriation. The whole operation was also exempted from the obligation to prepare an environmental impact assessment study. These conditions contrasted with the normal running of a municipal department for the submission of planning applications. Of course, for developers and builders the speeding up of the process meant significant financial savings.

Parque Expo prepared the Urbanization Plan and co-ordinated the production of six detailed urban zoning plans. Using the special statute of the area, the approval and publishing of the different plans took place without the otherwise required public inquiry. Table 11.1 summarizes the content of the Urbanization Plan.

For the commercialization of the land, Expo Urbe signed contracts with five estate agents. The overall area to be commercialized was over 1,800,000 m², of which 1,173,000 were for residential purposes, 450,000 for office development, and 153,000 for commerce. A large shopping centre occupied an area of 60,000 m², which included ten cinemas, a hypermarket, and six mega-stores.

The exposition site itself consisted of five main pavilions, two international areas, three buildings for shows and concerts, a panoramic tower, gardens, and boulevards. The main buildings and facilities were the Oceanarium, an International Pavilion for hosting the exhibits of 150 participating countries (a record in international expositions), a national pavilion (Pavilhão de Portugal), a multi-purpose sports hall with a capacity of 17,000 people, two thematic pavilions (Future and Oceans), a new railway and Metro station, a marine complex, and outdoor theatres.

11.4. The Expo 98 Urban Project— the Strategy for Competitiveness

11.4.1. *The financial model and the institutional capacity for implementing it*

The characteristics of this UDP meant that there were particular difficulties involved with estimating its cost, which made financial planning difficult. However, from the very beginning, the administration of Parque Expo declared their intention to promote and implement the exposition at zero cost to the public purse. A financial model was put together on the basis of an initial cost estimate of 1,285 million Euro for the production of the exposition, for implementing the urbanization plan, and for preparing the site (which included expropriations, compensations, removing existing buildings and materials, and solving environmental problems). The financial mechanism for achieving that objective was based primarily on the sale of the public land of the Intervention Zone (IZ) for property development, although ticket sales and sponsorship for the exposition itself were also to be important. According to the initial budget, the revenues from the property development and the exposition itself represented 51 per cent and 24 per cent respectively of the total expected income of 1,285 million Euro. The use of real estate as a major source of funding turned the UDP into a long-term project, with 51 per cent of the revenues being realized between 1999 and 2009. However, most of the expenditure would take place during a short initial period in order to finance the construction of the exposition and run the event, with only 4.3 per cent of the total costs being spent after 1998. This, of course, created balance-sheet problems and required a significant reliance on banking credit to finance the project, which, in turn, increased total cost.

A third important source of income was the European Regional Development Fund (ERDF) in the Community Support Framework (CSF) for 1994–9 and the Cohesion Fund. This totalled about 305 million Euro (Parque Expo 98 Mar. 1999). This covered the primary infrastructure work in the IZ, the implementation of various projects with significant environmental impact, the access and transport infrastructure work, and the infrastructure for the Multipurpose Pavilion. The amount allocated directly to Expo 98 under the Urban Renovation Program of the CSF was around 240 million Euro, representing about half of the total sum for urban renovation for the whole country for five years.

As we write in 2002, the final budget balance of the Expo 98 project remains unknown. It was estimated that accumulated expenses until the year 2009 would run to a total of 1,850 million Euro, of which 375 million Euro were pure financial costs (Parque Expo 98 Mar. 1999). The actual construction costs for the buildings and infrastructure were higher than budget, while revenue from ticket sales and sponsorship (250 million Euro) was lower than expected. Parque Expo will receive additional revenues from the sale of a few of the Expo pavilions to the government (paid for by the public purse) for the installation of ministries and cultural facilities. The value of this agreement was 60 million Euro. When the increased size of the deficit became clear, a strategy to increase property prices was pursued. Parque Expo expects that revenue received from land sales will amount to 850 million Euro by 2009—30 per cent greater than the initial estimate. If this estimate is realized, Parque Expo will almost break even.[4] However, the implications of the project for the urbanization process, the city project, and the regeneration of the eastern zone are different matters.

The zero cost objective has actually corrupted the whole process. The feasibility model depends on the chosen variables and on how the economic gains of the intervention are evaluated. The Parque Expo approach was, however, similar to that of any real estate agent, in that it attempted to sell the property at a price to cover (at least) the costs. This was frustrated by a complicated development process which had the main (stated) objectives of creating a metropolitan infrastructure and of regenerating a deprived part of the city. The 'free-hand' given to an administration that is in itself a public company and a political compromise, while acting as a *de facto* private developer, emphasizes the conflicting role of the capitalist state in urban planning.

11.4.2. The strategy for spatial and functional integration

The 1992 municipal plan for the eastern zone considered the construction of adequate transport and road infrastructure to be a key element in the strategy for creating a multifunctional and economically viable Expo area. The shift from an enclosed and restricted port and industrial area to an open and accessible leisure space and complex of facilities required a new approach to transport connections and to the design of the urban environment. This municipal plan was not as ambitious as the plan proposed by Parque Expo. The Expo project was able, however, to mobilize the necessary financial resources for the spatial integration of new uses and the construction of new facilities. This involved a massive investment in roads and transport systems, as well as close collaboration and co-ordination between various transport and traffic agencies with varying degrees of autonomy and with a tradition of co-ordination problems. The joint process of promoting Expo and negotiating with the EU for funding under the second CSF (1994–9), helped to allocate ERDF funds for infrastructure projects and investments in the eastern zone, and particularly in the IZ.[5]

The creation of the conditions for the spatial integration of the Expo project into the LMA, supported through strong state involvement, was, therefore, fundamental to the success of the whole enterprise. The impact of the new and fast transport and road links has, however, contradictory aspects. One purpose is to provide mass access for people and vehicles, along with the provision of control and security conditions. However, the creation of a more private and exclusive residential and office area for the city, upon which the success of the real estate development part of the project was based, has different requirements.

11.4.3. The strategy for local urban regeneration— the role of real estate development

The promotion and the justification of the Expo project relied upon the regeneration of a derelict and neglected part of the city. This included the creation of new jobs, an exclusive new housing development, and the development of prime facilities and infrastructure. It was clear from the very start that the new residents and activities would have very little in common with the previous occupants and the surrounding areas. This realization, however, did not alter the direction of public intervention or lead to a change in the planning objectives. The Expo management was autonomous and free to influence investments with the aim of making the whole development a successful and profitable enterprise.[6]

In fact, the rhythms of the construction industry and the real estate market established the conditions for urban regeneration. Developments in the real estate sector and in office and housing markets tend to determine the future use and development of the area and the possibilities for spatial, social, and economic integration and/or exclusion. The principal view that the final price should be set by market demand favoured the construction of high quality flats. The Expo urbanization was, as a result, primarily aimed at the middle/upper income groups. There was no room, therefore, for social or cost-controlled housing schemes—the dominant form of housing in the eastern zone—and proposals for achieving social and urban integration through social housing provision were not heeded.

In September 1998, the total value of land sales realized by Parque Urbe amounted to 278 million Euro (*Expresso*, 26 Sept. 1998) and reached 630 million Euro in March 2001 (*Jornal do Imobiliário*, 1 June 2001). About 75 per cent of the total available land had been sold. The growth in sales was quite remarkable if one takes into consideration that Parque Expo's initial budget was estimated as 132 million Euro by the end of 1998, and 518 million Euro by 2009. This (unexpected) growth was related to a price increase explained by external and internal factors. The combination of low interest rates and the trend of investing in the property market as a reaction to a crisis in the financial markets actually helped sales. In addition, the Expo management also decided to intervene in the commercialization of the development. It raised land prices to take advantage of high demand for apartments in Lisbon. These trends pushed property values up and the Expo site became one of the most expensive areas in Lisbon.[7]

11.5. The Expo 98 Urban Project: The Question of Cohesion

11.5.1. Urban regeneration as a project for economic restructuring

Once the project had matured, it became apparent that its main logic was not the re-utilization of the eastern zone as a complementary and integral part of the activity of the city and the region, but rather the development of a competitive area in terms of urban and metropolitan structural development. This approach raises questions concerning the process of integration of the Expo urban project in the surrounding areas and in the development of the Lisbon Metropolitan Area. The shift from an outdated industrial complex to a commercially promoted service, leisure, and residential area leads to a different perspective on the role of territories. In the eastern zone, the disintegration of territorially based activities and their replacement by centres for mass consumption and supplies of services whose success depends on a capacity to influence and to attract demand from outside, has implications for urban and social integration. In the present context, we shall just outline some of the differences in uses and functions taking place.

The eastern zone was characterized by a significant number of industrial activities, mainly composed of large and medium-sized firms, whose location advantage was linked to the proximity of the international airport, the port of Lisbon, and the main railway line. In 1993, only 19 per cent of the land in the IZ was privately owned, with the remainder being in the hands of the state or of public institutions. The Port of Lisbon Authority owned 42.4 per cent of the publicly held land and used it primarily for the storage of containers, 22 per cent of the public land had no use, the privately owned land consisted of unused space or disused buildings, and housing represented only a small part of the area (1.19 ha), with 123 temporary accommodations and 66 old and derelict buildings. In 1993, 117 firms were located on the 310 ha of the IZ. These firms were mainly commercial (30.8 per cent) or manufacturing (24.8 per cent) companies, and employed around 3,000 people. Small-scale businesses dominated, although the eleven largest firms employed 44.4 per cent of the workforce.[8] During the 1990s, the labour and industrial structure of the eastern zone went through significant transformations, characterized by a decrease in industrial employment and the growth of the service sector. This trend is associated with the closing of firms in a context of greater competition; a relocation process, especially of larger firms, to the periphery of the LMA where the cost of land is lower; and market pressures that pushed land prices up, which, in turn, led to more service and residential uses.

The Expo project and the world exposition accentuated these tendencies—both directly through the closure and displacement of a significant number of industries and transportation services located in the Expo site, and indirectly through the growth of demand for other uses and increased land values. The overall impact of these transformations is difficult to assess.[9] On the basis of the closures taking place during the 1990s, the communist trade union (CGTP) estimated the total loss of jobs to be around 25,000. The local institutions (e.g. the parishes (*Juntas de Freguesia*), Employment Centre, Department of Social Security) also acknowledge rapid changes in the labour market as a result of the relocation of activities and the threat of more firm closures in the area surrounding Expo.

The UDP has ushered in a significant shift from industrial to tertiary activities in the eastern zone, the consequences of which are difficult to assess for this area and for the LMA as a whole. The Lisbon Trade Fair, the 46,000 m² shopping centre, and ten cinemas opened in April 1999 and attracted large crowds. Other private commercial investments included two hotels, and offices for two car manufacturers and for two large companies. A few public buildings and facilities are also located in the IZ: a private hospital, offices for the Ministry of Health, university services and technical departments, student accommodation, and a youth centre.

11.5.2. Social impacts on the local community

The social impact of the Expo project has to be understood in the context of its integration into the eastern zone of Lisbon. It is part of the traditional periphery of the city, characterized by a mixed rural–industrial environment with a high percentage of social housing estates and a low income population. Overall, the area shows the characteristics of a deprived community: low income levels (associated with poorly qualified workers in poorly paid jobs); unemployment, under-employment, and precarious employment (the eastern zone has one of the highest rates of unemployment in Lisbon); a high percentage of derelict land; and old (and frequently poorly constructed) housing estates. Parque Expo did not take the social characteristics of the surrounding districts into consideration. They were more concerned with the development of the riverfront than with the economic and social history of the eastern zone. Issues of social integration were dealt with within the boundaries of the IZ and the internal labour relations (e.g. the displacement and rehousing of squatter settlements) after the negotiation of a contractual arrangement with the trade unions.

Although the final impact of the Expo UDP will not be evident for some time, there are several aspects that are already worth stressing. Local interlocutors stressed the important positive aspects of the Expo development, such as the new transport and access facilities that contributed to improved territorial cohesion. This infrastructure provides better links with the centre of Lisbon and connects the eastern part of the city with the metropolitan urban system. The modernization of the railway system and the new Metro line also represent a major improvement for the local communities. Social integration of traditionally poor and marginalized communities was enhanced by rapid and cheap access to the city centre through the public transport network.

In contrast to this, some argued that the construction of major transport infrastructure, particularly roads, creates new physical barriers, which undermine the idea of promoting 'urbanity' and the sense of neighbourhood communities. Another argument points to the limited level of the development of social infrastructure such as buildings and facilities. These are low in relation not only to the needs of the new housing development, but also to those of the large, poor, surrounding communities. This contrasts sharply with the high concentration of public buildings and facilities with metropolitan and national importance that cluster on the Expo site. Of course, negative effects are associated with the closure and relocation of firms with the consequent job losses. The new commercial and service-oriented jobs have little connection to the industrial tradition of this part of the city, and the value of establishing high level services and technologically advanced firms is still open to question. In addition, the increasing value of the surrounding properties has pushed up the price of property and has accelerated the substitution of industrial premises for office space. These changes have major impacts on the local labour market. There are new job opportunities in the tertiary sector, which address the aspirations of young people, especially women. However, most of the new jobs are in the shopping areas, which, according to the local Employment Centre, recruit an unskilled labour force that is poorly paid and works long hours under intensive time schedules. The site preparation involved the displacement of 278 poor families living in old quarters and squatting in temporary accommodations. Although some of the rehousing was rather problematic (particularly among the group of gypsy families), the environmental upgrading and the urban landscaping represented a substantial improvement in the quality of life of the local communities.

11.5.3. The role of the local community

During the preparation, construction, and implementation of the Expo project, Parque Expo negotiated and established agreements with various elected local bodies and associations. The municipalities of Lisbon and Loures were the obvious partners: they are shareholders of Parque Expo and will eventually be responsible for the management of the site. In practice, however, these relationships were not unproblematic. Although the municipalities were full members of the technical commissions overseeing the whole project, there were disagreements resulting from different perspectives with respect to solving problems and establishing priorities. There were particular disparities between Parque Expo's resources, short-term objectives, and investment capacity on the one hand, and the municipalities' concerns and responsibilities for administrative, territorial, and social integration on the other. In addition, the institutional mechanisms that were behind the formation and consolidation of Parque Expo created conditions for corporatist forms of management. These conditions promoted the relative autonomy of this institution, which, in turn, blocked access to external influences, affected the establishment of clear feasibility criteria, and veiled some of the less benevolent economic and social priorities. Under such institutional arrangements, communications at and with the lower levels were even more tenuous. The lower-scale elected bodies, the two parishes (*Juntas de Freguesia*) Olivais and Moscavide, were not represented. According to the Presidents of the *Juntas*, their role was of mere spectators and recipients of information. The *Juntas*, however, put pressure on and filed repeated complaints to Parque Expo. The main ones related to the immediate impact of the project caused by the construction site (noise and dust, obstruction of roads, traffic congestion) and by the physical barriers (new highways) built around the existing housing estates.

11.6. Conclusion: Conditions for Competitiveness and Cohesion in the Expo 98 Urban Project

Table 11.2 summarizes the main features of the implementation of the Expo 98 urban project. This list allows a comparison between the particular conditions that contribute to urban competitiveness and cohesion objectives. Thus, urban redevelopment projects are usually linked to the conditions for economic restructuring supported by a new economic policy (see Chapter 2) the promotion of new environmental and urban infrastructures (the production of the next layers of construction in ways that match future needs (Harvey 1995); the supply of accommodation for new urban residents and to re-house existing dwellers; and a sort of implicit plan or hidden agenda for shaping city expansion and city development.

Table 11.2. The Expo 98 urban project in Lisbon: conditions for competitiveness and cohesion

PROJECT	Urban redevelopment objectives	Evaluating urban competitiveness	Evaluating social and territorial cohesion
	Economic restructuring	• Replace industrial area and jobs with service and leisure industries • Creation of office and commercial space for 18,000 jobs • Relocate port and industrial activities • Creation of conditions for marketing the city (theme park ideas, facilities for large international events)	• Forced relocation of polluting industries and cleaning up of industrial soil and infrastructure • New job opportunities require low qualifications and skills • Job creation is not articulated with training programmes and incentives • Impact in the local economic activities and land market is not anticipated and integrated in project development
	Provision of environmental and urban infrastructure	• Implementation of new and modern infrastructures and a clean environment • New road network and transport system promoting urban accessibility • Implementation of public facilities with regional and national importance	• Solving long-term environmental problems of an unused port and polluted industries through an integrated plan • Access to the river front and to the new infrastructures integrated in the regional context • Access to social facilities are not planned for the neighbourhood community • Local needs were not integrated in the planning of the project
	Housing development / promotion of real estate market	• Construction of houses for 25,000 people in the high-middle class groups • State company and developers competing with the local market for raising house prices	• Does not address the problems of housing shortage and housing access for the surrounding communities • Project for an environmentally friendly and energy efficient housing development
	City planning and development	• Create a new centrality for Lisbon • New high-profile, design-oriented, residential area • New access and transport network for territorial integration	• New uses, supply conditions, and facilities are not integrated in the planning of the city • Transport network promotes territorial integration and cohesion • Absence of a strategy for regional integration (the region as an outlet for absorbing negative effects of intense urbanization)

Table 11.2. *Continued*

	Urban redevelopment objectives	Evaluating urban competitiveness	Evaluating social and territorial cohesion
PROCESS	Market enablement	• Privatization of land development • State company and private developers speculate together • State finances site preparation and infrastructures	• Sole criteria for development based upon profitability
	Political enablement	• Public company replaces local elected authorities • Decentralization of functions and decision-making to public company • Quasi-private control over the allocation of public funds	• Absence of an integrated supra-municipal authority • Autonomy of public company and professionals with discretionary decision-making processes • System facilitates and promotes élite creation • Responsibility for long-term site management and administration not defined
	Community enablement	• Public consensus as a hegemonic process • Discretionary system for selecting development options, projects, and consultants without public discussion and participation	• Absence of public inquiries and consultations • Economic rationale for articulating the interests of pressure groups • Total autonomy of public company regarding articulation of local interests

In addition, conditions for urban redevelopment are facilitated by new processes of design, formulation, and implementation, which are mediated by new forms of institutional arrangements representing changes in the relations between the state, the market, and civil society. Following Burgess *et al.* (1997: 138–62), these new institutional arrangements correspond to three policy transformations that relate to the theory of enablement: market enablement, political enablement, and community enablement. These three levels correspond to strategies established by the central state for mediating conflicts of interest around urban development projects and the urbanization process. Market enablement is exemplified by policies aimed at deregulation and privatization; political enablement by policies aimed at decentralization and subcontracting, and community enablement by regulatory and participatory reforms (ibid.).

Table 11.2 shows an apparent contradiction between processes and projects that contribute to productivity, and therefore to improving urban competitiveness on the one hand, and those that contribute to achieving conditions for social and territorial cohesion on the other. These two levels of objectives express two main goals. The first level refers to the creation of a new centrality for Lisbon (with important new facilities, modern infrastructure, and communication systems), making the city more efficient and more accessible, and therefore more competitive. The logic for achieving productivity and a competitive edge is highly debatable. Consensus around the opportunity and the size of the project is, however, the dominant trend, sustained by the expectations of positive trickle-down effects.[10]

The second level refers to the regeneration objective, which affects a local community and calls for greater social integration and articulation with the planning of the city. This side has suffered from constant neglect, and conditions for preventing further exclusion and creating social and territorial cohesion have not been included in the project. The long-term results of this are as yet unknown, but neo-liberal ideology assumes that the trickle-down effects will contribute to long-term integration and the convergence between centrality and regeneration.

The two conflicting policy levels show, however, contrasting aspects in terms of the adopted enablement processes. As shown in Table 11.2, urban development projects in Lisbon are implemented at the expense of democratic processes, undermining the social mechanisms for reconciling efficiency and equity. The entrepreneurial logic behind this hegemonic project has been instrumental in asserting the position of élites and their dominant interests (political parties and economic groups). The growth of Lisbon is, however, no longer a direct consequence of the development of the national accumulation regime. Urban projects led by economic élites in association with political élites and based on criteria of profitability, however, are not a viable means to achieve social and territorial cohesion.

Notes

1. An earlier version of this paper, entitled 'Urban Development and City Planning in a Global Economy—a Framework for the Evaluation of the Expo '98 Urban Project in Lisbon', was presented at the Regional Studies Association International Conference, Regional Potentials in an Integrating Europe, the University of the Basque Country, Bilbao, 18–21 Sept. 1999.
2. Minus 19 per cent in 1991–2001, according to provisional results from the last population census.
3. 4.8 per cent in 1991–2001, according to provisional results from the last population census.
4. According to an Audit of the project in 2000 by the 'Tribunal de Contas', the expected deficit amounted to 568 million Euro, excluding the investments and the current expenses of Parque Expo in the period between 1999 and 2010 (*Público*, 13 July 2001). However, the good returns on the land sales allowed for a decrease of the debt to 500 million Euro in 2001 (*Diário Económico*, 26 Mar. 2001).
5. The main investments in the road system were for new roads and for the upgrading of existing ones to create direct links to Lisbon's airport, to the centre of the city, to the inner and outer ring roads, and to the north and south highways. This programme of investments involved an investment of approximately 42 million Euro (Parque Expo 98, Mar. 1999). The main investment was, however, linked with the restructuring of Lisbon's public transport system through the construction of a new Metro line, with seven new stations, and the construction of a modern intermodal station (Gare do Oriente), which included a train and bus terminal and parking for 2,000 vehicles. The construction of the complex Gare do Oriente (designed by architect Santiago Calatrava) was estimated at 130 million Euro for which the ERDF contributed 60.5 per cent of the total investment.
6. That was indeed the task, stated in a Resolution of the Council of Ministers, to prepare for the management of the site for the period post-exposition. This document explicitly stated the 'strategic objectives for the post-Expo phase': (*a*) to guarantee urban and environmental quality in the intervention zone; (*b*) to guarantee the rapid establishment of urban activities to minimize transition periods; and (*c*) to maximize financial revenues to reduce the deficit and to pursue a rigorous cost-benefit policy.
7. According to Parque Expo, planning permission has been given for the construction of 5,400 flats since 1995. The 1,700 flats already built correspond to a population of 4,200 people (*Arquitectura e Vida*, July/Aug. 2001). The idea of a ghost town described by a weekly paper (*Expresso*, 27 Mar. 1999) is, therefore, changing, but the urban characteristics of the whole development are not much different from most of the suburban areas of the Lisbon periphery.
8. In 1991, the industrial sector represented 34 and 19.8 per cent of total employment in the Lisbon *freguesias* (parishes) of Marvila and Sta. Maria dos Olivais respectively. In Olivais, jobs in transport and communications linked with Lisbon Airport employed 41.1 per cent. The municipality of Loures and the *freguesias* in the area of the Expo site were also dominated by large industrial firms. In Lisbon, the dominant branches were chemistry (petrol and gas)—around 22 per cent of the industrial employment in the whole eastern zone. Other sectors were machinery, tools, and

transport material, which represented 37 per cent of industrial employment in Mar-vila and 46 per cent in Olivais.

9. Most of the firms had financial and economic problems. One set of problems had to do with landownership as many firms were tenants or were leasing public land with old and unresolved contracts. The operations of the large industrial units also had environmental and security problems as a result of being located in what was becoming an urbanized and residential part of the city. Some of the firms closed down and others relocated, for which Parque Expo negotiated forms of com-pensation. The large firms, mainly oil companies, moved to locations close to the metropolitan area. According to published studies, these closures and processes of relocalization did not have major negative impacts. These studies have, indeed, pointed out the advantages acquired from these delocalization processes in terms of growth in productivity levels and promoting economic development in much less affluent municipalities (see Seabra 1993).

10. This trend was used by the government in 2000 to promote an investment programme for major infrastructure projects in 18 Portuguese cities (*Programa de Requalificação Urbana e Valorização Ambiental de Cidades, POLIS*). This has been portrayed as a way to compensate a few cities (and projects, considered best prac-tice, selected on a discretionary basis) for the over-concentration of EU funds in the Lisbon Expo site during the previous CSF. For promoting the whole event and to run half of the redevelopment projects, lucrative commissions were given to Parque Expo. The company has, therefore, gained institutional weight and autonomy, sus-tained by this long-term financial project and the human and technical resources linked to the Expo-related urbanization process. These commissions are also seen as a way of maintaining and reproducing the heavy and expensive human and mate-rial infrastructure created in 1996. The process has been criticized since it clashes with the autonomy of local authorities and raises critical questions about the artic-ulation of regeneration policies and city planning.

References

BURGESS, R., CARMONA, M., and KOLSTEE, T. (1997) (eds.). *The Challenge of Sustainable Cities: Neoliberalism and Urban Strategies in Developing Countries*. London: Zed Books.

Câmara Municipal de Lisboa (1995). *Plano de Urbanização da Área Envolvente da Expo'98*. Lisbon: Direcção de Projectos e Planeamento Estratégico; Direcção Municipal de Planeamento e Gestcão Urbanística.

Comissão de Coordenação Regionat de Lisboa e Vale do Tejo (April 1999). *Protaml—novo contexto de elaboração e conteúdo—Estratégia territorial*, Plano Nacional de Desenvolvimento Económico e Social (PNDES). Lisbon: CCRLVT.

DUNFORD, M., LOURI, H., and ROSENSTOCK, M. (1999). 'Competitiveness and Cohesion: Competition, Competitiveness and Enterprise Policy' in R. Hall, A. Smith, and L. Tsoukalis (eds.), *Competitiveness and Cohesion in EU Policies*. Oxford: Oxford University Press.

FERREIRA ANTÓNIO FONSECA (1987). *Por uma Nova Política de Habitação*. Lisbon: Edições Afrontamento.

GASPAR, JORGE (1997). 'Lisbon: Metropolis Between Centre and Periphery', in C. Jensen-Butler, A. Shachar, and J. van Weesep (eds.), *European Cities in Competition*. Aldershot: Avebury.

GONÇALVES, F. (1989). 'Evolução Histórica do Direito do Urbanismo em Portugal', in *Direito do Urbanismo*. Lisbon: Instituto Nacional de Administraço.

HARVERY, D. (1995). 'Cities or Urbanisation?' *City*, 1/2: 38–61.

MATIAS FERREIRA, VÍTOR (1987). *A Cidade de Lisboa: de capital do império a centro da metrópole*. Lisbon: Dom Quixote.

——and INDOVINA, FRANCESCO (1999) (eds.). *A Cidade da Expo '98*. Lisbon: Editorial Bizâncio, Colecção Documentos.

——*et al.* (1997). *Lisboa, a Metrópole e o Rio*. Lisbon: Editorial Bizâncio, Colecção Documentos.

——LUCAS, JOANA, and CASTRO, ALEXANDRA (1997). 'A Expo '98 em Lisboa'. *Sociologia Problemas e Práticas*, 24: 185–230. Lisbon: Centro de Investigação e Estudos de Sociologia do Departamento de Sociologia, Instituto Superior das Ciências do Trabalho e da Empresa.

MOULAERT, F., and SWYNGEDOUW, E. (1999). 'UDP's, Socio-political Polarisation and Urban Governance in Metropolitan Cities', in *Urban Redevelopment and Social Polarisation in the City—URSPIC*, Rapport mois 18, Recherche réalisée dans le cadre du 4ème Programme Cadre, DG XII 1997–1999. Lille: IFRÉSI.

Parque Expo SA (1995). *Acordo Social para a Expo'98*. Lisbon.

——(1996). *Macro-Impactes Expo'98*, Documento Síntese. Lisbon.

——(1997). *Orçamento Plurianual da Parque Expo'98, S.A.* Lisbon.

Parque Expo 98 (Mar. 1999). *Report to the European Investment Bank*. Lisbon.

PORTAS, N. (1999) 'O pós-Expo e o resto à volta', in Vítor Matias Ferreira and Francesco Indovina (eds.), *A Cidade da Expo'98*. Lisbon: Editorial Bizâncio, Colecção Documentos.

——DOMINGUES, ALVARO, and GUIMARÃES, ALBERTO (1998). 'Portugal', in *National Urban Policy in the European Union*. Rotterdam: European Institute for Comparative Urban Research, Erasmus University.

SEABRA, JORGE (1993). *Expo'98—Dimensão Sócio-Laboral: Da situação actual às perspectivas futures*. Lisbon: Parque Exp 98 SA.

SILVA, CARLOS NUNES (1994). *Política Urbana em Lisboa—1926–1974*, Colecção Cidade de Lisboa. Lisbon: Livros Horizonte.

SOARES, LUIS BRUNO (1996). 'Lisbon: A Riverside City Looking for its Future', in L. Trigueiros and C. Sat (eds.), *Lisbon World 98 Projects*. Lisbon: Blau.

12

Business as Usual:
The Naples Business District
(Centro Direzionale di Napoli)

Serena Vicari Haddock

12.1. Introduction

Visitors to Naples cannot help but be struck by the natural beauty of the city's location and buildings and at the same time by how they have been disfigured over time. This double image is not a recent phenomenon; it has been a constant feature of the 'beautiful monster', as Braudel (1966) called the city, for hundreds of years. In some ways the new business centre of the city, which towers over its skyline, is a further addition to its monstrosity. Beauty and desolation, wealth and poverty reside side by side in all parts of the city—glaring evidence of the constant conflict among different economic, social, and cultural groups, which is at the heart of a fragmented southern European society. Throughout its history the city has been the object of large investments in fixed capital, yet these recurrent injections of capital have failed repeatedly to produce a reorganization of the city's economic system and to induce endogenous development. Political instability, corruption, and crime have been constant companions of the city's fragile and unbalanced development. In 1993 a new coalition came to power at City Hall. Led by a union leader, Antonio Bassolino, the coalition enjoyed strong popular support and remained in power almost eight years (just short of two terms), a unique achievement in the politics of Italian cities in recent years. During this period the city's fiscal crisis was solved, comprehensive planning was approved, signs of industrial development appeared, along with a boom in tourism: what has been called 'the Neapolitan renaissance' is in full bloom. At the same time Naples remains in an emergency situation. The city is frequently brought to a halt by demonstrations organized by the various groups of unemployed and by workers employed in so-called 'public utility jobs' demanding permanent employment in the agencies and public institutions for which they are currently working. On the

Plate 12.1. The Centro Direzionale di Napoli

security front, after years of unopposed domination by organized crime in the area, a number of successful police actions have brought leading figures of the main criminal organization (*camorra*) to justice. The resulting struggle for leadership and control of the organization has brought death and injury to innocent bystanders and citizens in the metropolitan area as well as to the competing criminal factions.

In this chapter, I analyse the planning and implementation of the new business centre, a major redevelopment of a large derelict area in the centre of the city, which at present remains half-finished (see Plate 12.1). The project is first placed against the background of the socio-economic crisis of the city and the larger processes of social polarization and spatial segmentation. Second, the institutional context of urban policy and the relative role of the national and local governments and economic actors are discussed. Third, an analysis of the decision-making and implementation process highlights the interaction between political and economic élites in the metropolitan area. It will be maintained that since the end of the Second World War urban policy in the city has consistently been the product of governance structures centred on the public sector. The new business centre was the product of one such coalition led by a state agency, which subordinated local government to its interests and mobilized land interests and construction companies around the project. In the minds of this agency's leaders, the project was to become the emblem of their modernizing role. But in its implementation the state élite performed more as rentiers than modern civil servants or state entrepreneurs. Analysis shows the specific impact of this property-led development on the fabric of the city. The mechanisms of redistribution set in motion by such a development are also presented.

12.2. The City: Socio-economic Crisis and Spatial Segmentation

12.2.1. Socio-economic crisis

Up to the end of the 1980s Naples could still be considered the industrial capital of both the Campania region and the entire Mezzogiorno of Italy. This position was due to the presence in the city of a vast array of medium and large companies, some private, but more often state owned, active in many sectors. In the middle of the 1960s, state-owned industrial companies accounted for almost 80 per cent of industrial production in the south. Today, Naples has clearly lost its supremacy and is experiencing a process of profound de-industrialization accompanied by substantial growth in the tertiary sector. In addition to more general factors leading to de-industrialization, the Neapolitan industrial system was particularly affected by European Union action to reduce iron and steel production in Europe and its policies protecting fair competition that limited state aid to industries.

De-industrialization has also been particularly extensive because the disappearance of heavy industry has not been counterbalanced by the rise of a system of medium and small companies. Four factors have been identified to account for the weakness of the local economic system. The first has to do with the quality of the local government: the instability of governing coalitions and their inability not only to produce policies conducive to local development but also to ensure the 'normal' provision of public services and infrastructures. The absence of this important location factor has increased costs for companies—a second factor that has damaged the business environment. The third factor is the distortion of the labour market, due to the presence of a strong movement of 'organized unemployed'. Local politicians have responded to the recurrent mobilization of this group with jobs in the public sector, expansion of the Cassa Integrazione Guadagni,[1] and subsidies of all kinds. This policy has in turn favoured the consolidation of the informal sector and penalized formal entrepreneurial activity. A fourth factor is the presence of organized crime, which impacts on economic activities both directly as they become subject to extortion and indirectly through adding uncertainty to the business environment.

The process of de-industrialization is particularly concentrated in the metropolitan area of Naples. While in the 1970s there had been an 11 per cent reduction in the number of industrial companies but still some job growth (14.7 per cent), in the period between 1981 and 1991 the metropolitan area of Naples lost 36 per cent of its manufacturing companies and 27 per cent of all industrial jobs. In the Mezzogiorno as a whole there was a decrease by 20 per cent of industries and 16 per cent of jobs compared to 18 per cent and 14 per cent respectively for Italy as a whole. All industrial subsectors shrank considerably, with the exception of construction, which grew by 30 per cent (officially, but much more in terms of irregular workers) as a consequence of public works programmes (ISTAT 1971; 1981; 1991).

Turning to the service sector, we find the rate of employment in this sector rising sharply during the 1970s, continuing to rise (although less rapidly) during the 1980s, and remaining more or less stable during the 1990s, both at the metropolitan and at the regional level. The growth is concentrated in less advanced services, i.e. retail trade and traditional professional occupations, and in the public administration, providing evidence of the difficulties the city has experienced in making the transition towards a service economy (Cavola and D'Antonio 1994).

The minor gain in service jobs has in no way compensated for the huge losses of jobs in the industrial sector. As a result Naples has become the capital of unemployment: the unemployment rate is the highest of all large Italian cities, and has been rising constantly since the end of the 1970s and by 1991 had reached 42.7 per cent.[2] Unemployment is particularly severe for young people (between 14 and 29 years old); this group shows an unemployment rate of 57.3 per cent (for young women the rate of unemployment rises to 78 per cent) (Kazepov 1999; Morlicchio 1996).

It might be argued that the unemployment rate could be overestimated by including people that in reality work in the informal sector of the local economy. In Italy the informal economy is large and growing.[3] Although by no means an exclusively southern phenomenon, the informal economy is certainly more widespread in the south and in Campania in particular. In industrial areas of this region and in the metropolitan area of Naples, in textile, clothing, and shoe production, the percentage of undeclared work reaches 80–90 per cent of the total number of jobs (Meldolesi 1998). Informal work in Naples is not of the same kind as that found in the Third Italy areas, however.[4] It is deskilled, precarious, and poorly paid. Informal manufacturing activities have transformed themselves from traditional crafts—what used to be an urban subsistence economy—to a sweatshop system of production, which is not directed towards innovative sectors of the market, but to residual sectors such as those serving the market for unauthorized imitations (knock-offs) or second-quality goods. In this context, work in the informal economy does not provide a substitute for a formal job. At the same time, the processes that create, reproduce, and permit the continuing existence of the informal economy bring about specific forms of exclusion (Goddard 1996; Vicari 2001).

Naples is the capital of unemployment but also of organized crime. In the last two decades a mafia-type organization known as the new Neapolitan *camorra* has gained control over all illegal activities related to drug dealing in the area, and as such has accumulated a great deal of capital, which is then laundered and invested also in local economic activities. The *camorra* also controls votes, which it exchanges with political leaders who are able to ensure privileged treatment of its members by police and judges or to provide opportunities for profits. The connection between organized crime, local entrepreneurs, and local political leaders in the management of public works is well documented in the records of a mounting number of judicial cases (Allum 1996; Barbagallo 1997).

12.2.2. Spatial segmentation

Naples is at the centre of a densely inhabited conurbation extending across all municipalities of the city's province/metropolitan area.[5] It is a metropolitan area which has remained strongly divided between its core—the central part of the municipality of Naples where resources, infrastructures, and services, aspects of the quality of the built environment, are concentrated—and the periphery of the city and surrounding municipalities, which are particularly lacking in services. In the 1980s and 1990s large-scale projects have contributed to and consolidated this dualistic and monocentric model (Gasparini 1991).

Comparison among metropolitan areas in Italy shows first that within a general trend of polarization of the Italian social structure in the 1980s, Naples is unique in the degree of social contrasts between the core and the periphery of its metropolitan area. Secondly, in Naples as in most Italian cities, there are no upper-class residential quarters outside the core: the upper class remains in the city centre, showing the traditional attachment of the bourgeoisie to the sites that it had built for itself at the time of its formation (Becchi 1996). It must be emphasized, however, that pockets of poverty still exist also in central areas: in the inner city there are still low cost dwellings, often in severe physical decay, where less privileged social groups can afford to live. The main axis of spatial and social segregation, however, remains the great divide between the historical centre of the city and its surrounding areas on the one hand, and the peripheral areas of the Neapolitan and adjacent provincial communes on the other.

12.3. Institutional Framework and the Changing System of Governance

Italian local governments are part of a three-tier administrative system in which centralization is slowly giving way to regionalization and decentralization.

The regions have seen their functions greatly expanded in recent years, and regional governments now have full authority over social and health services, economic development, and spatial and environmental planning. At the same time, however, regional financial autonomy has been reduced and the central state has retained the right to issue administrative guidelines and provisions for policy co-ordination, even in areas of exclusively regional competence. Municipal governments are permitted even less financial autonomy and are subject to tight controls at regional and central level. They have, however, full authority over spatial planning and are also in charge of providing basic health and social services, as well as all public works related to these services and to the transportation infrastructure. In 1990 Parliament approved a general reform of local government,[6] to improve the effectiveness of municipalities and provinces and to eliminate the overlap of functions and joint-decision traps built into the system.[7] The process of reforming local public administration is very slow, as it runs against traditional Italian administrative culture.[8] On the other hand, the new electoral law, which prescribes that mayors be elected directly, has given greater visibility and leverage to mayors of large cities in their bargaining for resources with the centre. This new power has proved to be an important factor in fostering new urban strategies and in improving the effectiveness of local government in the last decade.

In the south of Italy three additional factors further complicate the institutional context of developmental policy. First, the direct role that the state has played, in lieu of a national policy for urban areas, through 'exceptional' or 'emergency' programmes, which the state defines and finances. 'Exceptional' programmes have been designed to address specific problems, as in the case of urban traffic.[9] Urban redevelopment and infrastructures have been promoted through policies related to a national 'event',[10] but also via capital investment in the construction of specific infrastructures, such as university campuses, prisons, and law courts. Concern about the competitiveness of the industrial system and lack of technological innovation brought about a policy programme for the promotion of technology parks in the south. In the 1980s and early 1990s, major transformations in Italian cities resulted from such programmes, which were often administered by *ad hoc* agencies and in disregard of local government planning policies. For the city of Naples, in particular, 'emergency' policies were quite obviously called for in the case of the 1980 earthquake. Massive funds (about 25,000 million Euro) were made available during different phases of the reconstruction process under the management of *ad hoc* authorities. In the reconstruction programme—one of the major scandals in public expenditure of the post-war period—we see at work a model of public intervention that has at its centre national and local political leaders and entrepreneurs in construction and related businesses, a coalition of interests known as the 'party of public expenditure' (Sales 1993).

A second factor concerns the role played by national and European aid to the south. Until very recently the main instrument for funnelling national and European money into the south has been the Cassa per il Mezzogiorno. The Cassa gave rise to a cross-party coalition of politicians and their clients monopolizing the distribution of public resources with clear preferences for large infrastructure projects. Abolished in 1986, its successor SVIMEZ ceased functioning only in 1991: by that time the gap between the regions of the south and the rest of Italy was greater than at any time during almost thirty years of special interventions. Most major infrastructure works in the Naples area were financed with some aid from the EU. In the specific case of the Centro Direzionale di Napoli (CDN) project, EU funds came both under the form of a co-funding operation of the European Regional Development Fund (ERDF) and FIO (Fondo investimenti occupazione (Investment Fund for Employment Promotion)), and under the form of a loan of 110 billion lira (55 million Euro) for infrastructure from the European Bank for Investment (BEI). EU funds were to be managed by the promoter of the CDN project, thus strengthening the former's role *vis-à-vis* the local government.

Politics is the third factor shaping developmental policy. In Naples in the thirty years between 1963 and 1993, twenty-six city governments tried to run the city, with very poor results both in terms of their ability to direct urban development and effectively to oppose illegal building.[11] Political instability *per se* impedes the policy decision-making process, but it is mainly the clientelist relationship between political leaders and their constituencies which shapes urban policy. The nature of this relationship favours the building of large-scale projects and infrastructure, as these channel to the area significant financial resources which can be distributed to companies involved in the redevelopment process at various levels, and to local bureaucracies and dominant parties. Because of their large and selective redistributive potential, large-scale projects have a higher probability of being accomplished and have become the major if not the sole outcome of urban policy.

The intrusiveness of the central state, various forms of national and EU aid mediated by specific agencies, the politics of local development: all these factors have reduced the involvement of local government and its capacity to produce comprehensive urban policy. Local government planning is of little relevance in explaining urban development. On the other hand, dominant market forces, which are traditionally used as the opposite pole in such an explanation, are not so clearly responsible for it either. Because of the characteristics of the local economy described above and its transformation over time, interests are diverse and extremely fragmented, forming unexpected and unstable coalitions of power.

I would prefer to define these coalitions as different governance structures overseeing the reproduction of the city. Four types of such governance structures can be distinguished, each one of which had a dominant role in a specific period and produced a concrete urban policy. The first can properly be called a 'growth machine' (Molotch 1976), as landed interests dominated local government, presiding over the unregulated growth and speculation of the 1950s and

1960s. Land interests and construction companies are not distinguishable from local politicians running the city's council; they formed a compact bloc of interests,[12] which expressed itself in a *laissez-faire* policy of overbuilding. In the second type, state-owned enterprises and public agencies play the leading role (1970–82). Policies to regulate urban growth and population concentration signalled some distance between the new ruling coalition and old landed interests. State holding companies and local agencies of the central state administration controlling investment in the city were the most prominent actors in local governance. Urban policy was oriented mainly towards maintaining the city's industrial base through repeated public investment, directly into state-owned companies and indirectly into redevelopment for the transition of the local economy into services. In this framework, and as we shall see in detail in the following section, the new business centre is a typical example of the urban policy of this second type of governance structure. In the third type, pivotal roles are played by political leaders at the national and local levels, and large redevelopment projects directly promoted by them—such as the renewal of the stadium and related infrastructures, a new university campus, the new ring road around the city—are the specific and only outcome of urban policy during the period 1983–93. The economic and political interests of Neapolitan ministers in Rome, politicians in Naples, and national and local entrepreneurs in construction and related businesses are determining factors. This governance structure included for the first time among its actors organized crime, which in the 1980s and 1990s became heavily involved both as a result of direct investment in local companies and through its connections and exchanges with local political leaders. Urban policy was determined by public funds available under various national 'emergency' or 'exceptional' programmes and chiefly under the frame of the post-earthquake reconstruction programme. National leaders with their constituencies in the region channelled enormous financial resources to the area. These were distributed to companies (mainly builders) involved in the redevelopment process and to local bureaucracies and dominant political parties. This clientelist strategy constituted the main framework of the urban development process (Barbagallo 1997; Indovina 1993). A fourth governance structure has begun to take shape in recent years (from 1993 to the present) and has at its centre the local government, which has regained its power of regulation over urban development. Urban regeneration has become the central focus of urban policy, and a different approach, which foresees integration between building initiatives and socio-economic actions, has been gaining ground over the last decade. Policy networks are being opened up to new actors from civil society and public–private partnerships are pursued forcefully. These changes are being driven by EU policy and by a new political and administrative culture at the national and local level. They face, however, tremendous challenges in the building of new forms of co-operation between public and private sectors.

12.4. Naples Business District
(Centro Direzionale di Napoli, CDN)

The project for the new Naples business district (Centro Direzionale di Napoli, CDN) concerns an area of approximately 110 ha at the eastern edge of the city's historical centre, close to the Central Station and not far from the city's airport, the harbour, and major entry points to the motorway network (see Plate 12.1). In terms of property ownership the area is divided into two distinct parcels: a western part of about 50 ha owned by Italstat, a finance company of the 'state-holdings' corporation IRI,[13] and an eastern part of about 60 ha owned by the municipality (90 per cent) and by a group of small property owners (10 per cent).

The rationale for the development of a business centre in such a location reflects a number of different discourses. The first discourse took shape around the idea that the city of Naples, which had grown tremendously as a built environment in the 1950s and 1960s, needed to be 'modernized', i.e. transformed into a modern metropolis conceived as a centre of services. The second discourse was based on the need to relocate administrative and management functions from the city's centre, which had become overcrowded and overrun by traffic. A third rationale for the project lay in the need to regenerate an urban area where abandoned industrial sites and decaying neighbourhoods were located. Last but not least, there was growing pressure to renew an urban economy plagued by unemployment and a deep crisis in one of its most important sectors, the construction industry.

The idea to build a business centre in Naples took shape in the early 1960s; the actual planning of the project, however, began only twenty years later.[14] In this long incubation period two unrelated processes came to completion and determined the conditions which, in retrospect, can be regarded as necessary for the successful planning and implementation of the project. First, a company called Mededil was formed which gradually acquired land in the area and was endowed with adequate capital as it came under the control of the 'state-holdings' corporation IRI. Second, state investment in the area came with the decision to build new Law Courts for the city. Over time the project for the new Law Courts in the area was included in the 1972 city Master Plan and funds for it were made available within an *ad hoc* national programme in 1981. The location of the Law Courts is the result of what can be considered the single most important marketing action of the CDN's promoter; it was supposed to attract other public bodies and private offices and to provide an additional rationale for the extension of public transportation to the area.

The CDN project, presented by the Japanese architect Kenzo Tange, integrated a range of buildings into a comprehensive design—a unique phenomenon in Naples. It called for the construction of over 5 million m³ (30 per cent for residences and 70 per cent for service functions). In the western area, the municipality licensed the building of a total of 2,250,000 m³ (360,000 m³ of residences and 1,890,000 m³ for offices) all of which were built between 1983 and 1991, resulting in 1,000 residential units and about 500,000 m² for service functions. Parking facilities were built for approximately 10,000 cars (40 per cent of the total amount) in private and public parking lots. One school (of six) and one church (of two)—those assigned to the western area—were built by September 2001. The eastern area of the CDN was also granted substantial building rights: 2,100,000 m³ for the municipality and 480,000 for private owners. To date, these rights have yet to be exercised; the eastern part of the CDN still awaits development, which will be carried out on a smaller scale under guidelines defined by the new Master Plan approved in 1999.

In order to explain the non-development of the eastern area, it is necessary to look at the dynamics of the relationship between Mededil and local government and to position them in the context of the city's urban policy. Despite its substantive power in urban planning, the local government has consistently acquiesced to the requests of Mededil and accommodated them in subsequent planning documents. Even when leftist parties governed the city council, it was unable to bargain for substantial trade-offs in the development process. As shown in the previous section, by the time the CDN was built urban policy was restricted to the promotion of large-scale projects which failed to trigger urban regeneration either in the historical centre, which continues its slow decay undisturbed, or in the periphery. Local government proved unable to produce a different kind of urban policy addressing the severe problems of the city or to direct the reconstruction process after the 1980 earthquake or even to exercise authority over its own territory to stop illegal building.

The case of the CDN exemplifies the ways in which political and economic resources are played out in urban development. Because Mededil controlled public funding which could not be invested in other development projects, the construction of the CDN was never an issue even for the opposition. In addition, it never had to face any kind of protest or public opposition. On the contrary, there were demonstrations every time construction work was suspended or delayed. Mededil is a peculiar type of investor and developer with accesses to specific financial and political resources, which made it very powerful *vis-à-vis* the municipality.[15] Mededil proved very effective in activating its links upward, first to IRI in order to secure a constant flow of financial resources to the project, second to the central state, in order to promote the location of important functions, such as the Law Courts, and the related investment in the CDN, and third to other public agencies and companies in order to sell them office buildings in the CDN. Furthermore, Mededil, as a state-owned company, was able to present itself as an actor supposedly pursuing higher social interests, an actor with an aura totally different from a 'normal' private real estate speculator and therefore commanding greater attention from public officials. At the same time, as a private body, it was able to escape the procedures for public sector contracts and to grant these contracts to national and local companies and professionals close to its political affiliation.

These self-reinforcing factors explain the successful working of a specific governance structure of which the CDN was a product. They also lead to an understanding of the breakdown of that structure and the consequent end to the CDN operation. Funds under the umbrella of the 'state-holding' corporation IRI dried up and political changes and reforms at the national and local level, coupled with a new urban policy framework influenced by the EU, gave new power and a different orientation to local government. In November 2000 the approval of a new Master Plan signalled that the local government had regained control over urban development. As a result the completion of the CDN project was subjected to intense scrutiny. The new leftist administration formally accused previous administrations of having taken action prejudicial to the public interest, specifically having allowed Mededil to appropriate rights to build that belonged to the municipality.[16] Public scrutiny of the CDN operation has brought to light other liabilities resulting from how the project was implemented. First, the absence of public control has resulted in a severe lack of public services and infrastructures, which the developer failed to provide. A study by the municipality planning office also revealed that Mededil built the large infrastructures using EU funds—provided under a co-financing agreement—without contributing its own financial share.

At present, in the western area, the CDN remains incomplete in terms of certain public transport infrastructures such as the Circumvesuviana station and the connection with the Alifana railway, for which some preliminary work was carried out but for which major work remains to be done. An additional missing piece concerns the Law Courts, a building complex which cost 1,000 billion lira (about 500 million Euro, ten times the original estimate) but which is still missing the 'tower' dedicated to civil justice.[17] The Criminal Law and Attorney General's offices lack adequate access roads and parking facilities.[18] The eastern area, which remains undeveloped, is in certain respects more significant than the area actually built. In fact, it was the eastern part of the project that provided for the location of the most important public structures: the region and municipality headquarters and five of the six schools, together with an 8 ha public park with sports and cultural facilities. All these structures were intended to serve also the neighbouring quarters Luzzati and Ascarelli, which are particularly lacking in services. Moreover, together with the missing pieces in the western area noted above, they would have made the whole CDN more attractive to people and business. Instead, in 1999, five years after the completion of the project, the CDN had a vacancy rate of about 30 per cent for the office and residential units.

12.5. Impact of the CDN on Neighbourhoods and the Larger Metropolitan Community

The city has gained half a business district, which has been planned and implemented outside local government control and removed from public scrutiny and democratic control. It has been built in large part in disregard of labour and safety norms. The deficit in public services on the western side has to be compensated in the eastern part, reducing the commercial value of that future development for the municipality, the landowner of the area. This is the result of the unbalanced relationship between local government and developer analysed above. We turn now to the specific impact of the CDN on the city.

12.5.1. The physical impact on the city

Despite the fact that the project is only half-built, the very scale of the developed area makes it a landmark for the city. Apart from scale, its physical impact on the city is conspicuous because of the high-rise design of its residential buildings and particularly because of the two towers which mark the entrance to the CDN. Set against the background of the surrounding hills and the Vesuvio volcano, it orerrides the traditional skyline of the city and constitutes, in public opinion, an eyesore. On the other hand, the project, and these towers in particular, were featured in the most important journals in the field for the architectural quality of their design and for their innovations in anti-seismic technology. Whether welcomed by supporters of the need to modernize the city or criticized by many others on different grounds, it remains unquestionable that the design of the project makes it completely foreign to the urban fabric of the city. The project is also poorly connected to the adjacent neighbourhoods because of its introverted urban layout. To people working and living in the CDN, it appears to be an island separated from the city, a foreign territory enamoured of its own grandeur and advanced technology. Among other complaints expressed are feelings of insecurity and uneasiness associated with living and/or working in the CDN.[19]

12.5.2. The economic impact

It has been estimated that the construction of the CDN created about 1,500 jobs and provided indirect employment for an additional 800 people for the six central years of the construction process.[20] Apart from the construction phase, job creation in the CDN can be said to have been disappointing and totally incommensurate with the size of the investment. Company registries show that in 1997 there were 1,130 companies located as owners or renters in the CDN; Mededil claimed that in 1996 there were 12,000 employees and that by 1997, with the (partial) opening of the Law Courts, the number would rise to 25,000.

The large majority of these jobs, however, are not new but the result of companies' relocation from other parts of the city. Moreover, Mededil's figures appear to be inflated: in fact no shopping facilities of any significance have moved to the area, an indication that the number of people moving through the CDN has not yet reached the critical point where it would be attractive to business. Nor has the clustering of companies from the central districts into the CDN generated new real estate developments and commercial enterprises in the surrounding areas. The relocation of public administration offices has suffered major delays and is far from complete; to date no related services have been generated. Only in 1999 did the decision to locate the newly formed Authority for Telecommunications in the CDN bring a large new employer to the area. Current estimates of vacancy rates confirm the difficulty that the CDN encounters as a location for business. In conclusion, all the evidence points to a much more conservative estimate of a few hundred new jobs being generated by the project.

12.5.3. The social impact

As of 1999, according to the phone registry, only 716 families lived in the CDN, totalling some 2,200–2,300 residents. They form an extremely homogeneous social group of middle-class families *vis-à-vis* the surrounding working-class communities.[21] In addition to the physical barriers discussed above, the social profile of the residents contributes to isolate them further. From the perspective of neighbouring quarters, which are particularly lacking in public services, the CDN has failed to improve their quality of life, firstly, because the location of public services, schools, public parks, and sports and cultural facilities were intended to be in the eastern part, which has yet to be built; secondly because even in the western area, the CDN remains incomplete in terms of some public transport infrastructures. Mobility within the CDN and accessibility to the CDN from outside remain problematic, both because of lack of public transportation from these neigbourhoods to the CDN and because of the physical barriers still in place. The result is that the gains in terms of better public transportation are still minimal for the neighbouring communities. Last but not least, there have been only minimal opportunities for employment in the CDN. From the perspective of the city as a whole, the CDN is not living up to expectations of improving life in the city centre. The relocation of public administration offices has proceeded quite slowly so that the expected decrease in overcrowding and congestion within the city centre has not occurred.

12.5.4. Impact of the CDN on the city's real estate markets

The CDN operation has been a commercial success for Mededil, the promoter, but less so for investors. Real estate sales in housing and offices in the CDN reached higher prices than in other valuable parts of the city, indicating probable high levels of profit for this promoter of the development. Secondly, from 1992 on, the housing and office stock of the CDN appears to have depressed the demand for housing and office space in the more exclusive quarters of the city, which experienced their lowest increase in value over this period. Also, the CDN seems to have absorbed some of the demand for shops that otherwise would have been satisfied in the centre or in the more exclusive quarters.

For investors, the CDN has not proved particularly rewarding to date. In the rental sector the CDN performed quite poorly, as the area's rental prices did not rise on a par with the city's average increase in land value. The high vacancy rate (50 per cent for offices, 35 per cent for commercial units) five years after completion of the project confirms this conclusion. In this respect the CDN has not proved to be competitive with regard to other parts of the city, despite the fact that all its units are newly built. Several factors account for this outcome. First, the CDN is not competitive because firms and shops, as well as residents, still find the city centre and the more exclusive quarters a more prestigious location, despite the assumed high quality of the CDN built environment. These central districts are able to yield higher returns and to perform as an insulated sub-market uninfluenced by what the CDN offers. Second, the CDN requires intensive maintenance, which translates into high fees that in turn contribute to depressing the real estate market of CDN offices, shops, and residences. Third, real estate investors and operators failed to provide the services and amenities which could have brought higher value to their investment.

12.6. Conclusions

I began this chapter with an image of a fragmented city where stunning beauty and desolation are present in each fragment of its territory. The piecemeal development of the last decades, centred as it was on large-scale projects, reinforced the fragmented character of the city. In the same period the already severe problems of the city, unemployment and poverty, were exacerbated. The traditional 'physical' approach to urban regeneration, which privileged large-scale projects, failed to generate local development. The benefits were in each case harvested by the governance machines that promoted this approach during the period from the 1950s until the early 1990s (see section 12.3 above). In the case of the CDN, developmental benefits were distributed within a closed circle. Great wealth was generated by Mededil, which collected rents as landowner and profits as developer. Some of that wealth had to trickle up, to bureaucracies and parties—not to mention organized crime—which made the development possible. Downward, the main beneficiaries were construction companies and related services, but nothing flowed down any further. Public benefits such as urban spaces and services, transportation and employment, were simply not produced.

The CDN is a case of property-led development where the property belongs to the state. It shows all the shortcomings of a property-led development and little or no responsiveness to social needs. The investment in the CDN privileged, once again, central areas to the detriment of already deprived peripheries and thus contributed to the reproduction and reinforcement of the 'divided' model of urban development in Naples. It also clearly represents a decision not to develop and invest in projects that might effectively address the social and economic conditions that continue to nourish the unending Neapolitan 'emergency'.

This case is not exceptional in Italy, as similar outcomes have resulted from other publicly funded large-scale projects. And in the Italian south this strategy is not even new, as traditional aid policies to the south have repeatedly set in motion similar dynamics and have similarly proved incapable of generating endogenous local development. In Italy the state has long played the role of an entrepreneur in the south and has consistently failed to achieve the socio-economic objectives necessary to justify the repeated massive investment of public capital and resources.

In part as a result of these failures and in part due to pressure from the EU, national and local development policies have undergone tremendous change, and the city has begun to show signs of a different approach to development. As in other metropolitan areas, new actors have begun to emerge in the local economy and society, particularly in what is known as the 'made in Italy' sector and in the social economy, or 'Third sector'. Within this new policy framework and with these new economic actors, it has become possible, for the first time, to pursue new forms of social and economic development, to seek new forms of collaboration among local actors, and to promote an approach to development that is both more integrated and more inclusive. The city is thus at a crossroads: the new direction faces enormous challenges on all fronts, but the alternative is to return to 'business as usual' based on large-scale projects and an élite governance machine driving a specific form of local development in which rewards are limited to a select few.

Acknowledgements

This chapter draws on a previous analysis carried out by the author and Lucia Cavola of Iter, whose contribution was significant and whose generosity and invaluable co-operation are gratefully acknowledged.

Notes

1. The CIG is a provision for unemployment which was implemented in 1975, whereby the state pays approximately 80 per cent of wages to workers temporarily made

redundant in firms facing problems of reduced demand (Cassa Integrazione Guadagni Ordinaria) or structural adjustment (Cassa Integrazione Guadagni Straordinaria). These two measures have been used intensively and increasingly over the years, in lieu of unemployment subsidies, which were almost non-existent. Although they have two/three year limits, extensions are fairly common and instances of people receiving this 'temporary' subsidy for more than ten years are not exceptional.

2. The 1991 Census provides the most recent data at the city level. Official estimates for the region of Campania indicate that it remained at least at this level throughout the 1990s.

3. Three different studies commissioned by the EU (Orseu 1995; Deloitte and Touche 1997; Schneider 1997) estimate the Italian shadow economy at between 20 per cent and 36 per cent of the GNP.

4. Recent investigation shows that, contrary to experts' expectations, signs of 'light' industrialization are emerging also in the south and in Campania in particular. Clusters of small industries produce porcelain in Capodimonte in the periphery of Naples, bathing suits in the municipalities in the southern part of its province, clothing and shoes in the northern part of its province. Even in these small companies, which are almost all hidden in the informal economy, working conditions and compensation are in general much lower than those typical in the Third Italy industrial districts. See Baculo (1997).

5. In the case of Naples the territorial definition of the province coincides with that of the metropolitan area. Its designation is in fact 'provincia metropolitana'.

6. Public Law No. 142/1990, subsequently amended regarding the provision of metropolitan areas by Public Law No. 463/1993.

7. Public Law No. 57/1997 and Public Law No. 127/1997 in particular simplified and rationalized procedures and relations among different levels of local government.

8. For large cities, for example, the reform provided for the designation of the provinces of the nine largest cities, including Naples, as *aree metropolitane* (metropolitan areas), in which a metropolitan council (with its own executive and 'metropolitan' mayor) exercises the most important functions, leaving only residual functions to the municipal councils within the metropolitan territory. So far this specific provision of the law has remained a dead letter (Rotelli 1999). Naples has changed the name of the province to 'provincia metropolitana' leaving for the moment unchanged the respective distribution of powers among the three levels of government.

9. Special funds are made available for underground public transportation systems (L. 211/1992), connections between urban and national railway networks (D.L. 77/1989), or the construction of parking facilities (L. 122/1989).

10. Examples of such events are 'Colombo 92' (L. 373/1988 and L. 99/1991), the celebration of the 500th anniversary of Colombus's voyage, or 'Italia 90' (L. 205/1989), the football world cup.

11. The Campania region and the metropolitan area of Naples have the highest percentages in the country of buildings without building permits, exceeding allowed volumes, or in violation of regulations.

12. At the national level the same coalition of interests—called 'blocco edilizio'—is said to have been responsible for the lack of attention paid to the definition of planning policy and regulation in the same period. See Parlato 1978.

13. IRI stands for Istituto Ricostruzione Industriale (Institute for Industrial Recon-
    struction). Together with ENI (Energy and Chemicals) and EFIM (Manufacturing
    Industry), IRI makes up the group of holding corporations which were the respon-
    sibility of the Ministry for State Holdings.
14. A more detailed account of the process is provided in Cavola and Vicari 1999.
15. An analysis of the Mededil board of directors shows the prominence and centrali-
    ty of its members in the network of the old Christian Democrat regime and suggests
    a considerable command of resources in different domains.
16. This action followed earlier legal action taken by the municipality against Mededil
    with regard to the cost of infrastructural works that the company had carried out.
    Both actions were settled in Apr. 1999 with Mededil receiving from the munici-
    pality 25 million Euro (instead of the 100 million Euro previously requested) as
    payment for infrastructural works.
17. The 'tower' burned down in July 1990, shortly before construction was completed;
    the cause of the fire has yet to be determined and the case remains open.
18. These infrastructures cannot be constructed because the area is still occupied by the
    wholesale food market.
19. According to Newman's analysis (1972) high-rise buildings placed in an undiffer-
    entiated open space, as in the CDN, create an impersonal environment which is con-
    ducive to crime; 'Gridded space . . . subdues those who must live in the space, but
    disorienting their ability to see and evaluate relationships' (Sennett 1990: 60).
20. The completion of the project on the eastern part of the area would provide 3,000
    jobs (1,000 of item indirectly) for five years.
21. Because the residential complexes are owned by INPDAP, a pension fund for
    public companies, only families working for state agencies are entitled to rent
    those apartments.

References

ALLUM, P. (1996). 'The Resistible Rise of the New Neapolitan Camorra', in S. Gundle
  and S. Parker (eds.), *The New Italian Republic: From the Fall of the Berlin Wall to
  Berlusconi.* London: Routledge, 87–112.

BACULO, L. (1997). 'Segni di industrializzazione leggera nel Mezzogiorno'. *Stato e
  Mercato*, 51: 377–418.

BARBAGALLO, F. (1997). *Napoli fine Novecento. Politici, camorristi, imprenditori.* Turin:
  Einaudi.

BECCHI, A. (1996). 'Città e forme di emarginazione', in F. Barbagallo (ed.), *Storia
  dell'Italia repubblicana*, iii. Turin: Einaudi, 838–910.

BRAUDEL, F. (1966). *La Méditerranée et le monde méditerranéen à l'époque de Philippe II.*
  Paris: Armand Colin.

CAVOLA, L. and D'ANTONIO, M. (1994). 'Gli effetti perversi della de-
  industrializzazione'. *Nord e Sud*, 1: 44–54.

——and VICARI, S. (1999). 'Naples: The Centro Direzionale', in F. Moulaert, E.
  Swyngedouw, and A. Rodriguez (eds.), *Urban Redevelopment and Social Polarisation
  in the City*. Research report 1997–1998. Lille: IFRESI.

Deloitte and Touche Consulting Group (1997). *The Black Economy and Taxes and Social Charges*, commissioned by the Task Force 'Statutory Contributions and Charges', D.G. XXI. Brussels: European Commission.

GASPARINI, C. (1991). 'La "città divisa": un modello urbano che si è andato consolidando', in AA.VV., *La costruzione della città europea negli anni '80*. Rome: Cresme, 335–407.

GODDARD, V. A. (1996). *Gender, Family and Work in Naples*. Oxford: Berg.

INDOVINA, F. (1993). *La città occasionale*. Milan: Franco Angeli.

ISTAT (1971). *XI Censimento generale della popolazione*. Rome: ISTAT.

——(1981). *XII Censimento generale della popolazione*. Rome: ISTAT.

——(1991). *XIII Censimento generale della popolazione*. Rome: ISTAT.

KAZEPOV, Y. (1999). 'La povertà urbana', in G. Martinotti (ed.), *La dimensione metropolitana*. Bologna: il Mulino, 243–74.

MELDOLESI, L. (1998). 'L'economia sommersa nel Mezzogiorno'. *Stato e Mercato*, 53: 319–34.

MOLOTCH, H. (1976). 'The City as a Growth Machine: Toward a Political Economy of Place'. *American Journal of Sociology*, 82/2: 309–32.

MORLICCHIO, E. (1996). 'Exclusion from Work and the Empoverishment Processes in Naples', in E. Mingione (ed.), *Urban Poverty and the Underclass: A Reader*. Oxford: Blackwell.

NEWMAN, O. (1972). *Defensible Space: Crime Prevention through Urban Design*. New York: Collier.

Orseu (1995). *Measurement of the Shadow Economy: Study of Five European Countries (Germany, Bergium, France, Great Britain, Italy)*. Brussels: Orseu.

PARLATO, V. (1978). 'Il blocco edilizio', in F. Indovina (ed.), *Lo spreco edilizio*. Venice: Marsilio, 189–200.

ROTELLI, E. (1999). 'Le aree metropolitane in Italia: una questione istituzionale insoluta', in G. Martinotti (ed.), *La dimensione metropolitana*. Bologna: il Mulino, 299–330.

SALES, I. (1993). *La camorra, le camorre*. Rome: Editori Riuniti.

SCHNEIDER, F. (1997). *Further Empirical Results of the Size of the Shadow Economy of 17 OECD Countries Over Time*, Dept. of Economics, University of Linz, Austria.

SENNETT, R. (1990). *The Conscience of the Eye*. New York and London: W. W. Norton and Co.

VICARI, S. (2001). 'Naples: Urban Regeneration and Exclusion in the Italian South'. *European Urban and Regional Studies*, 8/2: 103–115.

13

The Contradictions of Urbanizing Globalization

Erik Swyngedouw, Frank Moulaert, and Arantxa Rodríguez

> There is an acute contradiction here: it is not in the interests of the politi-
> cal establishment and the hegemonic class to extinguish this spark, for to
> do so would effectively destroy the city's worldwide reputation—based pre-
> cisely, on its daring, its willingness to expose the possible and the impos-
> sible, its so-called cultural development, and its panoply of actions and
> actors (working class, intelligentsia, students, artists, writers and others).
> Yet at the same time the political powers and the bourgeoisie controlling
> the economy are afraid of all such ferment, and have a strong urge to crush
> it under suffocating central decision-making.
>
> (Henri Lefebvre 1991: 386)

The preceding chapters illustrated in their rich diversity a number of common themes and features that characterize the urban development process in the European Union. Notwithstanding the profound reorganizations of the urban fabric that the political-economic élites of these cities have pursued in their attempts to insert their urban economies within a neo-liberal and global-izing world order, the concrete transformations exhibit a number of contradic-tions that stand in sharp contrast with the professed objectives. First of all, while economic competitiveness and social integration are spearheading the rhetoric of urban renewal and regeneration, the one-sided emphasis on pursu-ing strategies of urban redevelopment anchored around emblematic landmark events and/or projects parallels a social restructuring that actually often accen-tuates social polarization and re-enforces dynamics of social exclusion and/or marginalization. Secondly, and on a related point, spatially targeted policies partly replace Keynesian-style support mechanisms and welfare-based redis-tribution mechanisms. Thirdly, while urban redevelopment is envisaged, the initiatives have to fulfill the requirements of economic profitability. In an urban context, particularly, it is through the production of increased land rents that positive balance sheets can be achieved, although this is by no means guar-anteed. 'Development', then, becomes a mediated objective that should be engendered as the result of expected multiplier and trickle-down effects.

Fourthly, despite the rhetoric of market-led and market-based forms of development, the state remains an active, if not the central, actor in shaping the physical, institutional, and regulatory order on the variety of interlocking spatial scales that are required to permit these forms of development to proceed. Fifthly, and finally, organizing the operation of market forces is predicated upon a strong regulatory state and the structuring of forms of governance that support market-driven development. Despite the 'local' character of large-scale urban development projects, the new forms of urban governance that accompany and permit such interventions exhibit disturbing autocratic touches and less democratic and non-transparent forms of political organization. In this concluding chapter, these contradictions will be briefly explored, and the key conclusions and insights drawn from the case-study analysis summarized.

13.1. Urban Redevelopment Strategies in the European City: Autocratic Governance, Monumental Spaces, and Mythical Imaginations

13.1.1. From planning to projects

Large-scale urban projects are often presented as project-focused market-led initiatives, which have replaced statutory planning as the primary means of intervention in cities. Planning through urban 'projects' has indeed emerged as the main strategy for stimulating economic growth and 'organizing innovation,' both organizationally and economically (see Table 13.1). Large-scale projects and events are perceived as strategic instruments aiming at reshaping the city. Against the crisis of the comprehensive plan—the classic policy instrument of the Fordist age—the large, emblematic project has emerged as a presumably viable alternative, allegedly combining the advantages of flexibility and targeted actions with a tremendous symbolic capacity.

Essentially fragmented, this form of intervention goes hand in hand with an eclectic planning style where attention to design, detail, morphology, and aesthetics is paramount. The emblematic project captures a segment of the city and turns it into the symbol of the new restructured/revitalized metropolis cast with a powerful image of innovation, creativity, and success. And yet, despite the rhetoric, the replacement of the plan by the project has not displaced planning from the urban arena. In fact, the case studies reveal that in most examples there is a strong strategic component and a significant role for planning. However, in the process, there has been a drastic reorganization of the planning and urban policy-making structures and a rise of new modes of intervention, planning goals, tools, and institutions.

13.1.2. Urbanizing globalization and competitive restructuring

Despite the differences between the case-study projects and the distinct political-economic and regulatory regimes of which they are part, they share a new approach in urban policy that strongly expresses, at the scale of the urban, the main ingredients of a New Economic Policy (NEP). This neo-liberal NEP seeks to reorient state intervention away from monopoly market regulation and towards marshalling state resources into the social, physical, and geographical infra- and super-structures that support, finance, subsidize, or otherwise promote new forms of capital accumulation by providing the relatively fixed territorial structures and facilitating the institutional arrangements that permit the accelerated circulation of capital and the relatively unhindered operation of market forces. At the same time, the state withdraws to a greater or lesser extent from socially inclusive blanket distribution-based policies and from Keynesian demand-led interventions and replaces them with spatially targeted social policies and indirect promotion of entrepreneurship, particularly via selective deregulation, stripping away red tape, and investment 'partnerships'. The city's economic and political élites promote visionary images and boosterist discourses that strive to legitimize these projects and their associated institutional and regulatory frameworks.

13.1.3. The myth of the absent state

In contrast to their market-led and entrepreneurial activity (risk-taking, market-led investments) and despite their predominantly privatized management structures, the UDPs are decidedly and almost without exception state led and often state financed. In the context of liberalizing European metagovernance by the European Commission, and of national deregulation, UDPs are portrayed as anchoring interventions to reorganize metropolitan spaces. In some cases—such as Brussels, Copenhagen, or Berlin—a mix of projects is presented. Regardless of the efficacy of such a mix, the main objective of these projects is to obtain a higher social and economic return and to revalue prime urban land. Urban redevelopment is considered to be a central strategy in re-equilibrating the problematic fiscal balance sheet of local government. Of course, closing rent gaps or producing high rent-yielding spaces requires the production of built environments that permit significant surplus-value creation and/or realization. Indeed, a common theme is that most of the projects are decidedly rent extraction based. Their success rests fundamentally on: (1) the production of potential extra rent; and (2) the subsequent realization of the produced land rent. The employment and economic activity that are generated by the projects, however important they may turn out to be, are all subject to the successful appropriation of the 'manufactured' land rent embodied in the new built environment. The public–private or public–public initiatives rework the urban fabric such that the potential rent from new developments is significantly higher than existing rent levels. Sinking capital and investment into the production of a new built environment revalues, at least potentially, the monetary value of the land and the built environment—benefits that are almost always reaped by the private sector, although the public sector covers a significant part of the sunken investment capital. This is particularly noticeable in the cases of Dublin, Brussels, Bilbao, Berlin, Athens, Copenhagen, and Naples.

13.1.4. Fragmented institutions/autocratic governance

The newly emerging regimes governing urban revitalization involve the subordination of formal government structures to new institutions and agencies, often paralleled by a significant redistribution of policy-making powers, competencies, and responsibilities. In the name of greater flexibility and efficiency, these quasi-private and highly autonomous organizations compete with and often supersede local and regional authorities as protagonists and managers of urban renewal. Moreover, the fragmentation of agencies and the multiplicity of institutions, both formal and informal, are often portrayed as positive signs, suggesting institutional thickness, a considerable degree of local embedding, and significant local social capacity building. In addition, these institutional and regulatory configurations are celebrated as a new form of governing, signalling a better and more transparent articulation between government (state) and civil society. The 'stakeholder' participation on which partnerships are based becomes a normative model that is presented as a democratic forum that permits open and non-distorted communication and action.

Yet the actual configurations of such project-based institutions reveal an extraordinary degree of selectivity. Although a varying choreography of state, private sector, and non-governmental organization (NGO) participation is usually present (see Table 13.1 for a comparative overview), these forms of urban governance show a significant deficit with respect to accountability, representation, and the presence of formal rules of inclusion or participation. Indeed, accountability channels are often grey, non-formalized, and non-transparent, frequently circumventing traditional democratic channels of accountability (e.g. to a representative elected body). As Table 13.1 suggests, the structures of representation of the participating partners are diffuse and unregulated. There are rarely formalized mechanisms of representation, and it is often difficult, if not impossible, to identify who represents what, who, and how. Finally—and most importantly—participation is rarely statutory, but tends to operate through *ad hoc* co-optation and invitation, usually by the key power brokers within the institutions. This invariably influences the regulatory environment, shapes the interventions, and produces a particular imagination of the urban in line with the demands, dreams, and aspirations of the included, while marginalized or otherwise excluded groups remain symptomatically absent. This process has become the dominant mode of institutional organization and suggests a shift from a system of representative urban government to one of stakeholder urban governance that is centred on newly established institutional arrangements. In our case studies (and this is especially clear in Berlin, Athens, Brussels, Lisbon, and Bilbao—see Table 13.1), a complex range of public, semi-public, and private actors shape an interactive system in which different, but allied, views and interests are 'negotiated.' Public–private partnerships epitomize the ideal of such a co-operative and co-ordinated mode of 'pluralistic' governance.

The emergence of a more fragmented and pluralistic mode of urban governance has also contributed to the redefinition of the roles played by local authorities. In particular, it has served to reinforce the tendency towards a more proactive approach, letting local authorities act simultaneously as enablers, partners, and clients. At the same time, the new structures of governance also express the outcomes of an ongoing renegotiation between the different levels of government—local, regional, and national—regarding competencies and powers in the management of urban revitalization. These institutions are bulwarks against popular participation and influence by local community groups and, indeed, against democratic control and accountability. The cases of Lisbon, Brussels, and Bilbao reveal an extraordinary degree of autonomy and non-permeability in the managing organizations. This organic autonomy has often helped to reinforce the tendency to avoid a social and political debate over alternative paths and strategies.

Of course, as Table 13.1 illustrates, the extent of institutional reorganization of the systems and institutions of urban governance is highly variegated and context dependent. Moreover, as the process of planning and implementation is confronted by social protest or critique, institutional and organizational forms adjust or transform in order to maintain legitimacy, social cohesion, and sufficient political support. Despite the great diversity of local, regional, and national changes in the forms of urban governance and despite the often very different agendas of participating institutions (ranging from merely economic growth-based initiatives to integrated projects aimed at improving social conditions in the city), the project-based nature of these interventions is accompanied by new institutional configurations, characterized by power geometries that differ from those of the traditional arenas of government. A veil of secrecy pre-empts criticism and discussion, and a highly selective leaking of information is justified on the grounds of commercial confidentiality and technical impartiality. Indeed, a conspicuous feature of these large-scale projects is the relatively low resistance and conflict they generate. With the exception of Dublin and Brussels, there has been no major 'grassroots' contestation of the UDPs. In this sense, the role of local growth coalitions is critical in framing a discourse of renewal, innovation, achievement, and success.

Table 13.1. From planning to projects: exceptionality measures and local democracy

UDP	Territorial fragmentation	Exceptionality measures/ accountability	Inclusion of neighbourhood population in decision-making	Institutional complexity	Social returns
London The South Bank	Detachment from adjacent wards; bridge with central London	One of the most democratic models in URSPIC sample	Yes	No; from grassroots organization to partner-dominated planning	Yes
Berlin Adlershof	Detachment; filling gaps	Democratic control on public overspending	No	Partnership between the public sector (Berlin) and semi-private developer; little state/ municipality co-ordination	Indirect
Brussels Espace Leopold (EU)	Detachment	Permissive attitude of authorities towards private developers	No	Proliferating number of private developers and of 'informal' public/private relations	No (negative)
Lisbon Expo 1998	Few or no links with eastern zones of Lisbon	Discretionary planning agency	No	No relations with overall planning in Lisbon; no links with other UDPs in Lisbon	Ambiguous

Copenhagen Orestad	Attempt to connect Orestad to the city	Linked to the Oresund regionalization strategy; democratic deficit in the initial phase	No; no linkages to community empowerment programmes in deprived districts of Copenhagen	Very complex; independent state–municipal partnership/company; in reality controlled by the Ministry of Finance in Denmark	Ambiguous; perhaps social returns to the city as a whole and in the long run
Dublin Dublin Docklands Development Project with International Financial Services Centre as flagship	Detachment in early phase—attempt to create new sector to the east of existing CBD; attempt to build bridges and fill gaps in latest phase	Development authority: responsible to national government; initially local government and local communities excluded from decision-making, now the most democratic model in the URSPIC sample	Initially no, but subsequently yes: local neighbourhood excluded in first phase but now directly represented on the Governing Council of the UDC	Initially, an exclusive executive style quango with own complete planning powers; changed to local social partnership model of regeneration in 1997 with own planning powers coexisting alongside those of local government with dual planning regime (local authority and UDC) now yielding complex development scenarios	Local, none in the initial stage of the project but local social programmes now well developed and other initiatives coming on stream (including social housing); a major contributor through IFSC activities and tax revenues to GDP and exchequer resources

Table 13.1. *Continued*

UDP	Territorial fragmentation	Exceptionality measures/ accountability	Inclusion of neighbourhood population in decision-making	Institutional complexity	Social returns
Bilbao Abandoibarra	Filling gaps; building bridges	Combination of statutory planning instruments and discretionary management by a special purpose urban development company (mixed economy firm)	No	No, but innovations in managing structures and public–public partnerships for 'concerted' urbanism	Ambiguous; benefits for adjacent areas but no trickle-down effects
Athens Olympic Village	Detachment; undermining social and economic coherence of surrounding localities	Central state controls the redevelopment process and contains involvement of the local authorities and the local population.	No; virtually nothing has been done to involve neighbourhood populations in the decision-making process	The development project depends on two governance/government systems, a 'normal' and an 'exceptional' one; the 'normal' system deals with regular developmental issues while the 'exceptional' is the system that prepares and administers the Olympics	Ambiguous; the project's social returns include some potential gains in employment during the construction phase and the Olympic Village includes a public housing scheme for the post-Olympic era, but no central commitment exists that guarantees housing for local population

Vienna Donau City	Filling gaps; bridge to central city	Only superficial democracy: hearings without power	Ambiguous	Proliferation of private developers and public authorities	Negative social returns: institutionalization of public private partnerships, high income groups as clientele of social democracy
Naples Centro Direzionale	Yes, the project has increased fragmentation in the city	The private developer had a dominating influence on national, regional and local government	No, only through formal political representation in the city council; no provision of information and/or direct consultation	No co-ordination with other projects; no relations with planning in the city and metropolitan area	Improvements of public transport infrastructures

Key: Territorial fragmentation: functional and physical separation from adjoining poorer neighbourhoods; building bridges with neighbourhoods; filling gaps in abandoned, de-industrialized or emptied-out zones.
Exceptionality measures: special laws, special planning tools, new non- or quasi-governmental systems or agencies, avoidance of democratic control, etc.

13.2. Urban Projects and the Neo-Liberal Urban Order

13.2.1. Visioning the city as an élite playing field

The UDPs included in our study have a variety of characteristics, but their sheer dimensions elevate them to central icons in the scripting of the image of the future of the cities in which they are located. Invariably, the main aspiration is to turn the city into a global competitive actor in the domain in which the élites feel it has some competitive advantage. Needless to say, the imaging of the city's future is directly connected to the visions of those who are pivotal to the formulation, planning, and implementation of the project. Consequently, these projects have been, and often still are, arenas that reflect profound power struggles and position taking by key economic, political, social, or cultural élites. The scripting of the project highlights and reflects the aspirations of a particular set of local, regional, and national—and sometimes also international—actors that shape, through the exercise of their socio-economic, cultural, or political power, the development trajectories of each of the areas. As such, the UDPs can be considered as élite playing fields, on which the stake is to shape an urban future in line with the aspirations of the most powerful segment(s) of the participants.

Clearly, the association of coalitions of élite players changes over time and from place to place, and alliance formation and break-up redefines development trajectories in important ways. Struggles for inclusion in, or exclusion from, élite circles become pivotal in shaping the wider process of social, cultural, political, and economic integration or exclusion.

Each case study narrates the socio-historical dynamics of alliances in the choreography of this struggle for power. In conjunction with structural socio-economic changes, they are instrumental in shaping the fortunes of urban environments, as they decide fundamental rights to housing, access to services, access to land, and the like. Again, the role of the state, the system of governance, and the position of the citizens *vis-à-vis* these institutional forms will be central in determining the mechanisms of inclusion/exclusion that are shaped by the new urban development trajectories. Yet the underlying motive is to reinvigorate a successful accumulation strategy and accompanying hegemony of vision that revolves around the requirement to turn the projects into viable—that is, profitable—economic ventures.

13.2.2. From a social to a spatial definition of development: targeting places rather than people

Almost all of the case-study projects pay at least rhetorical attention to social issues associated with the planning and implementation of the project. The assumed trickle-down mechanisms, occasionally accompanied by targeted policies to facilitate social inclusion processes (see Table 13.1), are considered of sufficient strength to permit a socially balanced and successful development. However, in contrast to the universal, and inclusive, socio-spatial policies that characterized Keynesian and welfare-state interventionism, economic regeneration is now primarily achieved via place-bound and spatially targeted redevelopment schemes. While national funding and incentives are diminishing, private development capital (from local, national, or extra-national origin) is being mobilized for the implementation of territorially defined urban projects. In addition, given the reduction in universal welfare programmes, the 'territorial' approach or 'targeted'-area approach has replaced universal support structures. Moreover, the slimming down of national socio-spatial redistribution is accompanied by policies that direct funds and attention to particular social groups, identified on the basis of their location, their place, and the characteristics of their living environment. Similarly, the European Union's urban social programmes take on an outspoken, spatially focused character.

In sum, there has been a shift from universal to spatially targeted and place-focused approaches in the 1990s. Targeting policies/interventions to geographically circumscribed areas and to economically dynamic or promising activities is presented as a path to remedy socio-economic exclusion. Indeed, in the policy discourse, UDPs are presented as instruments that can also help to overcome social exclusion. The official rhetorical attention to social issues is mobilized politically to legitimize projects, while the underlying and sometimes explicit objective is different. The assumption of trickle down, however, does not hold true in a context characterized by an absence of regulatory (labour, financial, and income) standards or income redistribution systems at the national or EU level and by the limited local forward and backward linkages of the UDPs. This accounts, of course, for the significant differences in socio-spatial inequality between, for example, Denmark, with its long-standing social democratic tradition, and the UK, with its much more liberal–conservative legacy. The targeting of spaces for 'development' permits recasting particular social groups as problematic, excluded, marginalized, and non-integrated. Consequently—so the official argument goes—strategies of integration and inclusion should be pursued by means of territorial, place-based policies, rather than through national or European-wide socio-economic measures, redistribution, and political-economic strategies. From the perspective of this NUP, it is places that need to be integrated, not citizens; it is places that need redevelopment, not people that require jobs and income. Of course, the above is not a plea for dismissing community capacity-building and local-level initiatives, but an expression of the view that they need to be framed within general redistribution and regulatory polices at a higher level—that of the national state and, more importantly, the European Union.

13.2.3. Inter-urban competition for national or European funds

As most of the UDPs are nationally or EU (co-)funded, municipalities or other forms of local governance compete for targeted funding. In general, the concentration of public investment in these large-scale project locations involves redistributing resources away from other uses and areas. In addition, funds are allocated on a project-formulation basis, not on the basis of social needs or considerations of fostering the social economy. Either explicitly or implicitly, the competitive tendering process by national or international organizations favours projects that have a sound institutional and organizational basis capable of engaging in the complex tasks of project formulation, lobbying, negotiation, and implementation. This requires not only a set of sophisticated skills, but also significant financial resources, as well as easy access to the centres of power. All of this is not usually available to the weaker social groups and areas in the city, which are consequently falling behind and are dependent on *ad hoc* measures imposed from above. Moreover, given the need to foster alliances between often rival economic and political élite groups to create the necessary hegemony of vision to compete successfully for state support and private investment, the development activities are often masked in a web of secrecy and hidden behind a screen of commercial confidentiality.

In the context of more targeted interventions and reduced universal social support, which is increasingly organized and conducted by and through élite coalition formation, public resources are drained from universal programmes to targeted territorial projects geared at supporting a particular social configuration—a process that itself harbours exclusionary mechanisms. The murky organizational structures in Brussels, the exclusive élite coalitions of Vienna, and the shifting alliances in Copenhagen and Naples illustrate the variety of processes through which this takes place.

13.2.4. Authoritarian management, exclusion, and client formation

The new systems of urban governance—the quasi-governmental institutional framework based upon forging synergies between the public sector and the élite sections of civil society—also justify the adoption of discretionary forms of management. Thus, the way the process develops creates the conditions for the establishment of centralized and more autocratic management, which privileges direct appointments. The role of lobbies, family ties, business connections, and forms of clientelism become dominant. These forms of coalition formation at the level of project formulation and implementation accentuate a growing gap between actual governance and civil society, intensify processes of political exclusion, and promote a dual society in terms of a coalition of public/private interests on the one hand and a growing group of the disenfranchised on the other. While the above suggests that growth machines, élite coalitions, and networks of power are centrally important in shaping development trajectories, it is evident from our case studies that different growth machines are associated with different interests and lead to different mechanisms of inclusion/exclusion.

None the less, the coalitions of public and semi-public actors invariably produce an exclusive group involved in a common discourse on the progress of the project, a discourse that is not easily opened to public scrutiny or that would invite or permit dissidence. Important decisions and arrangements are made by steering committees, boards of directors of operating companies, non-accountable quasi-governmental organizations, and the like, and are often kept away from public scrutiny. Outsiders are usually not tolerated. There is, at best, only a highly formalized form of public participation that maintains key power in the hands of the existing élite structure and even prevents newly emerging élites (such as, for example, immigrant entrepreneurs and an incipient group of socio-cultural élites in the trans-national communities of cities like Brussels or Vienna) to enter the established networks of governance and dominant élite coalitions. These coalitions create a public discourse on the importance of the project and define it as a particular milestone in the shaping of the future of the city, and their interventions are presented as essential to maintaining a viable position in the inter-urban competition at a pan-European or global scale.

The reactions of the local state to exogenous and endogenous pressures are manifest in the establishment of these new forms of urban governance (public—private partnerships, development co-operations, new administrative structures, and new political forums) that circumvent, bypass, ignore, or marginalize certain social groups. The national state itself is often instrumental in shaping and organizing such exclusive growth coalitions and in providing the extraordinary regulatory environment in which they can operate outside a system of public accountability. In some cases, such as in Copenhagen, Brussels, and Vienna, such growth coalitions reproduce or re-enforce existing but threatened corporatist forms of governance. Informal networks of a relatively small number of individuals occupying key positions in public administration, business, or design/architecture form a new field of power. In the tendering of large-scale projects, these networks are of crucial importance. Needless to say, the projects are therefore closely associated with the interests of the particular coalition sets (and their clients); they are usually self-referential, relatively closed circles that consolidate their power while preventing access to others.

13.2.5. UDPs, speculation, and the production of land rent

As producers of urban space, UDPs are inherently speculative and hence highly risky, in the sense that their financial and economic viability depends on the future realization of the produced increased urban rents. Of course, the latter depends not only on the particular characteristics of the project or the vitality of the local economy, but also on national and international economic conditions. In addition, such projects provide opportunities to extract further resources in terms of public investment for infrastructures, services, and buildings from the state (at a local, national, or EU level), in addition to its direct contributions. Most of the project's development costs are supposed to be met from the sale or renting of land or buildings—the value of which is jacked up through state support, re-regulation, zoning changes, infrastructure investment, and the like.

All this suggests that it is financially very attractive for real estate developers to concentrate on developing projects for the better off. The uncertain and, hence, intrinsically speculative character of the production of new land rent points towards the key role of the state as the preferred interlocutor for carrying the financial risks associated with such real estate-based urban restructuring. Whether successful or not, the dependence on rent returns for the feasibility of UDPs invariably targets high income segments of the population or potentially high productivity-based economic activities and makes the success of the project dependent on the dynamics of the real estate sector. This does not contribute to the alleviation of social segmentation and exclusion and often leads to the creation of islands of wealth in an impoverished environment, resulting in the city becoming a patchwork of socio-economically highly diversified and more mutually exclusive areas. To the extent that low cost or social housing is included in the project, the lower revenue from such targeted housing policy undermines the financial feasibility of the project and requires, in turn, considerable state support or subsidies. Table 13.2 summarizes the relationships between real estate development, the production of high rental returns, and a project's financing structure for seven UDPs. Moreover, given the real estate-based nature of these projects, the public funding is, through private rent appropriation, transferred to the private sector. Consequently, there is a flow of capital from the public to the private sector via the built environment, often without mediation by means of socially targeted policies or instruments.

13.2.6. The city as patchwork

Given the often radically new socio-economic functions associated with UDPs, a process of transfer and of dislocation of jobs inevitably takes place. Spatial labour markets become out of joint or are mismatched. Targeted labour market policies might remedy some of this disjuncture, but the sheer scale of labour market restructuring often implies prolonged stress on the labour market combined with painful processes of adaptation and, frequently, a growing separation between remaining local communities and the incoming new workforce. This separation is often accentuated through now-generalized processes of deregulation of labour markets at national and EU levels. This leads to a segmentation of labour markets. Although this is not a new phenomenon, labour markets are increasingly segmented, with a group of

Table 13.2. Relationship between dynamics in the real estate market and UDP development (seven cases)

Project	Real estate market, the production of rent, and the development of the UDP
Berlin Adlershof	The reunification of Germany was decisive for the development of Berlin's real estate market and triggered a sudden rush of initiatives from international and national investors and developers. This was re-enforced by a strong competition for attractive sites. Today, the Berlin real estate market shows increasing supply-side reserves and demand structures that fall short of expectation. These developments on the real estate markets have a major impact on the progress and the pace of the project implementation in Adlershof. Here, a high volume of office and housing sites have been planned without considering the decreasing demand. Due to the restraint of private investors, project development has slowed down in Adlershof.
Bilbao Abandoibarra	As in most other cities throughout Spain, since the mid-1980s, the real estate market in Bilbao has experienced an extraordinary boom. During the 1990s, housing prices in the city continued to rise, although the rate of growth decreased in the last third of the decade. Real estate prices in Abandoibarra both benefited from and contributed to this boom. In less than four years that separated the beginning of redevelopment works and the marketing of the first housing land slots, land prices in Abandoibarra more than doubled (2.3 times). Real estate price increases spread throughout the city but tended to be proportionally higher in Abandoibarra's adjoining neighbourhoods. And, while it cannot be said that land price increases in the city are exclusively related to Abandoibarra's redevelopment, it is none the less certain that this scheme is contributing significantly to this trend as well as to altering housing price differentials among different neighbourhoods across the city.
Brussels Leopold Quarter	Due to the continuous demand for additional office space in the Leopold Quarter, a demand led by the European Union institutions but also by the (both national and international) banking and insurance sectors, rental values have systematically increased over the past decades. Rents in the Leopold Quarter are now amongst the highest in the country (up to 200 Euro per square meter). It has also generated speculative activities in the area: remaining residential blocks are systematically bought by property developers and eventually demolished and replaced with offices, irrespective of land use planning regulations. Other residential pockets have been upgraded and made available for wealthy (international) residents, or they are now *de facto* (and illegally) used as offices for smaller organizations (for example, lobby groups, law firms). Globally operating real estate agents (such as Jones Lang Wootton, Healey & Baker) have come to dominate the Leopold Quarter market, while construction and property development remains mainly in Belgian (and French) hands.
Copenhagen Orestaden	In general, the prices on the housing market skyrocketed during the second half of the 1990s and the social geography within the city became more polarized. There still exists an important social housing sector, but the role of the social housing sector has gradually declined because housing construction subsidized by the municipality and the state has almost stopped since the beginning of the 1990s. The municipal housing policy has increasingly been used as a tool to regulate the tax base of Copenhagen favouring the middle classes. The UDP follows this trend.

Table 13.2. *Continued*

Project	Real estate market, the production of rent, and the development of the UDP
Vienna Donau City	Rents skyrocketed in the second half of the 1980s, and have been stagnating since then. This can be explained by a contradictory movement. On the one hand, there still exists an important public housing sector. Housing construction subsidized by the municipality was intensive until 1996 and restrictive rent laws were applied until 1982. On the other hand, liberal regulation is on the advance: subsidies for construction of housing have been dramatically reduced over the last years. Furthermore, publicly subsidized housing is increasingly oriented towards the upper middle classes. UDP is a paradigmatic case, illustrating these changes.
Naples Centro Direzionale	During the 1980s, prices in the real estate market grew dramatically to reach record levels in 1991 and 1992, particularly in selected central areas; they subsequently declined almost as fast as they had previously risen, continuing to fall until 1997, when the first signs of recovery appeared and prices stabilized or began to increase again. Apartments in the CDN became available at the peak of the market price for prime location units and thus could be expected to yield quite significant returns. The developer, however, sold 90 per cent of the residential units to a state-run pension fund for the employees of public companies and guaranteed his return. By law, only families working for state agencies are entitled to rent those apartments and rental prices are set lower than the market price according to the rules of the 1978 Fair Rent Act. This decision removed these units from the sale and rental markets, creating a separate segment, which is somewhat insulated from market dynamics. The project had also a depressing effect on the value of building land for other office projects in the city.
Dublin Docklands Development Project (with IFSC as flagship)	Property demand in both the housing and office markets, both within the UDP site and in the surrounding neighbourhoods, has grown rapidly in the 1990s and land prices in the area have soared due to the presence of the IFSC. With companies queuing to get into the successful IFSC site as the economy boomed in the 1990s, the intense demand for office space squeezed other real estate markets, most notably the provision of social and affordable housing within and around the UDP. Average house prices tripled in the decade 1989 to 1999 whilst the provision of social housing evaporated due to the post-1986 retrenchment of public sector welfare spending. The housing situation is particularly acute in the docklands UDP and neighbouring areas. Local residents cannot compete with investors or the predominantly young professionals who purchase or rent the limited supply of private residential units available in the area. The result has been gentrification of the initial UDC site and the exclusion from the life of the area, through the property market, of many of the latest generation of the indigenous population.

highly paid and skilled executives and professionals on the one hand and large groups of less secure—often informal—workers on the other, with many other categories in between. The segmentation of labour markets, which is today facilitated by the national deregulation of labour market rules and other changes in the national regulatory frameworks, becomes cemented in, and expressed by, the socio-economic composition of the UDPs. The inclusion of the existing local labour pool proves difficult or impossible, while retraining and targeted labour market entry policies tend not to be very successful, despite the prolonged support for such programmes.

This socio-economic restructuring, combined with a mosaic of newly constructed built environments with their associated increased rents, produces urban islands, a patchwork of discrete spaces with increasingly sharp boundaries (gated business centres, leisure, or community spaces). This is re-enforced through a combination of physical, social, and cultural boundary formation processes. The overall result is the consolidation of a fragmented city, which accompanies the reorganization of the socio-spatial fabric of the urban agglomeration. In some cases, this mosaic takes the form of the suburbanization of poverty, while internal differentiation accentuates socio-spatial differentiation and polarization, a process that often takes outspoken racialized forms (notably in Brussels, Berlin, and Vienna).

13.3. Neo-liberal Urbanism, Social Polarization, and Democratic Deficit: A Conclusion

Urban regeneration and development policies in the European city, in the context of national and EU-wide tendencies towards the implementation of neo-liberal socio-economic policies, have brought about critical shifts in domains and levels of intervention and in the composition and characteristics of actors and agents, institutional structures, and policy tools. Over the last decade and a half, urban regeneration policy has become an increasingly central component of urban policy. For the most part, urban regeneration schemes based on large-scale UDPs have emerged as a response to urban restructuring processes associated with the transformation of production and demand conditions locally, nationally, and globally; they generally combine physical upgrading with socio-economic development objectives. The search for growth and competitive redevelopment has become the leading objective of the NUP in an attempt to reassert the position of cities in the emerging global economy. Enhancing the competitive advantage of cities is seen as largely dependent on improving and adapting the built environment to the accumulation strategies of a city's key élites. Therefore, physical reconstruction and economic recovery tend to go hand in hand and are frequently perceived as quasi-simultaneous processes: mega-projects are viewed as providing a solid foundation for fostering future growth and functional transformation. At the same time, urban revitalization is projected beyond the cities' limits and linked to regional recovery and internationalization strategies.

How do the various UDPs reflect this NUP? Most UDPs have caused increased physical and social fragmentation in the city. Most projects, with the possible exception of Orestaden, have primarily filled gaps for the (higher) middle-class real estate and consumption-good markets, but not for other, usually poorer and/or immigrant sections of the urban population. While economic gaps have been plugged, greater social disparities and socio-spatial fragmentation have been produced.

A central issue involved in urban regeneration policies is the relation of UDPs to existing planning instruments and regulations. While these projects are generally inserted into prevalent statutory planning guidelines, the initial conception, design, and implementation lie at the margins of formal planning structures. The condition of 'exceptionality' associated with these initiatives favours a more autonomous, if not autocratic, dynamic marked by special plans and projects that relegate statutory norms and procedures to a secondary and subordinated place. Many local authorities and national governments justify the exceptionality of a UDP on the basis of different factors: scale; the emblematic character of the operation; timing pressures; the need for greater flexibility; efficiency criteria; and the like. Exceptionality is a fundamental feature of the new urban policy, based on the primacy of project-based initiatives over regulatory plans and procedures. These changes involve, among other things, the emergence of new policy tools, actors, and institutions, and they have important consequences for urban policy-making in general and for local democracy in particular. These projects are prime examples of the trends towards a new local mode of regulation of urban (re)development and management shaped by the pressures of competitive restructuring and changing social and economic priorities, as well as by major political and ideological shifts. Indeed, the emergence of the NUP rests significantly on the establishment of new forms of intervention at the local level that, to a large extent, constitute a rupture with traditional forms. Entrepreneurialism is about the public sector running cities in a more businesslike manner, in which institutions of local governance operate like the private sector or are replaced by private sector-based systems. Indeed, the NUP is closely associated with fundamental shifts from traditional government structures to a more diffused, fragmented, and flexible mode of governance. The combination of different spatial and administrative scales in urban policy-making and the increasing fragmentation of competencies and responsibilities is one of its most striking aspects. In most cities, the full dimension of urban regeneration cannot be adequately apprehended without reference to the multiplicity of agents, the articulation of spatial scales at which they operate, and the fragmentation of agency responsibility within the urban arena. In some cases, this trend seems to be linked to a shift from hierarchical relationships (in terms of the traditional territorial hierarchy of statutory planning procedures) to a more collaborative and stakeholder-based, but often socially highly exclusive, scheme in which partnerships and networks composed of a variety of élites play a key role. However, at the same time, fragmentation and diversity are also accompanied by tendencies towards the exclusion of certain groups and collectives from participating in the decision-making process. A democratic deficit emerges as a central element of this strategic approach.

The fragmentation of the mode of governance redefines the role and position of local authorities. Indeed, in the name of greater flexibility and efficiency, these new institutions compete with and often supplant local and regional authorities as protagonists and managers of urban renewal. In fact, the new governance structures express the outcomes of an ongoing renegotiation between the different levels of government—local, regional, national, and European—and between public and private actors over competencies, decision-making powers, and funding. The establishment of these new structures frequently involves massive redistribution of policy-making powers, competencies, and responsibilities away from local governments to often highly exclusive partnership agencies, a process that can be described as the 'privatization of urban governance.'

The fragmented character of many of the UDPs—which are often self-contained, isolated, and disconnected from the general dynamics of the city—contrasts sharply with the strong emphasis on co-ordinated action of different actors, the encouragement of partnerships, and the building of networks and support coalitions. These are presented as providing a potentially superior form of urban management, more flexible and efficient, and thus better adapted to the competitive trends of global urban change. The trend towards a more flexible and network-oriented approach is often perceived as a validation of bottom-up, less hierarchical, and participatory dynamics. However, participation is often limited to selected professionals—architects, planners, economists, engineers, and so on—who have become increasingly influential, while the non-professional sector and less powerful social groups are largely excluded.

In those cases in which neighbourhood movements reacted to the initial lack of local democracy (Dublin), participation had to be partly restored, and neighbourhood demands, as well as concerns about social issues, climbed a few notches up the policy priority list. Nevertheless, the limited and spatially targeted interventions associated with project-based urban restructuring policies prevent these movements from transcending the localized issues associated with a project's implementation and from translating these social demands into more generalized policy models at higher spatial scales. This is arguably the most significant implication of the NUP. The down-scaling of urban policies to place-specific interventions in a context in which traditional redistribution policies are being reduced at higher-scale levels forces social movements to operate through localized actions. This, in turn, militates against the urgent need to translate these place-specific actions and demands into more general social and economic programmes articulated at the national, European Union, or international scale.

Reference

LEFEBVRE H. (1991). *The Production of Space*. Oxford: Blackwell.

INDEX

Note: page numbers for chapters are **emboldened**.